Sailor Historian

The Best of Samuel Eliot Morison

EMILY MORISON BECK is editor
of *Bartlett's Familiar Quotations*,
at present working on the fifteenth
edition, and lives in Canton,
Massachusetts.

BOOKS BY SAMUEL ELIOT MORISON

The Life and Letters of Harrison Gray Otis, 2 vols., 1913
The Maritime History of Massachusetts, 1921, 1941
The Oxford History of the United States, 2 vols., 1927
Builders of the Bay Colony, 1930, 1964
The Tercentennial History of Harvard University, 4 vols., 1929–36
Three Centuries of Harvard, 1936, 1963
Portuguese Voyages to America in the Fifteenth Century, 1940
Admiral of the Ocean Sea: A Life of Christopher Columbus, 1942
History of U.S. Naval Operations in World War II, 15 vols., 1947–62
By Land and By Sea, 1953
Christopher Columbus, Mariner, 1955
The Intellectual Life of Colonial New England, 1956
Freedom in Contemporary Society, 1956
The Story of the "Old Colony" of New Plymouth, 1956
John Paul Jones: A Sailor's Biography, 1959
The Story of Mount Desert Island, 1960
One Boy's Boston, 1962
The Two-Ocean War, 1963
Vistas of History, 1964
Spring Tides, 1965
The Oxford History of the American People, 1965
Life of Commodore Matthew C. Perry, 1794–1858, 1967
Harrison Gray Otis, The Urbane Federalist, 1969
The European Discovery of America: The Northern Voyages A.D. 500–1600, 1971
Samuel de Champlain, Father of New France, 1972
The European Discovery of America: The Southern Voyages A.D. 1492–1616, 1974

WITH HENRY STEELE COMMAGER AND WILLIAM E. LEUCHTENBURG

The Growth of the American Republic, 2 vols., 1930, 1969
The Concise History of the American Republic, 1977

WITH MAURICIO OBREGÓN

The Caribbean As Columbus Saw It, 1964

Sailor Historian

THE BEST OF SAMUEL ELIOT MORISON

EDITED BY EMILY MORISON BECK

FOREWORD BY WALTER MUIR WHITEHILL

SOME REFLECTIONS ON STYLE BY DAVID McCORD

HOUGHTON MIFFLIN COMPANY BOSTON

LIBRARY

JAN 9 1979

UNIVERSITY OF THE PACIFIC

355460

Copyright © 1977 by Emily Morison Beck

All rights reserved. No part of this work may be reproduced
or transmitted in any form by any means, electronic or
mechanical, including photocopying and recording, or by
any information storage or retrieval system, without
permission in writing from the publisher.

Library of Congress Cataloging in Publication Data
Morison, Samuel Eliot, 1887–1976.
    Sailor historian.

    1. United States — History — Collected works.
2. America — Discovery and exploration — Collected
works.   3. Naval history, Modern — Collected works.
I. Beck, Emily Morison.   II. Title.
E173.M85   973'.08   77-9406
ISBN 0-395-25444-2

Printed in the United States of America
V 10 9 8 7 6 5 4 3 2

Calligraphy by Stephen Harvard

The editor is grateful for permission to reprint from the following works by Samuel
Eliot Morison:

The European Discovery of America: The Northern Voyages, A.D. 500–1600, copy-
right © 1971 by Oxford University Press; and *The European Discovery of America:
The Southern Voyages, A.D. 1492–1616,* copyright © 1974 by Samuel Eliot Morison.
Reprinted by permission of Oxford University Press, Inc.
    "Which European Discovered America?" in *European Community,* January–
February 1976. Reprinted by permission of *European Community.*
    Admiral of the Ocean Sea: A Life of Christopher Columbus, copyright 1942 by
Samuel Eliot Morison; *Samuel de Champlain: Father of New France,* copyright ©
1972 by Samuel Eliot Morison; *"Old Bruin": Commodore Matthew C. Perry,* copy-
right © 1967 by Samuel Eliot Morison; *John Paul Jones: A Sailor's Biography,* copyright © 1959 by Samuel Eliot Morison; *The Two-Ocean War: A Short History of the
United States Navy in the Second World War,* copyright © 1963 by Samuel Eliot
Morison. All reprinted by permission of Little, Brown and Co. in association with
the Atlantic Monthly Press.
    The Parkman Reader: Selected and Edited with an Introduction and Notes by Sam-

uel Eliot Morison, copyright © 1955 by Samuel Eliot Morison. Reprinted by permission of Little, Brown and Co.

By Land and By Sea, copyright 1928, 1929, 1944, 1948, 1951, 1953 by Priscilla B. Morison; *Vistas of History,* copyright © 1963 by Priscilla Barton Morison; *The Story of the "Old Colony" of New Plymouth,* copyright © 1956 by Priscilla Barton Morison; *Of Plymouth Plantation* by William Bradford, edited by Samuel Eliot Morison, copyright 1952 by Samuel Eliot Morison. All reprinted by permission of Alfred A. Knopf, Inc.

The Maritime History of Massachusetts, copyright 1921, 1941, 1949, 1961 by Samuel Eliot Morison, copyright © renewed 1969 by Samuel Eliot Morison; *The Ropemakers of Plymouth,* copyright 1950 by the Plymouth Cordage Company; *Harrison Gray Otis, 1765–1848, The Urbane Federalist,* copyright © 1969 by Samuel Eliot Morison; *One Boy's Boston,* copyright © 1962 by Samuel Eliot Morison. All reprinted by permission of Houghton Mifflin Company.

"Landing at Fedhala, Morocco, November 8, 1942" in *American Foreign Service Journal,* March 1942. Reprinted by permission.

"The Conservative American Revolution," copyright © 1976 by Emily Morison Beck. Originally published by the Society of the Cincinnati.

Reprinted by permission of the publishers from *Harvard College in the Seventeenth Century.* Cambridge: Harvard University Press. Copyright 1936 by the President and Fellows of Harvard College, renewed 1964 by Samuel Eliot Morison.

"Prescott, the American Thucydides," copyright © 1957 by The Atlantic Monthly Company, Boston, Mass. Reprinted with permission.

Sir Winston Churchill: Nobel Prize Winner," copyright 1953 by Saturday Review.

"Reminiscences of Charles Eliot Norton" from the *New England Quarterly,* XXXIII, September 1960, pp. 364–368.

Spring Tides, copyright © 1965 by Samuel Eliot Morison. Reprinted by permission of Curtis Brown Ltd.

"For the whole earth is the sepulchre of famous men, and their story lives on, woven into the stuff of other men's lives."

from the *Funeral Oration of Pericles*

Preface

I T IS FITTING that I am on this Maine island as I write the Preface to a selection of my father's writings. Here at an early age Sam Morison came to love passionately the sea and to learn the lore of the tides and the rudiments of navigation while "messing around in boats." This isle of the desert mountains, furthermore, was discovered by one of my father's heroes, Samuel de Champlain, whose biography he was to write in that intensely active period after his "retirement" from teaching. Here, too, he became aware of the magic of the forest and the lichen-covered granite ledges, as did another of his heroes, Francis Parkman, a volume of whose selected writings he eventually edited.

The range of SEM's knowledge of flora and fauna was amazing, as I discovered while voyaging with him around South America the year before he died. He was familiar with the terrain and wildlife of the continent from the Andes to Patagonia. This interest naturally added a special dimension to his writing of the explorers, and re-creating what they must have seen in their discovered lands. He had, in short, the explorer's eye.

And my father could have been an explorer, a choice he might readily have made — given the chance. But he married young and raised a family that had to be supported and educated, so he began his explorations on a modest scale and in libraries. Once free of family responsibilities, he launched into oceanic voyages, beginning by following the wake of Columbus. At an age when most men would be taking their ease on their laurels, he was zealously pursuing, by sea and by air, the European discoverers of America.

But explorers tend to be loners. SEM, though he preferred solitude when he was writing, rejoiced in the company of friends, both serious and fun-loving. His anecdotes found an ever-ready audience, for he was a witty raconteur. One sensed a keen understanding of character, an awareness of human greatness and frailty, qualities that he was quick to detect in the historical figures he wrote of. Seldom voiced, his deep religious faith made him understand how important faith was in the early centuries of European discovery.

His curiosity reached out to all forms of literature, in many languages, and to the arts. His comparing the Yankee clipper to a Gothic cathedral or the Parthenon was as natural for him as quoting José María de Heredia's alexandrines in reference to Vicente Yáñez Pinzón's crossing of the Atlantic in 1499.

His was a personal style, marked by le mot juste, honed from successively worked-over drafts, yet sparkling with his zest for life. Arthur Schlesinger, Jr., expresses poignantly his sense of SEM's style in a letter of May 18, 1976:

Your father was a most important man in my life. It was from him that I first understood the importance of *style* in history. He knew that the essence of history is the reconstruction of the past, and he used his enormous literary gifts to fuse narrative and analysis into a single texture. But I mean style in a larger sense too — his whole attitude toward life and society.

One feels that his death breaks a last link to the classic past. He was in the apostolic succession, the last heir of the great New England tradition — Bancroft, Parkman, Prescott, Motley, Henry Adams — and there is no one to come after.

This project has been long in the works. Or, rather, there was a long hiatus between now and the time it was originally conceived by a former editor of the present publishers. It was to be edited jointly by my father, Walter Whitehill, and David McCord, but not even a rough table of contents was drawn up. By 1975 when, because of the trio's separate commitments, nothing to speak of had been done, my father suggested that I, though no historian, tackle it, and the publishers agreed to the change in editorship.

SEM's oeuvre comprises over forty volumes and more than a hundred articles. It has been no easy task to winnow from such richesse the selections appropriate for a volume that I thought should be a highly readable treasury of the best and most representative of SEM's writings. After innumerable rereadings, I found a pattern taking shape, and the selections fell into certain categories — roughly, historical, critical, and personal, many selections overlapping, of course. I was fortunate that my father lived long enough to examine and approve the final choice, after discarding a number of pieces as "old hat," "hackneyed," or "of little interest to the general reader." For the volume is aimed to give pleasure to the general reader, who will find herein chapters from favorite books and prized articles, as

well as forgotten pieces never before reprinted in a book. In addition, my father has written an introductory passage for each selection,
finishing the very last for "An August Day's Sail" shortly before his
death. For reasons of space, some of the illustrations and maps
figuring amply in the original works have been omitted.

I am grateful for the advice and help of Walter Whitehill, above all,
Antha Card McDonald, David McCord, and for suggestions from Justice Benjamin Kaplan and Michael N. Morison. I also wish to give
special thanks to Alfred A. Knopf, Inc., for their cooperation.

EMILY MORISON BECK

Good Hope
Northeast Harbor, Maine
September 1976

Foreword

I N THE SPRING of 1976, when Samuel Eliot Morison had read and
approved the selection of his writings that forms this book, he was
still living in the house in which he had been born more than eighty-
eight years before. Few Bostonians have been so consistent in their
devotion to a home port, or have sailed so far from it in the course of
their lives. *One Boy's Boston*, extracts from which appear in Part
VI, 1, carries Samuel Eliot Morison's autobiography only from 1887
to 1901. This Foreword is designed to give the reader some idea of
the way in which the tastes and enthusiasms reflected in this book developed during the seventy-five years after 1901. When he asked me
to write it, he said that he would be pleased if I simply brought up to
date the chapter that I had written about him in 1969 in my *Analecta
Biographica, A Handful of New England Portraits*. As he liked that
piece, I have borrowed more freely from myself than I would ordinarily wish to do.

Number 44 Brimmer Street, a four-story red brick house at the foot
of Beacon Hill, looks from the outside much as it did on July 9, 1887,
when Samuel Eliot Morison was born there, or in the previous decade, when his grandfather built it. Although the interior had been
titivated at various times, it had never lost the character of a comfortable, high-studded Boston house of the years immediately following
the Civil War, filled with books and with portraits and furniture
inherited from two or three earlier generations. Indeed, photographs
of grandfather and grandson, taken in the second-floor library sixty-
four years apart, show startling similarities not only in furnishings but
in the physical appearance of the men themselves.

Only from the late 1930's onward can I write from personal knowledge, for in the autumn of 1922, when I entered Harvard College as a
freshman, Samuel Eliot Morison had just gone to Oxford. When he
returned to Harvard in 1925, I, as a senior, was too immersed in the
Spanish Middle Ages even to think of taking a course in American colonial history. Indeed, I first heard of him, and of the delights of
New England history, during evening conversations in a Bloomsbury
boarding house in the winter of 1934–35 with his sometime student

Raymond Phineas Stearns, who had taken a Harvard Ph.D. in 1934 and come to England on a fellowship. Ray Stearn's devotion to and admiration for his teacher excited my interest, although it was only when I had come back from Spain in 1936 and had gone to work for the Peabody Museum of Salem that I came to know him. Since the collections of that ancient museum, established in 1799 by the Salem East India Marine Society, were rich sources of the maritime history of New England, I immediately turned to Sam Morison's writings for guidance. Soon I made his acquaintance. Thus, although we never met in a classroom, I have regarded him for most of the past forty years as a uniquely valued teacher, friend, and ally.

Both of Samuel Eliot Morison's grandfathers were members of the Harvard Class of 1839, although they were of quite different origins and do not seem to have been friends. Samuel Eliot (1821–1898) was the grandson of the Federalist merchant of the same name who in 1810 had established the first professorship of Greek literature at Harvard College. His wife, Emily Marshall Otis, named for her mother, the greatest Boston beauty of the 1820's and '30's, was the granddaughter of Harrison Gray Otis, Federalist lawyer and statesman. Nathaniel Holmes Morison (1815–1890) hailed from Peterborough, New Hampshire, where his family were farmers, and reached Harvard by his own efforts after working in a woolen mill and a machine shop. Grandfather Eliot was a schoolmaster, and for a time president of Trinity College, Hartford. Grandfather Morison also became a schoolmaster, but in Baltimore, where he was the first provost of the Peabody Institute. Between Otises, Eliots, and Morisons there was an extraordinary brew of geniality and worldliness, asceticism and frugality, inherited wealth and country enterprise, with Harvard College entering the picture in various generations. After John Holmes Morison, Nathaniel's son from Baltimore, had been graduated from Harvard College with the Class of 1878, he stayed in Boston to practice law. In 1886, when he married Samuel Eliot's daughter, the young couple were persuaded to live on the third floor of her parents' house at 44 Brimmer Street; hence the incident (to be found in Part VI, 1) of Lizzie Doyle and the perambulator that bounced Samuel Eliot Morison at the feet of Dr. Green.

Sam Morison grew up on Brimmer Street, and at appropriate times was sent to Mrs. Shaw's School and to Noble and Greenough's. Each summer the Morisons spent July and August in Northeast Harbor, Maine, where their son acquired what he describes as his "almost passionate love for the sea and Mount Desert Island," and also stayed for a few weeks with the Eliots, in their summer home at Beverly Farms. It was at Northeast Harbor that he began his seafaring career, cruising around Mount Desert Island in the summer of 1901 with Samuel Vaughan in the sixteen-foot open North Haven dinghy *Leda*. During that cruise he met, at Bartletts Island, Augustus Peabody Loring (1885–1951), who was to be his valued friend for the next fifty years.

That autumn Sam Morison entered St. Paul's School in Concord, New Hampshire, and, in September 1904, Harvard College, with Gus Loring rooming near him. Midway in his undergraduate career, his parents took title to Bleakhouse in Peterborough, New Hampshire, a place purchased in 1857 by Nathaniel Holmes Morison, "who was never quite happy — as no Morison has a right to be — beyond the view of Monadnock." Thus Sam supplemented his early passion for Mount Desert Island with a love for the hills of southern New Hampshire.

After receiving his Harvard A.B. in 1908, Morison spent a year in Paris at the Ecole des Sciences Politiques (see Part VI, 2) before returning to Harvard as a graduate student in history. On May 28, 1910, he married Elizabeth Amory Shaw Greene, who, although of Boston origin, had been born in Paris and had lived there during her girlhood. After spending the summer in a newly built bungalow on Sawyers Cove, Blue Hill Bay, in a remote western corner of Mount Desert Island, far from the amenities of Northeast and Bar harbors, the Morisons settled in Otis Place in Boston. For the next half-dozen years they lived there or in lower Mt. Vernon Street, within a stone's throw of 44 Brimmer Street.

Readable history is written only by men who have some strong personal enthusiasm for their subjects. Furthermore, firsthand acquaintance with the scene and people, or their latter-day successors, never does any harm. Thus Morison's first book, a biography of his great-great-grandfather, Harrison Gray Otis, written because the subject interested him, is many times more readable than the run of doctors' theses. The chief source for the biography was a mass of Otis papers then in the 44 Brimmer Street house, which Morison was encouraged by Professor Albert Bushnell Hart to explore as a thesis subject. He received his Ph.D. in 1912; the book was published, in two volumes, by Houghton Mifflin the following year.

His second book, which followed in 1921, sprang also from personal enthusiasm. Of the circumstances, he tells in his introductory note to "Oh! California, 1844–1850" in Part II.

But there were interruptions before he wrote the history of the merchant marine of his native state. In the autumn of 1914, Morison substituted at Berkeley for a University of California history professor on leave. Toward the end of the academic year 1915–16, which he spent as an underpaid tutor in history at Harvard, Morison was asked by Professor Edward Channing to take over, in the autumn, his course in colonial history. That summer he and his family — eventually three daughters and one son — moved to Concord so that the children could be brought up in the country. After the United States entered World War I, Morison became a private of infantry, serving in such disparate posts as the Depot Brigade at Camp Devens and the American Commission to Negotiate Peace, in Paris. Returning to Harvard and Concord in the late summer of 1919, he found little that was congenial in the current state of the world, which was slipping either into high-finance capitalism or into communism, neither of which suited his essentially liberal turn of mind. So he immersed himself in aspects of the Massachusetts past that were sympathetic to his seagoing temperament, and in eleven months from the beginning of research — during half of which he was actively teaching — produced the finished copy of *The Maritime History of Massachusetts*.

The book became a classic almost as soon as it was published, in 1921. The Otis biography had been a good, sound, readable work, far above average, but *The Maritime History* had a flair, a sweep, that, combined with remarkable literary craftsmanship, put it in a class by itself. Moreover, after more than fifty years, its contents remain as valid and as useful as the day the book was finished. The fire and enthusiasm with which it had been written (see Part II, 4) gave it a character very different from books worried over intermittently for years, in the manner of dogs gnawing bones. Years later, when Morison told Bernard Berenson that he was about to attempt a one-volume history of the United States, Berenson advised: "Write it in one swoop; then it may have literary value." *The Maritime History* was, indeed, a one-swoop book, and it achieved a standard of literary distinction seldom equaled and never surpassed in American historical writing. Too few statesmen have spoken like Winston Churchill and John F. Kennedy; too few historians have written like Samuel Eliot Morison.

In the spring of 1922 Morison went to Oxford as the first holder of the professorship of American history endowed by Lord Rothermere in memory of his son, Harold Vyvyan Harmsworth, who had been killed in the war. There he remained for three years as a member of Christ Church, and there he wrote *The Oxford History of the United States: 1783–1917*, which was published in 1927, after his return to Harvard. In the twenties, American history was regarded as quite extraneous to the Honour School of Modern History at Oxford. This two-volume work was consequently addressed to literate readers who knew a good deal about history in general but nothing to speak of about the United States. In 1930, in collaboration with Henry Steele Commager, Morison produced a different treatment of the same matter in *The Growth of the American Republic,* designed as a textbook for use in this country. Although the 1927 *Oxford History* remains a special favorite of mine, the textbook too has literary value; that it has gone through many editions and has been translated into Italian, German, Spanish, and Portuguese is sufficient evidence of its usefulness.

On returning to Harvard in 1925, Morison was promoted to a professorship of history. The family was happily settled in Concord, with fields and horses within easy reach, but when 44 Brimmer Street became vacant on the death of his mother the following December, they regretfully left Concord and moved into Boston. As Bleakhouse, in Peterborough, kept open the year round, was available for spring and fall weekends, frequent visits there, with horses at hand, and summers at the Sawyers Cove bungalow, with boats, reconciled the Morisons to academic years in Boston. In 1934, after Bleakhouse had been given to the Society for the Preservation of New England Antiquities, the Morisons built Pleasance, in Canton, near the Great Blue Hill, to have a place for country weekends nearer home.

On coming home in 1925, Morison became president of the Colonial Society of Massachusetts, to which he had been elected in 1912, before he had published anything. During the dozen years that he held this office, he continued the tradition of making the society's meetings occasions when promising young scholars in colonial history might come to know their elders, might ventilate their ideas, and get them into print. In 1928 he joined with his colleagues Arthur M. Schlesinger, Kenneth B. Murdock, and others in starting *The New England Quarterly,* which provided another vehicle for publication of studies on New England life and letters. For the next forty-eight years he was the chief pilot of this journal.

In 1926 Morison was appointed historian for the three hundredth anniversary of Harvard College, which was to be celebrated a decade later. A visit to Toledo on the way home from Oxford, during which he surveyed the remarkable series of portraits of archbishops in the chapter house of the cathedral, had led him to wonder where a comparable sequence could be found in North America:

It suddenly dawned on me that my own alma mater, Harvard College, was about the oldest institution and certainly the oldest corporation in the United States. And as I had recently been steeped in the history of the universities from which Harvard stems — Oxford and Cambridge — why not write the history of my university?

President A. Lawrence Lowell promptly told him to go ahead. On the reasonable theory that the latest period in the history of a country or a university is the most neglected, Morison started with a collaborative volume, *The Development of Harvard University Since the Inauguration of President Eliot: 1869–1929,* which appeared in 1930, while he was at work on *The Founding of Harvard College,* published in 1935. As the tercentenary of the Massachusetts Bay Colony obviously preceded the Tercentenary of Harvard College, he fitted in *Builders of the Bay Colony* in 1930 — biographical portraits of nine men and one woman who "would have led obscure lives but for a dynamic force called puritanism which drove them to start life anew in a wilderness." In 1936, the year of the Harvard Tercentenary, he followed *The Founding of Harvard College* with two volumes entitled *Harvard in the Seventeenth Century* and the single-volume *Three Centuries of Harvard: 1636–1936,* designed for the reader who required less profusion of detail. *The Puritan Pronaos: Studies in the Intellectual Life of New England in the Seventeenth Century,* delivered as the Stokes Lectures at New York University in 1934 and published two years later, was closely associated in mood with *Builders of the Bay Colony* and the Harvard history.

In some hands the Harvard history might have been a pedestrian and bureaucratic effort, hardly more interesting than a telephone directory. In Morison's it was very different, for as he saw it,

it opened an opportunity to study the history of ideas as expressed through academic institutions. It carried me back to medieval universities, Paris, Bologna, Oxford and Cambridge, and to the Netherlands universities, which the founders of Harvard imitated so far as their slender means would permit. It gave me an opportunity to study the lives and the ideas of English Puritans who founded New England and Harvard.

But before he reached a volume on the eighteenth century, the sea called him back, for fifteen years had passed since the publication of *The Maritime History of Massachusetts.*

Some years ago I sat near Sam Morison in Trinity Church, Boston, during the consecration of Bishop Stokes. During a lull in the proceedings, he whispered to me that his family's pew had been near where we were sitting and that as a boy he liked to imagine that a stained-glass window of the Last Supper, which one could see only indistinctly from this spot, had depicted not Our Lord and his disciples but Columbus and the egg! With so precocious an enthusiasm for Christopher Columbus, it is not surprising that Morison wished to write his biography. Moreover, as he embraced the theory of his model, Francis Parkman, that the historian should visit the scene of the actions that he describes, such a project would provide an unassailable excuse for going to sea.

In 1916, when preparing to take over Edward Channing's History 10, Morison had become fascinated with the vast literature on the discovery of America and had vowed that someday he would sail at least to the West Indies, to examine Columbus's landfalls and coastlines, for that seemed "the only way to find what kind of seaman and navigator he was; or, indeed, exactly where he sailed." Twenty years later, with the Harvard Tercentenary over, he "decided that it was now or never," took leave from Harvard, chartered a yawl, and sailed to the Windward and Leeward islands with a party of friends that included the sea-born Lincoln Colcord, whom he always referred to as the "Sage of Searsport." This brief excursion, combined with further documentary investigation in Lisbon, Paris, and London, convinced Morison that he must undertake a definitive biography of his hero as a seaman, explorer, and navigator. Thus armed with proof "that Parkman's outdoor methods could profitably be applied at sea," he set about organizing the Harvard Columbus Expedition. Morison, Paul Hammond, and other friends purchased and fitted out the barkentine *Capitana* to cross the ocean in Columbus's wake and view islands and coasts as he had seen them. William D. Stevens provided his ketch, *Mary Otis,* as the *Niña* of the expedition. Sailing, in August 1939, into what soon became a war zone, the expedition visited the Azores, Lisbon, Huelva, Cádiz, Madeira, before returning along the route of Columbus's third voyage, from Gomera in the Canary Islands to Trinidad in the West Indies, with detailed reconnaissance in the Caribbean afterward. In the summer of 1940, further exploration through the Bahamas and around Cuba was carried out in *Mary Otis.*

As preliminary studies for his larger work, Morison published two small books, *The Second Voyage of Columbus* (1939) and *Portuguese Voyages to America in the Fifteenth Century* (1940). The biography that was the motive of the expedition, *Admiral of the Ocean Sea: A Life of Christopher Columbus,* appeared in 1942 in two forms: in two volumes with full notes and documentation, and in a condensed single volume, which was widely distributed by the Book-of-the-Month Club. It was awarded the Pulitzer Prize.

The way was now clear for another seagoing project that was to become the most extensive and difficult of any in Morison's career — *The History of the United States Naval Operations in World War II.* President Franklin D. Roosevelt, who had a lifelong taste for naval history, after reading some of *Admiral of the Ocean Sea,* accepted Morison's proposal to be the Navy's historian, based on actual participation. In May 1942, the professor was commissioned a lieutenant commander in the Naval Reserve and given a set of orders that permitted him to move about the world at will. But having such a set of orders is one thing, and getting to a good vantage point to observe an action whose planning has been cloaked in deep secrecy is another. That he was invariably in the right place at the right time for the next three and a half years was due more to his qualities as a man and a sailor than to his formal credentials. He later recalled the problem thus:

As my position in the Navy was unprecedented, I had to move warily and gingerly in order to obtain co-operation from those who were doing the fighting. Amusingly enough, their initial suspicions of a "long-haired professor in uniform" were dissolved by perusal of my *Admiral of the Ocean Sea,* which told them that I was a sailor before I became a professor, and thus exorcised the academic curse. So, thanks to Columbus, the Navy accepted me; and with many of its members I made warm friendships, which even survived what I felt obliged to write about some of their mistakes.

From November 1942 until July 1946, I was on duty in the Office of Naval Records and Library at the Navy Department, attempting to arrange and salt down records of current operations for future professional and historical use. Thus, at various periods during the war, I saw a good deal of Sam Morison between operations. As he worked for the Secretary of the Navy and I for the Commander in Chief, United States Fleet and Chief of Naval Operations, it would have been necessary for us to send memoranda up and down through extended and exalted channels had we desired to communicate with each other officially through the standard forms of Navy correspondence. But that did not prevent us from working in our shirtsleeves in opposite corners of an overcrowded room, whenever he was in Washington, in terms of informal scholarly harmony. Shortly after I reported for duty, he returned from the invasion of North Africa, but he was soon off to the Pacific to see the last phases of the Guadalcanal campaign; and so it went, until the surrender of Japan. He would return with firsthand observations and memoranda, filling longhand notebooks; plunge into any official reports that had reached Washington; and begin a first draft of a chapter. All too soon, an oblique word would reach him that Admiral Ainsworth, or some other friend, would be glad to see him if he turned up at Pearl Harbor at such and such a moment, and off he would go, soon to find himself on the bridge of a flagship in action.

As the war progressed, and amphibious operations multiplied in size and complexity, one often wondered how even Sam Morison could ever filter these events through his mind and reduce them to ordered volumes. And when the war was over, there remained the equally prodigious task of discovering and digesting the naval records of the enemy side, with the additional barrier of the Japanese language. Yet, between 1947 and 1962, he completed the history in fifteen volumes, publishing in addition in 1963 a single volume, *The Two-Ocean War: A Short History of the United States Navy in the Second World War*, which, far from being a scissors-and-paste condensation, was an original work that could be read with fascination and delight even by those already familiar with the fifteen volumes that had preceded it. Few other men, if any, could have done it. That one individual could produce a work of this quality is owing to his long experience in reducing complex sources to order, unremitting industry, and a lifelong concern for niceties of literary style.

On November 19, 1947, he and I took the morning train from Boston to Rockland, Maine, to attend the funeral of our friend Lincoln Colcord. The sun was low over Penobscot Bay as we drove up to the church in Searsport for the late afternoon service. Yet after a brief visit with Link's family, and the consumption of a piece of pie in the kitchen, Morison entered a waiting cab, which drove him to the Bangor airport, where he took a plane to Boston so as to spend the last hours of the evening in the library of 44 Brimmer Street working on the naval history. I, who was eighteen years younger, happily spent the night in Searsport and returned only the next day. But I had that day the clue as to how he often accomplished the seemingly impossible.

With the sudden death of his beloved wife, Elizabeth Greene Morison, on August 20, 1945, while he was still on active duty in the Navy, he was on his own for the first time in thirty-five years. He wrote a singularly moving memoir of her entitled *Fullness of Life*, which was privately printed for distribution to friends. When he returned to Harvard the following year, his youngest daughter, Catharine, then a Radcliffe undergraduate, ably shouldered the domestic responsibilities of 44 Brimmer Street. Although peace had returned to the world, Sam Morison had four solitary years, in which work and still more work on his naval history offered the only salvation.

New happiness lay ahead, however, for on December 29, 1949, he married in Baltimore his cousin, the beautiful singer Priscilla Barton, who proved, as the dedications of his later books attest, the ideal companion of his work and play. For a time many of his Boston friends feared that the newlyweds might be tempted to live in a pleasant house of Priscilla's near Baltimore, but for their twenty-four happy years of married life they continued to winter in 44 Brimmer Street. The chief change in the pattern consisted of turning over to the children Pleasance and the Sawyers Cove bungalow, and building on the wooded headland at the eastern entrance to Northeast Harbor a new house, called Good Hope, convenient and accessible, and adapted for longer stays in Maine. There Priscilla Morison's genius for horticulture enhanced the natural beauty of the evergreen forest by creating intimate terraces and bosks on a variety of levels where flowering beds, in which delphinium reflected the blue of the sea, enlivened the green of the woods. But her talents were by no means confined to music or to horticulture. Priscilla Morison constantly helped her husband, not only "running interference" (or, as he preferred to call it, "repelling boarders") socially, but listening as he read his manuscripts aloud and helping him to find the correct phrase and *le mot juste.*

Samuel Eliot Morison taught at Harvard for forty years — with time out only for two wars and the Harmsworth Professorship at Oxford — until his retirement in 1955 as Jonathan Trumbull Professor of American History, Emeritus. In the United States Naval Reserve he progressed on active duty from lieutenant commander to captain, retiring, on reaching the age limit in 1951, with the rank of rear admiral. But formal retirement either from history or the Navy was only a technicality, for he worked even harder for both than he had before. Although he resumed teaching at Harvard soon after the war, he maintained offices at the Navy Department and the Naval War College in Newport, where staffs so small as to contradict Parkinson's Law assisted him in organizing enemy documents and other tasks essential for the completion of the naval history. The fifteen volumes of that work, published in as many years, were by no means his sole occupation.

The variety of other books that appeared between volumes of the naval history was extraordinary. Like the wine-taster who can move from glass to glass without confusing or muddling bouquets, Morison enjoyed varying the taste of ideas. He once remarked that he liked to keep a major work and a minor one going at the same time. While the naval history was in progress, a dozen "minor" works appeared. *The Ropemakers of Plymouth*, a history of the Plymouth Cordage Company, which had since 1824 been an enterprise of the family of his boyhood friend Augustus P. Loring, appeared in 1950, followed by a new edition of William Bradford's *Of Plymouth Plantation* in 1952, and *The Story of the "Old Colony" of New Plymouth: 1620–1692* in 1956. For a volume of collected essays and addresses that Alfred A. Knopf issued in 1953, under the title *By Land and By Sea*, Morison wrote introductory headnotes that agreeably enhanced the book's quality. *The Story of Mount Desert Island, Maine* and *One Boy's Boston* similarly drew upon his own past, but *Freedom and*

Compromise dealt with global matters. *The Parkman Reader* (1955) and a Limited Editions Club edition of Prescott's *History of the Conquest of Peru* (1957) were editorial efforts to bring the writings of two of his historical heroes to a wide modern audience, while *John Paul Jones: A Sailor's Biography* (1955) gave him an opportunity to change the taste of World War II by a deep draft of the American Revolution. Nor was Columbus forgotten, for in 1955 he wrote a wholly new book, *Christopher Columbus, Mariner,* "in the hope of reaching a wider public." The success of that hope is indicated by translations into Japanese, Italian, Dutch, Hungarian, Polish, Russian, Persian, Arabic, and Marathi. Furthermore, in 1963 he edited *Journals and Other Documents on the Life and Voyages of Christopher Columbus,* a long-projected documentary companion to *Admiral of the Ocean Sea* that had been delayed by the war.

It is therefore small wonder that the Balzan Foundation, when it wished to award in history something comparable in distinction to a Nobel Prize in the sciences, chose from the entire world Samuel Eliot Morison as the first recipient. As the late Pope John XXIII was to receive a Balzan peace prize, the presentation ceremonies were held in Rome in May 1963, under circumstances of great splendor. *Vistas of History,* published in 1964, contains an account of the occasion, as well as the address "The Experiences and Principles of an Historian," which Admiral Morison gave after receiving the award. This address, taken with "History As a Literary Art" — which he originally allowed me to publish in 1946 as an Old South Leaflet and is reprinted here — gives the essence of his approach to the writing of history.

The story did not stop with the Balzan Prize, for in 1964 Admiral Morison received the Medal of Freedom, the highest civilian award that the President of the United States can bestow, which helps keep in balance the Legion of Merit received from the Navy, and honorary doctorates from Harvard, Yale, Oxford, Trinity, Amherst, Union, Bucknell, Maine, Notre Dame, Holy Cross, and Boston College. There is a nice ecumenical quality in a Harvard professor's being honored by Yale, and a devout Episcopalian — long a parishioner of the Church of the Advent, across Mt. Vernon Street from his house — receiving degrees from three Catholic institutions.

The next twelve months saw the publication of three very different books. *The Caribbean As Columbus Saw It,* written in collaboration with his Colombian friend Mauricio Obregón, illustrated Columbus's landfalls as observed from the cockpit of Obregón's Cessna-310 air-plane. *Spring Tides* was a prose poem on the sea that evoked cruis-ing both in Maine waters and the Aegean, while *The Oxford History of the American People* was an 1150-page retelling of the subject from the origin of man in America to the death of John Fitzgerald Ken-nedy.

This, the third of the histories of the United States that Morison wrote in the course of forty years, was an entirely new work. It was, "in a sense," as he stated in his Preface, "a legacy to my countrymen after teaching and writing the history of the United States for over half a century." It was a huge single volume, heavy to hold in the hand, but far from heavy in its approach. As it was designed for popular reading, it eschewed the scholarly apparatus of footnotes and references. "Readers may take a certain amount of erudition for granted," he noted. Through the literary artistry of which Morison was a master, this distillation of a lifetime of thought and research became a series of vivid characterizations that can be read with de-light, and will long stick in the mind of the reader. The American people are indeed reading it, for the New York *Times* of July 25, 1965, noted that after eleven weeks on the best-seller list, 60,000 copies (out of an initial printing of 122,000) had already been sold, in ad-dition to a quarter of a million distributed by the Book-of-the-Month Club. A decade later it is still widely read in a paperback edition.

A biography of Commodore Matthew Calbraith Perry, which Mori-son began in 1964, led him to make a visit to Mexico in 1965 and one to Japan in the autumn of 1966, followed by a voyage around the world. The book appeared in the autumn of 1967, a few weeks before his eightieth birthday. At that point, most men would have rested on their oars, but not SEM. In May 1968, a month before the sixtieth reunion of his Harvard Class of 1908, he decided to write a work that had been on his mind for forty years. *The European Dis-covery of America: The Northern Voyages*, A.D. 500–1600, completed in the last days of 1970 and published in 1971 by the Oxford Univer-sity Press, was designed, with a projected sequel on the southern voyages, to cover the entire field of New World discovery, a task that no one had attempted in the twentieth century. The research in-volved a second voyage around the world and visits to numerous archives in Italy, France, England, and Denmark.

In accordance with his principle of keeping a major work and a minor one going at the same time, he turned, while doing research on the northern voyages, to a revision of his first book. *Harrison Gray Otis, 1765–1848: The Urbane Federalist*, which appeared early in 1969, was a very different work from the first edition of fifty-six years before, for it presented more of the social history of Otis's times than of Federalist political squabbles. Another by-blow of this period was *Samuel de Champlain, Father of New France*, published in 1972.

The year 1967 was an anxious one, for soon after the publication of the Perry biography it was discovered that Priscilla Morison had a breast cancer. A harrowing series of x-ray and cobalt treatments followed, which, it was thought in January 1968, had proved successful. The reprieve was, alas, only temporary, for in 1971 Priscilla was ill again and once more receiving cobalt treatment. She refused to be an invalid, however, and with the highest gallantry accompanied her husband on the travels that were essential for the completion of his *Southern Voyages*. In June 1971, they both were in Rome, Amsterdam, The Hague, Brussels, Antwerp, Haarlem, and London, while at the end of the year they began the Morison Magellan Expedition. There could be no question of sailing in the wake of Magellan; this time the voyages had to be retraced by air in the company of Mauricio Obregón. Even so, Priscilla's determination to accompany her husband was, as he wrote later, "the supreme demonstration of her intrepid courage and tenacity." They met the Obregóns in Los Angeles on December 12, 1971, and flew to Tahiti, thence to Honolulu, Guam, and Manila. From the Philippines they went to Rome and to Spain, then by ship to South America, where the Argentine and Chilean navies provided means to reconnoiter the Strait of Magellan by air. In March, they returned to Boston.

While back in the hands of the doctors, and in frequent pain, Priscilla kept the flag flying through 1972. On New Year's Eve, 1972, she and Sam gave their last great reception, for ninety friends, on what they called "the hundred and first birthday of 44 Brimmer Street." Early in the morning of February 22, 1973, she died. Although the light had gone out of Sam Morison's life, he turned for a second time to hard work as the only salvation. In March he flew to South America to check rivers discovered by his early explorers, and to San Francisco to investigate the landfalls of Sir Francis Drake. By Spartan self-discipline, he completed his manuscript in April 1974; *The European Discovery of America: The Southern Voyages*, A.D.

1492–1616 was published before the end of the year. Before his eighty-eighth birthday, Sam Morison had completed his great task in spite of advancing years and personal grief.

The European Discovery of America, like *The Oxford History of the American People*, had a phenomenal popular success. *The Northern Voyages* received the Bancroft Prize. The Massachusetts Historical Society dedicated its 1975 spring exhibition to Samuel Eliot Morison. In *The Discovery of America*, the picture book issued to commemorate the exhibition, Thomas Boylston Adams wrote of the necessary boldness of master seamen, continuing:

Those who launch their careers onto the infinite seas of time take seamen's risks. There is room to wander forever in the dim backward. A gluttony for facts can induce the fate of Circe's swine. A waste of words can drown a man as surely as the sea. Those who project their lines back must know how simultaneously to project them forward. It takes more than a touch of genius to make a great historian.

Gibbon was surely not the first, nor will he be the last to sit musing on the steps of the Ara Coeli overlooking the ruins of the Capitol. Parkman was no mere tourist climbing the narrow path to the Plains of Abraham or following the Oregon Trail. Many ask why. Some spend a lifetime searching for the answer in how and where and when. They tunnel through libraries with the eagerness of moles hunting grubs. Each develops a method, based on the habits of the past, the innovations of the present, and the standards of safety and prudence which experience has taught. But like the great explorers, only a few come home.

Gibbon, Parkman, and Morison — some things they have in common. Scholarship they have, minds incessantly retentive of fact, faultlessly remembering the great sweep of events, quick to remember the trivial incident, the unique personal remark that sets the vast in perspective, makes the forgotten real. But the words flow forth at last from these crucibles of the mind with a quality so elusive, so breathtaking and interest-provoking and yet so different that in despair for any better word, we call it style. Something there is that makes us turn the page. Something makes us remember the turned page. These books indeed are, in Emily Dickinson's phrase, frigates that take us lands away.

Tom Adams concluded his Foreword: "The grandest style the oceans ever saw was carried abroad by American clipper ships. Admiral Morison is our *Flying Cloud.*"

Although we hoped that our *Flying Cloud* would make many more voyages, the admiral firmly but quietly stated that, with *The Euro-*

pean Discovery of America, he had come to the end of his historical writing. There remained only one personal matter to record: the account of over twenty-three years of happiness with his lost wife. *Vita Nuova, A Memoir of Priscilla Barton Morison* was privately printed for friends before the end of 1975. He then turned, with the help of his widowed daughter, Emily (Wendy) Beck, to the choice of the selections from his own writings that form this book. That task was completed in March 1976. He then went to London, where he had a glorious time with old friends and his daughter Catharine. On his return in April, just as he was about to start for Northeast Harbor, his doctor sent him to the Massachusetts General Hospital for tests. There he suffered a stroke too massive even for him to surmount; there he died on May 15, 1976. His work was completed "shipshape and Bristol fashion."

For his funeral on May 18 at the Church of the Advent two Roman Catholic priests joined the parish clergy in the sanctuary. A galaxy of admirals, scholars, Beacon Hill neighbors, and more distant friends filled the church as a naval guard of honor brought in the flag-draped casket. The rector, the Reverend G. Harris Collingwood, paid a tribute that revealed much about Sam Morison's life and work. Father Collingwood said in part:

Four years ago while crossing the Public Garden, by chance Admiral Morison and I fell into step together. He was about to leave for South America where he planned to retrace the Southern Voyages of Magellan by airplane and by ship. He was excited by the prospect. I remarked on the courage of the early explorers.

He was silent for a moment as we walked along. Then he said, "Courage, yes, but a courage sustained by prayer."

He told me in detail about the journals and logs of the early explorers, how they were filled with thanksgivings to God for the daily mercies vouchsafed to them through His Providence.

In his last days as I prayed with him in the hospital, I remembered that incident. Samuel Eliot Morison lived a life of courage, sustained by prayer. He wrote his own epitaph.

He suffered the death of his son. He suffered the death of two wives. Each day nevertheless remained for him an adventure into the unknown, an adventure on which he embarked with courage sustained by prayer.

His was a remarkable life. This was borne in on me two years ago, Maundy Thursday [April 11, 1974]. He waited to speak to me that day after the noon Mass.

"Would it be possible," he asked, "for you to make a public statement of my thankfulness for God's mercy? Today I finished the volume of the southern voyages; it was a plan of writing I began fifty years ago."

It is a remarkable achievement for any man to persevere for fifty years through a hard plan and bring it to its end. It is even more remarkable to wish to give thanks to Almighty God for the strength to complete the task. I used the example of Samuel Eliot Morison the next day, Good Friday, when I preached on the Sixth Word, "It is finished."

Courage sustained by prayer was a mark of the early explorers of the new world. It was a mark of Samuel Eliot Morison's character, and it is his legacy of wisdom to each of us.

As a cable reached me in Florence the day following Sam Morison's death, a Latin requiem Mass for the repose of his soul was said, through the kindness of a Franciscan, on Sunday morning, May 16, in the crypt of the cardinals under the high altar of the Duomo, at an altar before which was the inscription: IN PACE CHRISTI ARCHIEPIS-COPI FIORENTINORUM RESURRECTIONEM EXPECTANT.

Ovid would have enjoyed describing the metamorphoses of Samuel Eliot Morison. What other man ever has been, or is likely to be, a professor both at Oxford and Harvard, a private of infantry and a rear admiral? Like Proteus, another "Old One of the Sea," who was the source of much indispensable information to mariners, his aspect changed frequently, with disconcerting rapidity. I remember him resplendent in academic costume or blue naval uniform, as well as in oilskins at the wheel of the *Emily Marshall*. I recall his enjoying a clam chowder at Mount Desert made by the late Enos Verge of Thomaston, picnicking on Gus Loring's beach at Prides Crossing, carving with easy grace a roast suckling pig at a council lunch of the Colonial Society of Massachusetts, against the background of an Empire gold mirror, presiding at his own table in Brimmer Street, or leaving 20 Louisburg Square at midnight, after one of Sohier Welch's great dinners, wearing an opera hat and cape that gave him the aspect of the *noctambule* in *Louise*. I saw him perhaps most often on a midday route between 44 Brimmer Street, the Somerset Club, and the Boston Athenaeum, dressed with the restrained elegance of a conservative householder, but I recall occasions when clams were being dug at Sawyers Cove, when we were at Searsport, sitting on Lincoln Colcord's back porch, looking out on Penobscot Bay, or exchanging pleasantries with Waldo Peirce — *W. Peirsius Barbatus*, as he described that painter to me on an illegible postcard. I think of him presiding over the meetings of the American Antiquarian Society at Worcester, enlivening those of the Massachusetts Historical Society, and striding purposefully into Widener Library in well-cut riding costume, carrying green baize bags full of books. In all his manifestations there was the underlying basis of style and quality, whether in wine, food, company, conversation, or the writing of history. There was also limitless energy, and certainly in my friendship with him a great deal of human kindness. Many of his graduate students long remembered the way in which he asked them to 44 Brimmer Street, gave them his best wine and cigars as a matter of course, and made them part of the local scene. Even the corn-fed soon became, by example, gentlemen as well as scholars. Like many New Englanders, he could have moments of shyness, which might lead to an occasional awkward remark, or none at all, but that is part of the breed. And at other times he could speak as he wrote, mingling the periods of an Edward Gibbon or a Winston Churchill with the pithy homeliness of a New England general storekeeper.

Two quotations from the ancients, prefixed to books of Morison's, do much to explain the character and quality of his writing. At the beginning of *Operations in North African Waters,* the first volume of the naval history to be published, was set this extract from Thucydides:

Of the events of the war, I have not ventured to speak from any chance information, nor according to any notion of my own; I have described nothing but what I either saw myself, or learned from others of whom I made the most careful and particular inquiry. The task was a laborious one because eyewitnesses of the same occurrence gave different accounts of them as they remembered, or were interested in the actions of one side or the other. And very likely the strictly historical character of my narrative may be disappointing to the ear. But if he who desires to have before his eyes a true picture of the events which have happened, and of the like events which may be expected to happen hereafter in the order of human beings, shall pronounce what I have written to be useful, then I shall be satisfied.

And some years earlier appeared on the title page of *Builders of the Bay Colony* this significant "tag" of Horace:

Quamquam ridentem dicere verum
quid vetat?

Why, indeed, may one not be telling the truth while one laughs? Samuel Eliot Morison combined with diligence for the truth a lively sense of humor. Our good friend and former neighbor John Cardinal Wright, while Bishop of Pittsburgh in the 1960's, commented on "the deadly earnestness surrounding the discussion of the current problem of the intellectual life of America" and feared that this earnestness "suggests that knowledge and information may be on the increase and wisdom and understanding on the way out." He asked: "What has become of the humanistic touch that used to betray a humane preoccupation and that revealed itself in an occasional trace of a sense of humor?" It is this humanistic touch, revealed in more than occasional traces of wit and humor, that makes Morison's forty-three volumes so uniquely delightful.

In appraising the work of his great predecessor, Francis Parkman, Morison wrote:

> His unusual combination of superlative skill in the three qualities that make good historical literature — research, evaluation, and literary presentation — besides the fascination of his chosen field, have caused the works of Parkman to endure longer than those of any other American historian of his era . . . Parkman's work is forever young, "with the immortal youth of art"; his men and women are alive; they feel, think, and act within the framework of a living nature. Documents are, to be sure, the basis of his History; but to him documents were not facts; rather, the symbols of events, which the historian must re-create for his readers. In Parkman's prose the forests ever murmur; the rapids perpetually foam and roar; the people have parts and passions. Like that "sylvan historian" of Keats's "Ode on a Grecian Urn," he caught the spirit of an age and fixed it for all time, "for ever panting and for ever young."

And so, in Morison's prose the California clipper still comes into India Wharf, long after the ships, the wharf, and he himself have disappeared. I am glad that he filled the shoes of Francis Parkman for so many years, and that, guided by Thucydides and Horace, he covered so much territory in them. The pages that follow, selected by his daughter, will, I trust, cause many readers to wish for more.

WALTER MUIR WHITEHILL

Some Reflections on Style

Funes ceciderunt mihi in praeclaris:
etenim hereditas mea praeclara est mihi.
— PSALM 16:6

THE PROSE of any reputable historian, one may argue, reflects more surely than the prose of the novelist, biographer, essayist, or the fine critic with his systematic dyspepsia, what Wallace Stevens means or meant by "the weave of the world." The future historian of Darwin's and Hudson's Patagonia, Auden's Iceland, or Clarke's (the geologist's) Gaspé will need sophisticated training and background beyond the narrow specialist in order to function with truly worldly insight — and, yes, humility — on any such far outpost as these three.

That I make my own observations on the literary quality of him who in peace and war was always his own lone outpost on the sea, on tidal flats, on islands, continents; in bays and harbors; aloft, or in the classroom or the house where he was born, is not solely because I cared enough to have had some early hand in this big book. And even if I did originally suggest it to the author and his publisher in the wake of *The Parkman Reader* of 1955, it is now a reality only because of many similar proposals on the part of others in what the anthropologists call "converging evolution."

No one could write so much so well so steadily so long, and with such unabating gusto and momentum, as Sam Morison managed to do, unless "the lines" did fall, as Psalm 16:6 proclaims, "in pleasant places." Lytton Strachey makes a point of Gibbon's happiness; Gibbon made a point of it as well in telling us how he felt that night in taking leave — an unforgettable moment — of his monumental labor. Likewise the author of all that is in this book was happy in his profession, in its demands and discipline, and largely in his life. One should remember this; which is not to suggest — for I don't believe it — that the sometime Harmsworth Professor of American History at Oxford was born with a literary style, pronounced or otherwise. He was not. He worked hard to *achieve* a natural narrative style; he worked hard, book by book, to *secure* it; and he put a first-rate mind in charge: a mind which could control (and these are his own good words) "this quick, warm synthesis between research, thinking, and writing . . . to attain the three prime qualities of historical composition — clarity, vigor, and objectivity." For unswerving devotion to his ideal he was rewarded by countless honors and by — what mattered more — a wide responding readership.

Now very few writers of our time were born with even a semblance of literary style, as perhaps, at a guess, was Sir Thomas Browne; or Jane Austen, Kipling, Charlotte Mew, E. Nesbit, and the more surprising and difficult Doughty. Likewise for us in America there were surely Poe, Parkman, Thoreau, Emily Dickinson, Robert Frost, and E. B. White. White is for absolute certain; and I proved it only twenty years back by reading a short prose piece in *St. Nicholas* magazine (of more than sixty years ago) in the children's section called the "St. Nicholas League." I had come on a few paragraphs signed respectively Edna St. Vincent Millay, Cornelia Otis Skinner, Robert Hillyer, and was suddenly struck by a prose passage much more earthy and natural in voice than what I had been glancing through. This sounds like E. B. White, I said to myself. *Then* I looked at the signature: Elwyn Brooks White, age 11.

It is true, however, that "style in its finest sense," as Whitehead says, "is the last acquirement of the educated mind." Yet it can be over-acquired as well, and become so velvet-smooth that to read it, as some rough wag has said, is like getting caught in a revolving door. But what makes the Morison style so attractive to eye and ear is neither dazzling brilliance nor velvet smoothness, but the effortless, unaffected quality of vocabulary and cadence, and the full sense of partnership with the reader which, paradoxically, the surprise of discovering such informality on a high intellectual plane almost instantly conveys. There is something Homerically Greek and analeptic in its effect.

So whether the flag went up for Columbus, Magellan, John Paul Jones, Sir Francis Drake, or Commodore Perry, Admiral Morison set sail to see the action in his mind's eye while examining with 20-20 eyes the actual spot where it had taken place. Of conventional armchair anchorage he would have none. Parkman — first of his heroes — rode the dangerous plains to make immortal the longest trail on earth. Mark Twain had been a pilot on the Mississippi. So Morison, after the well-deserved success of his second book — *The Maritime History of Massachusetts* — began to follow in the wake (or occasionally in the tracks) of almost everyone he wrote about: the northern voyagers, the southern voyagers, the inland voyager (Champlain), the roving voyager (John Paul Jones), the Oriental papa-san in Commodore Perry. "My feeling for the sea," says sailor Morison in *Spring Tides*, "is such that writing about it is about as embarrassing as making a confession of religious faith." The more he wrote about the sea, the more the groundswell of it entered into the rhythm of his prose.

His life became a series of landfalls and departures. The needle of his compass was never still. Whenever and wherever he sailed, or flew mast-high in the wake of some inspired Magellan, or went ashore, or traveled by land — he saw, he listened, he acquired, he examined, he weighed, he valued, revalued, or rejected. And all that he had seen, heard, noted, and ultimately assembled comes through to us today in narrative as fresh as salt and pine and kitchen smoke commingling in a fishing village on the south shore of the St. Lawrence River.

Color? "Color is, in fact, of central importance to his style," says Sinclair Hitchings, a younger reader than am I. "He found it in many ways. His actors speak through letters, journals, accounts. Repeatedly, he takes one paragraph or a few to reconstruct a day in the lives of a group of people, or to tell how they did what they were doing, whether it was shipbuilding, navigating, trading, attacking, defending. He loved the details of everyday life: what was for breakfast, how people dressed, how they tied their hair, what they shopped for, how they carried on their daily business, how they found diversion. In his effort to capture the feeling of a time, he sometimes prints words and music of songs of the day. Contemporary poetry and contemporary doggerel he quotes frequently."

Which brings me to poetry. Among the writers quoted in *The Maritime History of Massachusetts* are Hawthorne, Emerson, Thoreau, Whittier, Melville, and Whitman. Two of these were full-time poets; Emerson was a poet as well as essayist, and a near idol of Robert Frost; Thoreau could and did write poems on occasion. I wonder if our historian ever noted one detachable poetic line buried in the lofty prose of *Moby Dick*?

> It is not down in any map,
> True places never are.

Morison cared much for poetry. His daughter, who has edited this volume, says that she remembers him reading aloud, when she was small, Whitman's "Out of the cradle, endlessly rocking," and being herself very moved. He was a great Keats man. You will find SEM contributing verse of his own to *The Southern Voyages* and elsewhere. And his prose style at its best proves patently how much the rapture and grace of genuine prosody was in his blood.

He spoke French well; knew Latin, Spanish, and Italian; and liked to translate — freely and in his own (sometimes not too accurate) way. He greatly admired St.-John Perse, whom he met in Washington; and the poet gave him permission to make such translations of him from *Amers* (*Seamarks*) as he cared to. Some of these bob up like lobster buoys in *Spring Tides* (1965), along with many others there and elsewhere out of Homer, Hesiod, *The Greek Anthology*, Aeschylus, Virgil, and Dante. Morison likewise loved sea chanteys; and the opening charm of such an anonymous English fragment as this quatrain on Captain Cook,* which I once quoted in his presence:

> Slices, the natives bore, of ham and tongue,
> While from the tree the ready breadfruit hung.
> Pleased with the sight, the Navigator smiles
> And calls the happy spot the Sandwich Isles.

The colloquial always fascinated Morison; it gave spice to his speech as well as to his writing. And the seaman's — the sailor's — technical language: "gear and tackle and trim," as Hopkins says. The same with pertinent anecdote. He told me once — more than once — that the English reviewers of his books chided him, not for being, as Nietzsche said of John Stuart Mill, "offensively clear," but for diluting his professional prose with slang phrases and expressions. Some of these offenders may have been:

"Nothing is more pathetic than the 'gonna' historian."

"Sold down the river."

" 'Singing like crazy.' "

"We often fall for them."

---

* Given me by Sir Ronald Syme, O.M.

"The contents fetched up on Francisco."

"That should have made Alma Mater's ears burn."

"Rarin' to go."

"Let off steam."

I think of two of Morison's own whittled phrases: "to relate the past *creatively* to the present": for what indeed is history but that? As to style itself: "Unfortunately there is no royal road to style." No royal road, of course; but even as he says this, he is pointing out a number of the best-marked trails; and he has blazed or reblazed not a few of them himself. Or, if you wish to go back (as he does) to the Greek, though in translation, just make a note of this: "To be subtle without ceasing to be simple; to be realistic, yet not crude; to be minute at the right moment but not all the time . . . This at their best, the Greeks achieved." That is F. L. Lucas (in *Style*); and what Lucas has said is a fair summary of the Morison credo and the stylistic discipline nowhere better in evidence than in *The Maritime History, Columbus,* "The Young Man Washington," "A Prologue to American History," parts of *Three Centuries of Harvard, The Oxford History of the American People,* and that rare little item (q.v.) called "The Scholar in America" — an optimistic post-Emerson essay delivered originally in Kansas City, heart of the heartland itself, and half a continent away from Cambridge. It contains one notable aphorism — and Morison is in general no aphoristic writer, as were Emerson, Thoreau, and Sarah Orne Jewett — which should stick in the mind: *"The direction we need is vertical, not horizontal — down to the roots, up toward the stars."* Let it ride here in italics, for it has about it all the magnificence of J. B. Priestley's observation in *Midnight on the Desert:* "This country is geology by day and astronomy at night."

Now mannerisms are not to be confused with style, to paraphrase Horace Walpole; and no crudely mannered writer could possibly produce the Morison and Priestley quotations above. The sole exception is when one's *consistent* style, conceived on a grand scale like Browning's at one end of the spectrum and S. J. Perelman's at the other, becomes a mannered continuum and is then, though not the equal of Marcel Marceau's exquisite mime, simply a perfection of its own curious kind.

Morison had great wit and a fine, normally open but sometimes subtle, sense of humor. Examples:

"Across the harbor, obscuring the southerly channel, Marblehead presents her back side of rocky pasture to the world at large, and Salem in particular."

"Respectable men clerks (female clerks, sir? — would you have female sailors?)."

"Trained in some juicier profession."

"No American since John Fiske [referring to Charles and Mary Beard] had been able to make a living by writing history, apart from an academic milch cow."

"A forcing-bed for the professions."

"In four years Washington had learned much from war . . . ill rewarded by the music of whistling bullets."

"The authority of the British Parliament extends only to low water mark," wrote Jefferson. Morison says: "Note that this excepted the clams of Cape Cod from parliamentary jurisdiction, but not the oysters of Virginia!"

He wrote with a pen on lined legal-sized yellow paper, leaving lots of space between lines. He would then go over this first rough draft for changes, corrections, additions, deletions. The result would be typed, and the process possibly repeated. Parkman had "loathed the drudgery of historical research," and he had said so in these most positive words. But one sure thing these two historians held in common: no sign of drudgery ever appeared on the printed page. Nor did either, in his writing, ever put the solitary pot to boil. Even the fifteen-volume *History of the United States Naval Operations in World War II*, the style of which reflects inevitably the leveling intrusion of eyewitnesses — often like staccato reflex from the bridge — shows no lethal sign of second-rate reporting. Two of the truly great climaxes in all those thousands of pages will be found due east of where we are. And even reading them completely out of context, one must sense that fifteen volumes written for the specialist of today and tomorrow could not possibly be undeserving of the critic's words: "*Il a superposé la magie du style.*" Or, as the admiral himself says elsewhere: "We humdrum historians do occasionally have a creative moment." And in writing of the sea, Morison's creative moments lift him to the level of — sometimes above the level of — such masters of sea-writing as Joseph Conrad, H. M. Tomlinson, and Erskine Childers. A trinity, I well may add, impossible to duplicate.

"All his days," says Admiral Morison, "Parkman had nothing but contempt for a 'way of life where nature's fruit is that pallid and emasculate scholarship of which New England has had too many examples.' " Morison's contempt for the same provender was, if anything, sharper. Parkman, as Morison is careful to explain, "was never tempted to write of sea voyages and discoveries." But Morison was seaborne while the Charles River up to Watertown was still a tidal basin. As the result of that, certain captains and sailors of fortune who paced so many quarterdecks long vanished and who themselves survived imperfectly in foreign languages, in portraits done in oil, or in bronze statues, stand here today for retroinspection. But reading of them as of a world apart, and at a time when man seems to have backed himself into an international parking lot, one must not fail to do the seaman equal honor when it comes to his writing of teachers, colleagues, friends; his university, and of his art itself. How well he understood Clough's all but forgotten couplet:

> But play no tricks upon thy soul, O man;
> Let fact be fact, and life the thing it can.

DAVID McCORD

Contents

Sailor Historian

The Best of Samuel Eliot Morison

Introduction

MY DAUGHTER EMILY M. BECK, who has made this compilation from my works published since 1922, has asked me to contribute a brief introduction to each selection, stating (so far as I can) how, when, and why it was written. This Introduction will serve also as one to Part I, "The Discovery of America."

Although this chapter includes extracts from my three latest works to be published, in the 1970's, its planning and composition go back sixty years. In 1916, Professor Edward Channing, one of my masters at Harvard College, turned over to me when I was twenty-nine his course on American colonial history. At Concord, Massachusetts, where I had taken up residence with my beloved first wife, Bessie, I started in August to prepare my lectures for the next term, opening about September 25. By the 24th I was still working on Christopher Columbus! The man, and the printed literature about him, fascinated me; and I then decided that the only way to solve the problems of this great navigator, really to "get at" him, was to explore, under sail, the coasts and islands that he discovered. This was no easy thing for a young and impecunious person to accomplish in a disordered world. And, since I already was looking ahead to writing the history of subsequent discoveries in the New World for a century or more, the project took over fifty years to finish.

First came World War I, in which my military service was brief but my contributions to the preparations for peace at Paris were time-consuming. When I returned to teaching American history at Harvard, the impending Harvard Tercentenary loomed, and most of my research for years was devoted to the origin and development of Alma Mater. By 1935, when the Harvard Tercentenary was about to be celebrated, I realized that if ever my youthful dream was to come true, it must be then; so (with the help of Paul Hammond, Bill Stevens, and many others) I organized the Harvard Columbus Expedition, which, first in a chartered yawl and then in barquentine

Capitana and ketch *Mary Otis*, covered most of the coasts and islands discovered by Columbus. The result was *Admiral of the Ocean Sea*, whose success encouraged me to write sundry more volumes on the great discoverer. By the time *Admiral* was ready for the press, we were engulfed in World War II, the writing of whose naval history fell to me. That took the greater part of my time until 1955, when, with the last volumes almost completed, I retired both from the Naval Reserve and from Harvard and was able to concentrate once more on the age of sail.

To this very happy period of my life, when I was married to Priscilla Barton Morison (Bessie having died in 1945), belongs more than half the remainder of my books. Priscilla and I traveled together to all parts of the world where there were books and documents on eras of discovery, including Magellan's great voyage, which she endured with me while dying of cancer. In 1973, shortly after we had struck sail and dropped anchor for the last time, she departed for "that undiscovered country from whose bourne no traveler returns."

SAMUEL ELIOT MORISON

I

The Discovery
of America

1

The Mysterious Ocean

From THE EUROPEAN DISCOVERY OF AMERICA: THE NORTHERN VOYAGES, A.D. 500–1600 (New York: Oxford University Press, 1971), *pages ix–xii, 3–9.*

THERE IS SOMETHING very special about these northern voyages. In contrast to the fair winds that Columbus experienced and that made an outward Atlantic crossing easy from the navigator's point of view, anything might happen to you in the North Atlantic, even in summer; and in the sixteenth century everyone but French fishermen avoided sailing in winter. Westerly gales hurled crested seas against your little barque and forced it to lay-to for days; easterly gales drenched the sailors with chilling rain; fierce northerlies ripped their sails and cracked their masts. Between weather fronts even the whisper of a wind would often die and a white calm descend, so calm that one might think that the winds were worn out; then the fog closed in and the sea became a shimmering mirror reflecting the filtered rays of the sun. In high latitudes in summer one could forget whether it was day or night, while the sails slatted monotonously and the yards and rigging dripped rime. Plenty of men died on these northern voyages, but never of thirst. In a big fishing fleet, two centuries later, days of white calm might pass with jollity and humor from ship to ship, but for little knots of men confined to a small vessel, and no other human being within a thousand miles, the experience might be maddening. In the era of discovery, sailors would break out their sweeps and try to row their heavy vessels out of the calm, just to have something to do. It was a life for strong men and boys, not for women; the Greenlanders did indeed take women on their short voyages to Vinland, but there is no record of French or English taking them to America before Cartier's second voyage; and they were *forçats*, convicts.

People ask me to compare the hazards of the early navigators and

those of the modern single-handed breed. The Atlantic was crossed
many years ago by a Gloucester fisherman rowing a dory; and since
Captain Slocum sailed around the world in his little *Spray,* with not
one modern gadget, there have been countless one-man ocean crossings and a number of nonstop circumnavigations with self-inflicted
hardships perhaps equal to those of the crews of Cabot and Frobisher. But these modern loners know where they are going; they
have accurate charts, many instruments, and an auxiliary engine; they
are in communication with the world by radio; naval vessels, air-
planes, and coast guards shepherd them, drop food and water, and
even, on occasion, take them on board for a rest; and, perhaps most
important, they have no unruly, timid, and suspicious crew to govern
and cajole into doing their duty.

Consider also the hazards of a sixteenth-century navigator exploring
an unknown coast in a square-rigged vessel, incapable of quick maneuvering like a modern sailing yacht. With an onshore wind, the discoverers had to sail close to shore if they wanted to learn anything;
yet it was always risky, especially on a fog-bound coast like Newfoundland. Submerged just below the surface, rocks capable of rip-
ping the guts out of a ship were difficult to see in northern waters —
dark green, opaque waters, not transparent like those of the Caribbean and the Coral Sea. Every harbor you entered added a new risk,
even if a boat were sent ahead to sound. Would your anchor hold, or
was the bottom hard rock, eelgrass, or kelp, along which your hook
would skid like a sled, requiring quick and efficient action to prevent
your ship's crashing? If the wind is offshore when you sight land, you
might be blown seaward again and have to beat back, which could
take weeks — we shall see many instances of this. As Alan Villiers
wrote, "The plain everyday difficulties of handling these ships . . .
are already so forgotten as to seem incredible. Their means of movement was the wind properly directed to their sails . . . They had to
fight for their way, fight for their lives at times."* And so many lost
their lives: John Cabot, both Corte-Reals, Sir Humphrey Gilbert, for
instance. North America became a graveyard for European ships and
sailors.

I wish that everyone who imagines that the "perils and dangers of

* Alan Villiers, *Captain James Cook* (1967), pp. 146–47.

the sea" have vanished before modern science would read Captain K. Adlard Cole's *Heavy Weather Sailing* (1967), with its hair-raising stories of sailing yachts no smaller than those of the era of discoveries, but laden with gadgets. There you have firsthand accounts of some of the hazards that the early navigators encountered as a matter of course — enormous freak waves, pitch-poling, capsizing; and although hurricanes were rarely encountered on these northern voyages of discovery, very strong gales and immense seas were common. Please remember, too, that these early seamen had no storm warnings, no "law of storms" enabling them to evade the eye; and that even sailing in a fleet gave little protection. Under certain conditions a ship that foundered, like Gilbert's, or crashed on a lee shore, could expect no help even from another ship within sight. There is no basis of comparison between the astronauts who first landed on the moon on July 20, 1969, and discoverers like Columbus, Cabot, Verrazzano, and Cartier. Those four were men with an idea, grudgingly and meanly supported by their sovereigns. The three young heroes of the moon landing did not supply the idea; they bravely and intelligently executed a vast enterprise employing some 400,000 men and costing billions of dollars; whilst Columbus's first voyage cost his sovereigns less than a court ball; and Cabot's, which gave half the New World to England, cost Henry VII just fifty pounds. The astronauts' epochal voyage into space, a triumph of the human spirit, was long prepared, rehearsed, and conducted with precision to an accurately plotted heavenly body. Their feat might be slightly comparable to Cabot's if the moon were always dark and they knew not exactly where to find it — and if they had hit the wrong planet.

Abbé Anthiaume, a pioneer historian of French navigation, wrote many years ago of the early explorers by sea: "What superhuman energy a captain needed to triumph over these terrors of the ocean, to free his mind of ancient prejudices . . . and to carry his crew through these obscurities! . . . He knew very well that he risked his life and that of his shipmates for a hypothesis." The Abbé asks us to remember the common sailor, who, "lost in an immensity of ocean that he suspected to be endless," imagined an island behind each cloud on the horizon, and anxiously followed with his eyes the birds, which, as evening fell, flew in the same direction, hoping to be able, like them, to sleep ashore again.

*

The European discovery of America flows from two impulses. One, lasting over two thousand years and never attained, is the quest for some "land of pure delight where saints immortal reign"; where (in the words of Isaac Watts's hymn) "everlasting spring abides, and never fading flowers." The other impulse, springing into life in the thirteenth century, was the search for a sea route to "the Indies," as China, Japan, Indonesia, and India were then collectively called. This search attained success with the voyages of Columbus and Cabot — who (by the greatest serendipity of history) discovered America instead of reaching the Indies — and with the voyage of Magellan, which finally did reach the Indies and returned around the world.

The story of how this happened — so far as we can piece it out from the imperfect records of the past — is the subject of this book. It is convenient to cover the northern voyages first, because they had a certain unity of purpose as well as of geography. But we must briefly consider the heritage of classical antiquity, which is basic to all European westward ventures.

When primitive man first reached the shores of the Mediterranean and the Atlantic, his first impulse, no doubt, was to cast a line into this new and apparently limitless fishpond; and his second, to wonder what lay "over there," beyond the ocean's rim. He built himself rafts, dugout canoes, and finally boats for fishing and coastwise trading. He discovered that manipulating a sail saved him a lot of manual labor, and in the course of experimenting with winds and currents, some men ventured, or were blown, out of sight of land. No matter how far they sailed beyond the Pillars of Hercules (the Strait of Gibraltar) or off the western coast from Scotland to Spain, the same watery horizon greeted them. So, naturally, poets and priests adopted the theory of a never-never land, where the souls of the meritorious faithful live happily without work before proceeding to one of God's many mansions. It must have been a consoling thought for the families of sailors who never returned, that God had provided for them in these Happy Isles.

Hesiod, a Greek poet of the eighth century B.C., was the first man (so far as we know) to give these Islands of the Blest literary expression. Speaking of a "godlike race of hero-men" who preceded us on earth, he said that some were killed in battles such as the siege of Troy, but to the others, "Father Zeus, at the ends of the earth, presented a dwelling place, apart from man and far from the deathless gods. In the Islands of the Blest, bounded by deep-swirling Ocean, they live untouched by toil or sorrow. For them the grain-giving earth thrice yearly bears fruit sweet as honey." These *Insulae Fortunatae,* or Happy Isles, which are also called the Hesperides, the Elysian Fields, and other names in every European vernacular, were believed in throughout the period of classical antiquity and well into the Middle Ages. Even the sophisticated Horace, despairing of the republic in time of civil war, urged his noble Roman friends to "cease their effeminate complaints and go," leaving the vile, indocile plebeians to fight it out among themselves.

Happy fields surrounded by Ocean await us and invite us to their shores. Go, then, to these fortunate islands, where the land without tillage produces grain abundantly, the vine bears grapes without pruning, ripe figs may be plucked the year round, the olive ever bears fruit, honey drips from the live oak, the streams make a pleasant murmur as they flow from the mountains and tumble over rocky ledges; she-goats with full udders beg one to milk them; neither bears nor vipers are there . . . The Argonauts never rowed along these coasts; Medea, the shameless woman of Colchis, never set foot there; neither sailors of Sidon nor shipmates of Ulysses have ranged this coast under sail. There is no pestilence to hurt the cattle. Eurus, the tempestuous east wind, here brings a gentle, fertile rain, and never is there drought . . . Jupiter has reserved for the just these happy countries, whenever the golden age turns to brass, and an iron era succeeds the brass. Only by following my advice may the just escape the horrors of this age of iron.

Carthage, founded by Phoenicians from Tyre and Sidon, became the greatest sea power in antiquity. Carthaginians certainly discovered and partially colonized the Canary Islands, whose salubrious climate caused them to be confounded with the *Insulae Fortunatae.* Unnamed Phoenicians, manning "a number of ships" in the navy of the Egyptian pharaoh Necho, who reigned from 609 to 595 B.C., performed one of the most remarkable voyages of history, the circumnavigation of Africa from east to west. These big row galleys took their departure from Egypt by way of the Erythraean Sea, weathered the Cape of Good Hope, entered the Mediterranean, and reported to pharaoh at the mouth of the Nile. Since seagoing row galleys, with little storage space, had to keep a crew of at least fifty officers and oarsmen live and healthy, this Egyptian fleet had to stop ashore "when autumn came" to plant, grow, and reap a crop of grain; that was their only means of solving the logistic problem. Thus the voyage consumed three years. Herodotus, our sole source, disbelieved the story because, as it came to him, "in sailing round Libya" they had the sun upon their right hand; and for over a thousand years almost everyone followed the Greek historian in writing off this voyage as fabulous. Alexander von Humboldt first noted that, on the contrary, this observation was good evidence that the voyage did take place. Except when they crossed the Gulf of Guinea, these galley sailors must have seen the sun rise on their starboard hand.

"No evidence from the classic writers justifies the assumption that the ancients communicated with America," wrote Justin Winsor in 1889; nor has anyone since discovered any evidence.

The Greeks were never "light-hearted masters of the waves," as Matthew Arnold described them; they, like Ulysses, regarded the sea as an element "laden with suffering," necessary as a means of fishing and transportation, but to be used cautiously and avoided whenever possible. Nevertheless, one of the boldest voyages of history was made by Pytheas, of the Greek colony in Marseilles, at a time when Alexander the Great reigned. In a sailing ship with auxiliary oar power he sailed beyond the Pillars of Hercules into the broad Atlantic, north along the coasts of Portugal, France, and Britain, reaching a place that he named "Thule," where he observed the midnight sun and was told that darkness lasted all winter. This voyage, which we know only through the works of Pliny and other ancient historians, gave Thule an almost fabulous importance as the uttermost land that man had reached — "Ultima Thule." Columbus's son, for instance, boasted that his father had fulfilled the prophecy in Seneca's *Medea,* that some future Argonaut would discover a vast new world, when Thule would no longer be the ultimate.

But where and what was Thule? The Faroes, Iceland, or the northern coast of Norway? Not that it matters; nobody sailed north to check on Pytheas. The importance of his voyage lay in the fact that he made a startling discovery that led other men of enterprise to believe that they could do even better.

A contribution of antiquity far more important to the cause of discovery was scientific geography — especially the determination of the shape and size of the earth, and the distribution of land, water, and climates. The Pythagoreans of the sixth century B.C. taught that the world was spherical; Aristotle proved it from the circular shadow of the earth on the moon during an eclipse. Plato rendered the concept popular, as did Virgil and Ovid, and although there were many "flat-earth" dissenters (and still are), Aristotle's authority, supported by the common observations of sailors, caused the spherical earth to be taught, not only in ancient schools of learning, but in mediaeval universities. The story that Columbus was trying "to prove the world was round," and that he was held up by flat-earth monks, is one of those vulgar errors that no amount of denial can dispel. Scientific demonstration of the earth's rotundity was enforced by religion; God made the earth a sphere because that was the most perfect form. In the Old Testament there is a reference to this in Isaiah 40:22: "It is he that sitteth upon the circle of the earth" — "circle" being the translation of the Hebrew *khug*, sphere. The ancients also drew logical conclusions from the earth's sphericity; they postulated a south temperate zone corresponding to the one with which they were familiar, and a land therein, the Antipodes, to balance Europe.

Three men especially moved people in the Middle Ages and Renaissance. A Greek whose name we do not know invented the degree, $1/360$ circle or sphere, as a unit of measurement. When Alexander the Great's armies marched to India and back, it became necessary, for logistic purposes, to have accurate measurements, and the school of geography founded by the Ptolemies in Alexandria studied the problem. Eratosthenes, librarian at Alexandria around 200 B.C., made a laudable attempt at measuring the degree by making meridian observations of the sun from the bottoms of wells at two distant points (Cyrene and Alexandria), supposedly on the same meridian of longitude. Although he made sundry errors in his calculations, they canceled each other out so that his answer was very nearly correct; translated into modern nautical miles, Eratosthenes' degree was 59.5 instead of the correct 60.

The most influential geographer of antiquity, though not the most accurate, was Claudius Ptolemy (c. A.D. 73–151). His geography spotted the position — so far as he could ascertain it — of some 8000 places in the known world, and he drew both general and detailed maps that were not superseded for fourteen centuries. Ptolemy's *Geography*, known in a Latin translation from about 1406 and printed in edition after edition after 1475, exercised a tremendous authority over the human mind. It is no exaggeration to say that the learned world was more interested in the discovery of Ptolemy than in the discovery of America.   A geography book with any pretense to authority was long called a "Ptolemy," just as manuals of geometry are still called "Euclids" and the official compendium of navigation a "Bowditch." The Bologna Ptolemy of 1477 has latitude and longitude grids on the margins, and the Ulm edition of 1482, edited by Nicolaus Germanus, includes a very early world map.   Anyone like the Scandinavians, who objected to his attenuated depiction of the northern kingdoms, had to prove their case; for *dixit Ptolemaeus* — Ptolemy said it — was generally held to be conclusive.   Ptolemy was grossly inaccurate in spots: his Mediterranean was far too long, his Italy sloped too easterly, his Scotland leaned over backward, his Ceylon was bigger than India.   But Ptolemy was the best, indeed the only, world geographer that Europe had in the fifteenth century.   And Ptolemy's biggest mistake, making the length of Eurasia from Cape St. Vincent to the coast of China 177 degrees (the correct figure being 131), was a happy mistake.   For it encouraged navigators like Columbus and Cabot to believe that the Atlantic could be crossed in a reasonable time.

Columbus liked Ptolemy because he marked down Eratosthenes' length of the degree to 56.5 nautical miles; but he loved Marinus of Tyre (of the second Christian century) even better.   For Marinus, by totting up what the silk-caravan camel drivers told him about the length of their journeys to China and back, and assuming that a camel walked an average of twenty miles per day for seven months, figured out that Eurasia measured 225 degrees from Cape St. Vincent to the coast of China — 48 degrees more than Ptolemy's already overblown reckoning.

Another and older Greek geographer who became known to Europe in the fifteenth century was the Greek Strabo (born c. 63 B.C.), extracts of whose *Geographika* and *Diorthosis* were copied by the Byzantine scholar Gemistus Pletho and printed as early as 1469. Columbus made much of Strabo's statements that it would be possible to sail from S̨ain to the Indies, and that certain sailors had tried to do it but gave up their quest for want of provisions.

Eratosthenes, as reported by Strabo, stated that it was theoretically possible to sail from Spain to the Orient along the same parallel of latitude.   Seneca the philosopher gave Columbus considerable comfort by writing that the ocean from Spain to the Indies could be traversed *paucis diebus;* but Seneca meant "few" in a sense relative to eternity and the higher interests of the soul.   Ancient seacraft were not adequate for an Atlantic crossing both ways. In the late twentieth century the ocean has been crossed successfully by men in open dories or tiny sailboats; but it is one thing to do that when you know exactly your destination and can rely on coast guards and aviators to feed or to rescue you; and another to thrust forth into the unknown on a voyage of undetermined length and dubious destination.

In the ancient world, moreover, there was no international competition for trade routes. The Roman Empire, which succeeded to and absorbed the commercial supremacy of the Phoenicians, had no competitors. Thus the motives for financing the voyages of Columbus, Cabot, Cartier, and the rest did not then exist. And whilst the scientific findings of the Greeks were of great help to navigators of the Renaissance, their offhand remarks about the Atlantic were anything but encouraging. Aristotle taught that the sea was shallow and becalmed a few miles out from the Pillars of Hercules. Plato declared that the mythical Island of Atlantis — created by his imagination — had submerged into a vast mudbank. Tacitus believed that there was a built-in resistance to sailing ships in northern waters: a sort of jellied or coagulated sea. Not far wrong, when we think of the pack ice.

In conclusion, the philosophers and other writers of ancient Greece and Rome laid a scientific basis for the discoveries of the fifteenth and sixteenth centuries. To what extent these theories reached the common people is unknown. Doubtless fishermen and sailors were familiar with the hypothesis of the Islands of the Blest, especially through the familiar story of Hercules' searching for the golden apples of the Hesperides. These Happy, or Fortunate, Isles shone as an enticing mirage through the Middle Ages and almost to our own times. Many, many attempts were made to locate them, notably the Voyage of St. Brendan. But there is no evidence from classic writers to justify any assumption that the ancients communicated with America.

2

Who Really Discovered America?

In 1975 Mr. Walter Nicklin, editor of EUROPEAN COMMUNITY,
*decided to devote a number of this official organ of the European
Common Market to the United States Bicentennial. As a starter, he
commissioned me to write a short article on who really discovered
America. As this wraps up the subject in the shortest possible scope,
we have decided to reprint it here from* EUROPEAN COMMUNITY
for January–February 1976.

WHO DISCOVERED AMERICA? Or rather, what European discovered America? For we now admit that the people whom Columbus
mistakenly named Indians came over from Asia via the Bering Strait,
somewhere between 25,000 and 40,000 years ago, and, by the time
the Europeans arrived, had spread from Alaska to Tierra del Fuego
and had developed several hundred languages. In three places at
least — Peru, Mexico, and the highlands of Colombia — the Indians
developed highly sophisticated societies before Columbus landed; and
if the Spaniards had come a century later, they might have encountered a strong, defensible Aztec empire that would have developed
into a powerful nation, like Japan in Asia.

However, that was not to be, owing to the superior strength of European sea power and weaponry. But first the Europeans had to discover America, and we must agree on what we mean by "discovery,"
a word so vague as to be confusing. You can "discover" America or
the North Pole, and you can "discover" a nice little restaurant where
you may dine well and cheaply. And is a terrestrial discovery a discovery if it leads to nothing? The Scandinavian discovery of America
around the year A.D. 1000 was a dead end; it led to nothing more important than a short-lived settlement on Newfoundland; it made no
dent on the native culture, and the Norse settlements in Greenland,
parents of the attempts on America, died out before Columbus sailed.
Shall we call these ephemeral scratches by Europeans on the vast,

unknown continent "discoveries"? I think we should, barren though they were in results. But the discovery by Columbus, on October 12, 1492, of an island in the West Indies had immense and immediate results. Spain within a year, Portugal within seven years, began their successive conquests and colonizations, which by 1600 had subjugated almost all South and Central America, and a part of North America also, to European rule. So, I call Columbus's voyage of 1492 the "real" discovery of America, even though Christopher Columbus himself never wholly realized what he had found, or even knew the name "America."

As the four hundredth anniversary of Columbus's discovery approached, historians of several European countries began claiming that one of their nationals — Irish, Norse, English, Portuguese, Catalonian, and others — on scanty evidence or mere hunches, "got there first." Let us first consider the Irish. In the first Christian millennium, the Irish were great navigators in frail little curraghs, boats built largely on a wicker frame and covered with ox hides. Monks, very numerous in Ireland, loved to go on long voyages, both to get away from the temptations of the flesh and to vary the tedium of monastic life. The most noted of these voyages was the sixth-century one by St. Brendan, with a crew of monks from his monastery of Clonfert in Galway. They were gone seven years and had all kinds of adventures (such as kindling a fire on the back of a big whale, which they mistook for an island, and encountering psalm-singing sea birds). Many loyal Irishmen today insist that in the course of these voyages the navigator-saint *must* have discovered some part of America. I for one reject this hypothesis, because on every island where the saintly crew called there was already an Irish monastery full of monks, except one, which was the seat of Judas Iscariot, banished thither for all eternity. I believe that St. Brendan sailed as far as the Azores and back; he well describes an iceberg, some of which in recent times have drifted as far as the Azores without melting.

However, hope of new evidence for pre-Columbian discovery springs eternal, and news reached us in this summer of 1975 that a boat like a curragh, big enough to hold St. Brendan's crew, is being built in Ireland to follow and check up on the monastic adventure. The promoter will, I hope, have a good time; but to stretch the saint's voyage to America will hardly be convincing. During the Middle Ages the nearly contemporary narrative of this seven-year cruise was widely believed; and on mediaeval maps the mythical island San Borondon is usually found south of the Azores. Columbus mentions it, and Canary Islanders were still searching for it in the eighteenth century.

It is also possible that another Irish monk or monks did hit the American shores before any other European. For in A.D. 870 the pagan Vikings reached Iceland and made things so uncomfortable for the Christian Irish there that they built curraghs and sailed away, most of them certainly to Christian Ireland. But the Norse Icelandic sagas state that one band, at least, "drifted over the ocean" to some northern part of America. This is the story in brief: A Norse Icelander named Björn got a local girl in trouble, took ship to escape her wrathful brother, and disappeared. Some years later, around 1025–30, a certain Gudleif Gunnlangson, sailing from Dublin for Iceland, was driven off his course and anchored in an unknown harbor. A band of natives who flocked to the shore and spoke Irish seized him and his crew, and were debating whether to kill or to enslave them when a tall, old, white-haired man approached on horseback and was saluted in a manner befitting the natives' leader. Gudleif recognized him as Björn, who warned him that these natives, all Irish, would kill the intruders if they stayed, so they had better get out quick, which they did after Björn had given Gudleif a gold ring to take to his former mistress, and a sword for their son.

So it is barely possible that Björn's men cohabited with Indian girls and kept an Irish-American community going for two or three generations. But the rest is silence. No early Irish artifacts have been discovered in America.

This takes us to the Viking age, c. A.D. 470–1000, when the Scandinavians (Norwegians, Swedes, and Danes) were the sea kings of Europe. The Vikings, in the beautifully constructed long ships (like those excavated in our time at Gokstad, near Oslo in Norway, and Sutton Hoo, in England), roamed the coasts and great rivers of Europe from Russia to the Black Sea, some trading but most of them raiding defenseless towns and monasteries, carrying off slaves, gold and silver, and all manner of valuable things they could not otherwise obtain at home.

In an era when the English, French, and South Europeans hardly dared sail beyond sight of land, Norsemen from Norway, Denmark, and Sweden conquered a good part of Ireland before 800, sailed to Greenland about 985, invaded Normandy in the tenth century and Sicily in the eleventh.   And in 1066, the date everyone knows, William the Norman conquered England.   And although Vikings were tough and ruthless freebooters, their countrymen were not lacking in the fine arts or in politics.   The eddas and sagas of Iceland are justly famous as literature; the Norman adaptations of Romanesque architecture are second only to Gothic, and the institutions that they established in Normandy were eventually woven into those of the Anglo-Saxon world.

In the far north Iceland, Greenland, Baffin Land, and the Labrador formed "steppingstones" to America.   We have documentary evidence that a Norse Icelander named Eric the Red, banished from Iceland, sailed west, discovered Greenland, and gave it that name to attract settlers.   Actually it was not an inaccurate description, for the ribbon of coastal plain on the west coast of this big, icy island is delightfully green in spring and summer, affording good pasturage. That is what the Norsemen now wanted.   The Viking age of violence and robbery was over; Norwegians, pushed by the limited supply of good land in their own country, wanted to expand to a land of green pasture where cattle might prosper, and the more hardy types of grain, such as barley, flourish.   Greenland was no cowman's paradise like Normandy, which Rollo the Ganger conquered in A.D. 911; but no other unoccupied agricultural land was available in the year of Eric's discovery of Greenland.   Returning to Iceland, he went up and down the land, praising the possibilities of his discovery, and as a result recruited some fifteen shiploads of emigrants.   They accompanied him to the west coast of Greenland in 985 and founded two settlements, the eastern, near the modern Julianehaab, and the western, near Godthaab.   Both are on the southwest coast of Greenland, around Cape Farewell, as the east coast then as now was sheathed with ice the year round and unapproachable.

This settlement of Greenland was about fifteen years old and doing well when Leif Ericsson, son of Eric the Red, sailed to Norway and met King Olaf Tryggvason, who persuaded him not only to become a Christian (the king was a recent convert) but to introduce the new religion to the West.   On his return to Greenland, Leif encountered a Norwegian named Biarni Heriulfson, commander of a trading ship, who had initially missed his Greenland destination and made landfalls on a level, wooded land, then on a second wilderness, and finally, sailing east, had hit one of the Norse settlements in Greenland. He and his crew never stepped foot on the new land, but as he told Leif about it and even lent him his ship, I think Biarni is entitled to be called the genuine, number one, indubitable European discoverer of America. After his brief moment of triumph, he returned to Iceland in another ship and disappeared from history.

If, however, Biarni was the number one discoverer of America, Leif Ericsson was number two. For the first thing he did upon returning to his father's house in Greenland was to buy or borrow Biarni's ship and organize an expedition of kindred and neighbors to explore the land that Biarni had reported. The thing that attracted him in Biarni's story was the forests, for nothing bigger than a dwarf willow bush grew in Greenland.

Biarni's ship, incidentally, was no Viking ship, and Leif was no Viking. Please don't think of him dressed as a sort of Wagnerian hero under a winged steel helmet, standing in the prow of a ten- to twenty-oared long ship of the Vikings and hollering whatever was the Old Norse equivalent of "Land ho!" His was the type known to Scandinavians as the *knarr*, or knörr. Several of these vessels, carbon-dated around A.D. 1000, were dug up around 1968 in the mouth of Roskilde Fjord, Denmark, and have been raised and restored. The one illustrated in my *European Discovery of America: The Northern Voyages* was about 54 feet long and 15 feet beam, stoutly clinker-built of oak, with pine planking, and fastened with iron rivets. There is no big figurehead of a supposedly terrifying sea monster, as she is no warship; but, like the long Viking ships, she was directed by a steerboard on the right side — hence the word "starboard." She was partly decked forward and aft, and could carry several head of cattle, as well as a cargo and thirty or more people. For auxiliary power, the crew pulled on long sweeps, for which holes were cut in the uppermost plank. There is no evidence of any means of cooking food on board; the crew must have subsisted on cold victuals and beer, or mead fermented from honey.

The first place of any consequence that Leif discovered he called the "Wonder Strands," and they are our first anchor for the location of Vinland. Without doubt the sands that aroused the Norsemen's wonder were on the unique thirty-mile stretch of beach on the Labrador coast between latitudes 53°45′ and 54°09′ N, broken only by the wooded Cape Porcupine. Here are magnificent yellow sand beaches with a gentle gradient, longer than any that the Norsemen could ever have seen, and the more wondrous because they occur almost miraculously in the middle of a barren, rocky coast. Behind these Wonder Strands a level, sandy plain — unique for southern Labrador — nourishes a fine stand of black spruce, and numerous streams wind through the forest and flow across the beach into the ocean.

This place, however, did not satisfy Leif. Again he put to sea and sailed south from the Wonder Strands for two days. The appropriate saga says that they sailed through the channel between a big island and a cape jutting out to the north of the mainland; these have been identified as Belle Isle and Newfoundland. The climate was warmer than that of Greenland, streams were teeming with salmon, and the meadows were full of wild berries, from which Leif's men pressed a kind of wine. For that reason, and to attract settlers (as his father had done with the name "Greenland"), Leif named this land "Vinland the Good."

When the Icelandic sagas were first presented, in translation, to the American learned world in Carl Rafn's *Antiquitates Americanae* in 1837, a frenzied hunt started along the east coast of the United States and Canada for Vinland. This search lasted for more than a century, most intensively in New England because that was the northern limit of wild grapes. In 1892, Norwegian-Americans, resenting the publicity that "that Italian Colombo" was getting, arranged for a newly built Viking ship to sail (or be towed) to Chicago, and even endeavored to project Vinland into Minnesota. The stone windmill tower in Newport, Rhode Island, was the favorite phony; after thorough archaeological exploration, the mill's attribution to early Norse builders cannot be sustained.

Finally, in 1960, a pair of Norwegian archaeologists, Mr. and Mrs. Helge Ingstad, located a spot in northern Newfoundland, L'Anse aux Meadows, which they thought might be "it." Years of summertime diggings by competent scientists have beyond reasonable doubt proved this place to have indeed been Vinland, where Leif Ericsson spent one winter, and where members of his family founded a short-lived colony. On the verge of the meadow and the bay at L'Anse aux Meadows, the Ingstads have excavated the sites of two great houses, closely corresponding to the Norse dwellings earlier uncovered in Greenland. The bigger is 70 feet long and 55 feet wide. The floors were of hard-pressed clay, the walls of turf, and the roof of timber, covered with sod. There is a central hall with a fire pit in the middle, and a little ember box of flat stones in which hot coals were kept alive during the night. Around the fireplace are raised-earth benches, which the Norsemen doubtless covered with polar bear and other skins.

In the meantime, experts in Old Norse have proved that *vinber*, the name translated as wine, could mean any wild berry from which a kind of wine can be — and was — made; or even just a green pasture country.

Leif and his men, in Biarni's old vessel (which might have become more famous than the *Santa María* or the *Mayflower* if we only knew her name), returned to Greenland the same summer in 1001. Vinland interested these Norsemen mostly for the opportunity to raise cattle and cut big timber. At least three attempts were made to plant a permanent colony there. The first colonists, led by Thorvald Ericsson, Leif's brother, used Leif's buildings, spent two winters in Vinland, and explored the nearby coast. Next, one Thorfinn Karlsevni, husband of Gudrid (widow of Leif's brother), with three ships and about 250 people, made a serious attempt to establish a community at L'Anse aux Meadows; it was they, probably, who built the "great houses" excavated by the Ingstads. In one of them, Gudrid, Karlsevni's wife, gave birth to a boy, whom they named Snorri. This Snorri, first European child born in the New World, grew up to be an important man in Iceland. After two winters at L'Anse aux Meadows, the Norsemen were attacked by natives, whom they called Skrellings, coming in a fleet of kayaks. The Norsemen were on the run when a woman colonist named Freydis, Leif Ericsson's half sister, won the day. She bared her breasts, slapped them with a sword, and screamed like a hellcat; this so alarmed the Skrellings that they broke off their attack and retreated.

Karlsevni now decided to give up and go back to Greenland; for the advantages of Vinland over Greenland were not enough to warrant the constant need of defense against hostile natives, and no Skrellings had yet appeared in southern Greenland. Freydis, however, loved Vinland. She initiated and led the last attempt at colonization. She persuaded two brothers, owners and mariners of a Norwegian ship that put in at Leif's Greenland settlement, to make another try. Upon arriving at L'Anse aux Meadows site in the summer of 1014, she insisted that the big house belonged to her, and made the Norwegians build another. Then, having her eye on the Norwegian ship as the bigger of the two, she stirred up her husband with a lie about the two Norse brothers trying to "make" her, and so teased and taunted him with the "are you a man or a mouse?" routine, that, with the aid of his crew, he surprised and killed all the men of the brothers' party — Freydis herself finishing off the women. "After this monstrous deed," says the saga, Freydis and her husband loaded the Norwegian ship to the gunwales "with all the products of the land," abandoned their own vessel, and sailed back to Greenland.

With this sordid episode the recorded history of Vinland ends; for the Yale Vinland Map's inscription is now conceded to be a modern fake. There is evidence, however, that the Greenlanders made repeated voyages to Leif's Wonder Strands in the Labrador to load timber.

Of the Norse settlements in Greenland we have abundant evidence, mainly archaeological, up to a point. Extensive digs by the Danish government and nongovernmental archaeologists have found evidence of flourishing agricultural communities; and there were at least a dozen parish churches, a neat little stone cathedral, and an estimated population of around 3000.

Greenland gradually faded out of European cognizance. The last bishop of Gardar, whom we know to have visited his see, died in 1372. Around 1492 Pope Alexander VI observed (in a letter addressed to two bishops in Iceland) that no vessel had touched at Greenland for 80 years, and that although his predecessor had appointed a bishop of Greenland, he had heard nothing from him, not even whether he went there.

What happened? The chief factor, no doubt, was bad communication with the outside world. Norse and Icelandic economy suffered grievously from the Black Death of 1349, which killed one person out of three; so the annual ship no longer came. The men, physically degenerate, as their skeletons indicate, grew too weak to hunt.

It is a sad picture, the gradual snuffing out of this faraway colony so gallantly planted by Eric the Red, his last descendants, short on food, staring their eyes out all through the short, bright summer for the ship from Norway that meant their salvation. By September it became certain that she would not come that year. The long, dark winter closed in, and there was no more oil for lamps. Cold and hungry, the people lived merely to survive until the next summer, when surely a ship would come; but it never did. At some time in the second half of the fifteenth century, the last Norse Greenlander died.

For about four centuries nobody, according to authentic records, was interested in Atlantic exploration and discovery. But a new era began when the Portuguese, after designing a fast and weatherly type of small craft, the caravel, began to push along the Atlantic coast, destination India, and to thrust out into the Atlantic, destination St. Brendan's Islands or beyond.

It began with a bachelor member of Portugal's royal house, the Infante Dom Henrique, or Prince Henry the Navigator, as the English renamed him in the nineteenth century — for his mother was a princess of the House of Lancaster. Henry, at Sagres near Cape St. Vincent, set up around 1430 a sort of information center for voyaging, collecting charts and other data, and encouraging shipmasters, with grants and awards, to push south along the African coast in the hope of reaching "the Indies" that way. Which Bartholomew Diaz finally did, in 1488.

Although Prince Henry and his royal successors (Alfonso V and João II) were primarily interested in African exploration and the eastern sea route to the Indies, they did not ignore the western ocean. On one of the Catalan charts collected by the Infante, he saw depicted St. Brendan's Islands a few hundred miles off the Strait of Gibraltar, and in 1431 he sent one Gonçalo Velho Cabral to locate them. Velho sailed well to the westward of where the Brendan chain was supposed to be, and discovered the Formigas rocks, which break the ocean into a hissing froth some twenty-five miles east of the nearest island of the Azores. The following year he returned and discovered Santa Maria. Thence São Miguel was sighted. Third to be discovered, as its name indicates, was Terceira. São Jorge, Graciosa, the volcanic Pico, and Fayal came next; and the group was named Ilhas dos Açores (Isles of the Hawks) by the Infante. King Afonso V, in 1439, conferred the privilege of settling and ruling these seven Azorean islands on his uncle, Dom Henrique; four years later the Infante and his brother Dom Pedro began to people this fertile group, where no natives or trace of former occupants was found.

Two more Azorean islands, Flores and Corvo, remained to be discovered. These were found by a Portuguese resident of Madeira named Diogo de Tieve in 1452. Diogo and a friend named Pedro de Velasco were sent by Prince Henry to try and find Antilia, the Isle of the Seven Cities. This was a mythical Atlantic island whither a band of Portuguese Christians was supposed to have fled before a Moorish invasion of Portugal about A.D. 714. The Tieve-Velasco ship sailed northeasterly from the Azores to the latitude of Cape Clear, Ireland, and on their return discovered Corvo and Flores, westernmost of the Azorean group.

Apart from its practical value, the discovery of the Azores had an immense psychological influence on discovery. Here, for the first time, the ocean had loosed her chains (as Seneca had prophesied), and lands hitherto unpeopled were found where before there was nought but myth and mystery. The crossing to a new world was now more than one-third accomplished; it is 745 nautical miles from the Rock of Sintra, Portugal, to São Miguel in the Azores, and 1054 miles from Corvo to Cape Race, Newfoundland. Furthermore, these newly discovered islands proved to be fertile producers of grain, cattle, and wine, suggesting that more oceanic discovery would be profitable.

Thus another fabulous island stirred men to discovery. St. Brendan's, Antilia, and, next, O'Brasil, the Irish home of the blest, which people have "sighted" off the Irish coast to this day, and which John Cabot meant to make "first stop" on his high-latitude voyage from Bristol to the Indies. Similarly, Columbus intended to make Antilia a staging point for his sea route to the Indies; and many efforts were made to find these islands. From 1462 to 1484, at least six "letters of donation" were granted by the kings of Portugal to mariners, allowing them to have and hold any hitherto undiscovered island if they could find it.

Although Dr. Armando Cortesão and other Portuguese historians insist that some or all of these enterprising sailors "must" have discovered Newfoundland or Hispaniola, there is no evidence that they found anything. With the exception of the Azores, the story of Portuguese westward search before 1500 is a chronicle of failure. The explanation is meteorological. They struck out into the western ocean at seasons and in latitudes where strong westerly winds, even today, make navigation for sailing vessels full of danger and uncertainty.

Dr. Cortesão's theory is that some of those bold westward-thrusting mariners, being Portuguese (which everyone will admit meant that they were the best sailors of that era), must have discovered something but never got the credit until the Cortesão brothers, in the present century, explained all this as part of a "policy of secrecy." This meant that the Portuguese kings, fearful of their rivals, impounded and kept secret these reports of western continents and islands, hoping to use them at some future time. One cannot prove that the "policy of secrecy" never existed, because it is a concept of negatives, which needs no facts. But I, for one, simply cannot believe anything so preposterous.

Not that I am denigrating the Portuguese. They were the best navigators and shipbuilders of the fifteenth century — the teachers of Columbus, Magellan, and other great mariners. And when, by a strange accident, Cabral, commander of a Portuguese fleet en route to India via Africa in 1500, blundered into the great transatlantic country subsequently named Brazil, Portugal joined the "big league" of American discoverers.

Even before the year 1500, when it became evident that Columbus had opened up a new world, other countries than Spain began putting in claims for one of their subjects' "getting there first." I shall do no more here than name the claimants, because they all turn out to be fictitious, or their transatlantic voyage has been updated.

Portuguese claims: Any mythical or doubtful Atlantic island on a pre-Columbian world map is claimed as a not-otherwise-reported find of an unknown Portuguese sailor.

Britain's claims: First, that men of Bristol found Newfoundland in 1480. (Why, then, did Henry VII call it "the New Isle" in 1497 and reward John Cabot for discovering it that year?) Next, Prince Madoc of Wales, who brought a Cymric colony to America in the twelfth century. By some mysterious process, this colony became a Welsh-speaking Indian tribe, which moved west from the Atlantic shore until it became the Mandan in the Far West. John Dee added this tale to his map of the 1580's in order to support England's title to North America; numerous travelers for three centuries have sought out Welsh Indians and compiled impressive (though phony) parallel vocabularies of several different Indian languages with Welsh.

Venetian claim: Fictitious story of the Zeno brothers having discovered big islands, which they named Estotiland, Drogeo, and Frislanda, in the fourteenth century. Printed in Venice in 1558, this claim has no basis in fact, but is still defended by a valiant few.

Danish and Polish claims: Pining, Pothorst, and Scolvus. The first two were Danish pirates; the last, a Dane or Polander who is supposed to have piloted them in search of the Northwest Passage in 1476. All three voyages, I believe, are bogus, but Polish-Americans have adopted Scolvus (whom they call Jan of Kowno) as their Leif Ericsson and Columbus rolled into one.

Many other claims there are — ancient Gauls, for instance, discovering America for France — but none is worthy of remembrance save as examples of human credulity. The really important discoverer of America was Christopher Columbus, because his discovery of 1492 was quickly followed up by Spain, and every subsequent exploration of the New World was inspired by or based on his.

It is fortunate that we know much about the man Colombo, christened Cristoforo in Genoa in the summer of 1451. He was the son and grandson of local woolweavers, born and raised as a Roman Catholic — distinctly not a Spanish or Catalan Jew, as many nationist Spaniards like to believe. His first twenty-two years were spent in Genoa or nearby Savona or at sea; he made one or two voyages to Chios, where Genoa maintained a trading factory. On this and other coastal voyages, Christopher learned to "hand, reef, and steer," to estimate distances by eye, to make sail, let go and weigh anchors properly, and other elements of seamanship. He learned seamanship the old way, the hard way, and the best way, in the school of experience. As yet illiterate, he could not navigate and thus rate an officer's billet. On his next voyage, off Portugal, his ship became involved in an all-day sea fight with a French war fleet. His ship went down, but he swam ashore near Lagos, six miles away, and walked to Lisbon, where his brother Bartholomé had set up a chart-making establishment. In 1476 he sailed in a Portuguese vessel several hundred miles north of Iceland; and this raises the question as to whether he ever picked up the story of Leif and Vinland. Not likely. In any case, there was nothing in the Greenland-Vinland story of polar bears, walrus ivory, wine, and white falcons to interest a young seaman already dreaming of an ocean route to the fabulous Indies of gems, spices, and precious metals.

We find Christopher at sea again in the summer of 1478 as captain of a Portuguese ship that Centurione, his former employer, had chartered to buy sugar in Madeira. Next year Christopher, at twenty-eight years a master mariner, contracted an advantageous marriage with Dona Filipa de Perestrello e Moniz, daughter of Bartolomew Perestrello, hereditary captain of Porto Santo in the Madeira group. The young couple shortly went to live in Porto Santo, where their son, Diego (later the second admiral and viceroy), was born, and where Dona Filipa's mother placed at Christopher's disposal the charts and journals of her seagoing husband. Not long after the birth of this, their one and only child, the Columbus couple moved to Funchal, Madeira.

In 1481, Afonso V died and was succeeded by his son João "the Complete Prince." Young (aged twenty-six), energetic, wise and learned, ruthless and ambitious, João II equaled any monarch of his age. The young king determined to build a castle or fortified trading factory on the Gold Coast, strong enough to beat off any European rival and to keep the natives in order. A fleet of eleven vessels was fitted out at Lisbon. Soldiers, stonemasons, and other artisans were engaged, and late in 1481 it set sail from Lisbon under the command of Diogo d'Azambuja. On the Gold Coast the men worked hard and well that winter, erecting a great stone castle of mediaeval design, complete with turrets, moat, chapel, warehouse, and market court; and a garrison was left in charge. São Jorge da Mina (St. George of the Mine), as this castle was named, upheld Portuguese sovereignty and protected her trade on the Gold Coast for centuries.

By 1484, when he returned from Guinea voyaging, Columbus was ready to make an amazing proposition to the king of Portugal.

Columbus's *Empresa de las Indias* ("Enterprise of the Indies"), as he called it and to the furthering of which he devoted all his time and energy from about 1483 on, was simple enough. It was to discover a short sea route to the Indies instead of thrusting along the African coast as the Portuguese were doing. He also hoped to pick up en route some island or archipelago that would be a useful staging area; but the be-all and end-all was to rediscover eastern Asia by sailing west from Europe or Africa. He expected to set up a factory or trading post, like Chios or La Mina, on some island off the Asiatic coast, where European goods could be exchanged for the fragrant and glittering wares of the Orient much more cheaply than by trans-Asia caravans, with their endless middlemen and successive markups.

Exactly when Columbus conceived this momentous plan, or had it planted in his brain, is still a mystery. All educated men of western Europe knew that the world was a sphere; all observant sailors knew that its surface was curved, from seeing ships hull-down. Columbus never had to argue the rotundity of the earth. When he had learned enough Latin to read ancient and mediaeval cosmographers, he ascertained that Seneca was reported to have written that you could cross the ocean from Spain to the Indies *paucis diebus,* in comparatively few days; and Strabo recorded that certain Greeks or Romans had even tried it but returned empty-handed, "through want of resolution and scarcity of provisions." He picked up from two famous mediaeval books, Pierre d'Ailly's *Imago Mundi* and Pope Pius II's *Historia Rerum Ubique Gestarum,* numerous guesses about the narrowness of the ocean; and fortunately we have his own copies of these works, amply underlined, and their margins filled with his notes. He combed the Bible and ancient literature for quotations that might apply to his enterprise, such as Psalm 71: (or 72:) 8: "He shall have dominion also from sea to sea, and from the river unto the ends of the earth." He cherished the prophecy in Seneca's *Medea* — "An age will come after many years when the ocean will loose the chains of things, and a huge land lie revealed; when Tethys will disclose new worlds and Thule no more be the ultimate." Against this passage in Columbus's own copy of Seneca his other son, Ferdinand, wrote this proud annotation: "This prophecy was fulfilled by my father the Admiral, in the year 1492."

The first trace we have of any outside influence on Columbus's forming his great idea is the Toscanelli correspondence, his earliest known scholarly backing. Paolo dal Pozzo Toscanelli was a leading Florentine physician in an era when the best astronomers and cosmographers were apt to be medicos, since they alone acquired enough mathematics to be men of science. In brief, it says that Paul the Physician is pleased to hear that the king of Portugal is interested in finding a shorter sea route to "the land of spices" than the one his mariners are seeking via Africa. Quinsay (modern Hangchow), capital of the Chinese province of Mangi, is about 5000 nautical miles due west of Lisbon. An alternate, and shorter, route to the Orient goes by way of Antilia to the "noble island of Cipangu" — Marco Polo's name for Japan — where the temples and royal palaces are roofed with massy gold. At some time not later than 1481 (Toscanelli died in May 1482), Columbus was shown a copy of this letter, became greatly excited over such exalted backing for his ideas, and wrote to Florence, asking for more. Toscanelli replied by sending a copy of his earlier letter, with a chart (long since lost) to illustrate his notion of the ocean's width, and a covering letter praising the young mariner's "great and noble ambition to pass over to where the spices grow."

Although none of the alleged portraits of Columbus was painted in his lifetime, we have several detailed descriptions of him from contemporaries. The best, to my mind, is the one by his son Ferdinand (Don Hernando) in his biography of the discoverer:

The Admiral was a well-built man of more than medium stature, long visaged with cheeks somewhat high, but neither fat nor thin. He had an aquiline nose and his eyes were light in color; his complexion too was light, but kindling to a vivid red. In youth his hair was blond, but when he came to his thirtieth year it all turned white. In eating and drinking and the adornment of his person he was always content and modest. Among strangers his conversation was affable, and with members of his household very pleasant, but with a modest and pleasant dignity. In matters of religion he was so strict that for fasting and saying all the canonical offices he might have been taken for a member of a religious order. And he was so great an enemy to cursing and swearing, that I swear I never heard him utter any oath other than "by San Fernando!" and when he was most angry with anyone, his reprimand was to say, "May God take you!" for doing or saying this or that. And when he had to write anything, he would not try the pen without first writing these words, *Jesus cum Maria sit nobil in via*, and in such fair letters that he might have gained his bread by them alone.

A quality of Columbus's that his son took for granted was persistence. Once convinced that God intended him to discover a new sea route to the Indies, nothing could divert him from his quest for the means. His objective was very simple: to sail west from Spain until he hit Japan, or one of the islands, like Okinawa, off the coast of China. For at least twelve years he promoted this idea at the courts of Spain and Portugal (and finally, through his brother Bartholomew, at the courts of England and France). He gave up seafaring and devoted all his time and energy to propaganda, searching ancient and modern authors for statements to support his plan. He figured out, by careful selection of the shortest calculations, that from the Canary Islands to Marco Polo's Cipangu (Japan) on latitude 28° N, was the equivalent of only 2400 nautical miles; actually it is nearer 10,000 miles, by air. That is why his proposition was turned down by several royal commissions. Nobody doubted that the world was a sphere ("Columbus was trying to prove the world was round" is just an old wives' tale); but all the experts doubted that the great Ocean Sea was so narrow, or that Asia stretched so far east, as Columbus insisted. But Columbus did convince a number of individuals, notably Doña Isabel, queen of Castile and León, with the somewhat sulky acquiescence of her consort, Don Ferdinand of Aragon.

Finally, after the last of the Moors had been expelled from Spain, Columbus got what he wanted in April 1492. The sovereigns agreed to furnish him with two ships, manned and equipped, and his friends contributed the flagship *Santa María*. He was to be admiral and viceroy over whatever lands he might discover, and was to keep one tenth of all gold, silver, precious stones, and other merchandise thence obtained. The sovereigns also gave him a passport and letter of credence to any and every Oriental potentate he might meet.

The fleet sailed from Palos, where it had been equipped and most of the crews recruited, on August 4, 1492. In accordance with his plan to cross the ocean on latitude 28° N, Columbus dropped down to the Canaries, spent a few weeks topping off with provisions and making repairs. The admiral there indulged in a flirtation with the ruler of Gomera, the young and beautiful widow Doña Beatriz de Pereza. The three ships sailed from the roadstead of San Sebastian, Gomera, on September 6, 1492. By the 9th, all land had disappeared under the horizon, and the three ships had an uncharted ocean to themselves.

This famous first voyage of Columbus to America was one of the easiest — a fair northeast trade wind almost all the way; "weather like April in Andalusia," noted Columbus in his sea journal. On September 25 he thought he had found Antilia; but it was only a cloud on the horizon. After they had been at sea for a month (longer than any of the seamen had been out of sight of land), the crews became mutinous, and Columbus had to promise to turn back if they did not not discover land in three days' time. They just did.

At two in the morning of October 12, 1492, in the light of a waning moon, the cry *"Tierra! Tierra!"* went up from the deck of *Pinta,* and this time it was land — an island of the Bahamas that Columbus named "San Salvador," its name today. As this is where the Indies should have been, Columbus named the friendly Arawaks, who greeted him, "Indians." And with two or three of them volunteering as pilots (the language barrier was surmounted, supposedly, by sign language), Columbus's fleet made off for other Bahamian islands, and then for Cuba and Hispaniola. There the admiral found gold but lost his flagship. He planted a small colony (later wiped out by the natives), and took off in *Niña* on January 16, 1493. After a stormy voyage and calling at Santa María in the Azores and at Lisbon, he entered the port of Palos on March 15.

That was it: the real discovery of America. Not that Columbus recognized it as such, or ever did; he died believing he had discovered the eastern regions of China, and to him "America" was simply the name of a Sevillian shipchandler. But Columbus's 1492 discovery was quickly followed up. All American voyages of the first twenty-one years (1492–1513) were inspired by, or derived from, the four voyages of Columbus. The only exception is the independent discovery of Brazil for Portugal by Pedro Alvares Cabral in 1500. Cabral, a well-born country gentleman, was conducting a great fleet to India to follow up Vasco da Gama's first voyage. Sailing from Lisbon on March 9, 1500, he crossed the Atlantic Narrows to get a good slant on the southeast trade wind, and on April 22 raised a conical mountain on the Brazilian coast, which he named "Monte Pascoal." He spent several days ashore and continued his voyage to India. As the Spanish and Portuguese sovereigns had already agreed to partition the New World on a certain longitude, and Cabral's discovery lay west of that line, the further development and colonization of this great land was left to Portugal. And to such good purpose that Brazil is the biggest and wealthiest country south of the Rio Grande today.

So I conclude that the real, operative discoverer of America was Christopher Columbus. But the New World was not to be named after him, but after Amerigo Vespucci, a Florentine. His plausible but prevaricating book, *Lettera di Amerigo Vespucci,* printed at Lisbon in 1506 (the year that Columbus died), in which he claimed that he, not Columbus, discovered the mainland in 1497, came to the notice of a young professor at Saint Diá in the Vosges, who was getting out a new edition of Ptolemy. Martin Waldseemüller (the name of this enterprising geographer) suggested that since a fourth part of the world had been discovered by one Americus Vespucius, and as the other three parts — Asia, Africa, and Europa — had been named after women, why should not this be called "America"? And on a world map that he finished the same year, he placed America on the interior of Brazil.

3

Columbus

From ADMIRAL OF THE OCEAN SEA: A LIFE OF CHRISTOPHER COLUMBUS (Boston: Atlantic–Little, Brown, 1942), *Conclusion.*

Here is the conclusion to the end product of my long quest for Columbus, and of a book that led to my favorable reception by modern mariners, since it caused them to accept me as one of them. It led directly to my being commissioned lieutenant commander in the U.S. Naval Reserve for the special purpose of writing THE HISTORY OF U.S. NAVAL OPERATIONS IN WORLD WAR II. *The original edition (also 1942) was in two volumes, with extensive footnotes after every chapter, and a somewhat enlarged text. I owe to Roger Scaife of Little, Brown the suggestion to so reduce its length that the Book-of-the-Month Club was able to adopt it for its first choice in 1942. As very many naval officers were subscribers, I, the Johnny-come-lately in the Navy, was welcomed everywhere afloat and ashore as "the guy who followed Columbus under sail." And this Conclusion — which does not appear in the two-volume edition — was suggested by Ellery Sedgwick of the Atlantic Monthly Press, who remarked to me, after reading the manuscript, "Why, Columbus really had a good time, didn't he?"*

Since 1942 my Columbian research has never wholly ceased; but my high opinion of Columbus as a navigator and a man has, if anything, grown; although I do regard Magellan's circumnavigation, all things considered, as the greater voyage.

ON MAY 20, 1506, the vigil of the feast of the Ascension, Columbus suddenly grew worse. No news yet from the Adelantado at the new sovereigns' camp, alas. Please God to prosper his suit! Diego, the beloved younger brother; Don Diego, the son and heir; Ferdinand, the son and shipmate; Diego Méndez and Fieschi, valiant captains of *Capitana* and *Vizcáina* and leaders of the canoe journey; and a few faithful domestics rallied around the bedside of the dying discoverer. It was a poor enough deathbed for the Admiral of the Ocean Sea and Viceroy and Governor of the Islands and Mainlands therein; but no pomp or circumstance could help him now. A priest was summoned, a Mass said, and everyone in this little circle of friends, shipmates, and relatives received the sacrament. The viaticum was administered to the dying admiral; and after the concluding prayer of this last office, remembering the last words of his Lord and Saviour, to whose sufferings he sometimes ventured to compare his own, Columbus was heard to say *"In manus tuas, Domine, commendo spiritum meum."*

And having said this, he gave up the ghost.

So died the man who had done more to direct the course of history than any individual since Augustus Caesar. Yet the life of the admiral closed on a note of frustration. He had not found the strait, or met the grand khan, or converted any great number of heathen, or regained Jerusalem. He had not even secured the future of his family. And the significance of what he had accomplished was only slightly less obscure to him than to the chroniclers who neglected to record his death, or to the courtiers who failed to attend his modest funeral at Valladolid. The vast extent and immense resources of the Americas were but dimly seen; the mighty ocean that laved their western shores had not yet yielded her secret.

America would eventually have been discovered if the great enterprise of Columbus had been rejected; yet who can predict what would have been the outcome? The voyage that took him to "the Indies" and home was no blind chance, but the creation of his own brain and soul, long studied, carefully planned, repeatedly urged on indifferent princes, and carried through by virtue of his courage, sea knowledge, and indomitable will. No later voyage could ever have such spectacular results; and Columbus's fame would have been more secure had he retired from the sea in 1493. Yet a lofty ambition to explore further, to organize the territories won for Castile, and to complete the circuit of the globe sent him thrice more to America. These voyages, even more than the first, proved him to be the greatest navigator of his age, and enabled him to train the captains and pilots who were to display the banners of Spain off every American cape and island between 50° N and 50° S. The ease with which he dissipated the unknown terrors of the ocean, the skill with which he found his way out and home, again and again, led thousands of men from every western European nation into maritime adventure and exploration. And if Columbus was a failure as a colonial administrator, it was partly because his conception of a colony transcended the desire of his followers to impart, and the capacity of natives to receive, the institutions and culture of Renaissance Europe.

Columbus had a proud, passionate, and sensitive nature, which suffered deeply from the contempt to which he was early subjected, and the envy, disloyalty, ingratitude, and injustice that he met as a discoverer. He wrote so freely out of the abundance of his complaint as to give the impression that his life was more full of woe than of weal. That impression is false. As with other mariners, a month at sea healed the wounds of a year ashore, and a fair wind blew away the memory of foul weather. Command of a tall and gallant ship speeding over blue water before a fresh trade wind, shaping her course for some new and marvelous land where gold is abundant and the women are kind, is a mariner's dream of the good life. Columbus had a Hellenic sense of wonder at the new and strange, combined with an artist's appreciation of natural beauty; and his voyages to this strange new world brought him to some of the most gorgeous coastlines on the earth's surface. Moreover, Columbus had a deep conviction of the immanence, the sovereignty, and the infinite wisdom of God, which transcended all his suffering and enhanced all his triumphs. Waste no pity on the Admiral of the Ocean Sea! He enjoyed long stretches of pure delight such as only a seaman may know, and moments of high, proud exultation that only a discoverer can experience.

One only wishes that the admiral might have been afforded the sense of fulfillment that would have come from foreseeing all that flowed from his discoveries; that would have turned all the sorrows of his last years to joy. The whole history of the Americas stems from the four voyages of Columbus; and as the Greek city-states looked back to the deathless gods as their founders, so today a score of independent nations and dominions unite in homage to Christopher, the stouthearted son of Genoa, who carried Christian civilization across the Ocean Sea.

4

Magellan

The first circumnavigation of the globe, by Ferdinand Magellan and Sebastian de Elcano (1519–22), appealed to me, from the time I first read Edward G. Bourne's SPAIN IN AMERICA *(1905), as the greatest and most difficult of all voyages under sail. I always meant to write about it, but the organization of a Magellan expedition, in accord with my principle of trying to see every coast and island that the discoverer did, was much more difficult and expensive than following Columbus. A sailing voyage, which would have started in 1942 had the world been at peace, had to be given up for many reasons, including expense; but we finally got going, in December 1971, with the help of two good friends I had met in middle life, Mauricio Obregón of Bogotá, and James F. Nields of Ware, Massachusetts, both famous aviators with a taste for history. And I had the good fortune to be accompanied by my second wife, Priscilla, whose personal charm melted everyone she met, and whom no difficulties daunted.*

The following is Chapter XVI from my EUROPEAN DISCOVERY OF AMERICA: THE SOUTHERN VOYAGES, A.D. 1492–1616 *(New York: Oxford University Press, 1974). It is entitled "The Strait That Shall Forever Bear His Name," a translation of the felicitous statement in Camoëns's* LUSIADS.

Strait Discovered

ON OCTOBER 21, 1520, the feast of St. Ursula and the Eleven Thousand Virgins, the fleet raised a prominent peninsula, which Magellan named after that seagoing Cornish princess and her martyred shipmates. Cabo Vírgenes, or Cape Virgins, it still is, on latitude 52°20′ S, longitude 68°21′ W. Albo was only twenty miles off in latitude, and made a good guess at the longitude. The cape is a long, flat stretch of grass-topped clay cliffs rising about 135 feet above the water. The landmarks for it (said Uriate on Loaysa's voyage) are a white sandhill four leagues north and "three great mountains of sand which look like islands but are not." On top of this cape the Chile-Argentine boundary turns a right angle and reaches the Atlantic a few yards east of the Chilean lighthouse on Punta Dungeness, the flat and gravelly extension of Cape Virgins. It then drops due south, leaving to Argentina one third of Tierra del Fuego down to the Beagle Channel, and giving Chile both sides of the strait.

Although the cape is conspicuous enough, the fact that a strait opens here is by no means obvious, and the tidal currents are so strong and confusing that an uncertain mariner would be tempted to sheer off. Joshua Slocum in 1898 was blown outside Cape Virgins for thirty hours by a southwest gale; the next loner, Louis Bernicot, in *Anahita,* also without power, was twice blown out to sea. Even steamers have been forced to scud all the way to the Falklands and there await a change of wind. Pigafetta wrote that but for Magellan they would never have found the strait, "for we all thought and said that it was closed on all sides." (The men evidently imagined a strait as something one could look through, like that of Gibraltar.) Pigafetta continued: "But the Captain General found it. He knew where to sail to find a well-hidden strait, which he saw depicted on a map in the treasury of the king of Portugal, made by that excellent man Martin de Boemia." That "excellent man" must have been Martin Behaim, but what was the map? Behaim died in 1507; he never, so far as we know, went on a voyage of discovery, and no chart by him, subsequent to his famous globe of 1492–93, is known to exist.

Every biographer of Magellan, and many historians, have discussed the question, "What chart did Magellan see in Lisbon?" To me, the most reasonable answer is that he had seen one or more charts that ended South America with a strait, on the south side of which was the supposed Antarctic continent, running around the world. The globe made in 1515 by the German geographer Johannes Schöner (1477–1547) is a good example of the chart that Magellan might have seen and thought to be Behaim's, since both Behaim and Schöner were Nurembergers, and their style was very similar. Magellan had brought a painted globe to the Spanish court to prove his point; may not this have been a copy of Schöner's? Pigafetta's word *"carta"* need not put us off, since in those days the word could mean a flat map or one spread on a globe.

A globe like this could have assured Magellan that a strait existed either at the River Plate or farther south. And Schöner makes the Pacific Ocean encouragingly narrow. "Zipangri" (Japan) is smack up to "Parias" (Central America), and the Spice Islands are no farther from the west coast of South America than the Lesser Antilles are from Florida. Had they indeed been so near to America, Magellan's idea that a round-the-world extension of the Line of Demarcation would give them to Spain would have proved correct. Spain, in fact, would have got all Asia up to the Ganges.

Two geographical factors unknown to Magellan thwarted him, although, curiously enough, he discovered both. One was the strait's extreme southern position and the other was the enormous breadth of the Pacific Ocean. These, combined, made the western route to the Far East so long and arduous as to be almost impracticable until ways were found to cross Mexico. Even so, the Portuguese Cape of Good Hope route remained the shorter and less difficult of the two. Magellan shared Columbus's basic idea of sailing from Europe to Asia "in a few days." America and the unexpected width of the Pacific thwarted both discoverers. And Magellan's exploits were never properly appreciated until Schouten and Le Maire capped them with the discovery of Cape Horn.

From Cape Virgins to Cape Pillar

It was now October 21, 1520; moon two days past first quarter. Having passed Cabo Vírgenes and avoided the many offshore rocks and shoals that there await unwary mariners, the captain general determined to investigate this break in the coast, and make sure whether it really was *the* strait. He nipped around Punta Dungeness, the flat southern prolongation of Cabo Vírgenes. Mooring his flagship and *Victoria* in Bahia Posesión, hoping that this would turn out to be fair holding-ground (which it was not), the captain general sent ahead *Concepción*, now commanded by his faithful friend Serrano, and *San Antonio*, commanded by his kinsman Mezquita, to reconnoiter.

One of the sharp northeast gales characteristic of this region blew up the night of October 21–22. *Trinidad* and *Victoria* weighed and jilled around inside the bay; the two others, too deeply embayed to beat against the gale, sailed west, giving themselves up for lost. Miraculously, as it then seemed, the two-mile-wide Primera Angostura

(First Narrows) opens up, and they roared through into Bahia Felipe, where they found shelter and holding-ground. Farther on, they found another and broader narrows (Segunda Angostura), which led to a big bay, Paso Ancho (Broad Reach). Serrano and Pilot Carvalho put their heads together and decided that they really were in *the* strait. After the gale had blown itself out and the wind turned west, *Concepción* and *San Antonio* returned to Bahia Posesión and announced themselves to *Trinidad* and the captain general by breaking out gay banners, sounding trumpets, firing gun salutes, shouting, and cheering. Each pair had feared the loss of the other.

When all four ships were safely anchored, they "thanked God and the Virgin Mary," and Magellan decided to follow whither *San Antonio* and *Concepción* had led. Since it was now November 1, All Saints' Day, the captain general named the strait "Todos los Santos." On early maps that name appears only for sections of the strait; the whole strait is almost invariably called "Estrecho de Magallanes," Magellan's Strait.

The captain general and his shipmates would have roared with laughter, could they have read the modern official sailing directions for the strait: "The passage is safe for steamers"; but in thick weather, "both difficult and dangerous, because of incomplete surveys, the lack of aids to navigation, the great distance between anchorages, the strong current, and the narrow limits for the maneuvering of vessels." Magellan might say, "What about us? With no power, other than sail and oar, no survey, no aid to navigation?" The same manual assumes that no ship without power would be so foolhardy as to try the strait.

Captain James Cook stated in his journal of the *Endeavour*'s voyage in 1769, "The doubling of Cape Horn is thought by some to be a mighty thing, and others to this Day prefer the Straits of Magellan." After Cook's fast passage of Cape Horn became known, the big sailing ships in general shunned the strait and suffered all the buffetings of "Cape Stiff" rather than face the dangers of the shorter route. But the strait has since come back as a major sea highway. Not only small freighters destined for Chile and Peru, but the mammoth oilers of the 1970's, use the strait regularly, and an average of about three a year run aground or are lost there. Few realize how long the strait is — 334 nautical miles. This is equivalent to the entire length of the English Channel from Bishop Rock to Dover Strait, or from the Gulf of St. Lawrence to Montreal, or from the Panama Canal entrance to Barranquilla.

Magellan and his captains wisely did not attempt to sail here at night; but darkness during the Antarctic spring, when they entered the strait, lasts but three to five hours.

A boat sent ashore from *Trinidad* in Bahia Felipe, between the two Angosturas, reported a dead whale and a native cemetery with a couple of hundred corpses raised on stilts, but nothing alive. No Magellan source mentions his fleet's having had any contact with live natives in the strait. He saw their signal fires almost every night — hence the name that he gave to the country on the south side, "Tierra del Fuego." The name is particularly applicable today; since this region has struck oil, the gas from sundry oil wells burns in smoky flares on each side of the strait's eastern entrance.

In seeing no Fuegians, Magellan's men missed viewing these examples of human fortitude in the face of hostile nature. Probably among the first arrivals from the Asiatic invasion tens of thousands of years earlier, continually pushed south by more powerful and enterprising tribes, these Indians had reached a dead end. Accommodating themselves to available food, though not to dress, as the Eskimos did in the far north, they lived on the big, succulent mussels of the strait and on such fish and birds as they could shoot or snare, burning the wood of the tepu tree (*Tepularia stipularis*), and stripping bark for canoe hulls from various species of the evergreen Antarctic beech (*Nothofagus antarctica pomilio*, and the like) that clothe the lower slopes of the mountains. Charles Darwin thus described a canoeful of Fuegians whom he encountered in the *Beagle:* "These poor wretches were stunted in their growth, their hideous faces bedaubed with white paint, their skins filthy and greasy, their hair entangled, their voices discordant, and their gestures violent." They seemed not to mind sleet falling on their almost naked bodies.

Undeterred by sinister hints of the native graveyard, Magellan's fleet worked through the wider Second Narrows and came to an anchor in Paso Real, between Isabel Island and the main. Here, and well into Paso Ancho, or Broad Reach, the landscape on each side is pampas: green-to-brown rolling country with no hint of a strait. Even Paso Ancho looks like a dead end because in clear weather, sixty miles to the southward, the mountains on Dawson Island and on the Cordillera Darwin rise like an impenetrable barrier. On the land side the aspect today is pastoral. In February, hayfields white with daisies roll down to the sea, sheep and cattle pastures are everywhere, and a few neat villas, planted with evergreen to shield them from the furious winds, indicate that this region is livable winter or summer. Paso Ancho (fifteen miles broad), when low-hanging clouds hide the distant snowy mountains, looks very much like any broad bay in Maine, Nova Scotia, or Scotland. The great scenery begins within sight of Cape Froward.

Magellan's fleet, continuing south through Paso Ancho and passing the site of Punta Arenas, again separated. The captain general sent *San Antonio* and *Concepción* to investigate two openings eastward, which turned out to be dead ends — Bahia Inútil (Useless Bay) and Seno del Almirantazgo (Admiralty Bay) — while he in the flagship, with *Victoria*, sailed along what fortunately turned out to be the real strait.

Just before this separation, Magellan held a captains' conference to decide whether or not to push on. All were in favor of doing so except Esteban Gómez, now pilot of *San Antonio*. Although a Portuguese, Gómez "hated the Captain General exceedingly," wrote Pigafetta, because he had hoped to command the entire fleet, and his simmering hate blew hot when Magellan, after eliminating Cartagena, conferred the captaincy of *San Antonio* on his cousin Mezquita instead of on Gómez. Magellan, *muy compuesto* (with his usual cool), replied that he was resolved to go on, "even if they had to eat the leather chafing-gear on the ships' yards." And that is exactly what they did.

While *San Antonio* was exploring Useless and Admiralty bays, Esteban Gómez pulled off the one successful mutiny of this long voyage. He managed to suborn the stoutest fellows in the crew; clapped weak Captain Mezquita in irons; gave his fellow conspirator, Hierónimo Guerra, command of the ship; and piloted her back to Spain, arriving at the end of March 1521. He made no attempt to put in at San Julián to pick up marooned Cartagena and the priest. At Seville, both Gómez and his victim, Mezquita, were flung into jail. Gómez managed to parley his way out of jail and into the royal favor to such good purpose that he got a new ship to go in search of a better strait than Magellan's. But poor Alvaro de Mezquita, the most frustrated officer of the fleet, remained in jail until after *Victoria* arrived home, when he found witnesses to put his conduct in a more favorable light. Charles V eventually ordered Mezquita to be released, and he returned to Portugal on Dom Manuel's invitation.

In the meantime, Magellan in *Trinidad,* with *Victoria,* sailed west again down Broad Reach. About thirty miles south of the site of Punta Arenas, they passed, behind Punta Santa Ana, the site of Rey Don Felipe, one of two outposts established by Sarmiento de Gamboa in 1583 to guard the strait. Port Famine, the name given to it by Cavendish in 1587, is still the southernmost settlement on the strait; not a soul lives to the south and west. Near here, wrote Captain Slocum in 1900, "I had my first experience with the terrific squalls called williwaws, which extended from the point on through the Strait to the Pacific. These were compressed gales of wind that Boreas handed down over the hills in chunks. A full-blown williwaw will throw a ship, even without sail set, over on her beam ends." Sailing directions warn mariners always to be prepared for williwaws. They give no notice of their coming, and are apt to hit a vessel with such force as to strip off her sails, or even to capsize her.

Magellan's fleet sailed into spectacular scenery as soon as it passed Mount Tarn, which Darwin was the first to climb. Magellan's people had never seen anything like this combination of ocean strait with snow mountains, nor had Darwin. They rounded Cape Froward, a noble headland rising almost 1200 feet at latitude 53°54' S, the southernmost point on the American continent. Here the strait, about five miles wide, turns abruptly northwest, and after another twenty-five to thirty miles becomes a deep, narrow cut through the Andes, as if some giant hand had cleft the mountains millions of years ago.

Entering this part of the strait, as we did in February 1972, one seems to be entering a completely new and strange world, a veritable Never-Never Land. The strait never freezes except along the edges, and the evergreen Antarctic beech, with its tiny, matted leaves, grows thick along the lower mountain slopes. The middle slopes support a coarse grass that turns bronze in the setting sun; and above, the high peaks are snow-covered the year round. When it rains in the strait, it snows at 6000 feet. One misses, in the Antarctic autumn, the brilliant colors of New England and Canada, since Patagonia and Tierra del Fuego lack birch and other deciduous trees; but by way of compensation, they harbor no mosquitoes, which cannot stand the wind! There is no sign of human life south and west of Port

Famine except for a few small unattended lighthouses at dangerous points. The Indians are extinct, and with no coastal road or path or any means of land transportation, neither Chilean nor foreigner has attempted to settle or even to camp here.* Even the birds are different — the sinister gray *carnero*, which picks out the eyes of shipwrecked sailors; the steamboat duck, whose whirling wings, resembling the churning paddle wheels of early steamers, enable him to pace an eight-knot vessel on the surface. In spring, when Magellan sailed through, both banks are gay with many-colored flowers, and saturated peat moss makes a sort of tundra in the hollows. Although glaciers are everywhere visible and some descend nearly to the sea, icebergs are missing; the glaciers "calve" only small bits of ice, not bergs. Waterfalls tumble directly into the bays. It is "fascinating sailing," wrote H. W. Tilman, who sailed through in his little sloop, *Mischief,* in an Antarctic summer not long ago. One rounds miniature capes and peeps into hidden coves: "It had the powerful appeal of an untrodden land." In several places, such as Paso Inglés by Rupert and Carlos islands, and Crosstides, the channel is less than a mile wide, but in the center the depths run to 800 fathom; and from the narrow ribbon of practicable holding-ground near shore, a ship is likely to be wrenched by a sudden williwaw.

The little bight that Magellan named "River of Sardines," because its waters were swarming with small edible fish, one can identify as Fortescue Bay, just east of Cabo Gallant at latitude 53°42' S. The captain general may even have entered the inner landlocked harbor, Caleta Gallant. Both have excellent holding-ground; the Chilean *Derrotero* (Sailing Directions) calls Fortescue the best anchorage in the strait for all classes of vessels. And it is an exceptionally charming spot. The soft summer night of February 24, 1972, when we lay there in *Orompello* of the Chilean navy, will be ever memorable for the Milky Way rising in a great "whoosh" of sparkling light, and on top of it the Southern Cross flashing brilliantly. Next morning we went ashore on the pebble beach of Bahia Fortescue, which was wreathed with white flowers resembling gigantic marguerites; a few rods inland we found other flowers, brightly colored, and calafate bushes, bearing big red berries. Magellan evidently chose this fair place to celebrate the first Mass in the future Chile. The inner Caleta Gallant, "difficult

---

* An exception: Bahia Cutter, up the Canal San Jerónimo, where there is a small copper mine with about a dozen employees.

of access," says the modern *Derrotero*, but not too difficult for Magellan's ships, offers perfect protection and holding-ground, with two rivers to replenish water and plenty of beechwood for fuel.

While he waited here, the captain general fitted out, provisioned, and manned his flag longboat to explore the strait further in the hope of finding an outlet. "The men returned within three days," wrote Pigafetta, "and reported that they had seen the cape and the open sea." Roldán de Argote, a Flemish gunner of the fleet, climbed a mountain (later named after him), sighted the ocean, and reported it to the captain general, who "wept for joy," said Pigafetta, "and called that *Cabo Deseado*, for we had long been desiring it." The name is still applied to one of the two prongs of Desolation Island that mark the Pacific entrance to the strait; Cabo Pilar, the better-known later name, is the northern prong.

Solicitous about his other two ships, Magellan turned back to search for them. Having already roughly charted the eastern half of the strait, he avoided the great masses of kelp that still mark the rocky ledges, and had leisure to examine the striking scenery. Here, as Herrera tells us, "is the most beautiful country in the world — the Strait a gunshot across, separating high sierras covered with perpetual snow, whose lower slopes were clothed with magnificent trees."

Soon they met *Concepción* sailing alone. Captain Serrano had no news of *San Antonio*, but Magellan refused to write her off, and spent five or six days searching for her, even up Admiralty Sound; *Victoria* sailed all the way to Cape Virgins to look for the errant ship. The captain general now turned to his chief pilot, Andrés de San Martin, who combined astrology with navigation. After plotting the stars and consulting a book, Andrés reported that she had returned to Spain with Captain Mezquita in chains. He was right, as we have seen.

After *Victoria* rejoined the flagship, Magellan decided to press forward, and information from the boat exploration saved him from wasting time on dead ends. He sailed up the main channel, Paso Inglés, the most dangerous reach of the strait (although not the most narrow), and passed Carlos III Island (where Captain Joshua Slocum in his sloop *Spray* foiled an attack by Fuegians by sprinkling carpet tacks on her deck at night). On this island of many hills Magellan erected a cross.

As one approaches the meeting of waters, which some English navigator appropriately named Crosstides, where Canal San Jerónimo empties into the strait, anyone might wonder which was the strait and which the canal. But the longboat crew must have observed as they got nearer, what Ensign Thornton of *Orompello* pointed out to me, that the waters of the canal are lighter in color than those of the strait, and that the nearer one approaches, the wider the real strait appears to be. So Magellan wasted no time, and avoided the dead end. He passed safely through Paso Tortuoso with its 330-fathom deep, and entered Paso Largo with depths up to 810 fathom.

Here again the character of the scenery changes. The mountains of Desolation Island on the port hand are of ribbed granite with stunted vegetation only in the clefts, reminding one of the Labrador; no more trees. Great Pacific surges roll in and break on both sides. You feel that you are coming out into something enormous and unpredictable. Magellan passed Bahia Corkscrew, Cape Providence, and the bold island of Tamar, off which a 2½-fathom rock has wrecked many an incautious ship. Here in midstrait, with 800-foot deeps on each side, is the dangerous Bajo Magallanes, which breaks when heavy swells roll in from the ocean. At the end of Paso del Mar is the worst of many bad places in the strait in which to be caught in a strong westerly.

After thirty miles of this, on November 28, 1520 (moon four days past full), *Trinidad, Concepción*, and *Victoria* passed Cabo Pilar (which Magellan named "Deseado") on Desolation Island. Only one of these ships, and about 35 out of the 150 members of their crews, ever returned to Spain.

Antonio de Herrera, the late-sixteenth-century Spanish historian who seems to have cared most for Magellan, wrote of his entry into the great Pacific: "On the 27th of November he came out into the South Sea, blessing God, who had been pleas'd to permit him to find what he so much desir'd, being the first that ever went that way, which will perpetuate his Memory for ever. They guessed this Streight to be about one hundred Leagues in Length . . . The sea was very Black and Boisterous, which denoted a vast Ocean. Magellan order'd publick Thanksgiving, and sail'd away to the Northward, to get out of the Cold."

All in all, Magellan had a "very good chance," as sailors say, especially as he had sailed thrice over at least 250 miles of the 334-mile length of the strait, looking for *San Antonio*. He did not experience, or at least none of his three literary shipmates noted, any sharp squalls or particular hazards. He managed to moor safely every night by running a hawser from the stern to a tree ashore in one of the many anchorages suitable for small ships. Frequently the sailors landed to gather an excellent antiscorbutic, the wild celery (*Apium australe*), which grew in abundance near springs or rivers. Later voyagers described the natural bowers that wind-blown beech and pine made in the woods. Their matted branches kept out excessive snow and cold; in this shelter herbs flourished the year round, and in the spring there is a gorgeous show of wildflowers. Magellan's men caught plenty of fish — albacore, bonito, and flying fish. After they had passed safely through, Pigafetta wrote, "I believe that there is not a more beautiful or better strait in the world than that one." Beautiful, yes, but terrible as well; and one must study the history of later voyages through the strait, and if possible traverse it oneself, to appreciate the grandeur and the magnitude of Magellan's achievement. For say what you will of him, detractors, *he did it.* As Alonso de Ercilla wrote in *La Araucana,*

> *Magallanes, Señor, fué el primer hombre*
> *Que abriendo este camino, le dió nombre.**
> Magellan, Sir, was the first man
> Both to open this route and to give it name.

"Wednesday, November 28, 1520," wrote Pigafetta, "we debouched from that Strait, engulfing ourselves in the Pacific Sea." One of the great moments of a great voyage. The Pacific, shimmering under a westering sun, spread for half a circumference before Magellan's eyes. Vasco Núñez de Balboa, to be sure, had seen the ocean from a peak in Darien seven years before, and even earlier Abreu had sailed into its western edge, which laved the Moluccas. But Magellan now faced a waste of water thousands of miles wide, and entered it without fear or hesitation. Here, too, he navigated well, for this forefront of the great ocean is studded with breaking reefs; the entire coast is smoky with their white spray. If you let a west wind and flood tide throw you off from Cabo Pilar, you are likely to strike the extensive rocky shoals hopefully if unsuitably named by early sailors "Buena Esperanza" and "Las Evangelistas" — Good Hope and The Evangelists.

Albo tells us that from Cabo Deseado they steered northwest,

---

* Canto 1, strophe 8: first published in 1569.

north, and north-northeast for two days and three nights, and on the morning of December 1 sighted land and found their latitude to be 48° S. They were well on their way to penetrating the greatest of oceans, hitherto unknown to Europeans except by rare glimpses of its distant verges.

5

Giovanni da Verrazzano

From THE EUROPEAN DISCOVERY OF AMERICA: THE NORTHERN VOYAGES, A.D. 500–1600 (New York: Oxford University Press, 1971), *Chapter IX.*

Verrazzano, the Florentine explorer in the service of France, is one of my favorites. His explorations of the North American coast from the site of New York (which he discovered) to Newfoundland were already well known to me from yachting voyages, when in 1970 my friend James F. Nields undertook to fly me along the coast from South Carolina to New York in his Beechcraft. Here I may say that coastal research by air rather than sea has the advantage of speed, and that a low-flying plane gives one a view of the coast approximately equal to that from the round-top of a ship of the sixteenth century, although such research requires more care and imagination than does research done on a voyage under sail. In our case it settled many controversies over the original navigator's actual course, while leaving the exact spot of his tragic death, at the hands of Carib Indians, open to doubt. So, here goes —

IN TUSCANY, thirty miles south of Florence, one enters the Chianti country and a Tuscan landscape that has hardly changed since the painters of the *cinquecento* used it for background. Sparkling streams and rivers, bordered by conical hills, whose slopes are planted with vines almost to the summits; each hilltop crowned with a villa or a castle. By no means the least of these is the Castello Verrazzano, ancestral home of that noble family, whose arms are a six-pointed star. It is a real castle, with two stone towers for defense, but in the sixteenth century modern rooms were built, and a detached chapel, and a fishpond. Long has it been "comfortably accepted" (to quote Dr. Lawrence C. Wroth) that our Giovanni was born here in 1485. A recent French biographer denies this, giving Giovanni a new pair of parents, Alessandro da Verrazzano and Giovanna De Guadagni, and a Lyons birthplace. This is indignantly denied by everyone in the Chianti country, and ascribed to French chauvinism! Castello Verrazzano near Greve is indubitably the ancestral home, and as Giovanni and his brother were always referred to as Florentines, there is no sense quarreling about whether they were born here or in the Florentine community of Lyons.

"This valiant gentleman," as Ramusio called him, differed from other heroes of northern exploration in that he was well born and well educated. All contemporary documents refer to him as such; some even call him a nobleman.

If born in France, he was sent to Florence for his education, for the language of his Letter on the voyage of discovery and its literary allusions indicate that he received an upper-class Renaissance education. It also reveals that he knew more mathematics than most gentlemen of his time — or of ours.

The earliest actual fact that we know about him is that on attaining his majority, about 1506–1507, he removed to Dieppe, in order to pursue a maritime career. A gossipy annalist of Dieppe, writing nearly three centuries later, stated that "Jean Verason," presumably our man, sailed in Ango's *La Pensée* to Newfoundland in 1508. In any case, the allusions to Carthage, Damascus, and the Saracens in the famous Letter prove that Verrazzano made voyages to the Levant; and there are hints that he was friendly with Magellan at Seville before the great circumnavigator's departure in 1517. A gentleman-navigator, yes; but thoroughly professional.

None of the existing portraits of Verrazzano is contemporary with him, but as they all derive from one by Zocchi, painted in his lifetime or shortly after, they may be assumed to be roughly correct. All show him with strong, confident features, black or dark brown hair, heavily bearded and mustachioed, with a prominent Roman nose; a thoroughly attractive and impressive figure.

By 1523, when he had attained the age of thirty-eight, Verrazzano had an impeccable maritime record, and as an Italian he appealed to the king. In the sixteenth century there was no hard-and-fast line between official voyages and privately financed voyages. Verrazzano borrowed *La Dauphine*, a ship of the royal French navy, and reported to the French king; but the Florentine bankers of Lyons and

Rouen supplied most of the funds as well as the second ship, *La Normande*, which did not go far. *La Dauphine*, built in the new royal dockyard of Le Havre in 1519, was named after the dauphin François, heir to the throne, for whose birth the year before the great bell at Rouen tolled for twenty-four hours. She measured 100 tuns and carried a crew of fifty; this was twice the burthen of John Cabot's *Mathew*, and almost thrice the number of his crew. She probably flew the royal ensign of azure sprinkled with gold fleurs-de-lys. *La Normande* was a merchant ship chartered by the Lyons bankers from Jean Ango.

La Dauphine carried provisions for eight months. Her outfitting took place at Dieppe, probably under the eyes of Jean Ango. Spies reported to Dom João III of Portugal that French mischief was afoot; this Florentine boasts that he is going "to discover Cathay," but his real objective may be a raid on Brazil. Be on your guard, Your Majesty!

Verrazzano should have had a fleet of four ships, but a tempest in the autumn of 1523 disposed of two, and only *La Normande* and *La Dauphine* were left. They put in for refuge at a Breton port, and after repairs started south in company, taking a number of prizes off the coast of Spain. For reasons unexplained, probably because she had to escort the prizes to France, *La Normande* peeled off, and *La Dauphine* alone continued to America.

We have not the name of a single shipmate of Verrazzano's except that of his brother Girolamo the mapmaker. Giovanni, even less generous than Columbus in giving credit to subordinates, does not mention a single person in his official Letter to François-premier, and he refers to the crew as "*la turba marittima*" — the maritime mob. They had good reason to dislike him, as *La Dauphine* almost always anchored in an uncomfortable roadstead, and they had shore liberty but once in the entire voyage.

Before sailing, Verrazzano made his will: "*Le noble homme Jehan Verrassenne, capitaine des navires esquippez pour un voiage des Indes,*" named brother Girolamo his heir and made him co-executor with Rucellai, his banker-cousin. And in his official Letter to François-premier he made the object of the expedition perfectly clear: "My intention on this voyage was to reach Cataia and the extreme eastern coast of Asia, not expecting to find such a barrier of new land as I did find; and, if I did find such a land, I estimated that it would not lack a strait to penetrate to the Eastern Ocean" — that is, the Pacific.

We have no hint as to what navigational instruments Verrazzano had at his disposal. That he took a keen interest in scientific navigation is indicated by his keeping a day book, or journal (which has not survived), and by making an honest effort to determine longitude. His latitudes, more accurate than any prior to Cartier's, suggest that he was not confined to Columbus's imperfect instruments, the triangular wooden quadrant, with its tiddly plumb-bob on a thread, and the mariner's astrolabe; that he had at least one of the newly invented *balestilas*, or cross-staffs. But we cannot be certain, for it took a long time for new inventions to be adopted by sailors. The Ribero World Map of 1529, made subsequent to the voyages of Verrazzano, Gomez, and Ayllón, illustrates the quadrant and astrolabe, but no cross-staff.

From Deserta to the "Isthmus"

Verrazzano's plan for his ocean-crossing ran parallel to that of Columbus's in 1492; but instead of dropping down to latitude 28° N and the Canaries, he chose to take off from Las Desertas in the Madeira group at latitude 32°30' N. French corsairs had already been preying on the Spanish treasure fleets, Spanish warships were looking for prowling Frenchmen, and Verrazzano obviously wished to avoid hostile confrontations in order to carry out his mission. The Madeiras were Portuguese.

On January 17, 1524, *La Dauphine* said farewell to the Old World. The latitude the captain chose for the crossing lay well above the normal range of easterly trade winds, but for about three weeks *La Dauphine* enjoyed them: "Sailing with a zephyr blowing east-southeast with sweet and gentle mildness," as he puts it in his Letter. Like Columbus, Verrazzano appreciated the beauty of smooth seas and prosperous winds, and on the northerly edge of the trades he had them at their best.

On February 24 he ran out of luck, and encountered as sharp and severe a tempest as he or his shipmates had ever experienced. "With the divine help and merciful assistance of Almighty God and the soundness of our ship, accompanied with the good hap of her fortunate name, we were delivered," wrote Verrazzano. He altered course to west by north, and then turned west on latitude 34° N. Thus he made landfall on or about March 1, 1524, at or near Cape Fear, which is on latitude 33°50'47" N; Verrazzano said it was on 34°, "like Carthage and Damascus." Near enough — Damascus is on 33°30'. Note that this navigator, like Cabot, compared latitudes of his discoveries with known points in Europe, which meant something to those who read his report.

Cape Fear, southernmost of North Carolina's three capes (Fear, Lookout, and Hatteras), is a long alluvial promontory where the Cape Fear River has been depositing detritus for many millennia. The tip is formed by Bald Island, a tract of still unspoiled dunes and wet marsh where birds, fish, and turtle breed, and a live-oak forest grows, and the Frying Pan Shoals extend some fifteen miles farther out to sea. Verrazzano did not tarry, as he wished to explore the coast between there and Florida before turning northward. His distances are difficult to follow on the map, because every unit is "fifty leagues" (about 110 nautical miles), recalling St. Brendan's "forty days."

So, from her landfall, *La Dauphine* sailed south for "fifty leagues," then turned north again "in order not to meet with the Spaniards." Since she had not found any "convenient harbor whereby to come a-land," the turning point must have been short of Charleston; on Girolamo da Verrazzano's map this point is called "Dieppa," after *La Dauphine*'s home port. Returning to the place of her landfall, she anchored well offshore, probably in the lee of Cape Fear. Unlike other mariners of the period, Verrazzano liked anchoring in an open roadstead, provided he found good holding-ground. However, he sent a boat ashore on or near Cape Fear, and briefly consorted with a group of natives who "came harde to the Sea side, seeming to rejoyce very much at the sight of us; and, marveiling greatly at our apparel, shape and whiteness, showed us by sundry signs where we might most commodiously come a-land with our boat, offering us also of their victuals to eat."

Verrazzano here describes their manners and customs "as farre as we could have notice thereof":

These people go altogether naked except only that they cover their privy parts with certain skins of beasts like unto martens, which they fasten onto a narrow girdle made of grass, very artificially [that is, artfully] wrought, hanged about with tails of divers other beasts, which round about their bodies hang dangling down to their knees. Some of them wear garlands of birds' feathers. The people are of color russet, and not much unlike the Saracens; their hair black, thick, and not very long, which they tie together in a knot behind, and wear it like a tail. They are well featured in their limbs, of mean [average] stature, and commonly somewhat bigger than we; broad breasted, strong arms, their legs and other parts of their bodies well fashioned, and they are disfigured in nothing, saving that they have somewhat broad visages, and yet not all of them; for we saw many of them well favoured, having black and great eyes, with a cheerful and steady look, not strong of body, yet sharp-witted, nimble, and great runners, as far as we could learn by experience; and in those two last qualities they are like to them of the uttermost parts of China.

This reference to China indicates that Verrazzano was familiar with *The Book of Ser Marco Polo.*

Continuing some distance northward, the Frenchmen again landed, noted sand dunes fronting the upland palmettos, and bay bushes and cypresses, "which yield most sweet savours, far from the shore" — even a hundred leagues out. So he named this land "Selva di Lauri" (Forest of Laurels), and "Campo di Cedri" (Field of Cedars). Like Columbus, Verrazzano had a genius for giving newly discovered places beautiful and appropriate names; but, unlike those given by Columbus, few of his names stuck. Unless an explorer is shortly followed by others, or by colonists of his nation, his names are quickly forgotten.

As laurel and cedar grow all along the coasts of Georgia and South Carolina, we cannot identify these places. Strange that neither the Florentine, nor the Englishmen who came here in 1585–90, mentioned the yucca palm, with its spiky fronds and great clusters of white blossoms. Possibly it did not grow that far north in the sixteenth century.

Continuing north-northeasterly, *La Dauphine* anchored again in an open roadstead and sent a boat ashore. Here is how Hakluyt translates Verrazzano's story of the encounter:

While we rode on that coast, partly because it had no harbour, and for that we wanted water, we sent our boat ashore with 25 men; where, by reason of great and continual waves that beat against the shore, being an open coast without succour, none of our men could possibly go ashore without losing our boat. We saw there many people, which came unto the shore, making divers signs of friendship, and showing that they were content we should come a-land, and by trial we found them to be very courteous and gentle, as your majesty shall understand by the success. To the intent we might send them of our things, which the Indians commonly desire and esteem, as sheets of paper, glasses, bells and such trifles, we sent a young man, one of our mariners, ashore, who swimming towards them, cast the things upon the shore. Seeking afterwards to return, he was with such violence of the waves beaten upon the shore, that he was so bruised that he lay there almost dead, which the Indians perceiving, ran to catch him, and drawing him out, they carried him a little way off from the sea.

The young man, fearing to be killed, "cried out piteously," but these Indians had no sinister intention. They laid him down at the foot of a sand dune to dry in the sun, and beheld him "with great admiration, marveling at the whiteness of his flesh." They then stripped him down and "made him warm at a great fire," which caused his shipmates to expect him to be roasted and eaten.

The young man having recovered his strength, and having stayed awhile with them, showed them by signs that he was desirous to return to the ship; and they with great love clapping him fast about with many embracings, accompanying him unto the sea; and, to put him in more assurance, leaving him alone they went unto a high ground and stood there, beholding him, until he was entered into the boat. This young man observed, as we did also, that these are of color inclining to black, as the other were; with their flesh very shining, of mean stature, handsome visage, and delicate limbs, and of very little strength; but of prompt wit. Farther we observed not.

This spot Verrazzano named "Annunziata" because the day was March 25, the feast of the Annunciation of the Virgin. It must have been on the Outer, or Carolina, Banks between Capes Lookout and Hatteras, or a few miles north of Hatteras. According to his own marginal note, Verrazzano here committed his great geographical error. He found "an isthmus a mile in width and about 200 long, in which, from the ship, we could see *el mare orientale* [the Pacific Ocean], halfway between West and North"; that is, northwesterly. This sea, he says, "is the same which flows around the shores of India, China and Cataya . . ." To this isthmus the discoverer gave the name "Verrazzania," and the entire land discovered was called "Francesca," after King François.

This passage has attracted a good deal of scorn to the Florentine mariner, but without justice. You may sail for twenty miles south and twenty miles north of Cape Hatteras without seeing the mainland from the deck or mast of a small sailing ship. We flew Verrazzano's route on a beautiful June day with high visibility at an altitude of 200 feet, and for fifty miles could see no land west of the banks. Even from the modern motor road, which (spliced out with car ferries) extends along the banks, the far shore is commonly invisible. Verrazzano is, however, open to two criticisms: (1) In view of his preference for open roadsteads, why did he not anchor off one of the inlets and send in a boat to explore? These inlets are always shifting, but we cannot imagine that there was none in 1524, since the flow of fresh water always breaks out new ones when an old one closes. Sir Walter Raleigh's colonists found at least three in the 1580's with two fathom of water in each. (2) Verrazzano must have been familiar with a similar topography, on a smaller scale, in the Venetian lagoon; but there you can almost always see foothills from outside the Lido.

The Letter continued: "We sailed along this isthmus [the Outer Banks] in continual hope of finding some strait or northern promontory at which the land would come to an end, in order to penetrate to *quelli felici liti del Catay*" — those happy shores of Cathay.

Rather pathetic, is it not? Verrazzano and his shipmates straining their eyes to find a bold, northward-looking promontory like Cape St. Vincent or Finisterre, which *La Dauphine* could whip around in a jiffy, and everyone on board would shout and yell, and the musicians would strike up the "Vexilla Regis," knowing that they had found the long-sought Passage to India?

Thus Verrazzano assumed that he had sighted the Pacific Ocean across an isthmus much narrower than that of Panama! This tremendous error was perpetuated for a century or more by his brother Girolamo and the Italian cartographer Maiollo. Their world maps give North America a narrow waist around North Carolina, with the Pacific Ocean flowing over some 40 percent of the area of the future United States.

Et in Arcadia Ego

The next place where *La Dauphine* called, after the usual "fifty-league" sail from Annunziata, "appeared to be much more beautiful [than the other Outer Banks] and full of very tall trees." "We named it *Archadia* owing to the beauty of the trees," recalling the Arcady of ancient Greece.

The Arcadian concept, an ideal landscape inhabited by simple, virtuous people, is derived from Virgil. In his *Eclogues* (x) he has the lovesick Gallus say, "Arcadians, you will sing my frantic love for Phyllis to your mountains, you alone who know how to sing; for you have cool springs, soft meadows, and groves. Among you I shall grow old, now that an insane love enchains me, and in the forest amidst the dens of wild beasts carve the story of my loves on the tender bark of trees: *crescent illae, crescetis amores* [as they grow, so shall my loves]." Virgil's story took a new lease on life in Jacopo Sannazzaro's fifteenth-century novel *Arcadia*. This opens with a tribute to the tall, spreading trees that grow wild on mountains, especially to the grove "of such uncommon and extreme beauty" that flourishes on the summit of Mount Parthenius in Arcadia. If not Virgil, Sannazzaro's novel, so popular as to be printed at least fifteen times before *La Dauphine* set sail, must have inspired Verrazzano to call this fair land after the fabulous province of ancient Peloponnesus.

After flying along the entire coast from what is now Cape Fear River to the site of present-day Barnegat, New Jersey, in search of a hilly section with big trees, I have no hesitation in locating Verrazzano's Arcadia at Kitty Hawk, North Carolina, the scene of the Wright brothers' pioneer flights in 1900–1903. Kill Devil Hill, Kitty Hawk, although but 91 feet in elevation, is the highest natural eminence except Cape Henry (105 feet) on the coast between Florida and the Navesink Highlands. Already bare in the Wrights' day, as in ours, it was undoubtedly heavily wooded in Verrazzano's. Nearby, under a high dune of tawny sand now called "Engagement Hill," there is still a heavy forest growth of pine, live oak, red oak, bay, laurel, holly, and dogwood. Undoubtedly this was the most beautiful spot — to European eyes — that Verrazzano encountered on his voyage prior to our New York Bay, and it is no wonder that he called there and spent three days, despite the lack of a harbor.

Moreover, Girolamo Verrazzano's map, immediately east of a misspelled Annuntiata, places "Lamacra" — a misspelled L'Arcadia — and there are a dozen place names between it and New York Bay.

The doings of the Frenchmen were anything but Arcadian. Here is Verrazzano's account of a kidnaping:

That we might have some knowledge thereof, we sent 20 men a-land, which entered into the country about two leagues, and they found that the people were fled to the woods for fear. They saw only one old woman with a young maid of 18 or 20 years old, which, seeing our company, hid themselves in the grass for fear; the old woman carried two infants on her shoulders, and behind her neck a child of 8 years old; the young woman was laden likewise with as many. But when our men came unto them, the women cried out; the old woman made signs that the men were fled unto the woods as soon as they saw us; to quiet them and to win their favor, our men gave them such victuals as they had with them to eat, which the old woman received thankfully; but the young woman disdained them all, and threw them disdainfully on the ground. They took a child from the old woman to bring into France, and, going about to take the young woman (which was very beautiful and of tall stature), they could not possibly, for the great outcries that she made, bring her to the sea, and especially having great woods to pass through, and being far from the ship, we purposed to leave her behind, bearing away the child only.

Loud screaming, woman's first line of defense, here worked very well; but one would like to know what became of the poor child, snatched from his Arcadian people at a tender age.

"In Arcadia," continued Verrazzano, "we found a man who came to the shore to see what [manner of men] we were . . . He was handsome, naked, his hair fastened in a knot, and of an olive color." Approaching near a group of twenty Frenchmen, he thrust toward them "a burning stick, as if to offer us fire." This must have been a lighted tobacco pipe, and the poor fellow was simply making a friendly gesture, offering the intruders a pipe of peace. They, having neither seen nor heard of tobacco, took his intentions to be hostile and fired a blank shot from a musket. At that the Indian "trembled all over with fright" and "remained as if thunderstruck, and, like a friar, pointing a finger at sky, ship, and sea as if he were invoking a blessing on us."

Verrazzano described the dugout canoes, which the Indians constructed by burning out the interior of a hardwood log, and wild grapevines that climb trees "as they do in Lombardy"; "roses, violets, lilies, and many sorts of herbs, and sweet and odoriferous flowers, different from ours." The Indians wore leaves for clothing, and lived mostly by fishing and fowling; but they offered him pulse (beans) "differing in color and taste from ours, of good and pleasant taste." *La Dauphine* remained in Arcadia for three days around April 10, anchoring, as usual, offshore; and the captain states that he would have stayed longer but for the absence of a harbor.

Arcadia is one of three place names of Verrazzano's that have survived, but later mapmakers continually moved it eastward until it became "L'Acadie," the French name for Nova Scotia, New Brunswick, and part of Maine. Verrazzano must have been very bored, as he sailed northward, to find the same long, thin, sandy islands fronting lagoons, with only two breaks — the Virginia capes and the Delaware capes. He missed these entrances to Chesapeake and Delaware bays, which he surely would have explored as possible straits to Cathay. Prudently avoiding shoal water, he evidently sailed *La Dauphine* so far out to sea that these great bays were not visible.

After sailing past what is now Barnegat, New Jersey, he closed the shore and began observing places more to his liking. He anchored every night offshore; named one promontory "Bonivet," after the grand admiral of France; and a river "Vendôme," after Charles de Bourbon, duc de Vendôme; but it is impossible to locate these from his vague directions. A coast "green with forests" which he called "Lorraine," after one of the titles of Jean Cardinal Guise, was probably New Jersey.

Verrazzano was the first North American explorer to name places newly discovered after personalities and beloved spots at home. His predecessors generally confined themselves to descriptive names, such as "codfish," "grapes," "boldness," or "flatness," adding a few saints' names appropriate to the date of the landfall. The Florentine set a precedent that most of his successors honored; Cartier, for instance, used some of the same names, and a few of them have survived.

One thing is certain: *La Dauphine* was favored by extraordinarily good luck in weather. To sail along the coast from South Carolina to New York, in the turbulent spring of the year, and anchor offshore without mishap is an exploit that any merchant captain under sail, and some steamship masters, too, might well envy. The United States Coast Guard estimates that there are 600 wrecks off the Carolina Outer Banks. On *The National Geographic*'s map of them, the names of known wrecks in historic times are so close together as to seem continuous. When Verrazzano's *Letter* was published in 1841, many a practical seaman said, "It cannot be — the fellow is a fraud and a fake!" But there the record is, in black and white, from an honest captain; and who are we to deny it? But for his tragic end, we might conclude Verrazzano to have been especially favored by the gods of the sea and the winds.

Angoulême and Refugio

"In space of 100 leagues sailing," continues Verrazzano, "we found a very pleasant place, situated amongst certain little steep hills; from amidst the which hills there ran down into the sea a great stream of water, which within the mouth was very deep, and from the sea to the mouth of same, with the tide, which we found to rise 8 foot, any great vessel laden may pass up."

This description well fits New York Bay; the hills, the first he had seen since Kitty Hawk, might have been the present Navesink Highlands, Staten Island, or Brooklyn Heights. The day was April 17, *La Dauphine* sailed gently before a soft southwest wind, and New York Bay never looked fairer than on this very first day when European eyes gazed upon it.

The rest of Verrazzano's brief account indicates that he anchored in the Narrows, now renamed after him and spanned by the Verrazzano Bridge:

But because we rode at anchor in a place well fenced from the wind, we would not venture ourselves without knowledge of the place, and we passed up with our boat only into the said river, and saw the country very well peopled. The people are almost like unto the others, and clad with feathers of fowls of divers colors. They came towards us very cheerfully, making great shouts of admiration, showing us where we might come to land most safely with our boat. We entered up the said river into the land about half a league, where it made a most pleasant lake about 3 leagues in compass; on the which they rowed from the one side to the other, to the number of 30 of their small boats, wherein were many people, which passed from one shore to the other to come and see us. And behold, upon the sudden (as it is wont to fall out in sailing) a contrary flaw of wind coming from the sea, we were enforced to return to our ship, leaving this land, to our great discontentment for the great commodity and pleasantness thereof, which we suppose is not without some riches, all the hills showing mineral matters in them.

Verrazzano showed good judgment in weighing anchor and standing out to sea, rather than risk dragging ashore in the Narrows. But we wish he could have spent more than one day at the site of the future city, and not confined himself to this brief description of it and the feather-clad natives. His short boat tour indicates that he regarded the Narrows as part of the river, and that the "pleasant lake" about ten miles in circumference was the Upper Bay. Of the Hudson River he viewed only the mouth; and if he noticed the East River he probably figured that it flowed from the same source as the "Great" (Hudson) River, verdant Manhattan Island dividing the river's lower course so that it emptied into the sea by two mouths. He named this part of the country "Angoulême," the title of François-premier before he became king, and the bay "Santa Margarita," in honor of the king's sister, Marguerite, duchesse d'Alençon, who, he explained, "surpassed every other woman for modesty and intelligence." (She is best known as the authoress of the *Heptaméron,* which she wrote after she had become queen of Navarre.) He also named a promontory "Alençon" after her, somewhere on the Jersey coast.

"We weighed anchor," continues the Letter, "and sailed towards the East, for so the coast trended, and always for 80 leagues,* being in the sight thereof, we discovered an island in the form of a triangle, distant from the mainland 10 leagues, about the bigness of the Island of the Rhodes. It was full of hills covered with trees, well peopled, for we saw fires all along the coast. We gave it the name of your Majesty's mother, not staying there by reason of the weather being contrary." From the fact that *La Dauphine* immediately scudded into Narragansett Bay to escape foul weather making up, it is clear that this triangular island, which recalled Rhodes to Verrazzano, and which he named "Luisa," after the queen mother, was Block Island. The French later called it "Claudia," after the queen of France, and the Dutch renamed it after one of the navigators in the early seventeenth century.

Here, inadvertently and astonishingly, Verrazzano named a future state of the Union. Roger Williams, founder of the colony and state to which Block Island has always belonged, wrote a letter in 1637 dated "at Aquednetick, now called by us Rode Island." On March 13, 1644, the colonial assembly declared, "Aquethneck shall be henceforth called the Ile of Rhods or Rhod-Island." And in 1663 the name "Rhode Island" was applied to the colony. Roger Williams, a

---

* That is, 176 miles, if I have the right factor for the French league; and that is not far off. From the Narrows outside Long Island to Block Island is about 150 nautical miles.

well-read gentleman and scholar, must have brought to New England a copy of either edition of Hakluyt, which contains a translation of Verrazzano's Letter, and interpreted his island "about the bignesse of the Ilande of the Rodes . . . full of hilles, covered with trees" as Aquidneck. That is the big island in Narragansett Bay, the future seat of Newport; and its shape does resemble that of Rhodes in the Aegean. Thus, the smallest state of the Union owes her name to Roger Williams's mistaken notion of the island that Verrazzano compared to Rhodes!

The natives who flocked around *La Dauphine* in canoes as she anchored a few miles outside Narragansett Bay on a hard, boulder-strewn bottom were so friendly that Verrazzano (doubtless to the joy of his crew) decided to make an exception to his practice of mooring in the open. Piloted by an Indian, he sailed *La Dauphine* into the bay. Leaving the future Point Judith and Beaver Tail to port, he noted the little rocky islands now called "The Dumplings" as a suitable place for a coast-defense fort; the American patriots of 1775 agreed with him and fortified the biggest islet. Verrazzano punningly named this cluster of rocks "Petra Viva," after the wife of Antonio Gondi, one of his banker-promoters; her maiden name was Marie-Catherine de Pierre-Vive. The native pilots conducted *La Dauphine* to a completely sheltered anchorage, the present Newport Harbor, behind the highest point of Aquidneck. There he spent a fortnight palavering with the natives.

These Indians were the Wampanoag, whose domain extended over the eastern side of Narragansett Bay and southeastern Massachusetts. They had lately taken Aquidneck from the Narragansett tribe, and were apprehensive about a comeback. This in part accounts for their friendliness to the Frenchmen and, almost a century later, to the Pilgrim Fathers.

Verrazzano's description of the Wampanoag corresponds closely to what Roger Williams later wrote about them. They came on board fearlessly after the captain had caused a few "bells and glasses and many toys" to be tossed into their canoes. Among the visitors were two "kings," one about forty and the other about twenty years old. Each was clothed in a deerskin artistically embroidered with dyed porcupine quills, and, as an emblem of office, "a large chain garnished with divers stones of sundry colors." "This is the goodliest people, and of the fairest conditions, that we have found in this our voyage," wrote Verrazzano. "They exceed us in bigness," are comely, "with long black hair, which they are very careful to trim"; their eyes are "black and quick," and their color, various shades of "brasse." Their bodies are well proportioned, "as appertaineth to any handsome man." The women, too, are "very handsome and well favored," and "as well mannered and continent as any women of good education. They are all naked, save their privy parts, which they cover with a deer's skin, branched or embroidered, as the men use." Some "wear on their arms very rich skins of leopards." They use elaborate head-dressings "like unto the women of Egypt and Syria," and ornaments made of their own hair hang down on both sides of their breasts. "When they are married, men as well as women wear divers toys, according to the usage of Asiatics." For "toys" we should read trinkets or gewgaws; and for "leopard" skins, those of wildcats or lynxes.

Verrazzano particularly noted the Wampanoag's most valued possessions, "plates of wrought copper, which they esteem more than gold." These copper plates, which they obtained by trade from tribes of the Great Lakes region, were the native jewelry; they were mistaken for early Norse on the Indian remains that Longfellow celebrated as "The Skeleton in Armor." The bells that Verrazzano gave them, and that he says they "esteemed most" after copper, were tiny spherical hawks' bells, which Columbus found to be greatly prized by natives of the Caribbean; and the blue crystal beads next in favor were no doubt Venetian. These were used as earrings or necklaces. Strangely enough, the Wampanoag had no use for cloth — peltry suited them better — nor did they want iron or steel implements to replace their stone axes.

The one disappointing thing about these natives, from the crew's point of view, was the men's concern for the chastity of their women. Every day, when anchored in the future Newport Harbor, "the people repaired to see our ship, bringing their wives with them, whereof they are very jealous." While they came on board and stayed "a good space," their poor wives had to sit stolidly in canoes. If it was a royal visit, the queen and her ladies stayed in a canoe at Goat Island "while the king abode a long space in our ship . . . viewing with great admiration all the furniture," and demanding to know its use. "He took likewise great pleasure in beholding our apparel, and in tasting our meats, and so courteously taking his leave departed." Landing on the island, "the king, drawing his bow and running up and down with his gentlemen, made much sport to gratify our men."

During the fifteen days that *La Dauphine* tarried in Newport Harbor, parties of sailors explored the interior for some thirty miles. They noted plains near the present Pawtucket, fertile soil, and woods of oak and walnut; they flushed game, such as "luzernes" (lynxes) and deer, which the Indians took in nets or shot with flint and jasper arrowheads; they admired the native houses covered with mats, and the cornfields; and they undoubtedly found means to frolic with Indian girls when their lords and masters were away hunting.

Verrazzano also wrote that the Wampanoag were "very pitiful and charitable towards their neighbors . . . make great lamentations in their adversity," and at their death "use mourning, mixed with singing, which continueth for a long space." These prolonged bouts of mourning were a characteristic of the Algonkin and other Indian nations of the Northeast. Roger Williams recorded that Wampanoag families went into mourning for "something a quarter, halfe, yea a whole yeere," during which time they considered it "a prophane thing" to play, or "to paint themselves for beauty." As bad as English court mourning in the reign of Queen Victoria!

Following Cabot's practice of noting comparative latitudes, Verrazzano adds, "This land is situated in the parallel of Rome, in 41 degrees and 2 terces"; that is, 41°40″ N. The center of Newport is on 41°30′ N, and the Vatican is on 41°54′ N. This proves, even better than his earlier comparison of his landfall with Damascus, that the captain was a competent celestial navigator. He must have "taken" the sun and Polaris frequently and averaged them; Rome's latitude he could have obtained from any printed Ptolemy or rutter (manual of instruction).

Maine — "Land of Bad People"

On May 5 or 6, *La Dauphine* resumed her voyage eastward, passing Sakonnet Point, which Verrazzano named "Jovium Promontorium," after his friends the Giovio family of Como. The captain sailed through the present Vineyard Sound, Nantucket Sound, and Pollock Rip (which daunted the *Mayflower* in 1620) rather than around Martha's Vineyard and Nantucket. The treacherous shoals, where, in spots, there were only three feet of water, he called "Armellini," possibly by way of a crack at Francesco Cardinal Armellino, a prelate much disliked for his avarice and his success at collecting papal taxes. Next, the ship rounded *un eminente promontorio*, which Verrazzano named "Pallavisino," after Pallavicini, one of the king's Italian generals. This must have been Cape Cod; *eminente* means "outstanding," which that cape certainly is.

Stretching across Massachusetts Bay, *La Dauphine* hit the coast of what is Maine at or near Casco Bay. Verrazzano described the land as fair, open, and bare, with high mountains (the White Mountains) visible far inland. But the Abnaki natives, although they looked like the Wampanoag, were "of such crudity and evil manners, so barbarous, that despite all the signs we could make, we could never converse with them. They are clothed in peltry of bear, lynx, 'sea wolves' and other beasts. Their food, as far as we could perceive, often entering their dwellings, we suppose to be obtained by hunting and fishing, and of certain fruits, a kind of wild root." These were groundnuts, which the early settlers of New England found to be a good substitute for bread.

Wherever the crew came ashore, these Indians raised loud war whoops, shot at them with arrows, and fled into the forest. But they consented to trade meagerly with a French boat crew from a rocky cliff on the seashore, letting down in a basket on a line "what it pleased them to give us . . . taking nothing but knives, fishhooks, and tools to cut withall." The latitude of the place where this happened, wrote Verrazzano, was 43°40′ N, and the only two spots in that area whence one could let down a basket on a line into a small boat are Seguin Island (latitude 43°42′) and Bald Head, at the tip of Cape Small (latitude 43°43′ N), the eastern entrance to Casco Bay. Both are cliffy and steep; Bald Head is the more probable place, as it is on the mainland. What displeased the Frenchmen more than the awkward method of trading was the Indians' uncouth manners; at parting they used "all signs of discourtesy and disdain, as was possible for any brute creature to invent, such as exhibiting their bare behinds and laughing immoderately." One can well picture this scene — glowering Frenchmen in the boat, braves exhibiting bare buttocks, little boys urinating, and men, women, and children raising just such an unholy clamor of whoops, laughs, shouts, and yells as only Indians could make. Since North American natives were usually friendly to the first Europeans they encountered, and hostile only after being abused or cheated, this attitude of the Abnaki suggests an earlier visit by foreigners who raided the Maine coast for slaves. However that may be, Verrazzano gave this coast a bad name, "Terra Onde di Mala Gente" (Land of Bad People), as it is called on his brother's map.

La Dauphine continued northeasterly along the Maine coast, counting in the space of fifty leagues some thirty-two islands "lying all near the land, being small and pleasant to the view, high, and having many turnings and windings between them, making many fair harbors and channels, as they do in the gulf of Venice in Illyria and Dalmatia." A very apt comparison: the Dalmatian coast always reminds one of Maine, and Maine of Dalmatia.

May on the Maine coast is a joy to all seamen — when the fog does not roll in. Verrazzano not only admired the excellent harbors, but appreciated the beauty of this region — white fleecy clouds, turquoise sea flashing in the sunlight, islands where the shad bush flings out masses of white blossoms among somber evergreens. He named the three biggest islands that he passed after three young princesses at the French court — "le tre figlie di Navarra" (the three daughters of Navarre). These were Anne, Isabeau, and Catherine, daughters of Jean, duc d'Albret, and Catherine de Foix, queen of Navarre. They were then between fifteen and eighteen years old, celebrated for their beauty, and, being orphans, spent much time at the French court. The islands thus honored were Monhegan, Isle au Haut, and Mount Desert. These stand out above all others as one sails wide along that coast, and all have a natural beauty worthy to be compared to that of the lovely daughters of Navarre.

Here Verrazzano added another word to American nomenclature. Near the Daughters of Navarre, on his brother's Vatican map, appears "Oranbega." This is obviously Norumbega, which in the Abnaki language means a stretch of quiet water between two falls or rapids. That fits in well with the spot on the Penobscot River that later writers magnified into the capital of a region. Its appearance on the Verrazzano map is puzzling; his brother's relations with the Abnaki were brief and brusque, yet it is the only native Indian name on the map. After the voyage, mapmakers and writers began to expand Norumbega to cover the entire region between the Hudson and the St. Lawrence, complete with a rich and noble city of the same name on the Penobscot River, and in the first printing of Verrazzano's Letter, by Ramusio, it is captioned as "Della Terra de Norumbega."

La Dauphine now ran into easterly winds and had to beat to windward, making good an east-northeast course. This neatly covered the rest of Maine. After sailing for 150 leagues, missing the Bay of Fundy and most of the future Nova Scotia, she "approached the land that in times past was discovered by the British, which is in fifty degrees." There, wrote Verrazzano, "having spent all our naval stores and victuals, and having discovered 700 leagues and more of new country, we topped off with water and wood and decided to return to France." In view of his remarkable accuracy in taking latitudes, we may conclude that Verrazzano sailed along the east coast of Newfoundland and took his departure from Cape Fogo or Funk Island (latitude 49°50′). Both his brother's and the Maiollo map cover Newfoundland. They use the old Portuguese place names instead of applying new French ones, suggesting that they had a Portuguese chart on board and claimed no new discovery.

The ship made a speedy passage, a little more than two weeks, and had safely anchored at Dieppe by July 8, 1524, the day that Verrazzano dated his Letter to François-premier. It concludes with the gallant captain's prayer that God and his majesty may help him to bring this initial step to a perfect end, so that, in the holy words of the evangelist (Romans 9:18), "*In omnem terram exivit sonus eorum . . .*" "Their sound went into all the earth, and their words unto the ends of the world."

End of the Voyage, and of Giovanni

Near the end of his Letter, Verrazzano makes some interesting observations on the longitude of his discovery. He states that if a degree on the equator is 62.5 miles (as he was using Italian miles of 1480 meters, or 1619 yards, this was an underestimate), a degree of longitude at latitude 34° N, upon which he endeavored to cross the Atlantic, is 52 miles. He and his officers kept careful estimates of distance, making daily meridian elevations of the sun, and decided that they had sailed 4800 miles, land to land. This, divided by 52 assured Verrazzano that *La Dauphine* had crossed 92 degrees of longitude. But the true difference in longitude between Deserta and Cape Fear is about 61.5 degrees! This 50 percent overestimate was due in part to the captain's underestimate of the length of the degree, and in part to his exaggerating the speed of his ship. Columbus erred similarly; any sailor will condone a mistake of that nature.

Nevertheless, this miscalculation enabled Verrazzano to state emphatically what his predecessors had said less firmly: that the coast between Florida and Newfoundland belonged to a completely new world. It might, he admitted, be joined to northern Europe in the Arctic regions, but the land he had coasted was no promontory of Asia, as many mapmakers had depicted it, and would long go on doing. This insistence on the newness of the New World cancels Verrazzano's earlier mistake about the false isthmus. Unfortunately, Ramusio omitted this from his early version of the Letter, so it did not circulate. Verrazzano and Cartier were not the last navigators to look for "Cathay" just around the corner. Frobisher thought that the north side of his bay in Baffin Island was part of Asia. As late as 1638, when Jean Nicolet was sent as envoy to the Winnebago tribe, he provided himself with an embroidered robe of Chinese damask, just in case he should meet Chinese mandarins!

Verrazzano sounded a note of reasoned optimism. Although he had not found the Northern Strait and had written it off as nonexistent in those latitudes, he had discovered a vast continental mass that could be of immense value to France. He hoped to be allowed to follow it up. Unfortunately for France, he returned at the very worst time for organizing a second voyage. François-premier, preparing to resume his interminable war against Charles V and to carry it into Italy, gave the discoverer an audience at Lyons and, in a moment of enthusiasm, allotted him four ships for a second voyage; but he decided that they were needed for coastal defense and canceled the order. His Italian campaign ended disastrously in the battle of Pavia on February 26, 1525; the king lost his army and for a year his freedom, and would have lost his throne but for the sagacious regency of his mother, Louise of Savoy. Nor did Verrazzano impress his banker-supporters; the samples of drugs, gold ore, and "aromatic liquors" that he brought home proved to be spurious or worthless, and the bankers were not interested in a long view of future values. They missed the chance to obtain Manhattan Island for even less than the traditional $24 worth of goods.

The discoverer, after considering (it was rumored) and rejecting good offers from Henry VIII and Dom João III of Portugal to enter their service, turned for support to Jean Ango of Dieppe and Philippe de Chabot, sieur de Brion and admiral of France. Giovanni received the command and the right to one sixth of the profits. In the spring of 1527, the fleet sailed from Dieppe. Off the Cape Verde Islands one ship separated in a gale and the sailors of the two others mutinied, insisting on returning home; but as they knew nothing of navigation, Verrazzano fooled them, nipped across the Atlantic Narrows to Brazil, cut and loaded a cargo of logwood, and returned to Dieppe in mid-September of the same year. The fourth vessel eventually made the Brazilian coast and she, too, loaded logwood. This "Brazil wood," in great demand for dyeing cloth, sold well to the clothiers of Rouen.

Verrazzano had never renounced his ambition to find a new strait through the Americas. The dyewood profits suggested to him and his backers a means of combining exploration with profit — seek the strait in a region where, if you failed to find it, you could cut a cargo of logwood. Accordingly, they arranged a third voyage, consisting of two or three ships, with Verrazzano's flag in *La Flamengue* of Fécamp. They departed Dieppe in the spring of 1528. Our sole knowledge of what happened on this voyage, which ended fatally for the captain, is derived from a few words in Ramusio's collection of voyages, and a poem by Giulio Giovio, nephew and disciple of the humanist Paolo Giovio. Girolamo the mapmaker, who survived, told the tragic tale to both Giovii, and Giulio wrote of it in a long narrative, *Storia Poetica*.

This fleet crossed the Atlantic by a route slightly north of Columbus's. First raising the coast of Florida, Verrazzano sailed to the Bahamas and then shaped a course for the Isthmus of Darien, intending probably to investigate the Gulf of Darien for a possible strait. En route he changed his mind, and followed the chain of the Lesser Antilles. There he made the mistake of anchoring well offshore, as he customarily did. Unfortunately, the island where he chose to call — probably Guadeloupe — was inhabited by no gentle tribe of Indians, but by ferocious, man-eating Caribs. The Verrazzano brothers rowed shoreward in the ship's boat. A crowd of natives waited at the water's edge, licking their chops at the prospect of a human lunch; but the French as yet knew nought of this nation of cannibals. Giovanni innocently waded ashore alone while Girolamo and the boat's crew plied their oars far enough off the beach to avoid the breakers. The Caribs, expert at murder, overpowered and killed the great navigator, then cut up and ate his still quivering body whilst his brother looked on helplessly, seeing the "sand ruddy with fraternal blood." The ships were anchored too far offshore to render gunfire support.

"*Questo infelice fine hebbe questo valente gentilhuomo,*" wrote Ramusio. "To so miserable an end came this valiant gentleman."

From subsequent lawsuits we know that *La Flamengue* continued her voyage to Brazil, and, in March 1529, brought back a cargo of logwood to Brittany. Girolamo, after finishing his chart showing the 1524 voyage, sailed back to Brazil in 1529 as master of the ship *La Bonne Aventure* of Le Havre.

Verrazzano may have opened for France a lucrative trade with Brazil, but the results of his voyage along the North American coast were largely negative. The "Isthmus" and "Sea" of Verrazzano, his only positive contributions, turned out to be pure fantasies — but they influenced North American cartography for over a century. By reporting the absence of any strait between Florida and Nova Scotia, he turned the exploratory efforts of France and England northward; Jacques Cartier took up the quest where Verrazzano left off, and Frobisher continued it farther north. Neither discovered "the happy shores of Cathay," but empire followed in their wakes, whilst France completely ignored that of *La Dauphine*, which subtended a land of riches immeasurable — the Carolinas, Virginia, New York, New England. But it was not Verrazzano's fault that the French government remained indifferent to the opportunities that he opened.

There is no blinking the fact that Verrazzano missed many important places, and that he was singularly incurious. His habit of avoiding harbors caused him to miss great bays, such as the Chesapeake, the Delaware, and the Hudson estuary, leaving them for the English, Dutch, and Swedes to explore and colonize in the following century. His failure to take a good look at the mouth of the Hudson River is perhaps the greatest opportunity missed by any North American explorer. But no sailor will blame him for missing things, since most of them have done so themselves. The great Captain Cook missed Sydney Harbor. Drake and all the Spanish navigators missed the Golden Gate and San Francisco Bay, which were discovered by an overland expedition. Why, even Des Barres's Royal Navy team of surveyors in 1770 missed my home port, Northeast Harbor, Maine!

Let us, however, judge Verrazzano by what he tried to do, rather than by what he accomplished. If he failed to find the strait "to the happy shores of Cathay," it was because it was not there; his attainable vision of a New France stretching from Newfoundland to Florida faded because king and country were not interested. His greatest ambition, as his brother told Ramusio, had been to people the regions he discovered with French colonists, to introduce European plants and domestic animals, and to bring the "poor, rough, and ignorant people" of North America to Christianity. When one contemplates the fate of the North American Indians, one cannot be very enthusiastic over these benevolent gestures of European pioneers; but at least they tried.

6

Drake in California

From my EUROPEAN DISCOVERY OF AMERICA: THE SOUTHERN VOYAGES, A.D. 1492–1616 (New York: Oxford University Press, 1974), *Chapter XXVIII.*

Anyone who has heard of the English sea dogs of the sixteenth century knows something of Sir Francis Drake, and most readers have formed for themselves a definite opinion: was he a mere pirate, or a pioneer of English sea power whose name should be cherished? What, if anything, did he discover? His entire career bristles with controversy; the records are abundant, and, now that this four hundredth anniversary approaches, all California is torn by conflicting opinions of where, in that golden land, he spent five weeks in June and July of 1579.

None of my contributions to Drake's career is original, but I have taken nothing for granted, and the last of my sea reconnaissances was in the spring of 1973, to settle the last question. The Coast Guard lent me a cutter, and with my daughter Emily Beck (the compiler of this book) and John Gordon as company, we ranged the coast fifty miles north of the Golden Gate and out to the Farallons. The results are here.

Nova Albion

EVERYONE, INCLUDING DRAKE, with whom the Spanish prisoners talked on board *Golden Hind* reported that he intended to sail home around the world. Nuño da Silva, however, felt confident that he was going north first. Did Drake change his mind, or had he always intended to seek the fabled Strait of Anian, the Northwest Passage, which attracted so much misguided effort by his English contemporaries? We simply do not know. It has been surmised that he picked up from the Spanish pilot, his unwilling captive, the timetable of the Manila galleons, which always cleared Acapulco by March 27, and that he considered mid-April too late for fair winds on a Pacific crossing. Hardly credible; weather reports of the Manila ships were not so accurate as to deter a navigator like Drake, who had successfully threaded the Strait of Magellan in winter. Or he may have felt that the fifty days' supply of water that he took on board at Guatulco was not enough for a trans-Pacific voyage. Or he may have decided he must find a safe place to repair *Golden Hind*, whose heavy cargo of silver had started a number of leaks. Actually, this leg of the voyage, to somewhere in Alta California on June 5, 1579, took almost exactly fifty days: a very neat calculation, or merely Drake's usual good luck.

Golden Hind and the Tello pinnace made a wide sweep into the Pacific and then headed for the west coast, close-hauled on the port tack. The mariners at sea were "grievously pinched" with "extreme and nipping cold," says *The Famous Voyage*, "complained of the extremitie thereof, and the further we went, the more colde increased upon us." Hence Drake started his sheets "to seeke the land." The wind veered northward on June 5, 1579, when Drake's ships "were forced by contrary windes to runne in with the Shoare, which we then first descried, and to cast anchor in a bad bay, the best roads we could for the present meete with." This bay spoken of so disparagingly was probably the little cove just south of Cape Arago on the coast of Oregon at latitude 43°20' N. There the two vessels were subjected to "extreme gusts and flawes" and these were succeeded by "most vile, thicke, and stinking fogges." "In this place was no abiding for us," wrote Fletcher; the only direction in which anyone wanted to go was south. And that is what Drake did. He abandoned his search for the Strait of Anian — if that had ever been his goal.

In June they coasted south for a good 5 degrees, always with moonlight, saw snow-covered mountains of the Coast Range in the distance, and suffered from more "nipping cold." Master Fletcher, anticipating criticism from "chamber champions," men "who lye on their feather beds till they go to sea," and whose teeth chatter when they drink "a cup of cold Sack and sugar by the fire," became indignant over slugabed criticism of this southerly turn, as are we. California weather is not all golden sunshine and gentle rain; there were ten days of frost and snow at Oakland in the winter of 1972–73, and why should Fletcher have reported foul weather had it been fair? The cold cannot possibly have been anything like what northern discoverers such as Frobisher and Davis had endured, but the temperature did drop to the point where the lines froze; and by comparison with the equatorial heat they had been through, and lacking winter clothing, the men doubtless were very uncomfortable. So was the crew of the famous Captain Cook on this same coast almost two centuries later.

Most astonishing to us (and repugnant to West Coast tourist bureaus) is Master Fletcher's statement that the face of the earth all along the west coast appeared "unhandsome and deformed . . . shewing trees without leaves, and the ground without greenes in those moneths of June and July." But that may be explained by drought, or normal midsummer parching. We, in May 1973, found the coast beautifully green.

Since Drake's shipmates seldom if ever recorded their impressions of scenery, we cannot scold them for not alluding to the beauty of the California coast that they followed so assiduously. Rolling hills come right down to the shore and, as often as not, break off as cliffs. Trees are scarce except in sheltered valleys, as the prevalent west and northwest winds will not let them grow tall. Surf continually roars upon the shore, and even today sea birds are plentiful; we plowed through vast sheets of tiny paddling phalaropes dipping for plankton, and there was hardly a moment when gulls, terns, cormorants, and many others were not crossing our bows in flight. The water is chilled summer and winter by a southward flowing current, into which the cold Japan current feeds. Partly because this makes bad sea-bathing, but mostly because Californians have foresightedly made this shore into state parks or reservations, the coast that Drake examined has escaped "development." One can gaze on a Drake's Bay almost as untouched by humans as when the "Generall" passed that way.

From the 43° landfall (state two out of the three original narratives) *Golden Hind* coasted south in search of a comfortable harbor and found it at 38° N. (The third narrative says 38°15'.) Here they put in on June 17, 1579, and tarried until July 23; and 38° N is the exact latitude of Point Reyes, some thirty-six miles north of the Golden Gate.

Before examining the question of where Drake spent those five weeks in June and July of 1579, let us relate what happened there. The most important thing, after the graving of the *Golden Hind,* was the friendly attitude of the natives, Indians known as the Coast

Miwok tribe, who lived from about Cape Mendocino to San Francisco
Bay. When Drake careened his flagship on a beach so that her leak
could be got at, he built a fortified camp ashore. This drew a multitude of Indians armed with bows and arrows; for like other natives of
America, they instinctively resented foreigners who gave the impression of having come to stay. Drake was expert enough at the universal sign language to allay their suspicions, especially after he had
distributed liberal gifts of cloth, shirts, and "other things."

These Miwok were great talkers, delivering lengthy orations in a
language that no Englishman could make head or tail of, and relentless singers and dancers after their fashion. The men went completely naked; and the women, who wore miniskirts of bulrushes, had
a curious habit, which has puzzled later ethnologists, of lacerating
cheeks and torsos with their fingernails until the blood flowed in tor-
rents, and, as further self-punishment, casting themselves on rough
ground or briars. The English sources say nothing of sexual relations
between the two races, but it is difficult to believe that they did not
occur, considering the long time that Drake's men had been at sea.*
These natives amiably augmented the Engishmen's rations during
their five weeks' stay, mostly with broiled fish and a root that they
called "*petáh*." This was the bulb of a wild lily, which they ground
into meal and ate, and they also made bread of acorns; but they had
no corn or manioc to offer, and it puzzles one how Drake managed to
provision his ship for the long voyage ahead. Presumably his men
shot and cured the small rodents they called "conies." The cony has
been identified recently as *Thomomys bottae bottae*, the Bötta pocket
gopher, although some authorities still assert that it was the common
ground squirrel. Maybe they cured fish on shore, as in Newfoundland. But where could they have obtained salt?

One of the earlier yelling and lacerating orgies by native visitors
was broken up by Drake's calling on Preacher Fletcher to conduct
divine service, complete with psalm-singing. The Indians then
stopped their clamor to listen, stare, and occasionally shout. "Yea,
they tooke such pleasure in our singing of Psalmes, that whensoever
they resorted to us, their first request was commonly this, *Gnaáh*, by
which they intreated that we would sing." The historian J. Franklin
Jameson once sagely observed that *gnaáh* proved that all English-

---

* It may be significant that in the numerous Spanish reports of Drake's incursions on the west
coast, his men were never accused of raping, or even molesting, the Indian girls.

men, and not only the Puritans, sang psalms through their noses!

On one occasion, at least, the native visitors brought their chief, distinguished by several necklaces of local shells, a mantle of gopher skins, a wood "septer or royall mace," and a knitted cap in which feathers were stuck, as a crown. He greeted Drake with the title of *Hyó*, "set a rustic crown on his head, inriched his necke with all their chains," and laid on a special song and dance. What the natives meant by all this is anyone's guess, but Drake chose to regard it as a feudal ceremony in which these humble creatures placed themselves under the protection of Queen Elizabeth. Consequently, shortly before his July departure, Drake named the country "Nova Albion," "for two causes; the one in respect of the white bancks and cliffes, which lie toward the sea; the other, that it might have some affinity, even in name also, with our own country, which was sometime so called." (Albion was the Latin name for England.) He then "set up a monument of our being there . . . a plate of brasse, fast nailed to a great and firme post; whereon is engraven" the queen's name, the date, and the fact that the native king and people freely acknowledge her sovereignty, the queen being represented by a silver sixpence with her effigy, and "our Generall" by his name. So says Fletcher; more about this plate anon. But the white cliffs are right there on Drake's Bay, outside the Estero, and they bear a striking resemblance to those on the English Channel.

After *Golden Hind* had been graved, repaired, and floated, Drake, "with his gentleman and many of his company, made a journey up into the land." The inland parts they found "farre different from the shoare, a goodly country, and fruitfull soyle, stored with many blessings fit for the use of man," such as great herds of deer. It is, indeed, a beautiful rolling country, reminding one of the downs along the English Channel. Those who do not know this region may wonder why this inland excursion did not reveal San Francisco Bay to Drake and his merry men. The answer is simple: on a day's walk along the valley as far as Olema at the head of Tamales Bay, one finds one's view of San Francisco Bay screened by high ridges and Mount Tamalpais of 2600 feet altitude.

Drake's men never wore out their welcome. As the Indians observed preparations for departure, "so did the sorrowes and miseries of this people" seem to increase; more lacerations by the women, more "wofull complaints and moanes . . . refusing all comfort."

Which certainly indicates that those Engishmen had behaved with singular kindness and patience, and suggests that if only the Northwest Passage had opened up, Nova Albion might have become an earlier New England, with a more salubrious climate and better race relations.

Tello's pinnace was abandoned, probably because Drake no longer had enough men to work her as well as *Golden Hind.* The flagship left California with between fifty and sixty men on board.

"The 23 of July," says Fletcher, the Indians "tooke a sorrowfull farewell of us, but being loath to leave us, they presently ranne to the top of the hills to keepe us in their sight as long as they could, making fires before and behind, and on each side of them." Drake never returned, nor did any other Englishman for centuries.

Now, in which bay did *Golden Hind* spend those five golden weeks?

The Good Bay of Nova Albion

Numerous scholars and amateurs from California and elsewhere have attempted to answer this question. Each selects his bay and despises any other solution. And, after my short coastal reconnaissance, I have become as positive as any!

If we accept the contemporary statements that the bay lay on or around latitude 38° N, the choice boils down to Bodega Bay at 38°20′ N, Drake's Bay at 38°00′ N, or San Francisco Bay, entering by the Golden Gate at 37°49′ N.

Data available in the three contemporary accounts are as follows:

1. Drake hit the coast at or around latitude 43° N (Cape Arago) on June 5, sailed southward looking for a suitable harbor to careen and repair *Golden Hind,* and found it between 38° and 38°30′ N on June 17. These latitudes we must accept, for Drake and his pilots knew perfectly well how to take accurate sights ashore, and they had five weeks in which to find fair days and clear nights to shoot the sun and Polaris.

2. Fogs were common, and lasted for days on end; but the grass was still brown and the weather chilly.

3. "White bancks and cliffes which lie toward the sea" were seen, reminding Drake of the familiar south-coast cliffs in old England, and suggesting the name Nova Albion.

4. Fish, clams, mussels, and pocket gophers were abundant, and the natives ground meal out of a lily root.

5. Jodocus Hondius's map of about 1589–90 has an inset of "Portus Novae Albionis." Everybody thinks this fits "his" bay neatly; and ingenious attempts have been made to identify it as Bodega Harbor, the Estero of Drake's Bay, and the part of San Francisco Bay where the brass plate was last picked up. I cannot see any resemblance to any of them. It looks a bit like Trinidad Bay up north, but that was no place to careen a ship safely, and the three contemporary authorities state that the bay was at 38°30′ or 38° N.

If you round Cape Mendocino at latitude 40°26.5′, the next good harbor you reach is Bodega Bay, latitude 38°20′ N, one of the favorites. Bodega Head is a fistlike, conspicuous headland, altitude 228 feet. Passing it, sailing south, you find a narrow inlet with (nowadays) a dredged depth of seven feet at the entrance, leading into Bodega Harbor, home port for several hundred salmon-fishing boats. The neighboring country resembles the downs along the English Channel, but no more so than the country around Drake's Bay.

The absence of white cliffs is the principal reason for rejecting Bodega Bay as Drake's. The outer shores of the Tamales Peninsula are indeed bold, and the cliffs are of a pale gray color flecked with yellow, which might by a stretch of the imagination be called white; but they certainly do not resemble those of the south coast of old England. As for the long but shoal Tamales Bay running thirteen miles southeasterly from Bodega Bay, no careful seaman would have let his ship be trapped in that pocket.

Eighteen to twenty miles to the southward of Bodega Head, and right on latitude 38° N, is Point Reyes, protecting what is now officially called Drake's Bay. When we visited it in May 1973, we found the shores to be almost as wild and devoid of human touch as they were four centuries ago. The first thing that strikes one here is conspicuous white cliffs, highest on the coast, and closely resembling the group called the Seven Sisters of Beachy Head, on the English Channel. In the northern bight of Drake's Bay there opens a shallow estuary now officially named Drake's Estero. Its mouth is now closed by a bar of sand and silt, but according to the U.S. Coast Guard chart of 1860 it could be entered by a channel with least depth of eight feet, and there are records of coastal schooners using it as a refuge early in the twentieth century. The anchorage in the outer bay is hard and bad,* but the Estero, with a good mud and sand bottom, is ample in extent, and would have offered Drake a perfect shelter to careen and repair the leaks in *Golden Hind.* George Davidson, professor of geodesy and astronomy at Berkeley, made a special study of Drake's California in the 1880's, and decided that he had landed there, which led both state and nation officially to name the locations Drake's Bay and Drake's Estero. I see no reason to disagree.

The subsequent history of Drake's Bay is interesting. Sixteen years after Drake's voyage, Sebastián Rodríguez Cermeño, in command of the Spanish ship *San Agustín,* examined this coast on his way from Manila to Mexico. *San Agustín* was cast away in November 1595, in the same bay, which her captain named "San Francisco." In his narrative, Cermeño reports three fathom of water on the bar to the Estero. He heard nothing about Drake from the Indians, who were still friendly, and saw nothing to suggest that anyone had been there before. He explored the Estero, which he valued largely for its supply of fresh water. Before he got around to bringing *San Agustín* inside, an onshore wind drove her on the beach and he never got her off. Some old ship timbers that are still in Drake's Bay may be hers. Cermeño then caused a pinnace to be assembled on the spot, and in her sailed to Mexico, arriving January 31, 1596, at Acapulco, with some eighty people on board. His name, "San Francisco," has led to much confusion, but everyone now agrees that Cermeño's bay was the one now named "Drake's."

The next important Spanish voyage thither was that of Sebastián Vizcaíno in January 1603. Although first to chart the Farallons, Vizcaíno never sighted the Golden Gate, which was so named by John C. Frémont in 1849. The annual Manila galleons returning to Acapulco passed along this coast, within sight of the shore, for 200 years, without ever seeing the Golden Gate. San Francisco Bay was finally discovered in 1769 by an overland expedition led by Gaspar de Portolá, the first Spanish governor of Alta California; and the first ship known to have entered it is Juan Manuel de Ayala's *San Carlos* in 1775.

No mariner who knows the California coast will find this surprising. The lay of the land is such that one can sail almost up to the Golden

* In March 1973, the German training ship *Deutschland,* 4400 tons, anchored here, hoping to clean up in preparation for an official visit to San Francisco, but found it too rough to launch a boat, and dragged her anchors.

Gate without realizing that there is an opening; headlands and the Berkeley-Oakland hills look like a continuous land mass. On a clear May day in 1973 we could not see the Golden Gate when we were eight miles away, at the outer buoy to the dredged ship channel. Approaching it from the north, as Drake might have done had he clung to the coast before sighting the Farallons, one cannot see the Golden Gate from three miles away. And that Drake could have entered this gorgeous bay, one of the world's finest, without describing it, is incredible. In the great gold rush of the 1850's it was not infrequent for sailing ships coming from Cape Horn to miss the Golden Gate and pile up on a rocky shore nearby. Innumerable cases of the sort could be cited; almost any seaman with experience of this coast will think it preposterous that Drake could have seen this entrance.

Nevertheless, there are many advocates for San Francisco Bay having been Drake's bay. Edward Everett Hale, in Justin Winsor's *Narrative and Critical History*, predicted that "it will not be long, probably, before the question is decided," and did "not hesitate" to give the palm to San Francisco Bay. Too bad Dr. Hale could not have lived another fifty years, when he would have found the dispute blown sky-high and the site thrown into San Francisco's lap by the discovery of the now famous "Drake Plate of Brass."

My conclusion, and that of my shipmates on our brief examination of the Marin County coast, is that Drake's Bay is correctly so named; that here he spent five weeks, repaired *Golden Hind,* sang psalms for the Indians, and marched upcountry. The white cliffs like those of Albion "on the side of the sea" (from the Estero) were for us the determining factor. If Drake or any of his men had climbed Mount Tamalpais, they would have seen the magnificent panorama of San Francisco Bay and probably sailed in to investigate it; but Englishmen in those days did not climb a mountain for fun.

The Plate of Brass — or Was It Lead?

The World Encompassed states that Drake caused a plate of brass to be engraved with a record of his taking possession, and nailed it to a post, together with an English sixpence bearing Queen Elizabeth's effigy. *The Famous Voyage* in Hakluyt says substantially the same thing, without stating the metal of the plate. The *Anonymous Narra-*

tive, however, says that in this "harborow where he grounded his ship to trim her, while they were graving of their ship . . . in this place Drake set up a greate post and nayled there on a sixpence which the contraye people woorshipped as if it had bin god [space]. Also he nayled upon this post a plate of lead and scratched therein the Queenes name."

So, brass or lead? Lead is the more probable, because every sea-going ship in that era carried sheet lead for covering leaks, keckling (wrapping) cables to prevent their chafing in a hawse-hole, and a variety of uses. Brass, on the other hand, was then little used on ships, and it would have been unusual to find a sheet of this size among *Golden Hind*'s sea stores or in her shipboard forge.

For many years Professor Herbert E. Bolton, of the University of California at Berkeley, lecturing to his classes on early west-coast history, quoted *The World Encompassed* story about the brass plate and begged his students to keep their eyes open. If the plate was found, the finder was to bring it to him. Anyone with a knowledge of undergraduate humor would regard that as an invitation to a student "rag" or "gag."

In the summer of 1936 a man named Beryle Shinn picked up a tarnished brass plate "on a pile of rocks on the brow of a hill on the north shore of Corte Madera Inlet, in Marin County, overlooking the waters of San Francisco Bay," near San Quentin. He tossed it into the trunk of his car, thinking it might do for making repairs; but in February 1937 a neighbor who had been a pupil of Professor Bolton's, and who helped Shinn to cleanse it, noticed the name "Francis Drake." He then took it to Bolton, who promptly pronounced it genuine, as did Mr. Allen L. Chickering, president of the California Historical Society. Shinn played coy about selling the plate, but finally accepted $3500 as an "award," and the plate is now prominently displayed in the Bancroft Library, Berkeley. Here is the inscription:

BEE IT KNOWNE VNTO ALL MEN BY THESE PRESENTS
IVNE 17 1579
BY THE GRACE OF GOD AND IN THE NAME OF HERR
MAIESTY QVEEN ELIZABETH OF ENGLAND AND HERR
SVCCESSORS FOREVER I TAKE POSSESSION OF THIS
KINGDOME WHOSE KING AND PEOPLE FREELY RESIGNE
THEIR RIGHT AND TITLE IN THE WHOLE LAND VNTO HERR

MAIESTIES KEEPEING NOW NAMED BY ME AN TO BEE
KNOWNE VNTO ALL MEN AS NOVA ALBION.
FRANCIS DRAKE

At the lower right corner is a jagged hole through which, presumably, the bemused Indians could see the effigy of their new queen on a silver sixpence.*

The place where Shinn found the plate has ever since been a leading argument of the proponents of San Francisco as having been Drake's bay. But it is difficult to see what the plate contributes to this argument. For, during the early publicity about this "discovery," a chauffeur named William Caldeira alleged that he had picked up the plate in 1933 on a roadside about two and a half miles from the shore of Drake's Bay, washed it enough to see the word "Drake," but, since his employer was not interested, discarded it as useless about half a mile from the place where Shinn later found it. Nobody seems to have reflected that a heavy object like a brass plate, after the post to which it was attached had rotted, would in the course of over 350 years have buried itself in the ground and been completely overgrown by turf; so if Caldeira found it on the surface, someone must have dug it up, or forged it, and placed it there. Shinn does indeed describe the position of his find as "embedded in the ground with a rock partly overlaying it"; but it could not have been deeply embedded since he saw a corner of it sticking out, and the rock was small enough for him to pick up and roll down the hill. Thus the claim of sundry writers that the plate had been right there, waiting for 350 years to be discovered, cannot be sustained.

Experts disagree as to whether or not the brass is contemporary with Drake. Analysis by Colin J. Fink, of Columbia University, and George R. Harrison, of Massachusetts Institute of Technology, declared it to be hundreds of years old. But Henry R. Wagner, a practicing metallurgist before he shifted to the less exact field of history, declared that, judging from its zinc content, this particular piece of

* Here, for comparison, is exactly what Fletcher wrote in *The World Encompassed* (Penzer ed., p. 62; facsimile ed., p. 80): "Before we went from thence, our Generall caused to be set vp a monument of our being there, as also of her maiesties and successors right and title to that kingdome; namely, a plate of brasse, fast nailed to a great and firme post; whereon is engrauen her graces name, and the day and yeare of our arriuall there, and of the free giuing vp of the prouince and kingdome, both by the king and people, into her maiesties hands: together with her highnesse picture and armes, in a piece of sixpence currant English monie, shewing itselfe by a hole made of purpose through the plate, vnderneath was likewise engrauen the name of our Generall, etc."

brass could not have been more than sixty or seventy years old. And
Professor Calley, of Princeton, who also analyzed it, states that the
zinc content was much too great for it to have been Elizabethan. A
faker could have picked it up in an old junk shop.

Apart from provenance, the contents condemn the plate as a fraud.
No such odd lettering, especially the capital B, which resembles a
four-paned window, can be found in the British Isles. Mr. Reginald
Haselden, curator of manuscripts at the Huntington Library at the
time of the discovery, declared it to be a forgery. Experts in the
British Museum pronounced it an undoubted fake; no such letter
forms for the M and N exist in Elizabethan graffiti or manuscripts.
The language, too, is wrong for the era. "By the Grace of God"
should have come after "Elizabeth" and before "of England," as anyone with Drake's or Fletcher's education would have known.*
Among other spellings, *herr,* used twice, is also suspect. *The New
English Dictionary,* V, 228, gives over twenty different spellings to
this possessive of the pronoun *she,* but not one of them is *herr.* I am
reminded of the remark of an eminent philologist at Copenhagen with
whom I discussed alleged runic inscriptions in America: "If you dig
up an alleged Greek vase sitting on a telephone directory, there is no
need to argue further." Since the letters and language of the Drake
plate are not of the period, there is no sense quibbling about the age
of the brass or who picked it up and where.

In my opinion, the plate is a hoax perpetrated by some collegiate
joker who knew little about Drake except what he had heard from
Dr. Bolton and read in one of the modern editions of *The World Encompassed.* He naturally chose that text to be blown up for the
inscription, tried to give it a "quaint" look by odd lettering and spelling, then dropped it at a place where it was likely to be picked up.
"Drake's Plate of Brass" is as successful a hoax as the Piltdown Man or
the Kensington Rune Stone.

Voyage Home

On July 24, 1579, the day after *Golden Hind* left her anchorage,
she sighted the Farallon Islands and "called them the Islands of St.
James," as it was the vigil of that saint's feast. They landed on the

* For instance, the grant to Adrian Gilbert in 1583 begins, "Elizabeth, by the Grace of God,
of England, France and Ireland Queene."

Southeast Farallon, the biggest, whose 350-foot hill, from a distance, looks like a miniature Rock of Gibraltar. Here Drake topped off his provisions with sea-lion meat and the eggs and flesh of numerous wild fowl that nest there. This seems an odd thing to do at the beginning of a long voyage; but maybe the native provisions obtained at Drake's Bay were deemed insufficient.

Golden Hind made a westerly passage of sixty-five or sixty-six days without sighting land. Her first call was on September 30, at a group of islands where the natives were great thieves and pestered the English sailors by hurling stones at them from outrigger dugouts. One remembers Magellan's experience at Guam in the Ladrones; but Fletcher gives the latitude as "about" 8° N, which won't do for Guam, latitude 13° N. It was probably an island of the Pelew or Palau group. From this Isle of Thieves, *Golden Hind* sailed along the south coast of Mindanao and then took off for the fabulous Ternate, where the ships of Magellan and Loaysa had tarried after the death of their captain general. Drake found Ternate to be much the same as Elcano had reported it sixty years earlier. The rajah, Babù by name, sent out to check the strange ship, and, having ascertained that she was neither Spanish nor Portuguese, invited her into port, sending four big canoes to tow her in during a calm. Babù was enchanted to open trade with a rival to the monopolizing Portuguese. He flew into a rage when Drake declined to pay heavy export duty on six tons of cloves that he bought, but the captain appeased him with valuable gifts, and discussed the possibility of setting up an English factory at Ternate.

Drake spent but four or five days at Ternate, departing on November 6, 1579. *Golden Hind* again needed a complete bottom-cleansing and rummaging, so Drake sought out an uninhabited island to do it.* He found one, which the men called "Crab Island" because it was full of big king crabs, "one whereof was sufficient for hungrie stomachs at a dinner." Drake stayed there twenty-six days, "a wonderful refreshing to our wearied bodies." Upon departing, he left behind two blacks he had picked up somewhere in the eastern seas, "and likewise

---

* Heaving down and graving left a ship and her company as defenseless as a lobster changing its shell. That is why captains from Columbus down, if unable to do it in a friendly civilized port, had to seek out a lonely spot. Drake's place is identified by Wagner as one of the small islands in the Banggai Archipelago.

the negro wench Maria, being gotten with childe in the ship." Maria had been a slave to Francisco Zárate, and as she had been on board about eight months, Fletcher's statement is probably correct. Drake's purpose in leaving these three on the isle of the king crabs, says the *Anonymous Narrative,* was to start a settlement. What became of the marooned blacks we know not.

Departing Crab Island on December 12, *Golden Hind* followed the east coast of Celebes, blown by the northeast monsoon. On the night of January 8 or 9, 1580, Drake almost lost his ship and his voyage. *Golden Hind* ran on a shelving reef offshore. To get her off, he jettisoned several big bronze cannon, half his precious cargo of Ternate cloves, and even some sacks of flour and beans; but nothing could move her. Then Preacher Fletcher tried prayer and administered Holy Communion to every member of the crew, which now numbered but fifty-eight. That seems to have done the trick. The wind changed, and by setting all sail, the ship slid off into deep water and resumed her voyage, undamaged. The poor parson, instead of being thanked for invoking divine aid, was disgraced for remarking, when things looked very bad, that this accident was divine punishment for the execution of Doughty. Drake, incensed, played God himself, excommunicated the minister from the Church of England, and condemned him to wear about his arm a paper declaring, FRANCIS FLETCHER YE FALSEST KNAVE THAT LIVETH. But Drake seldom stayed angry long, and within a few days Fletcher was again leading shipboard prayers and preaching sermons.

Golden Hind, following much the same course as Elcano's *Victoria* sixty years earlier, called frequently and with no trouble at Moslemheld islands for provisions, Drake even signing treaties with the local rajahs. At Tjilatjap, Java, "as many as nine kings came and entered the vessel," and were much pleased with the music and the banquets that the Englishmen gave them. From there, the ship crossed the Indian Ocean, rounded the Cape of Good Hope about June 18, 1580, and, avoiding the islands under Spanish or Portuguese sovereignty, called at a river mouth in Sierra Leone to replenish water (which was down to half a pint a day for three men) and provisions. It is obvious that Drake had learned from Pigafetta's narrative, a copy of which he had on board, the urgent necessity of keeping his crew well fed. Sailing from Sierra Leone on July 24, *Golden Hind* avoided the usual route of Portuguese East Indiamen returning home, and sailed into Plymouth on September 26, 1580, the day of full moon. It was three years less eleven weeks since the day she left England.

The first question Drake is said to have asked ashore was about the health of his queen. For he sensed that had she died, he might be repudiated as an unauthorized pirate. His second request was to straighten out his calendar; for, like Elcano, he had lost a day sailing west and could not make out why.

By any standards, this was a great and memorable voyage, even thought it came sixty years later than Magellan's and brought meager results in actual discovery. Drake had shown consummate seamanship throughout. He had kept most of his men alive, well fed, and healthy. Despite one nonstop run of sixty-three days in the Atlantic, two of fifty and sixty-eight days in the Pacific, and a third of at least seven weeks' duration in the Indian Ocean and South Atlantic, they suffered very little from illness. Only seventeen men, including those killed in brawls with Indians or Spaniards, lost their lives during the voyage. That is a remarkably good record for the sixteenth century, or, indeed, for the next two centuries. Moreover, he took good care of his ship, heaving her down often enough to keep her bottom clean and tight. For his countrymen he opened a new seaway to wealth and glory in the East Indies. The proposed English "factory" at Ternate was never set up; but after a few years both English and Dutch were plucking the feathers of Portugal in the Far East.

Golden Hind brought home more valuable plunder than any ship of any nation, prior to Cavendish's prize, *Santa Ana*. Exactly how much, historians have been unable to figure out because there was a great deal of smuggling bars of silver ashore at night. She sailed to London in November 1580 and unloaded considerable bar silver at the Tower. Drake had already delivered some of it to a royal treasury official, who stowed it in Saltash Castle, at Plymouth, and he sent a few horse-loads of silver and gold to Sion House, Richmond, where the queen was staying, as a harbinger of plenty to come.

Bernardo de Mendoza, the Spanish ambassador to England, made every effort to persuade Elizabeth to repudiate Drake and return his booty to Spain. Characteristically, she stalled him along for months, not being ready for a complete breach with Spain, and in the meantime secretly ordered £10,000 of the spoil, lying in the Tower, to be

delivered to Drake personally. Wagner estimated the total value of
his booty in gold, silver, and precious stones at 950,000 pesos d'oro,
equivalent to £332,000 in the currency of the day. Contemporary
rumor, which Treasurer Tremayne vainly tried to verify by interrogat-
ing leading members of the crew, put it at £1,500,000. A good part
went to the government; but the "undertakers," who paid for fitting
out the fleet at an estimated cost of £4000, were said to have received
1000 percent on their investment.

Drake enjoyed the queen's personal favor to a high degree, and he
presented her with a diamond cross and a new crown made of Peru-
vian silver and emeralds. At her orders he was knighted on April 4,
1581, on the deck of his flagship at Deptford. That marked her
defiance of Spain, and the beginning of Philip II's organization of the
"invincible armada" to conquer England and depose Elizabeth.
Drake bought Buckland Abbey in his ancestral county of Devon,
where he set himself up as a country gentleman. His first wife, Mary
Newman, having died in 1583, he married, two years later, Elizabeth
Sydenham. They left no children; but Drake's heir, his brother
Thomas, is ancestor of the present Drake family.

Sir Francis never ceased to work for further humiliation of Spain.
He took a leading part in the defeat of the Spanish Armada, and
sailed to the West Indies on his last cruise against the dons in 1595.
The following year he died of yellow fever on board his flagship off
Nombre de Dios, Panama, and was buried at sea.

During his lifetime and ever since, Drake became a folk hero to the
English, in a class with King Alfred and Lord Nelson; and rightly so.
He loved God, loved England and hated her enemies, loved the sea,
loved fighting, loved fame and fortune. The late Alfred Noyes wrote
an epic on Drake in twelve books. Another legend of the gallant captain is told in "Drake's Drum," Sir Henry Newbolt's poem:

Drake he's in his hammock an' a thousand mile away,
    (Capten, art tha sleepin' there below?),
Slung atween the round shot in Nombre Dios Bay,
    An' dreamin' arl the time o' Plymouth Hoe.
Yarnder lumes the Island, yarnder lie the ships,
    Wi' sailor lads a-dancin' heel-an'-toe,
An' the shore-lights flashin', an' the night-tide dashin',
    He sees et arl so plainly as he saw et long ago.

Drake he was a Devon man, an' ruled the Devon seas,
   (Capten, art tha sleepin' there below?),
Rovin' tho' his death fell, he went wi' heart at ease,
   An' dreamin' arl the time o' Plymouth Hoe.
"Take my drum to England, hang et by the shore,
   Strike et when your powder's runnin' low;
If the Dons sight Devon, I'll quit the port o' Heaven,
   An' drum them up the Channel as we drummed them long ago."*

* Stanzas 1 and 2 from "Drake's Drum," Six Henry Newbolt, *Poems: New and Old* (London, 1912); reprinted by permission of Peter Newbolt.

7

Samuel de Champlain

This book, SAMUEL DE CHAMPLAIN: FATHER OF NEW FRANCE, *my penultimate, was published by Atlantic–Little, Brown in 1972. It needs no preface but its own.*

Preface

SAMUEL DE CHAMPLAIN was the most versatile of colonial founders in North America; at once sailor and soldier, writer and man of action, artist and explorer, ruler and administrator. Sailors admire him, not only for exploring the rugged coast of New England without serious mishap, but for his *Treatise on Seamanship,* in which his description of "The Good Captain" well applies to himself: "An upright, God-fearing man, not dainty about food or drink, robust and alert, with good sea legs." Canoeists admire him for his explorations up rugged Canadian rivers, and his uncomplaining acceptance of hardship and danger in the long, long carries and the *sault.* Historians admire him for his detailed records of voyages and of events in Canada, the best source we have for the first third of the seventeenth century.

Champlain's accounts of his coastal cruises and explorations of the interior were embellished with drawings of flora, fauna, and fights with the natives, which, though not of great artistic merit, are marvelously informing; and they are accompanied by maps that for fifty years were not surpassed in accuracy. Loyal to his king, his church, and his wife, he endeavored with success to lead the New Testament life in an age of loose morals. The life of this great man encompassed those efforts that led to the founding of New France.

My interest in Champlain goes back to my boyhood, when, in 1904, I saw the tercentennial monument to him erected on Mount Desert Island — at the wrong place. His *Voyages,* in the Slafter translation, was my companion in sundry cruises along the coasts of New England and L'Acadie — Nova Scotia and New Brunswick.

Later, I became the proud possessor of the Champlain Society edition of his *Works,* and as early as 1950, when my wife and I resumed cruising along the Maine coast, I planned to write a new biography of my hero. Other and more pressing matters interrupted the work; but herein it is brought to fruition.

To conclude, here is my best effort to honor one of the greatest pioneers, explorers, and colonists of all time.

Quebec Founded and Iroquois Attacked

The third day of July 1608, when Champlain stepped ashore at Quebec * and unfurled the fleur-de-lys, marks the birth of that city and province, and, indeed, of Canada as a nation. One cannot wholly separate Champlain the explorer from Champlain the empire-builder, because the one served the other; but why did he shift his efforts from L'Acadie to the St. Lawrence?

When he returned to Paris in October 1607, Champlain sought out the sieur de Monts and begged him to write off his Acadian ventures as a loss, reorganize his company, and concentrate on Quebec. There they would be hundreds of miles nearer the source of peltries than in L'Acadie or Tadoussac, and at a strategic point on the great axis of penetration of North America. De Monts agreed, and he and Champlain persuaded the king to restore their monopoly for one more year. De Monts then equipped three ships for the season of 1608: one, name unknown, to operate in L'Acadie; *Le Levrier,* commanded by Pont-Gravé, to trade at Tadoussac; and *Le Don de Dieu,* commanded by Champlain, to establish a permanent trading post at Quebec. She and *Levrier* carried workmen, supplies, trade goods, weapons, a knocked-down pinnace, and materials for a new habitation.

Don de Dieu sailed from Honfleur on April 13, 1608, and raised Cape St. Mary's, Newfoundland, on May 26, passed through Cabot Strait, made Tadoussac on June 3, and met Pont-Gravé, who had both sailed and arrived earlier. The tough Breton was practically a

---

* The name in its present form, Quebec, first appears on the Levasseur map of 1601. Champlain's earliest use of it is in *Des Sauvages* (1603, *Works* I, 129): *"Nous vinsmes mouiller l'ancre à Québec qui est un destroit de ladicte rivière de Canadas . . ."* H. H. Langton, footnoting this passage, states that the word, in Micmac, is *Kĕbĕc,* and means simply "the narrows of a river." The popular derivation, from a French sailor exclaiming, *"Quel bec!"* when he first sighted Cape Diamond, is a modern romantic invention.

prisoner of some even tougher Basques, who laughed at de Monts's renewed monopoly and declared they would trade wherever they chose. They had fired on Pont-Gravé, wounded him, killed one of his men, and disarmed his ship. Champlain, who must have been a consummate diplomat, made peace with the Basque captain; and, while his pinnace was being assembled, took a trip in a shallop up the Saguenay as far as the Chicoutimi waterfall. He decided that this river had no possibilities for settlement, but he heard about Hudson Bay from the natives; they said it was a forty to fifty days' journey. "I have often wished to make this discovery," wrote Champlain in his 1613 *Voyages*, "but I couldn't do it without the savages, who don't want one or any of our people to go with them." This was the first of many frustrations experienced in Canada by Champlain. No Indian wished to show him any new country; all tried to keep him out, suspecting that to let the palefaces into the source of their peltries would be bad business. And, of course, they were right.

Resuming his course up the St. Lawrence on June 30 in the assembled pinnace, a 12-tunner, Champlain arrived off Cape Diamond and the Rock of Quebec on July 3. Choosing "the point of Quebec," as the natives called it, he set men to work felling the butternut trees with which it was covered, laboriously sawing them into planks by the old sawpit method, digging a cellar, and building a storehouse to get all supplies under cover. The habitation was on the site of the little eighteenth-century Church of Notre-Dame-des-Victoires. A too big and pretentious building of three stories, it had a gallery running around the outside. A quaint if useless embellishment was a dovecote, which only nobles were allowed to set up; de Monts, being a nobleman, rated this *colombier*. The whole structure had a moat running around it and a drawbridge before the main entrance, and "round about there are very good gardens." It is evident from Champlain's description that most of the building materials were prepared on the spot, but the handsome glazed windows and probably the doors had been brought from France in *Don de Dieu* and brought upriver from Tadoussac in several trips of the pinnace.

Before completing the habitation, Champlain had to deal with an incipient mutiny. Several workmen planned to murder their captain and sell out to the Basques. One conspirator blabbed, Champlain arrested the lot, and with the aid of Pont-Gravé, who sailed up from Tadoussac, tried five men by judicial procedure. The court found all guilty, hanged Jean Duval, the ringleader, and stuck up his head on a pike; the other conspirators were sent to France in chains. That was the last trouble Champlain ever had with his own people. But he had plenty of trouble with others, both white and red.

After September 19, when Pont-Gravé left with the prisoners, work was resumed on the habitation, and ground cleared for planting winter wheat and rye. Everything was made snug before snow fell, but the first winter at Quebec was very severe; half the French died of scurvy. And it was even worse for the Montagnais, who lived thereabout. They never made any provision for winter except to trap and smoke eels. When these gave out they went into the woods on snowshoes (which Champlain called *"raquettes,"* as they reminded him of the courtly tennis rackets of France), to hunt beaver, deer, and moose. That winter game was so scarce, and the snow so light, that on February 20, 1609, the hunters with their women and children appeared on Pointe Lévis, across the river, shouting for help. When they tried to cross, ice floes roaring down the river crushed their frail canoes, and the survivors swam to a big floe, which providentially grounded not far from Champlain's habitation. "They looked like skeletons," he wrote; most of them were unable to stand. He gave them bread and beans, but could not spare nearly as much as they wanted; and he also provided bark to cover a new set of lodges near the habitation. So famished were the Montagnais as to eat stinking carrion — a dead dog, cat, and sow — which the French had earlier set out as fox bait. The stench this made when being half-cooked by the Indians was so overpowering that Frenchmen vomited when they approached the bark-covered cabins; and for people who were used to the odors of Paris at that era, this was saying a good deal. Finally, the spring shad run enabled the Montagnais to feed themselves. Champlain's compassion for these Indians was genuine. Especially he pitied the babies, who died of starvation when their mothers' milk gave out. These savages had their good points, but were "full of wickedness, revengeful, and great liars whom you can't trust." He wished that he could teach them to grow corn and cache it for winter use, as their neighbors did; and that they could be converted.

Champlain knew enough of the savages by that time to realize that feeding the hungry would not make them faithful allies; charity would soon be forgotten. What he must do was to help them and their allies, the upriver Algonkin and Huron, to make headway against the dreaded Iroquois, the Five Nations, in what is now New York State. He had earlier talked to the Indians he met in Maine about "reconciling them with their enemies," but those northern savages had no use for peace. Intermittent but perpetual warfare was their way of life. The Iroquois had forced the Huron out of the St. Lawrence Valley, and they intended to raid that valley every year, as part of their life pattern. If the French, with gunfire, could aid the Montagnais-Huron-Algonkin alliance to defeat these raids, they might win their friendship and depend on them for trade. If not, and the French tried to remain neutral, Quebec would need a garrison of hundreds of trained soldiers to survive. It is folly, therefore, to criticize Champlain for what he did next.

When spring broke up the ice in April 1609, only eight of the twenty-four Frenchmen who wintered at Quebec were alive: half the survivors consisted of Champlain and his pilot and two boys, Etienne Brûlé and Nicolas Marsolet. The lads had well employed the long winter months by learning the Montagnais language, and became valuable interpreters; but eventually they turned traitor.

Champlain, reinforced by men from Pont-Gravé's ship (anchored at Tadoussac), now held a conference upriver with chiefs of the Huron, Algonkin, and Montagnais. As a result, he began his fateful incursion against the Iroquois on June 28, 1609. He and the Sieur de Marais (Pont-Gravé's son-in-law) traveled in two shallops with twenty men, three or four of them armed with the arquebus, a handgun fired by a slow-burning match. "The country becomes more and more beautiful as you advance," wrote Champlain. "The country is all covered with great and high forests." About forty-five miles above Quebec they reached a "very delightful" river, which they named Sainte-Marie (now Sainte-Anne de la Perade); and, a little beyond, Champlain encountered a muster of two to three thousand Huron and Algonkin. With them, he planned a campaign against the Iroquois, but first had to invite them to Quebec for five days' dancing and feasting — indispensable preliminary to a warlike expedition. Pont-Gravé arrived with more Frenchmen, but he did not join the war party. On July 3, 1609, Champlain made a fresh start from Sainte-Croix (now Pointe Platon) about thirty miles upstream from Quebec. Passing Trois-Rivières at the mouth of the St. Maurice River and "very fair and open forests," they reached the mouth of what is now the Richelieu River, which Champlain named after the Iroquois. There they tarried some time, feasting and haranguing, as a result of which a good part of the Indians who had been clamoring for war went home "with their wives and the wares they had bartered."

Almost half the month of July was now spent. What was left of the war party, about sixty Indian warriors in twenty-four canoes, moved up the Richelieu. Balked by the rapids at Chambly, Champlain decided to leave his heavy shallop behind and accept canoe transportation. Completing the portage around the rapids on July 12, and after a seventy-five-mile journey from the Richelieu River mouth, they reached the great lake that Champlain, with pardonable pride, named after himself. The Adirondack Mountains, some still snow-topped, were seen far off. The canoe flotilla paddled south up the lake, the guides being certain that the Iroquois would come that way. Nor were they mistaken.

The war party moved slowly and deliberately, camping every night. Champlain described the Indians' tactics and organization in forest warfare: separate groups of scouts, warriors, and hunters to supply the food. He criticized their practice of sleeping all night without posting guards, exposing themselves to surprise; but they answered, "We get so tired scouting and hunting in the daytime we must sleep at night!" This time they were not surprised.

After dark on July 29 they found a war party of the Mohawk nation entrenched in a temporary camp behind a beach on a narrow meadow, which is now overlooked by the restored Fort Ticonderoga. All night Champlain's party remained in the canoes close to shore, exchanging boasts, threats, and bawdy insults with the Mohawk, "such as is usual at the siege of a city" in Europe, wrote Champlain.* About 200 Mohawk sortied from the barricade; "strong, robust men," wrote Champlain, who "came slowly to meet us with a gravity and calm which I admired; and at their head were three chiefs," distinguished by eagle feathers.

Champlain's allies ran some 200 yards toward the Iroquois, then called on their leader to come forward and do his stuff. Clad in a plate corselet and wearing a steel helmet with a white plume like Henry of Navarre, he loaded his arquebus with four bullets, drew a

* Romain Rolland's *Colas Breugnon* has a classic description of one of these sieges.

bead on the three chiefs, and fired. All three fell, two dead and the third mortally wounded. Arrows then flew on both sides. One of the arquebusiers whom Champlain had cannily posted on the flank immediately fired; and that panicked the Mohawk. Running into the forest, they were hotly pursued, losing several more dead as well as ten prisoners. The allies lost nobody.

Champlain's drawing of the fight at Lake Champlain, which has survived, is his second attempt to draw something superior to charts; his first was on Cape Cod. He had no sense of perspective; but he had an eye for native forts, weapons, and artifacts. Both in this and in his later battle pictures, his greatest error was to depict the natives, both enemies and allies, as fighting stark naked, which they never did. Why did he do it? Because it was the fashion! Théodor de Bry, in his earliest illustrated books on the New World, almost invariably depicted the savages naked, the more easily to distinguish them from Europeans.

On the day that this fight took place on the shores of Lake Champlain, Henry Hudson in the Dutch East India Company's *Half Moon* was sailing up the great river named after him. Upon reaching the site of Albany, *Half Moon* was boarded by a band of Indians. Hudson invited them below, plied them with bread and brandy, "which made them sweat awhile," and sent them ashore happily tipsy. One of the favorite stories in the early history of North America is the contrast between Hudson serving cocktails to the Mohawk (as his guests were assumed to be) and Champlain giving them hot lead. From these two incidents, we have often been told, stemmed the enmity of the Five Nations toward the French, and their friendship toward the Dutch and their legatees, the English. Alas, this is all nonsense. The natives who were given a shipboard dram by Captain Hudson were not Mohawk but the (not quite) "last of the Mohicans" destined to be rubbed out by the Mohawk within a few years; and the Five Nations' choice of friends was dictated by economic and political factors that long preceded European settlement. They had already driven back the Huron and Algonkin from the St. Lawrence Valley in the sixteenth century. And there was nothing decisive about this battle of 1609. Far from frightening the Iroquois into a passive policy, Champlain merely exacerbated a long-standing enmity, the North American Hundred Years' War. A compassionate man, he may have doubted the wisdom of tangling in savage warfare when compelled to witness the torturing of Mohawk prisoners by his allies. All they would concede to his protest was to let him dispatch one poor wretch with a bullet in the head.

At the Chambly rapids the Huron and Algonkin parted to return home, and the Montagnais paddled themselves and their French leader downriver, a 120-mile journey in two days, so eager were they to exhibit scalps and perform a victory dance before the women.

Champlain, leaving Captain Pierre Chauvin, of Dieppe, in charge at Quebec, departed for France with Pont-Gravé on September 5, to support de Monts in a plan for extending his monopoly. They arrived at Le Conquêt, the little seaport behind Ushant, on October 10. Henri IV received the partners graciously at Fontainebleau, expressed "pleasure and satisfaction" with Champlain's account of his adventures, and accepted his gifts of a Mohawk scalp, a belt of porcupine quills, the skull of a garfish, and two live scarlet tanagers. But he refused to do anything more for the company.

De Monts and Champlain decided nevertheless to carry on, as the fur trade at Quebec had proved profitable, and they might as well profit from their victory over the Mohawk. And Rouen merchants provided them with more money. Two ships were equipped: Champlain's carried eleven more workmen to Quebec, and supplies for the following winter. Embarking at Honfleur on March 7, 1610, they were driven back by foul weather into three different French harbors, and did not really get going for another month. Champlain, suffering from *une forte grande maladie*, was set ashore at Honfleur for treatment part of this time. When they finally did sail, on April 8, a brave east wind gave Champlain's ship a record passage of eleven days to the Grand Bank. That seems to have cured him. Three days later, and only two weeks from France, they sighted Saint-Pierre, and on April 26 they made Tadoussac.

Arriving at Quebec in early May 1610, Champlain found the garrison in good shape after a phenomenally mild winter; no day had passed without fresh game to eat. "Which goes to show," wrote Champlain, "that you can't expect to have everything nice your first year, but that by doing without salt provisions and having fresh meat, one's health is as good there as in France." Captain Chauvin reported that "their greatest trouble was to amuse themselves" — they had nobody like Lescarbot to plan masques and feasts.

Some sixty Montagnais were at Quebec, eager to take the warpath against the Iroquois, whom they rightly guessed would be seeking revenge for the battle on Lake Champlain. What Champlain wanted of them was to be guided up the St. Maurice River to the great salt sea that they talked about, and to return by Lac Saint-Jean and the Saguenay. Had they accepted, Champlain might have found Hudson Bay before the English. But the northern Indians were always cagey about exploration; they instinctively objected to opening their country up to Europeans, whom they tolerated only as military allies and traders. Champlain could never get farther than Lake Nipissing, and then only on the excuse of recruiting a war party.

On this occasion his Algonkin and Huron allies, instead of waiting for Champlain and the Montagnais, made a premature attack on the Iroquois' improvised fortress near the mouth of the Richelieu, and were beaten back. Champlain and his arquebusiers then arrived and turned the tide of battle. Arrows flew "thick as hailstones." Champlain was wounded in the ear by an arrow, which split his ear lobe and stuck in his neck; he pulled it out himself. But he was more troubled by the swarms of mosquitoes, "so thick that they hardly let us draw breath," which worked their way inside his armor.

Seeing his powder running out, Champlain persuaded his Indian allies to take the fort by storm, and directed the assault himself. Indians shot arrows and the French poured a deadly fire into the fort. In the meantime one Sieur des Prairies of Saint-Malo, an independent trader, had come upriver in a shallop to help. Champlain sketched this fight and had it engraved for his *Voyages* of 1613. He depicted a group of allies advancing under cover of oak-and-deerskin shields to make a breach in the wall, and an Indian helping them by cutting down a tall tree to crash on it. Champlain and five other arquebusiers are shown rendering fire support on the right, while the Sieur des Prairies and friends do the same on the left. When the wall was breached, both French and Indians swarmed in and gave the defenders cold steel, killing all but a few who escaped by the river. Fifteen poor wretches were captured.

There can be no doubt from the way he tells this story that Champlain relished a good fight, but he was sickened by the torture of prisoners by the Montagnais women and children. "The wives and daughters," he wrote, "surpass the men in cruelty; for by their cunning they invent more cruel torments and it affords them great delight." He gives us the horrible details, which we are fain to omit.

This fight, on June 19, 1610, appeared to be more important than the one at Ticonderoga in 1609. The site on the Richelieu River, about a league above its mouth, became Cap de la Victoire, and is still so called. Of course it was not decisive; no battle or campaign in savage warfare could be, unless one side was exterminated.

Upon arriving at Quebec by canoe in the fast time of two days from the Richelieu, Champlain was deeply grieved to hear that his friend and supporter, Henri IV, had been assassinated. The king's nine-year-old son, the dauphin, became King Louis XIII, under a regency held by his mother, Marie de Medici, who cared little if anything for Canada. Yet fresh support must be sought for Quebec, especially as the fur trade had become a free-for-all. Illegal independent operators who took no part in the fighting, and shared no expenses of the habitation, were getting the best furs; and there was so much competition that the season of 1610 turned out disastrously for everyone. Accordingly, Champlain left one du Parc in charge at Quebec, with sixteen men; he and Pont-Gravé sailed for home on August 8, 1610. Their ship arrived at Honfleur on September 27. En route they ran right over a whale, and Champlain took this opportunity to describe the methods of the Basque whale fishery in the Gulf of St. Lawrence. They harpooned the whale offshore, killed him when he rose to the surface, towed him ashore, flensed him, and rendered his oil in large cauldrons.

Here is an opportunity to discuss Champlain's appearance and personality. All alleged portraits of him in modern biographies are phonies. The only existing contemporary portraits of him are the sketches by himself, in the best of which he is wearing a steel helmet with a big white plume, like one he doubtless remembered seeing Henri IV display in battle. Neck, chest, and waist are protected by a steel corselet with an extension to cover his hips, and under it the then-fashionable knee-length robe, worn with woolen breeches, woolen hose, and leather shoes. He is taking a wide stance — for the arquebus had a terrific kick — and appears to be taller than the conventionalized Indian allies and enemies. His features, except for eye and nose, are hidden by the butt of the arquebus; but like other sailors of the period he probably wore a beard.

Champlain exuded authority, whether on land or sea; but, as L'Ordre de Bon Temps proved, he could relax, sing, drink, and make merry with his men. Both toward them and the Indians he was ever an upright and merciful judge. He had an inexhaustible store of energy and an iron digestion; became as inured as a savage to cold, hardship, and hunger; and never complained of any physical ill. Uncompromisingly honest, he was severe toward the fur traders who practiced trickery and court politicians who indulged in evasions. Both before and during marriage, he rejected his very many opportunities to prove his masculinity on the native girls. His loyalty to king and Church never wavered; his frequent ejaculations of thanks to God were not conventional, but were genuine expressions of a profound faith, the faith in which he died.

II

Voyages and Sea Battles

1

A Day at Sea

From ADMIRAL OF THE OCEAN SEA: A LIFE OF CHRISTOPHER
COLUMBUS (Boston: Atlantic-Little, Brown, 1942), *excerpts from Chapters
XII and XIII, and from my* EUROPEAN DISCOVERY OF AMERICA: THE
SOUTHERN VOYAGES, A.D. 1492–1616 (New York: Oxford University
Press, 1974), *pages* 167, 168, 173–74, 175, 177–78.

*This was perhaps the most difficult chapter to write in all my accounts
of voyages. For it tells of everyday things that the contemporary log-
books and narratives ignored because everyone knew about them. So
it is only by chance, or when something goes wrong, that we are able
to pick up a little information. For instance, how do we know that
Columbus's ships were ballasted with cobblestones? Only because
one of the grommets, or ship's boys, in* Santa María, *according to the
admiral's Sea Journal, killed a bird with a stone; and where would one
find a stone on board a sailing ship if not in the ballast? Fortunately,
a humorous Spanish official, Eugenio de Salazar, wrote a very detailed account of his observations on a voyage from Spain to Santo
Domingo in 1573. Even earlier, the Dominican friar Tomás de la
Torre described minutely the discomforts of an American voyage from
Sanlúcar de Barrameda in 1544. Professor Irving A. Leonard, whose
translation of de la Torre appears in his* COLONIAL TRAVELERS IN
LATIN AMERICA *(Alfred A. Knopf, 1972) and, in part, in his* BOOKS
OF THE BRAVE *(Harvard University Press, 1949), has been kind
enough to point out to me significant details in de la Torre, and to
correct some of my translations from the rough nautical Spanish of
Salazar.*

A DECENT FORMALITY has always been observed in ships at sea.
The watches are changed and the tiller or wheel is relieved according
to formula, solar and stellar observations are made at fixed hours, and
any departure from the settled custom is resented by mariners. In
Spanish and Portuguese ships these formalities were observed with a

quasi-religious ritual, which lent them a certain beauty and served to remind the seamen every half-hour of the day and night that their ship depended for safety, not only on her staunchness and their own skill, but on the grace of God.

Until the late sixteenth century, the only ship's clock available was the *ampolleta* or *reloj de arena* (sand clock), a half-hour glass containing enough sand to run from the upper to the lower section in exactly thirty minutes. Made in Venice, these glasses were so fragile that many spares were usually carried — Magellan had eighteen on his flagship. It was the duty of a ship's boy in each watch to mind the *ampolleta* and reverse it promptly when the sand ran out. A very rough sea might retard the running of the sand, or the boy might go to sleep; Columbus on one occasion expressed indignation with a lazy lad who lost count. As a ship gains time sailing east and loses it sailing west, even the most modern ship's clock has to be corrected daily by radio. The only way one could mark correct sun time in the era of discovery was to erect a pin or gnomon on the center of the compass card, and watch for the exact moment of noon, when the sun's shadow touched the fleur-de-lys that marked north (or, if in the Southern Hemisphere, south) and then turn the glass. Even that could not be counted on to give true noon nearer than fifteen or twenty minutes.

The *marineros, grumetes,* and *oficiales* of the ship's company (able seamen, apprentice seamen, and petty officers such as caulker and cooper) were divided into two watches (*cuartos* or *guardias*) of four hours each. An officer commanded each watch according to a fixed rule of precedence: captain, pilot, *maestre* (master), *contramaestre* (master's mate or chief boatswain). From sundry entries in Columbus's Journal, it is clear that his watches were changed at three, seven, and eleven o'clock. These hours seem odd to a modern seaman, who by immemorial usage expects watches to change at four, eight, and twelve o'clock; and I believe they were so changed from 1500 on. Presumably the afternoon watch was "dogged" (that is, split into two two-hour watches) as the merchant marine still did in the nineteenth century, in order that the men might change their hours nightly. On a sailing vessel that might be many weeks or even months at sea, it was fairer to dog the watches daily so that each man would have the unpopular "graveyard watch" from midnight to 4:00 A.M. (or from eleven to three) on alternate nights.

Seamen in those days thought of time less in terms of hours than of *ampolletas* and *guardias*, glasses and watches, eight glasses to a watch. The system of half-hourly ship's bells that we are familiar with began as a means of accenting the turning of the glass. No ship's bell is mentioned in any of the Spanish sea journals of the sixteenth century that I have seen, and García de Palacio's *Instrucción Náutica* (1587), the Spanish seaman's first Bowditch, says nothing of them. Drake's flagship, *Golden Hind*, carried no bell, but his men "liberated" one from the church at Guatulco, Mexico, in 1579. They hung it in an improvised belfry on board, where a Spanish prisoner reported that it was "used to summon the men to pump." Since pumping ship was the first duty of every watch, it is evident that the bell was used for summoning, and that this use of the bell was new to Spaniards, if not to Englishmen.

At night in the Northern Hemisphere whenever the weather was clear and the latitude not too low, your sixteenth-century navigator could tell sun time from the Guards of the North Star. The Little Bear or Little Dipper swings around Polaris once every twenty-four hours, sidereal time. The two brightest stars of that constellation *beta* (Kochab) and *gamma*, which mark the edge of the Dipper furthest from the North Star, were called the Guards; and if you knew where Kochab (the principal Guard) should be at midnight, you could tell time as from a clock hand. The early navigators constructed a diagram of a little man with Polaris in his belly, his forearms pointing E and W, and his shoulders NE and NW. That gave eight positions for Kochab. As this star moved from one major position to another in three hours, you could tell time at night if you knew its position at midnight on that date. For that purpose a very simple instrument, the nocturnal, sufficed. It had a hole in the center through which you sighted Polaris, and a movable arm representing the Guards, which you moved until it pointed at Kochab; then you read the time off a scale on the outer disk. Nocturnals were in use for centuries. With a little practice, almost anyone on a long voyage can learn to tell time within a quarter-hour by this method.

In the great days of sail, before man's inventions and gadgets had given him a false confidence in his power to conquer the ocean, seamen were the most religious of all workers on land or sea. The mariner's philosophy he took from the Vulgate's 107th Psalm: "They that go down to the sea in ships and occupy their business in great waters; these men see the works of the Lord, and his wonders in the deep. For at his word, the stormy wind ariseth, which lifteth up the waves thereof." It behooved seamen to obey the injunction of the Psalmist, "O that men would therefore praise the Lord for his goodness, and declare the wonders that he doeth for the children of men!" That is exactly what they did, after their fashion. The Protestant Reformation did not change the old customs of shipboard piety, only the ritual; Spanish prisoners on Drake's *Golden Hind* reported a daily service that featured the singing of psalms.

Although the captain or master, if no priest were present, led morning and evening prayers, the little semireligious observances that marked almost every half-hour of the day were performed by the youngest lads on board, the *pajes de escober* (pages of the broom). This, I suppose, was on the same principle as having family grace said by the youngest child; God would be better pleased by the voice of innocence.

According to Salazar, the ritual that he describes always prevailed when venturing on unknown seas where the divine protection was imperatively needed. No pious commander would have omitted aught of these traditional observances. I repeat them here just as Salazar reports them, with a translation.

A young boy of the dawn watch saluted daybreak with this ditty:

Bendita sea la luz,	Blessed be the light of day
y la Santa Veracruz	and the Holy Cross, we say;
y el Señor de la Verdad,	and the Lord of Veritie
y la Santa Trinidad;	and the Holy Trinity
bendita sea el alma,	Blessed be th'immortal soul
y el Señor que nos la manda;	and the Lord who keeps it whole,
bendito se el día	blessed be the light of day
y el Señor que nos lo envía.	and He who sends the night away.

He then recited Pater Noster and Ave Maria, and added:

Dios nos dé buenos días; buen viaje; buen pasaje haga la nao, señor Capitán y maestre y buena compaña, amén; así faza buen viaje, faza: muy buenos días dé Dios a vuestras mercedes, señores de popa y proa.

God give us good days, good voyage, good passage to the ship, sir captain and master and good company, amen; so let there be, let there be a good voyage; many good days may God grant your graces, gentlemen of the afterguard and gentlemen forward.

Before being relieved the dawn watch was supposed to have the deck well scrubbed down with salt water hauled up in buckets, using stiff besoms made of twigs. At 6:30 or 7:30 the *ampolleta* was turned up for the seventh and last time on that watch, and the boy sang out:

Buena es la que va,	Good is that which passeth,
mejor es la que viene;	better that which cometh,
siete es pasada y en ocho muele,	seven is past and eight floweth,
mas molerá si Dios quisiere,	more shall flow if God willeth,
cuenta y pasa, que buen viaje faza.	count and pass makes voyage fast.

As soon as the sands of the eighth successive glass ran out, the boy, in turning up, said, instead of his usual ditty:

Al cuarto, al cuarto, señores marineros de buena parte, al cuarto, al cuarto en bueno hora de la guardia del señor piloto, que ya es hora; leva, leva, leva.

On deck, on deck, Mr. Mariners of the right side,* on deck in good time you of Mr. Pilot's watch, for it's already time; shake a leg!

The new watch need no time to dress, for nobody has undressed; when they went below in early morn, each man sought out his favorite soft plank, or some corner wherein he could brace himself against the ship's rolling and pitching. The mariners coming on duty are soon awake, rubbing their eyes and grumbling, and each man grabs a ship biscuit, some garlic cloves, a bit of cheese, a pickled sardine, or whatever is on for breakfast, and shuffles aft to the break in the poop. The helmsman gives the course to the captain of his watch, who repeats it to the new helmsman, who repeats it again. Little chance for error! A lookout is posted forward, another aft, the off-going captain of the watch transfers his reckoning from slate to logbook, and the ship's boy wipes the slate clean for the new captain. Chips the carpenter (or *calafate* the caulker, if he goes on watch) primes the pump, and if the ship has made water during the night two or three hands pump her dry. The off-going watch eat breakfast and curl up somewhere out of the sun to sleep.

Now the decks are dry, the sun is yardarm-high, and the ship is dancing along before the trades with a bone in her teeth. The cap-

---

* Meaning the watch, port or starboard, that is due on deck.

tain, whose servant has brought him a bucket of sea water, a cup of fresh water, and a bit of breakfast in his cabin, comes on deck, looks all around the horizon, ejaculates a pious *gracias a Dios* for fair weather, and chats with the master or pilot.

Each watch is responsible for the ship during its hours of duty, except in case of tempest or accident, when all hands are summoned. The usual duties are keeping the decks both clear and clean, making and setting sail as required, trimming sheets and braces; and when there is nothing else to do, scrubbing the rails, making spun yarn and chafing-gear out of old rope, and overhauling other gear. In the morning watch, as soon as the running rigging has dried from the night dews, it has to be swayed up, and every few days the lanyards or tackles that connect the shrouds with the bulwarks must be taken up taut.

One question to which every old salt wants the answer is about "Crossing the Line." Since the principal southern voyages after 1498 crossed the equator and entered the Southern Hemisphere, did they do it with ceremony? Did the Portuguese and Spanish navigators relieve the tension of a long voyage with the now time-honored ceremony of Crossing the Line? Did a burlesque Neptune and court come on board over the bows, subjecting the "pollywogs," or neophytes, to various humorous indignities to turn them into "shellbacks"? Existing sources indicate that they did not; this ceremony belonged to the northern nations. It was derived from the mediaeval custom of Norman, Hanseatic, and Dutch sailors holding a quasi-religious service when they passed a well-known landmark, such as the Pointe du Raz in Brittany or the Berlingas off Portugal.

The earliest known reference to a ceremony at the equator is a contemporary account of the voyage of the Parmentier brothers of Dieppe to Sumatra in 1529. "Tuesday 11 May in the morning, about 50 of our people were made *chevaliers* and received the accolade in passing below the Equator; and the mass *Salve Sancta Parens* was sung from notes to mark the day's solemnity; and we took a great fish called albacore and some bonito, of which a stew was made for supper, solemnizing this feast of chivalry." The next, in order of time, occurred on the voyage of a French ship, captained by Jean de Léry, to Brazil in 1557. Here is the first reference to the now traditional pranks: "This day the 4th of February, when we passed the World's Center, the sailors went through their accustomed ceremonies . . .

namely, to bind [a man] with ropes and plunge him into the sea, or blacken his face well with an old rag rubbed on the bottom of the kettle and then shave it off, so as to give those who had never before passed the Equator something to remember. But one can buy one-self off and be exempt from all that by paying for wine for all hands, as I did."

The Parmentier brothers' and Léry's ships were French. When did the Portuguese and Spanish adopt this genial way to break the monotony of a long voyage? Gossipy Pigafetta, who sailed with Magellan and Elcano around the world in 1519–22, never mentions anything of the sort, which suggests that they had not yet done so.

Sixty years passed, and the account by Jan Huygen van Linschoten of a voyage to Goa in an official Portuguese fleet indicates that sailors of this nation had taken over the custom and developed it in their own fashion. Linschoten's ship sailed in February 1583; on May 26 she passed the equator off Guinea, and on the 29th the business began. Each ship, following "an ancient custome," elected someone as "emperor," who became lord of misrule. On this occasion the pranksters and the drinking went too far, and "by meanes of certain words that passed out of their mouths, there fell a great strife and contention among us at the banquet; at the least a hundred rapiers drawne without respecting the Captaine or any other, for he lay under foote, and they trod upon him, and had killed each other," had not a distinguished passenger, the new Archbishop of Goa, burst forth from his cabin and commanded every man, under pain of ex-communication, to hand over his weapons. This they did, and the strife ended.

No record exists, to my knowledge, of any Spanish ship holding a Crossing the Line ceremony before the eighteenth century. The Portuguese must have adopted it from their many north European friends.

In daily life at sea, the master's or pilot's orders on big ships were transmitted to the men through the *contramaestre*, or chief boatswain, who carried a pipe or whistle on a lanyard around his neck and on it played a variety of signals. There is no mention of a pipe on Columbus's ships, probably because they were so small that the cap-tain of the watch gave orders orally. Salazar said he had never seen an order so well and promptly obeyed by soldiers as those of his pilot. Let him but cry, *"Ah! de proa!"* (Hey, up forward!), and they all come aft on the run "like conjured demons," awaiting his pleasure. Here are some samples of the orders:

dejad las chafaldetas	well the clewlines
alzá aquel briol	heave on that buntline
empalomadle la boneta	lace on the bonnet
tomad aquel puño	lay hold of that clew
entren esas badasas aprisa por esos ollaos	pass them toggles through the latches quick
levá el papahigo	hoist the main course
izá el trinquete	raise the foresail
dad vuelta	put your back into it
enmará un poco la cebadera	give the spritsail a little sheet
desencapillá la mesana	unbend the mizzen
ligá la tricia al guindaste	belay the halyard on the bitts
tirá de los escotines de gabia	haul in on the topsail sheets
suban dos á los penoles	two of you up on the yardarm
untá los vertellos	grease the parrel trucks
amarrá aquellas burdas	belay them backstays
zafá los embornales	clear the scuppers
juegue el guimbalete para que la bomba achique	work that pump brake till she sucks

Nautical Castilian, like nautical English of the last century, had a word for everything in a ship's gear and a verb for every action; strong, expressive words that could not be misunderstood even when bawled out in a gale.

For any lengthy operation, like winding in the anchor cable or hoisting a yard, the seamen had an appropriate *saloma,* or chantey, and of these Salazar gives an example, the translation of which is useless. The chanteyman sang or shouted the first half of each line, the men hauled away on the "*o*" and joined in on the second half, while they got a new hold on the halyard:

> *Bu izá*
> *o dio — ayuta noy*
> *o que somo — servi soy*
> *o voleamo — ben servir*
> *o la fede — mantenir*
> *o la fede — de cristiano*
> *o malmeta — lo pagano*
> *sconfondi — y sarrahin*

torchi y mori — gran mastín
o fillioli — dabrahin
o non credono — que ben sia
o non credono — la fe santa
en la santa — fe di Roma
o di Roma — está el perdón
o San Pedro — gran varón
o San Pablo — son compañón
o que ruegue — a Dio por nos
o por nosotros — navegantes
en este mundo — somo tantes
o ponente — digo levante
o levante — se leva el sol
o ponente — resplandor
fantineta — viva lli amor
o joven home — gauditor

And so on, improvising, until the halyard is "two-blocks," when the captain of the watch commands, *"Dejad la driza, amarrá!"* (Well the halyard, belay!).

When not ordering the men about, the captain of the watch kept station on the high poop, conning the helmsman through a hatch in the deck just forward of the binnacle. On all but the smaller vessels the helmsman had a second compass to steer by, but he could not see ahead, and so had to be an expert at the feel of the ship to keep her on her course. Salazar gives us some specimens of the orders to the helmsman:

botá a babor	port your helm
no boteis	steady
arriba	up helm
goberná la ueste cuarta al sueste	steer W by S

Besides a nautical language, a nautical slang had developed. Just as modern seamen with mock contempt speak of "this wagon" or "the old crate," a Spaniard called his ship *"rocín de madera"* (wooden jade) or *"pájaro puerco"* (flying pig, or filthy bird). The nickname for the firebox meant "pot island." People on board got in the habit of using nautical phrases for other things; Salazar, for instance, says, "When I want a pot of jam I say, *saca la cebadera,* break out the spritsail; if I want a table napkin I say, *daca el pañol,* lead me to the sail locker. If I wish to eat or drink in form I say, *pon la mesana,* set the mizzen.

When a mariner upsets a jug he says, *oh! cómo achicais,* Oh, how she sucks! When one breaks wind, as often happens, someone is sure to cry, *Ah! de popa,* Hey there, aft!"

In an era when every house in every town was pervaded by foul odors, the "pestilential Funkes," as one English voyager called them, were particularly potent on a crowded ship. For, despite repeated orders to the contrary, the sailors could not be prevented from urinating, vomiting, and casting all kinds of garbage into the hold, with the comfortable assurance that "the pump would take care of it." The pump did, after a fashion; but here is what de la Torre says of sanitary conditions on shipboard:

An infinite number of lice eat one alive, and clothing can not be washed because saltwater shrinks it. Everywhere bad odors pervade the ship, especially below deck, and the stench becomes intolerable when the ship pump is working. This operation varies according to whether the sailing is smooth or not, but it goes at least four or five times each day, pumping out the water that has leaked into the hold, and it smells very foul indeed.

For regular evacuations, but unavailable in rough weather, were the seats hung over the rail forward and aft. These were called "*jardines,*" perhaps in memory of the usual location of the family privy. Salazar writes in mock sentiment of the lovely views they afforded of moon and planets, and of the impromptu washings that he there obtained from the waves. A later voyager, Antonio de Guevara, complained of the indecency of thus exposing a Very Reverend Lord Bishop to the full view of the ship's company, and adverts bitterly to the tarred rope end, which performed the function assigned by North American folklore to the corncob.

The worst part of the voyage, for most passengers, was the first. In 1544, de la Torre's ship, overcrowded with clergy, had a bad time sailing before the "Portuguese Trades" between Sanlúcar and Tenerife. Here is what he says:

Since there were so many of us, the Father Vicar had arranged to have us all travel together, thinking in this way we would be a comfort to each other, help each other, and that we would thus get along with less baggage and fewer provisions. But it was a great mistake, for, when only two or three clergymen are on a single ship, they are waited upon, cared for, and treated with great respect, even though they bring no supplies with them. But with all of us together, they treated us like Negroes, making most of us go below deck to sleep and tramping over us as we were seated or lay sprawled about the deck floor. And often it was not just our ecclesiastical habits that they stepped on but right on our beards and faces without the least consideration for us as holy friars . . .

Everyone became so deadly seasick that nothing in the world could induce us to move from the spot where we lay; only the Father Vicar and three others remained on their feet. But the latter were in no shape to be of help and only the Father Vicar was able to wait on us and push the basins and containers near us to vomit in, and if they didn't happen to be close at hand, they were useless . . .

A more befouled hospital and one so filled with the moans of the sick can hardly be imagined. Some sufferers were cooked alive in the heat below deck, while the sun roasted others lying about the deck, where they were trod upon and trampled, and where they were so filthy that words are inadequate to describe the scene.

Apparently the seamen on Spanish and Portuguese ships enjoyed but one hot meal a day. This must have come around noon, so that the watch below could get theirs before coming on deck, and the watch who had been relieved could eat after them.

Who did the cooking? I wish I knew! There was no rating of cook on any of Columbus's ships or even on Magellan's. The earliest man especially designated as cook that I have found on a ship's roll sailed on Sebastian Cabot's flagship in 1526. García de Palacio's *Instrucción Náutica* of 1587, which gives all ratings and tells everyone's duties, mentions neither cook nor cooker; although the steward, he says, has charge of the fire. My guess is that the hard-worked ship's boys took turns at the firebox, except that the captain's servant would naturally have cooked for him, and pages of gentlemen-volunteers served their masters. On board the big Mexico-bound galleons described by Palacio, a table was set for the men forward, the boatswain presided, and the pages served and cleared away. On small ships, it is probable that foremast hands took their share in a wooden bowl and ate it with their fingers wherever they could find a place. How the little *fogón,* or open firebox, could cook food for over a hundred people on a small caravel, as it must have on *Niña's* voyage home in 1496, staggers the imagination.

The only drinks mentioned in Spanish or Portuguese inventories are water and wine, both of which were kept in various types of wooden casks. It was the cooper's job to see that these were kept tight and well stowed or lashed down so that they would not roll. South Europeans, unlike the English and French, did not carry beer or cider, which always went sour on a long voyage; coffee and tea did not reach Europe until the following century. The staff of life for Spanish seamen was wine, olive oil, salt meat, salt codfish, and bread in the form of sea biscuit or hardtack baked ashore from wheat flour and stowed in the dryest part of the ship. The only sweetening they had was in the form of honey, sugar being too expensive. Columbus's ideas of the proper provisioning of vessels on an American voyage are given in a letter of about 1498–1500 to the sovereigns:

Victualling them should be done in this manner: the third part of the breadstuff to be good biscuit, well seasoned and not old, or the major portion will be wasted; a third part of salted flour, salted at the time of milling; and a third part of wheat. Further there will be wanted wine, salt meat, oil, vinegar, cheese, chickpeas, lentils, beans, salt fish and fishing tackle, honey, rice, almonds, and raisins.

Olive oil, carried in huge earthenware jars, was used for cooking fish, meat, and legumes. Salted flour could be made into unleavened bread and cooked in the ashes, as Arab seamen do today. Barreled salt sardines and anchovies are frequently mentioned among ships' stores of the time, and garlic would certainly not have been forgotten. The sixteenth-century mariners fared as well as peasants or workers ashore, except during a storm, or weather so rough that no fire could be kept — or when provisions brought from Europe gave out.

Dinner for the afterguard was announced by a ship's boy in this wise:

Tabla, tabla, señor capitán y maestre y buena compaña, tabla puesta; vianda presta; agua usada para el señor capitán y maestre y buena compaña. Viva, Viva el Rey de Castilla por mar y por tierra! Quien le diere guerra que le corten la cabeza; quien no dijere amén, que no le den á beber. Tabla en buena hora, quien no viniere que no coma.

Table, table, sir captain and master and good company, table ready; meat ready; water as usual for sir captain and master and good company. Long live the King of Castile by land and sea! Who says to him war, off with his head; who won't say amen, gets nothing to drink. Table is set, who don't come won't eat.

Salazar describes how the pages would slam on the officers' table a great wooden dish of stringy, ill-cooked salt meat, when everyone would grab his share and attack it with a sheath knife as if he were a practitioner of anatomy; and how every bone was left "clean as ivory." The table conversation, he says, was mostly sighing for what you couldn't have — "Oh! how I'd fancy a bunch of Guadalajara white grapes! — I could manage a few turnips of Somo Sierra! — If we only had on board a plate of Ilescas strawberries!"

What they longed for, obviously, were antiscorbutics. Nothing then was known about vitamins; and, for want of fresh vegetables, fruit, or fruit juice, scurvy in its most hideous forms raged among the seamen on almost every long voyage. The officers fared better, as they always carried personal luxuries, such as figs, raisins, prunes, and pots of jam, which kept the dread disease away. By the end of the next century (as Abbé Labat tells us) the French managed to sail with salad plants set out in flats, so that the afterguard enjoyed green salad almost daily; but they had to set a twenty-four-hour guard over their shipboard garden to keep off rats and sailors.

Although Pierre Chaunu's compilation of voyages to the Indies mentions several instances of food giving out on an unduly long return voyage, that was comparatively rare on the West Indies routes. But no master mariner prior to Drake managed to feed his crew adequately on voyages that went south of the Line, especially those that reached the Pacific. There simply was not room enough, or storage tight enough, to preserve basic foodstuffs, such as wine, hard bread, flour, and salt meat, for so long a time. Hence the resort to penguin meat, seal, and other loathsome substitutes; and occasionally to the desperate eating of rats and chewing leather chafing-gear. Drake's men made out comparatively well, only because he stripped every prize ship of all desirable food stores, gear, and weapons. There is not one of these southern voyages on which the modern blue-water yachtsman, used to refrigeration and canned goods, would have been happy.

During the sixteenth century, rutters, or manuals of navigation, such as Medina's *Arte de Navegar* (1545), proliferated; but sailors, the most conservative of men, were reluctant to try anything new. It was the pilot's business to keep track of the ship's position; but despite the education given pilots before they could be licensed as such, throughout the sixteenth century most pilots depended on dead reckoning.

Captain Teixeira da Mota, after meticulous search into both manuscript and printed rutters of the sixteenth century, has concluded convincingly that the best Portuguese pilots early in that century had plotted the trade winds (which they called *"os ventos gerais"*), as well as the equatorial current, which runs from the bulge of Africa to the Caribbean. They pointed out very early the important fact — known to any square-rig master in the last century — that vessels sailing from the Cape Verde Islands to Brazil must not allow themselves to be carried to the north (leeward) to Cape San Roque, but steer for Cabo Santo Agostinho. Similarly, the Spaniards, owing to their increasing trade with Hispaniola, Cuba, and Mexico, found out about the Gulf Stream and so planned their return routes to Spain that this mighty ocean current would help them to whip around Florida and up into the zone of the westerlies.

If one studies the rutters rather than actual voyages, one too easily concludes that Portuguese pilots of the sixteenth century knew everything. But when we read the *Tratado da Sphera* of 1537 by Pedro Nunes (Nonius), the famous Portuguese-Jewish mathematician who discovered the vernier, we wonder how useful these pilots really were. "Why do we put up with these pilots, with their bad language and barbarous manners?" wrote Nunes. "They know neither sun, moon nor stars, not their courses, movements or declinations; neither latitude nor longitude of the places on the globe, nor astrolabes, quadrants, cross staffs or watches, nor years common or bissextile, equinoxes or solstices." Yet they were supposed to have learned all these things before being licensed by the Casa de Contratación, or by the corresponding board at Lisbon.

Columbus was a dead-reckoning navigator. He made colossal mistakes every time he tried to determine latitude from a star, until, marooned at Jamaica, he had plenty of time to make repeated observations. He knew no way (nor did anyone else in the sixteenth century) of determining longitude except by timing an eclipse. Regiomontanus's *Ephemerides* and Zacuto's *Almanach Perpetuum* gave the predicted hours of total eclipses at Nuremberg and Salamanca respectively, and by comparing those with the observed hour of the eclipse by local sun time, multiplying by fifteen to convert time into arc, you could find the longitude west of the almanacmaker's meridian. This sounds simple enough, but Columbus with two opportunities (1494 and 1503) muffed both, as did almost everyone else for a century. At Mexico City in 1541 a mighty effort was made by the intelligentsia to determine the longitude of that place by timing two eclipses of the moon. The imposing result was 8h 2m 32s (120°38') west of Toledo; but the correct difference of longitude between the two places is 95°12'. Thus the Mexican savants made an error of some 25½ degrees, putting their city into the Pacific! Even in the late seventeenth century Père Labat, the earliest writer (to my knowledge) to give the position of Hispaniola correctly, adds this caveat: "I only report the longitude to warn the reader that nothing is more uncertain, and that no method used up to the present to find longitude has produced anything fixed and certain."

Dead reckoning is still the foundation of celestial navigation, but the modern navigator checks his D.R. daily (if weather permits) by latitude or longitude sights or both, which Columbus never learned to do. And, as an error of half a point in your course will mean an error of about 250 miles in landfall on an ocean crossing, it is evident that Columbus's dead reckoning was extraordinarily careful and accurate. Andrés Bernáldez, who had information directly from the admiral after his second voyage, wrote, "No one considers himself a good pilot and master who, although he has to pass from one land to another very distant without sighting any other land, makes an error of 10 leagues, even in a crossing of 1000 leagues, unless the force of the tempest drives and deprives him of the use of his skill." No such dead-reckoning navigators exist today; no man alive, limited to the instruments and means at Columbus's disposal, could obtain anything near the accuracy of his results.

By the time Magellan sailed, in 1519, great advances had been made in taking meridian altitudes of the sun with a quadrant or mariner's astrolabe, and working out latitude from a simple formula. Albo, Magellan's pilot, whose logbook has been preserved, recorded latitudes of newly discovered places fairly accurately. And there was considerable improvement during the century, as we can ascertain by the positions recorded in Drake's voyage.

The most surprising thing about Columbus's voyages, after his uncanny perception of profitable courses, was the speed that his vessels made; *Niña* and *Pinta*, for instance, made 600 miles in four days of

February 1493, and approached a speed of 11 knots. He and the Pinzón brothers must have been what men in the clipper ship era called
"drivers," not comfortable joggers-along; they refused to shorten sail
every night or at the appearance of every black cloud. On his first
two voyages Columbus made the Grand Canary in six and seven days
from Andalusia. Compare that with the average time of that run for
Spanish merchantmen in the half-century from 1550 to 1600 — just
double. His first three ocean crossings, of 2500 to 2700 nautical
miles — thirty-three days in 1492; twenty-nine days in 1493; forty
days on the third voyage, in 1498 — were good. And that of twenty-
one days on the fourth voyage, 1502, was phenomenal. According to
Chaunu, it has seldom been equaled and has never been surpassed in
the colonial era. Even the twelve-ship convoy under Antonio de Tor-
res, by following his master's directions, arrived home in thirty-five
days from Isabela, a record never equaled under sail. For fifty-three
homeward-bound convoys from Havana, between 1551 and 1650, the
average time was over sixty-seven days.

Part of the explanation of these remarkable bursts and sensational
stretches of speed lies in the lines and sail plan of the caravel. Would
that one of these brave little vessels were dug up, like the Viking
ships in Norway, so we could guess at her secret! Naturally, a lightly
laden caravel, in the early voyages, could sail circles around a heavily
laden 200- or 300-tun *nao* on the later trade routes. But the design of
those full-rigged and wide-hulled ships also improved through the
century. The "round tuck" at the stern of the first *Santa María* gave
way to a square stern, upon which the high superstructure was built,
as an integral part of the vessel. Toward the end of the century, the
Dutch began to save manpower by cutting sails smaller and shorten-
ing the yards. Perhaps the most important improvement was that of
sheathing, to thwart the teredos. Drake's flagship was double-
planked, and toward the end of the century Henri IV of France,
when outfitting a fleet against Spain, insisted on not only double
sheathing but a pad of superior German felt between the planks, and
copper plating below the waterline.

At 3:00 or 4:00 P.M. the first dog watch is set. The day's work of
scrubbing, splicing, seizing, and making repairs is now done; and if
the wind is such that the sails need no handling before nightfall, the

men sit about talking and spinning yarns, tending a fishline, washing in buckets of salt water. Peninsular seamen were a cleanly lot. Columbus, at least twice on his first voyage, mentions their going swimming in a midocean calm, and they never missed a chance to wash themselves and their clothes upon landing near a river. They certainly needed it, since hygiene (in the sixteenth century) required them to wear woolen clothes from neck to feet, no matter how hot the climate.

In the second dog watch and before the first night watch is set, all hands are called to evening prayers. The ceremony begins with a ship's boy trimming the binnacle lamp and singing, as he brings it aft along the deck:

Amén. Dios nos de' buenas noches, buen viaje, buen pasaje haga la nao, Señor Capitán y Maestre y buena compaña.

Amen. God give us a good night and good sailing; may the ship make a good passage, Sir Captain and Master and good company.

The boys then lead the ship's company in what was technically called *"la doctrina cristiana."* All hands say Pater Noster, Ave Maria, and Credo, and sing Salve Regina. This beautiful hymn, one of the oldest Benedictine chants, fittingly closed the day. The music has come down to us so that we can in some measure re-create that ancient hymn of praise to the Queen of Heaven that floated over uncharted waters every evening as a fleet of discovery slipped along.

We are not to suppose that the seamen kept very close to this music. Columbus once refers to the "Salve Regina, which the sesmen sing or say after their own fashion," and Salazar wrote his friend:

Presently begins the Salve, and we are all singers, for we all have a throat . . . For as mariners are great friends of divisions, and divide the four winds into thirty-two, so the eight tones of music they distribute into thirty-two other and different tones, perverse, resonant, and very dissonant, as if we had today in the singing of the Salve and Litany a tempest of hurricanes of music, so that if God and His glorious Mother and the Saints to whom we pray should look down upon our tones and voices and not on our hearts and spirits, it would not do to beseech mercy with such a confusion of bawlings!

The boatswain or boatswain's mate, whichever is on watch, extinguishes the cooking fire before the first night watch is set. As the *ampolleta* is turned up, the boy chorister sings:

Bendita la hora en que Dios nació,   Blessed be the hour in which God
                                            was born
Santa María que le parió   Saint Mary who bore Him
San Juan que le bautizó.   Saint John who baptized Him.
  La guarda es tomada,   The watch is called,
  La ampolleta muele,   the glass floweth;
  buen viaje haremos   We shall make a good voyage
  si Dios quisiere.   if God willeth.

On sail the ships through the soft tropic night. Every half-hour the boy turns his *ampolleta* and sings his little ditty:

Una va pasada   One glass is gone
y en dos muele;   and now the second floweth;
más molerá   more shall run down
si mi Dios querrá   if my God willeth.
á mi Dios pidamos,   To my God let's pray
que bien viaje hagamos;   to give us a good voyage;
y á la que es Madre de Dios y   and through His blessed Mother our
  abogada nuestra,   advocate on high,
que nos libre de agua de bomba y   protect us from the waterspout and
  tormenta.   send no tempest nigh.

Then he calls to the lookout forward:

"*Ah! de proa, alerta, buena guardia!*" (Hey you! forward, look alive, keep good watch!)

At which the lookout was supposed to make a shout or grunt to prove that he was awake (like our "Lights burning brightly, sir!"). Every hour the helm and the lookout are relieved, but the captain of the watch keeps the quarterdeck for the whole watch, pacing up and down and peering into the binnacle to see if the helmsman is holding his course. If the night is quiet, all members of the watch not on lookout or at the helm lean over the fore bulwarks, watching entranced the phosphorescent sea, dreaming of epic morrows.

2

The Voyage of the *Mayflower*, 1620

From THE STORY OF THE "OLD COLONY" OF NEW PLYMOUTH 1620–1692 (New York: Alfred A. Knopf, 1956), *Chapters IV and V.*

There's more sentiment in America about the Mayflower *than about any other of the thousands of sailing vessels that brought immigrants from the Old World to the New in the colonial era. For almost everyone in the United States "relates" to her in imagination. This little book of mine originated when my friend Alfred A. Knopf suggested that I write a "juvenile" for him; and this selection is from two chapters on the subject I then chose. One of my fixed principles is never to "write down" to children; so the only concession I made to teen-agers was to write simply, never using a long word if a short one would do as well. For sampling, my daughter has selected chapters on the* Mayflower *and her voyage.*

The Ship

"SEPTEMBER 6. These troubles being blown over, and now all being compact together in one ship, they put to sea again with a prosperous wind, which continued divers days together, which was some encouragement unto them." Thus begins William Bradford's brief account of the voyage of the *Mayflower.*

Before we tell the story, let us look at the famous ship herself.

There are several modern models of the *Mayflower,* and our English friends are now [1956] building a full-scale replica, which they propose to sail across the Atlantic and moor in Plymouth Harbor. This was done, under the command of Alan Villiers, and *Mayflower II* is now on display at Plymouth. But reconstructing the *Mayflower* is like building the skeleton of a mammoth from one shinbone. The only facts we have are some records of her earlier voyages, a partial list of her crew in 1620, and her cargo-carrying capacity: 180 tons.

This means that she could load 180 "tuns" or double hogsheads of wine in her hold. She had been in the wine trade with France for at least twelve years before the London Adventurers chartered her for the Pilgrims, and she was probably at least twenty years old when she sailed for America.

She was a fine, staunch vessel. Employment in the wine trade had made her a "sweet" ship. Leakage from the wine casks over a space of years neutralized the garbage and other filth that sailors in those days threw into the hold instead of bothering to drop overboard. That explains why the Pilgrims lost only one of their number by illness on the long, rough, cold voyage. She was a fast ship, too, as her return voyage of thirty-one days from Plymouth to Plymouth proves. That would be a good run by a sailing vessel of her size today.

On the basis of the 180-tons burden, historians familiar with the proportions and build of seventeenth-century ships have worked out a fairly reliable table of the *Mayflower's* dimensions, rig, and appearance. Her overall length from bow to stern was around 90 feet; her beam (extreme breadth), 25 feet; the depth of her hold from the top deck to the inside of the keel, 17 feet; and she drew, loaded, about two fathom (12 feet) of water. The middle part of her main deck, which ran the full length of the ship, was exposed to the weather. This open part was called the "waist" of the ship, and canvas "waist cloths" could be rigged to keep out the spray. Below the main deck was the gun deck, with about five feet of head room; and below the gun deck was the hold.*

At each end, the bow and the stern, there was a high superstructure. The forward one, called the "forecastle," was where the crew lived and the cook had his galley — a crude brick stove that used wood for fuel. The larger sterncastle, or poop, had two short decks, one of which contained both the "great cabin," or wardroom, where the officers ate, and the master's stateroom; both had built-in bunks for the more important passengers. Here, too, was the bread room, where flour and hardtack were stored, since it was the dryest part of the ship. Under it was the steerage, where a sailor steered by a whipstaff, a vertical beam attached to the great tiller which ran

* These dimensions have been kindly furnished by Mr. William A. Baker of Hingham, Mass., who designed the *Mayflower II*.

through a sternpost to the rudder head. Steering wheels and gear were not invented until the eighteenth century.

The helmsman couldn't see where the ship was going, or, indeed, anything but the foot of the mainmast and the lower clews or corners of the mainsail. He was "conned," as we still say in the Navy, by the officer of the deck (the master or one of the two master's mates) through an open hatch in the poop deck. Samples of such orders are: "starboard a little," "steady now," "full-and-by," "luff her a little," "keep her off." The officer of the deck had a compass before him in a square box called the binnacle, which was lighted at night; probably the helmsman had a second compass to help him keep the ship on a steady course.

The *Mayflower* had three masts. The mainmast, the middle one, together with the main topmast secured to it, extended about 100 feet above the water. It carried a 54-foot main yard to which the square mainsail, 20 feet tall, was bent. The mainsail's area and height could be increased by a 9-foot "bonnet," which was laced to its foot, or lower edge, when the wind was light. The topmast carried a 20-foot topsail yard upon which the topsail was bent, its lower clews being secured to the main yard; and above the topmast was a 15-foot flagstaff, where the Union Jack could be displayed. Foremast and foretopmast, at least 12 feet shorter than the main, carried two sails similar in shape but smaller. The mizzenmast, about 60 feet tall with a 40-foot yard slung diagonally across it, carried a fore-and-aft lateen sail, like those still used by vessels in the Mediterranean Sea and the Far East. For headsails, since the jib had not been invented, she had a square spritsail bent to a short yard slung under the long, high-pointing bowsprit.

All the rigging was of hemp; there was not one piece of wire or Manila rope. Her sails were upheld by heavy lines called "shrouds," crossed by ratlines, like the steps of a ladder, to enable sailors to climb aloft quickly. Her yards were hoisted by halyards, a word still used on sailing craft. They were adjusted to the direction of the wind by braces. Each square sail was set, furled, or trimmed by a complicated series of ropes — clewlines, buntlines, leechlines, tacks, sheets, and bowlines. In all, there were probably seventy-five different lines in the running rigging of the *Mayflower*. They were secured to belaying pins at the foot of the masts or at the rail; and every sailor had to know how to lay his hand on the right one instantly in the dark — or else!

Every merchant ship of that day was armed, even in time of peace, and the *Mayflower* carried several long guns called "minions," which fired a four-pound cannon ball, and some lighter pieces called "sakers." Some of the larger ones were later mounted on the fort at Plymouth. She also carried muskets and cutlasses on racks for the men to use in case of a fight at sea. But that was one thing the Pilgrims did not have to go through, fortunately.

It is a puzzle how the *Mayflower* managed to accommodate all the passengers, who, after part of the *Speedwell*'s company joined, numbered 102. For she was a cargo carrier, not a passenger ship, and was not equipped to take many people. Some passengers, we know, slept in the shallop, a big ship's boat that could hold thirty or forty people, and was stowed on the gun deck. Double- or triple-tier bunks must have been built, or hammocks slung, on the gun deck. There can have been little privacy for anyone.

No live cattle or livestock of any kind was taken, but some of the passengers brought their pets. They used a mastiff and a spaniel to hunt deer the first winter ashore, and we may be sure that these were not the only dogs aboard the *Mayflower*. How they got on with the ship's cats — for every ship in those days had cats to cope with the rats — we don't know; but one can bet that any tough cat that had been on board ship for years could handle anything of the dog tribe.

Master, Officers, and Crew

The master, as a captain of a merchant ship is called, was Christopher Jones, of Rotherhithe on the Thames. He knew the *Mayflower* well, as he had commanded her for twelve years and had bought a quarter share of her with his savings. Master Jones has been depicted in a recent movie as a brutal ruffian who spent most of his time on board making love to Dorothy Bradford and the other girls, and who had been bribed to take the Pilgrims to the wrong place. That is sheer nonsense. The Pilgrims themselves spoke highly of him and named the biggest stream that flows into Plymouth Bay, Jones River, after him. Jones was an excellent seaman and a humane gentleman, who stood by the Pilgrims through their first hard winter ashore.

The two master's mates, corresponding to our first and second officers, had been in America before. John Clarke had been kidnaped by a Spanish caravel at the Chesapeake in 1611, kept in a Spanish prison for four years, and later employed to carry a shipload of Irish cattle to Virginia. Robert Coppin had previously been on a voyage to New England. Besides these, there were four petty officers called quartermasters (as they still are in the Navy), a boatswain, a surgeon, a gunner, a cook, and twenty or more seamen. They seem to have been the usual rough sailors of that era, religious in a way but disliking the frequent prayers and psalm-singing of their Puritan passengers. One "very profane" sailor, who was always cursing the seasick passengers and threatening to throw them to the sharks, was stricken himself and died at sea.

Just before weighing anchor at Plymouth, Master Jones divided his crew into two watches — "starboard" and "larboard" (the old name for port, or left side of the ship), each under one of the mates. Every four hours watches were changed, except that between 4:00 and 8:00 P.M. they were "dogged"; that is, divided in half so that different sailors would alternate the tough "graveyard watch" from midnight to 4:00 A.M. Time was kept by a half-hour sand glass hanging from a beam of the poop deck; for nobody on board owned a watch, and the pendulum clocks of that era would not work on a tossing ship. Every half-hour, as the sand ran out, a sailor reversed the glass and struck a bell that hung in a little belfry at the break of the poop. At seven bells, or a little after, he woke up the relieving watch; and as eight bells struck, the officer of the deck bawled, "Relieve the helmsman and the lookouts!" Then the sailors who had been working on deck, or pumping, or looking around the horizon, went forward for something to eat and drink, and a well-earned sleep. But if the wind blew very hard or something carried away, it was "All hands on deck!" and the watch below had to turn out and lend a hand, no matter how tired, wet, and sleepy they were.

When the dog watches were changed, the seamen sang a psalm and said a prayer in which the passengers joined; for you needed all the help God would give you on a night at sea in 1620.

*

Stormy Weather

Luckily the *Mayflower* had fair weather for a week or two after her final departure on September 6, so the passengers were able to shake down and get their "sea legs." Christopher Martin, one of the Pilgrims, was appointed their "Governor" on board ship to keep order among them. In those days people were used to being cold and uncomfortable on land, and the ship was not much worse except for drenchings and seasickness. There was no heat except in the galley, no chance to wash except in salt water. No plumbing, of course; if you were seasick or wished to ease yourself, you did it in a bucket and heaved the contents overboard, or you hung in the nettings under the bowsprit and got soused by the bow waves. There were no oilskins or rubber clothing for passengers or crews; if you got wet, you stayed wet until the sun came out. People never undressed, but wore the same clothes all the way across; we would have found them very, very smelly at the end of the journey! No mattresses or blankets were provided, except what the passengers themselves brought. The food was nothing but ship biscuit, salt beef and pork, and boiled peas or beans, although the leading passengers carried private stores of luxuries, such as sugar and raisins, and lemons to prevent scurvy. There was nothing to drink but water and beer, except that Bradford, Brewster, and a few others brought several bottles of wine and brandy.

The men and big boys among the Pilgrims helped the sailors haul on ropes, partly to get exercise and partly to learn how to sail; for they knew that in their new home the only way to get about, until roads were built, would be in a boat. The *Mayflower* had a well-balanced rig, so that when the yards and sails were trimmed properly she was as easy as a small boat to steer; and often youths like John Howland would be allowed to take a trick at the whipstaff, so long as a professional seaman stood by. The boys were certainly allowed to climb the masts and sit in the crow's nest with the lookout and listen to his yarns of the sea during the long watches. When it blew hard and sail had to be shortened, no "landlubbers" were wanted aloft. First the square sail would be clewed; that is, pulled up in loose bunches on the yard. It could not stay that way or it would slat and tear; so a gang of sailors climbed aloft to roll it tight and fasten it with short lines called gaskets. That was called furling.

Ships of those days could not sail closer to the wind than six points of the compass. For instance, if the wind was due west, the *Mayflower* could not sail nearer to west than north-northwest if on the port tack (wind blowing on her port side); or south-southwest if on the starboard tack (wind blowing on her starboard side). Master Jones had to judge which tack would get his ship nearer her destination, and when to "come about" on the other tack. For that complicated maneuver, all hands were called on deck. The mizzen was hauled in tight so as to kick her stern around, and the spritsail was furled. The helmsman put the tiller "hard down" and the great main yard was swung through an arc of about 90 degrees at the exact moment when the master shouted, "Let go and haul!" At that moment the crew were glad to have some "beef" from the passengers to apply to the main braces.

The women and children had the worst time on board. During the voyage a son was born to Elizabeth and Stephen Hopkins and appropriately named Oceanus; and just after the ship arrived at Cape Cod, a boy was born to Susanna and William White and named Peregrine, the Pilgrim. Four persons, including Dorothy Bradford, died on board in Provincetown Harbor before the *Mayflower* left Cape Cod. Thus, only ninety-nine were delivered at Plymouth. Peregrine, many years later, received a land grant from the colony as "the first of the English born in these parts"; he lived through the entire history of the colony and died at Marshfield in 1704.

The *Mayflower* made a slow and rough voyage because she left at the wrong time of year. If the Pilgrims' plans had been carried out promptly, she would have started in May and enjoyed fair winds. But in September the season of westerly gales had begun, and she encountered plenty.

How did Master Jones find his way across this "vast and furious ocean," as Bradford called it? He had some inaccurate charts of the Atlantic, and knew the straight course for Cape Cod; but for more than half the voyage the west wind prevented his steering the straight course. Every noon he checked his latitude by observing the sun with a crude instrument called a cross-staff, and applying figures from an almanac. But he had no means of measuring longitude or how far west he had sailed, except by tracing on the chart his compass course and estimated distance. He knew the *Mayflower* so well that he could judge the speed that she could make under various conditions.

In those days the usual route to Virginia followed that of Columbus, dropping down to the Canaries to get the easterly trade winds to waft you across to the West Indies and Florida, whence you followed the coast. Some ships, however, had had good luck following the short route straight across, and Master Jones decided to try it. The *Mayflower* took sixty-five days to sail from Plymouth, England, to Cape Cod, and one day more to her first American harbor. That was exactly twice what Columbus took on his first voyage. The *Mayflower* might have made a shorter and easier passage by the southern route, but she would have run the risk of being captured by the Spaniards or wrecked off Cape Hatteras.

It is too bad that we have no log, or sea journal, of the *Mayflower;* it would be priceless now. Master Jones doubtless kept one, but since he died shortly after returning to England, his widow probably used it for wrapping paper. All we know about the voyage, aside from a few incidents, is that after the first few days it was very, very rough. When the ship was half-seas over, a main beam (one of the thwart-ship timbers that strengthened the hull) cracked. This made the main deck leak rain or sea water, and everyone on the deck below was drenched. Some of the sailors wanted to turn back; but the passengers broke out a "great iron screw brought out of Holland" — probably for raising houses — and used it to shove the cracked beam in place. They then caulked the deck, "committed themselves to the will of God, and resolved to proceed."

In some of the westerly gales the ship had to lay-to, which meant taking in all sails and drifting with the wind. In one such gale John Howland fell overboard but managed to grab a trailing halyard and was pulled back with a boat hook.

Landfall and Change in Destination

On November 9, 1620,* at about 8:00 A.M., the *Mayflower* sighted the highlands of Cape Cod, which made everyone "not a little joyful," says Bradford. No wonder, after two months and three days at sea! "And the appearance of it much comforted us, especially seeing so goodly a land, and wooded to the brink of the sea." All good Cape Codders will approve.

---

* By the Julian calendar that the Pilgrims used. To find the equivalent date on our modern calendar, the Gregorian, add ten days.

Master Jones, now knowing where he was, turned the *Mayflower*'s bow south and sailed down the long, skinny arm of Cape Cod. He was en route, as he hoped, to the mouth of the Hudson River, the Pilgrims' intended destination. But by evening the *Mayflower* was off the elbow of the Cape, and involved in the dangerous shoals called Pollock Rip. The current was against her, the wind falling, and darkness coming on. Pollock Rip is a perilous passage for sailboats even today, when it is well charted, buoyed, and dredged; but on November 9, 1620, it was terrifying to approach those "dangerous shoals and roaring breakers." Rather than become entangled in them, Master Jones held council with Carver, Bradford, and other leading passengers, and decided to turn about and make for the harbor inside the tip of Cape Cod.

That was a sound decision. By next evening, November 10, the *Mayflower* was off Peaked Hill Bar. The weather was clear and cold; the moon, in her last quarter, rose shortly after one o'clock, lighting up the white sand dunes of Race Point. Most of the passengers were below, the "graveyard watch" had charge, and on the high poop deck Master Jones and Mate Clarke walked briskly to and fro, watching the sails, peering into the binnacle, looking up at the stars, and conning the helmsman in the steerage. Every quarter-hour the leadsman in the chains hove the hand lead and sang out the depths. It was a night of watchfulness but not of danger; the passengers were thankful for their narrow escape from the shoals, and joyful over the prospect of landing on the morrow.

The Landing at Provincetown

During the small hours of November 11, the *Mayflower* tacks to and fro, in order not to lose touch with the Cape. Daylight, breaking around six o'clock, finds her on a southeasterly course working in by Wood End with a fair tide. At seven, the sun rises red and clear above the Truro hills; and by the time eight bells are struck and the watch changed, the *Mayflower* is south of Long Point and heading into Cape Cod Harbor, as they then called it — Provincetown Harbor, as now renamed.

It is now nine or ten o'clock. The bulwarks are so crowded with passengers eager to look upon their new Land of Canaan that the mate orders them to stand clear of the tackle so that he may work his ship. About a mile off the tip of Long Point, Master Jones shapes a course southward for the land-locked part of the harbor, feeling his way with leadline so that he will not be in danger of running aground. At the same time, he is taking in sail. When the leadsman sings out, "By the mark, five!" (meaning 30 feet, in land language), the master says to Mate Clarke, "Well enough." Clarke says, "Aye, aye, sir," and bellows, "Hard down!" to the helmsman, who answers, "Hard down, sir!" and, presently, "Helm's a-lee!" Now, with no sail to give her headway, the *Mayflower* glides into the wind a couple of hundred yards from shore. At the proper moment the best bower anchor is let go, and the thick hemp cable, which the seamen have been flaking on the forecastle head since daybreak, is carefully paid out as the anchor fluke bites into the bottom, and the ship begins to make sternway. When the mate gives the word, the cable is snubbed on the capstan. Now, as Bradford notes in correct nautical language, "They rode in saftie." The *Mayflower* is snugged down in one of the best anchorages of New England.

Now the ship's longboat is lowered and an armed party of fifteen or sixteen men rows ashore, landing at the southern end of the present Provincetown. Bradford tells us that they promptly "fell upon their knees and blessed the God of Heaven, who had brought them over the vast and furious ocean, and delivered them from all the perils and miseries thereof, again to set their feet on the firm and stable earth, their proper element."

For all that, the Pilgrims were in a grim situation. It was too late in the season to strike around Cape Cod again for the Hudson. The settled part of Virginia, wherein they had permission to plant, was hundreds of miles away. The nearest white men were the French at Port Royal, Nova Scotia. Behind them was the mighty ocean, separating them from the civilized part of the world. Before them was the wilderness, whose only inhabitants were Indians, "readier to fill their sides full of arrows than otherwise." Master Jones said they must make up their minds promptly where to pitch their colony, for his ship's stores were running low, and he must keep enough to get home. It would be nine months, at least, before they could hope to reap a harvest. "What could now sustain them," writes Bradford, "but the Spirit of God and His grace? May not and ought not the children of these fathers rightly say: 'Our fathers were Englishmen which came over this great ocean, and were ready to perish in the wilderness; but they cried unto the Lord, and He heard their voice and looked on their adversity . . . ' "

The Pilgrims intended to keep the *Mayflower's* shallop for their own use and wished right away to explore the coast and find a good site for the settlement. But the shallop had been so banged about in rough weather as to be full of leaks. So they hoisted it out and floated it ashore, where the *Mayflower's* carpenter and some of the men went to work making repairs.

The Landing at Plymouth

Behind the island later named Clark's, the Pilgrims' shallop found quiet waters on the night of Saturday, December 9. Everyone went ashore, "and with much ado got fire" with flint and steel; and were mighty glad of it, as the wind whipped around to northwest and it froze hard that night.

In accordance with their religious principles, they "rested the Sabbath" on Clark's Island. On Monday, December 11, they rowed to the mainland in the shallop. The nearest land in Plymouth Bay where they might have landed was right where the Plymouth Cordage Company wharf used to stand, but they may have gone ashore anywhere between that point and the mouth of the Town Brook, where Plymouth Rock lies. From whatever place they did land, they marched for several miles along the shore, finding "divers corn fields and running brooks, a place very good for situation."

This is the day — December 11 in their calendar, the 21st in ours — that is celebrated as "Forefathers' Day," when the first of the Pilgrims landed at Plymouth.

After sounding the depth of water in the harbor, the exploring expedition sailed back to Provincetown Harbor and reported that Plymouth was the right place to settle. Their clinching arguments were that cleared cornfields ready for tillage were available and that there was an absence of live Indians, with plenty of bones as evidence that the natives were all dead. They had died in a pestilence a few years before, leaving their cornfields for the first comer to use.

For William Bradford, however, the expedition's return to the *Mayflower* was a tragic event, for during his absence his young wife, Dorothy, had fallen overboard and been drowned. One may suspect that she did it on purpose, disheartened by gazing on the barren sand dunes of Cape Cod. How many tender hearts of pioneer women must have grown faint when they first beheld the wilderness shores of New England, so different from those of the green and placid Old England that they knew!

On December 16 the *Mayflower* weighed anchor from Cape Cod, and that night she anchored in Plymouth Harbor. Since it was against Puritan principles to work on the Sabbath, everyone stayed on board during Sunday, December 17, and Elder Brewster conducted divine service. Exploring parties started going ashore on Monday, the 18th.

Thus, if you wish to be exact about dates, the first landing took place at the site of Provincetown on November 11; the exploring expedition landed at or near the present town of Plymouth on December 11; the *Mayflower* anchored in Plymouth Harbor on the 16th; and the first people went ashore from her on the 18th. There was no immediate or wholesale "landing of the Pilgrims on Plymouth Rock," such as you see in popular illustrations.

3

The Battle off Flamborough Head,
September 23, 1779

From JOHN PAUL JONES: A SAILOR'S BIOGRAPHY (Boston: Little, Brown, 1959), *Chapter XIII.*

Every once in a while an idea for a book strikes an historian when he has no time to do anything about it, so files it in memory's locker to be forgotten or pulled out whenever time and circumstance seem appropriate. Exactly when I first thought of writing about this controversial naval hero is now forgotten; but he kept cropping up in many of my researches, his ghost taunting me with being what I had called a "gonna" historian — one who is always "gonna" write some great opus but never does. Finally, however, the occasion came. My naval history almost completed, I had acquired a summer place, Good Hope, at Northeast Harbor, Maine — an ideal place for maritime work as well as play — and my beloved wife, Priscilla, was ready as usual to accompany me to the John Paul Jones country (or "operational areas") in the British Isles, Holland, Paris, and Brittany.

Paul Jones has had eminent biographers (or, what I call for want of a better word, mentioners), such as Alexandre Dumas (LE CAPITAINE PAUL), Herman Melville (ISRAEL POTTER), J. Fenimore Cooper (THE PILOT), Walt Whitman ("Song of Myself," a glorious poem on this battle), Thomas Carlyle (THE FRENCH REVOLUTION), and Rudyard Kipling ("Rhyme of the Three Captains"). My only excuse for a fresh biography is my maritime experience. And I wouldn't have had that if Franklin D. Roosevelt had been able to carry out his plan for a biography of Jones. But I shan't call him a "gonna" historian, since he was called to greater tasks. So, I stepped into the breach, and here is my account of Jones's greatest and best-known battle, that of the Bonhomme Richard *against H.M.S.* Serapis, *on September 23, 1779. I reconnoitered the scene of that battle in H.M.S. Wave, out of Scarborough, in May 1957.*

The task force which Jones then commanded consisted of:

	NO. OF OFFICERS AND MEN	COMMANDING OFFICER	ORDNANCE					
			18s	12s	9s	8s	6s	4s
Frigate *Bonhomme Richard*	380	Captain John P. Jones USN	6	28	6	—	—	—
Frigate *Alliance*	215	Captain Pierre Landais USN	—	28	8	—	—	—
Frigate *La Pallas*	253	Captain de V. Denis-Nicolas Cottineau	—	—	26	—	—	—
Corvette *La Vengeance*	66	Lieut. de V. Philippe-Nicholas Ricot	—	—	—	—	—	12

When he left France, he had also cutter Le Cerf *and two French privateers under his command, but they had long since gone their separate ways when he encountered* Serapis. *Jones was Captain, U.S. Navy, with the courtesy rank of Commodore; Landais, Ricot, and Cottineau had USN commissions.*

"JONES was a man to be obeyed," remarked Lieutenant Mackenzie, his early naval biographer. But he was often disobeyed. He had been disobeyed off the Blaskets, and so lost two boats, some good men, and the cutter. He had been disobeyed by Landais off Cape Wrath and Fair Isle. He had had to argue the French captains into the raid on Leith, and so lost a fair wind and surprise. Again, the commodore was thwarted as his squadron sailed southward along the rugged coast of Northumberland.

In order to elude British warships, which were searching for him offshore, Jones sailed close aboard the Holy Isle of Lindisfarne and stood into Skate Roadstead. When Bamburgh Castle loomed up, he playfully shot a cannon ball at the ancient edifice; it landed in a private garden and is treasured by the owner's descendants to this day.

His intention was to raid Newcastle-on-Tyne in order to cut off London's winter coal supply. On Tuesday, September 19, he had his boats' oars muffled, and next morning the Marines were readied for executing the Leith landing plan. Newcastle was gravely alarmed. A respectable inhabitant wrote to the Admiralty:

Paul Jones's squadron is *actually* off here, he stood in for Tynemouth Castle this *morning* with five ships — but seeing a Fleet of Colliers to the Southward he sent three of his smallest after them, the event of which we don't know. I have had the mortification of *seeing* him also this Afternoon with three prizes, the one a Brig that sail'd from this Port in the morning called the *Union* with other two small Sloops. His force is said to be [of] 86, 20, 28, 20 & 16 Guns *and nothing in the World to oppose him.*

Actually, Jones had only three warships with him — the two others were prizes — and Captain Cottineau, with whom Jones consulted, had no stomach for another shore raid. He argued that if the squadron tarried on the Northumbrian coast after the alarm it had created in the Forth, it would certainly be taken. Cottineau even told Colonel de Chamillard that unless the commodore turned southward, both *Pallas* and *Vengeance* would desert him. Jones considered attacking Newcastle with one ship only, and the officers of *Richard* were all for it; but he decided that the risk was incommensurate to the possible gain. So he abandoned the attempt when *Richard* was so close to shore that the houses of South Shields were clearly visible.

We must not judge Jones's captains by World War II standards. In the eighteenth century, even in the grand fleets of England and France, deliberate misunderstanding of the commanding officer's signals, unauthorized action by individual ships, and plain insubordination were frequent. Hood let Graves down in the battle off the capes of the Chesapeake; Bougainville disobeyed de Grasse in the Battle of the Saints; and the Bailly de Suffren, the greatest French naval officer of his day, was never able to obtain proper cooperation in his Indian Ocean operations. The more daring and original a commander might be, the less chance he had of being followed and obeyed. Historian Charles de La Roncière remarked on Suffren's experience, "New strategy and tactics, principles directly opposed to those of his time, impeccable concept from start to finish; that was the contribution of this great seaman. Feeble execution, total incomprehension, insufficient cooperation — such were the common faults of his lieutenants." This was certain to be the case under Paul Jones, an officer who never fought by the book but was alert to profit by opportunities, with a squadron whose commanding officers at best did not understand him, and one of whom was eager to destroy him.

But there was no insubordination on board the flagship. During the few months that he had commanded *Bonhomme Richard,* he welded her officers and men into a fighting man-of-war's crew. The officers were of his choice; and the enlisted men fought gallantly because they liked fighting and were devoted to their commander, even if he did lose his temper at times. Paul Jones was like a temperamental orchestra leader who enrages almost every musician under him, yet produces a magnificent ensemble.

Passing Scarborough on the starboard hand, around 1:00 A.M. on September 22, the squadron captured a Scarborough collier in ballast, forced another vessel ashore between Flamborough Head and the Spurn, and took an English brigantine from Rotterdam. Scarborough hoisted a red flag as signal that an enemy was off the coast; all maritime Yorkshire was in consternation. The militia beat to arms and went on twenty-four-hour duty, expecting a landing. The gentry packed off their women, children, and valuables; desperate letters were dispatched to the Admiralty, demanding protection. Hull was equally alarmed; a "general meeting," called by the mayor to decide what to do, decided there was nothing it could do, as the fort was decayed and its cannon dangerous only to the cannoneers. The Northumberland militia was called out and marched to Bridlington and Beverley. These preparations to repel a landing force continued long after Jones had fought the battle and sailed away.

By 8:00 A.M. on the 22nd, the squadron was off the Spurn, the northern cape to the Humber estuary. Commodore Jones, wishing to chase a merchant convoy that he had sighted, hoisted the British signal for a pilot — the Union Jack at the fore-topgallant masthead. That brought out two pilot boats. One pilot boarded *Richard,* thinking her to be British; the other boarded the prize from Rotterdam. He, too, was brought to Jones and detained, together with one of the boats, which was taken in tow. Jones tried to entice some of the ships anchored in the Humber to come out and fight, but in vain; and the wind became too light and variable to risk *Richard* inside the estuary. So, during the evening, when Spurn Light bore WNW distant eighteen miles, *Richard* turned north again toward Flamborough Head, to rejoin *Pallas,* which had already turned back to chase prizes in those profitable waters.

Shortly before midnight two sail were sighted from the flagship. All hands were called to quarters, and the night recognition signals — lanterns at the three mastheads — were hoisted. At 5:30 A.M. of the fateful 23rd, when day was breaking, the two ships were made out to be *Alliance*, which had not been seen for over a fortnight, and frigate *Pallas*. Counting little cutter *Vengeance*, the commodore now had four ships under his command.

The squadron sailed slowly before the light wind toward Flamborough Head. At 2:00 P.M., when the wind had almost died, the commodore sent one of the captured pilot boats, under command of Lieutenant Henry Lunt, to take a brig sighted to windward, which he suspected to be the one that he had formerly run ashore. An hour later, the commodore realized that his long-sought opportunity had arrived. A fleet of forty-one sail appeared off Flamborough Head, bearing north-northeast from *Richard* and standing in her direction. From what the captured pilots told him, Jones knew that this was a convoy from the Baltic escorted by frigate *Serapis* (44 guns) and sloop-of-war *Countess of Scarborough* (20 guns).

H.M.S. *Serapis* (pronounced Se-ray'pis; the keeper of *Richard*'s log called her "Searuppus"), commanded by Captain Richard Pearson, RN, was a new copper-bottomed frigate. Rated at 44 guns, actually she had 50; a main battery of 20 eighteen-pounders on a lower gun deck (compared with *Richard*'s 6 of that caliber); 20 nine-pounders on an upper covered gun deck (compared with *Richard*'s 28 twelve-pounders), and 10 six-pounders on the quarterdeck (where *Richard* had 6 nine-pounders). Captain Pearson had arrived at Elsinor on August 19 with a convoy from the Nore, and was there joined by H.M.S. *Countess of Scarborough*, Captain Thomas Piercy, to escort a convoy of seventy sail to England. The convoy departed Elsinore on September 1, anchored near Christiansund during an easterly gale, departed on September 15, and made landfall near Whitby on the 23rd. At that time the convoy numbered forty-four sail, as the ships bound for Scottish ports had parted company. Captain Pearson was much pleased with his new fast frigate, his only complaint being with the old eighteen-pounders that the Admiralty had furnished. Their vents were so big that too much gunpowder exploded through them, and their muzzles were so long that when the guns were drawn in there was no space left to coil down his hawsers properly. But there is no doubt that *Serapis* was a newer, faster, and more nimble frigate than *Richard;* and in fire power, owing to her far greater number of eighteen-pounders, she was definitely superior. In terms of recent warfare, it was as though a 14-inch-gunned battleship, with an additional advantage of speed, engaged an 8-inch-gunned heavy cruiser.

Flamborough Head, off which the famous night action was fought, is a broad headland of chalk cliffs rising 450 feet above the sea, cut by deep gullies with tiny beaches at the foot, and honeycombed by numerous caves, which were favorite resorts of smugglers. The tide splits at the Head; half the flood, running from north to south, sweeps seaward off a sandbar called the Smithics; the other half, running between the Smithics and the shore, makes a great "boil" over a reef jutting out from the Head, known as the Flamborough Steel. Just before low water, a strong inshore current sets northerly and the ebb current outside the Smithics starts two hours later than the ebb inside. It is dangerous ground for a stranger; the ten-fathom line is about three miles off the Head. At Flamborough Head today, only a lighthouse and a few small cottages on the cliff alter its 1779 profile, which was the last glimpse that over a hundred brave seamen had of the land to which they hoped to return. And *Bonhomme Richard* in her long career had never looked so beautiful as she did that last full day of her life, when the westering sun gilded her towering pyramid of sail and touched up the highlights on her elaborate quarter galleries and carving.

Captain Pearson was expecting Jones, since the bailiffs of Scarborough had sent out a boat to warn him; but his primary duty was to protect the convoy. Ordering it to sail as close to shore as the merchant captains dared, he stood offshore to cover. Shortly after noon on the 23rd, the convoy, which so far had ignored Pearson's signals, sighted *Richard, Alliance,* and *Pallas,* and promptly tacked inshore, "letting fly their topgallant sheets and firing guns" as an alarm signal and then turning north to seek refuge under the guns of Scarborough Castle. Light airs were blowing from the southwest. *Serapis* cracked on sail to get between her convoy and the enemy, and succeeded in so doing. "At one o'clock," wrote Pearson in his report, "we got sight of the Enemys ships from the masthead, and about four we made them plain from the Deck to be three large ships and a brig; upon which I made the *Countess of Scarborough* signal to join me, she being in shore with the Convoy . . . I then brought too, to let the *Countess of Scarboro* come up, and cleared ship for Action; at ½ past five she joined me, the Enemy's ships then bearing down upon us with light breeze at SSW; at six Tacked and laid our Head in shore, in order to keep our Ground the better between the Enemy's ships and the Convoy." Brave Pearson did not flinch from engaging an enemy that appeared to be double his strength; and the timid, uncertain maneuvering of the three smaller American ships made him the more brisk to offer battle.

Commodore Jones, who had always wanted to break up a Baltic convoy, knowing its importance for supplying the Royal Navy, made every effort to close; but the wind was so light that it took him three and a half hours to cover the ten or eleven miles between himself and *Serapis*, and he realized that he would have to take or sink the two escorts before he could get a crack at the convoy.

At 3:00 P.M. Jones sighted the enemy; at 3:30 *Richard* fired a gun (which Lieutenant Lunt did not hear) to recall the pilot boat, hoisted the signal General Chase, crossed royal yards, and set all three royals. At 4:00 studdingsails were set on both sides, and the gunners, seamen, and officers quietly took their assigned stations aloft, on deck, and below. At 5:00 the Marine drummers marched up and down beating the roll for General Quarters. At 6:00, just as the sun was setting, the commodore made the agreed signal "Form Line of Battle" — a blue flag at the fore, blue pendant at the main truck, and blue and yellow flag at the mizzen. Nobody paid any attention to it. *Alliance*, in the lead, prudently hauled her wind, leaving *Richard* alone to engage *Serapis*; *Pallas*, astern of *Richard*, sheered off, but later redeemed herself by engaging *Countess of Scarborough*; *Vengeance* simply sailed about, looking on.

By 6:30 *Richard* had hauled up her lower courses for better mobility and rounded-to on the weather (port) quarter of *Serapis*. Presently the two ships were side by side on the port tack, heading west, *Richard* to the southward and windward of *Serapis*, the wind then being southwest by south. Commodore Jones was on the quarterdeck; de Chamillard with about twenty French Marines on the poop; Lieutenant Dale had charge of the gun deck and the main battery; Lieutenant Stack commanded twenty sailors and Marines manning swivels and small arms in the main top, Midshipman Fanning commanded the foretop with fourteen men, and Midshipman Coram the smaller mizzen top with nine men. Midshipman Mayrant stood by the commodore to act as his aide. The guns were shotted and ready;

the gunners of the starboard battery, with lighted match in hand for each piece, were awaiting the word to fire. *Serapis* triced up her gun ports, revealing two decks of guns and making a formidable appearance. In Midshipman Fanning's words, "Just as the moon was rising, the weather being clear, the surface of the great deep being perfectly smooth, even as in a millpond," and the two ships being within pistol shot, Captain Pearson hailed, "What ship is that?" Paul Jones, in order to get into close action, was flying British colors. Playing for time, he caused Master Stacey to reply, "The *Princess Royal!*" "Where from?" asked Pearson. The answer, whatever it may have been, was not heard on board *Serapis*. She hailed again, "Answer immediately, or I shall be under the necessity of firing into you." Jones struck his British colors, caused a big red-, white-, and blue-striped American ensign to be raised, and gave the word to fire his starboard broadside. *Serapis* fired hers almost simultaneously. At the first or second salvo, two of Jones's eighteen-pounders burst, killing many gunners and ruining the rest of that battery, as well as blowing up part of the deck above.

"The battle being thus begun," wrote Jones in his Narrative, "was Continued with Unremitting fury." Each captain strove to maneuver his ship across the other's bow or stern, in order to rake. *Serapis*, the faster by reason of her slippery bottom, several times gained an advantageous position "in spite of my best Endeavours to prevent it," admitted Jones. After exchanging two or three broadsides, the commodore estimated that a gun-to-gun duel would be fatal for him; he must attempt to board and grapple. He backed *Richard*'s fore and main topsails, dropped astern on *Serapis*'s port quarter, both ships firing furiously at a range of 80 to 100 feet, "filled again, put his helm a-weather" (to port), ran *Richard* up on *Serapis*'s starboard quarter, and attempted to board. This was a very disadvantageous position from which to carry an enemy ship by boarding; it was like attempting an amphibious assault on so narrow a front that the enemy could concentrate his fire on a thin line of men. The English sailors repulsed the boarders, and Jones sheered off.

The next move was Pearson's, an attempt to cross *Richard*'s bow to rake her; but *Serapis* had not enough headway to make it; and Jones, following her movements, ran *Richard*'s bow into her stern. It was at this juncture — not near the close of the battle, as has generally been stated — that Captain Pearson called out, "Has your ship struck?"

Successive Positions in the Battle off Flamborough Head.

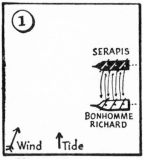

①

SERAPIS

BONHOMME RICHARD

Wind Tide

The battle opens.

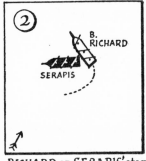

②

B. RICHARD

SERAPIS

RICHARD on SERAPIS' starboard quarter, hoping to board.

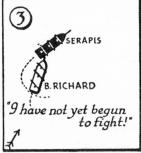

③

SERAPIS

B. RICHARD

"*I have not yet begun to fight!*"

SERAPIS tries to cross RICHARD'S bow, but has not enough headway. RICHARD'S bowsprit hits SERAPIS.

④

SERAPIS

B. RICHARD

They straighten out again. SERAPIS backs topsails to reduce speed.

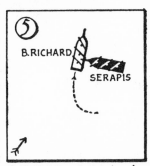

⑤

B.RICHARD

SERAPIS

RICHARD surges ahead, tries to cross SERAPIS' bow, her jib boom fouls RICHARD'S mizzen shrouds.

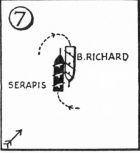

⑧ 3rd broadside

B.RICHARD

SERAPIS

ALLIANCE

2nd broadside

Tide

SERAPIS, anchored and locked to RICHARD, swings 180° with tide. They fight for two hours, when SERAPIS strikes. ALLIANCE sails around them firing broadsides mostly at RICHARD.

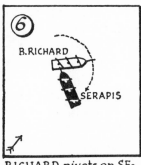

⑥

B.RICHARD

SERAPIS

RICHARD pivots on SERAPIS' bowsprit.

⑦

B. RICHARD

SERAPIS

They fall alongside, grappled. Night falls.

and Paul Jones made the immortal reply: "I have not yet begun to fight."

Nor had he. Unable to bring a single cannon to bear on *Serapis* from that position, *Richard* backed her topsails to get clear, *Serapis* wore briskly around "on her heel" from a northeasterly to a westerly heading, and *Richard,* too, pulled away and straightened out. *Serapis* being ahead, Pearson backed topsails to check headway and get broadside to *Richard* in order to bring his superior fire power to bear. Jones, divining his intent, ordered Master Stacey "to lay the enemy's ship on board." Taking advantage of a fresh puff of wind, which did not strike *Serapis* because *Richard*'s sails blanketed hers, Jones ranged ahead, ordered helm a-weather, and tried the same maneuver that Pearson had attempted on him. He laid *Richard* "athwart hawse" — like the cap of a T — in order to rake his enemy's decks.

"It did not exactly succeed to my wishes," admitted Jones, because, some of the yards' braces having been shot away, the people could not trim them properly and maneuver quickly enough to clear. The two ships collided, bow to stern; *Serapis* thrust her jib-boom (tip end of the bowsprit) right into *Richard*'s mizzen shrouds — the rigging that held up her aftermast. The wind acting on the sails of both ships caused them to pivot until they were on a north-south axis, bow to stern and stern to bow. A fluke of *Serapis*'s starboard anchor sealed this fatal marriage by hooking the bulwarks of *Richard*'s starboard quarter, and the two ships' topsides clapped together so that the muzzles of their guns were touching. Paul Jones, joyfully accepting this new situation, shouted, "Well done, my brave lads, we have got her now; throw on board her the grappling-irons and stand by for boarding!" And while waiting for Master Stacey to rouse out a spare line, the commodore with his own hands seized a forestay of *Serapis* that had parted and fallen across *Richard*'s quarterdeck and made it fast to his mizzenmast. At this juncture the master appeared with the line, swearing horribly; the captain checked him by remarking, "Mr. Stacey, it's no time to be swearing now — you may by the next moment be in eternity; but let us do our duty."

All this was as pretty a piece of maneuvering as you could see at the start of a modern yacht race, and the unforeseen clapperclaw was exactly what Jones wanted. He was outgunned even at the start of the action, and he had abandoned his eighteen-pounder battery —

his only cannon of the same caliber as the main battery of *Serapis* —
suspecting after two blew up the rest would follow. He knew that
his only chance of victory, or even survival, was to disable the rigging
of *Serapis* and kill off her crew by musketry and hand grenades, or to
take her boarding; and as the British frigate had two covered gun
decks, capture by boarding would be very difficult. Captain Pearson, on the contrary, had to shake off *Richard*'s deadly hug if he were
to bring his superior fire power to bear. To that end, he ordered the
grappling hooks to be cast off or severed; but *Richard*'s sharpshooters
picked off the sailors who tried to do that. Pearson then dropped
anchor in 15 to 20 fathom of water, hoping that the wind and tide
would swing *Richard* clear. On the contrary, the two ships, spitting
fire at each other, pivoted through a half-circle, for all the world like
one of those macabre dances of death by two skeletons in a mediaeval
engraving. *Serapis*, now held by her anchor, headed south into wind
and tide, while *Richard*, still fast grappled to her, pointed north.

It is now between 8:00 and 8:30; the harvest moon, two days short
of full, rises over heavy clouds on the eastern horizon and illuminates
the battle. "Flamborough reapers, homegoing, pause on the hillside;
for what sulphur-cloud is that which defaces the sleek sea; sulphur-
cloud spitting streaks of fire?" wrote Thomas Carlyle. Spectators,
attracted from Scarborough and Bridlington by the sound of the opening salvos, flock to Flamborough Head. They witness a naval combat
the like of which has never been fought before or since. Here, for
two long hours, *Bonhomme Richard* and *Serapis* are mortised
together, snug as two logs in a woodpile, guns muzzle to muzzle.
They are so close that the starboard gun ports of *Serapis*, shut during
the first phase of the battle, cannot be opened outboard, and have to
be blown off by her guns; and the gunners, in order to load and ram
their charges home, must thrust their staves into the enemy's gun
ports. At one point the sails of both ships are ablaze, and killing is
suspended while damage control parties fight the flames; then each
ship resumes banging away at t'other. The Englishman wants to
break off and fight at cannon range but cannot; the American clings
desperately to him, knowing that only by maintaining the clinch can
he survive. Deprived of his eighteen-pounder battery in the
gunroom by the bursting of the guns, and of his main battery of
twelve-pounders by the blast from *Serapis*'s two decks of eighteen-
pounders, Commodore Jones has no cannon left except three nine-

pounders on the quarterdeck, one of which he helps to trundle over from the port side and serves with his own hands.

Jones's one advantage, other than his own inflexible determination, is the good marksmanship of the French Marine musketeers on deck, and of the polyglot seamen and gunners in the fighting tops. Owing to their fast and accurate shooting with swivels, coehorns, small arms, and tossed grenades, *Serapis* can keep no man alive on deck, and her open-deck battery of ten six-pounders is deserted. But her eighteen-pounders, below deck, go on roaring and breaching through *Richard*'s topsides, and Jones has no means to counter them. French ship-builders must have put stout stuff into that old East Indiaman; for when the fight ended, only a few stanchions prevented her quarter-deck from falling into the gunroom, or her main deck from crashing into the hold, and her topsides were a mass of fragments and splinters. Jones's tactics of close grappling prevented the English guns from breaking his masts and yards, which continued to support his fighting men in the tops, even when the rest of *Bonhomme Richard* had been reduced to little more than a battered raft.

"During this time," reported Pearson, "from the great Quantity and Variety of Combustible Matters which they threw in upon our Decks, Chains and in short into every part of the Ship, we were on fire not less than Ten or Twelve times in different parts." It is a scene difficult to imagine, impossible to describe in detail. The yards of *Richard* so far overhung the deck of *Serapis* that her sailors were able to leap into the enemy's tops, throw out the English topmen, and then shoot directly down at her deck and even into the hatches.

Vengeance, during the battle, maneuvered at a safe distance; the boat commanded by Lunt stood by, not daring to come alongside; Pallas hotly engaged *Countess of Scarborough*, and Landais in *Alliance* played the rôle of a madman. During the early part of the clinch, he raked *Richard*, killing two sailors and driving others from their battle stations. He then sailed close to where the other two ships were fighting, but did nothing to help *Pallas*. After that, he beat up to windward in very leisurely fashion and, about two hours after his first blast at *Richard*, crossed the axis of the two locked ships to windward of them. Turning downwind, *Alliance* crossed *Richard*'s stern, and "while we were hailing her," said Midshipman Mayrant, poured into her port quarter a broadside that holed her between wind and water and even under water. He then passed ahead, returned athwart *Richard*'s bows, and — despite the commodore's hailing, "Lay the enemy on board!," the seamen shouting, "Don't fire — you have killed several of our men already!" and Lieutenant Stack calling from his fighting top, "I beg you will not sink us!" — Landais gave *Richard* a third and the most fatal broadside, fired into the forecastle, where men driven from the gun deck had gathered. It killed several more, including a chief petty officer.

This cannot have been accidental, as Jones had his night recognition signals burning; the scene was illuminated by moonlight, gun flashes, and fires; *Richard*'s topsides were painted black and those of Serapis bright yellow. The evidence is overwhelming that Landais did it on purpose. After the battle he confided to one of the French colonels that his intention was to help *Serapis* sink *Richard,* then board and capture the British frigate and emerge the hero and victor of the battle. Later he had the impudence to claim that his broadsides forced Captain Pearson to strike; and Pearson himself was not backward in claiming that he succumbed to two frigates, not one. But the testimony collected by Commodore Jones at the Texel is conclusive: *Alliance* was nowhere about in the last half-hour of the battle, Landais having fired his last malevolent broadside around 10:00 P.M. and retired to a safe distance to think up more mischief. His crew suffered not one casualty, and his ship no damage. She was hit only thrice by *Scarborough* at long range; one of the balls stuck in her topsides and the other two bounced off.

The commodore directed the nine-pounder guns on his quarter-deck and served one of them himself, since Purser Mease, the officer in charge of that one remaining battery, was badly wounded in the head. At one moment Jones became so exhausted that he sat down to rest on a hencoop, when a sailor came up to him and said, "For God's sake, Captain, strike!" Jones paused, then leaped to his feet and said, "No, I will sink, I will never strike!" and resumed his service of the nine-pounder.

His indomitable spirit and the sharp work of his topmen and Marines were the decisive factors in the battle. They picked off so many British gunners that the boy "powder monkeys" found few people on the gun deck of *Serapis* to receive the powder cartridges being brought up from the magazine, and dropped them on deck. An enterprising seaman of *Richard*'s crew, a Scot named William Hamilton, took a basket of hand grenades and a live match out to the end of a yardarm that hung directly above an open hatch of *Serapis*, and dropped a grenade right through it, which exploded the powder cartridges that the boys had left lying about. At least twenty men were killed and others frightfully burned. Jones followed this up by directing the fire of his three nine-pounders, loaded with double-headed shot, against the enemy's mainmast.

Immediately after the big explosion, Captain Pearson was at the point of calling for quarter when three of Jones's petty officers, two of whom had been wounded, put their heads together and decided that *Richard* would sink if she did not strike. The chief gunner, an Englishman named Henry Gardner, ran aft to haul down the ensign; but, finding that a cannon ball had carried away ensign and staff, he began bawling, "Quarters, Quarters, for God's sake!" At this the commodore, pulling a pistol from his belt, hurled it at the chief and felled him to the deck.* Pearson, however, had heard the cry and called over to Jones, "Sir, do you ask for a quarter?" He replied, "No, sir, I haven't as yet *thought* of it, but I'm determined to make *you* strike." Pearson's reply to that was to command, "Boarders away!" But by the time his boarding party had crossed *Richard's* bulwarks, "they discovered a Superior Number lying under Cover with Pikes in their hands ready to receive them, on which our people retreted instantly into our own ship, and returned to their Guns again." †

It was now 10:00 P.M. The battle went on for another thirty minutes, becoming even more bloody and desperate. *Richard's* master at arms liberated the prisoners from the hold, to the number of over a hundred, and assured them that they had better man the pumps if they valued their lives. Most of them did so; but one, the master of prize ship *Union*, leaped through an open port of *Serapis*, rushed on deck, and told Captain Pearson that if he could hold out a little longer

* This is the origin of the yarn about Jones shooting "Lieutenant Grub" (Midshipman Beaumont Groube) for hauling down the ensign.

† One of the strange things about this part of the action is that neither side attempted to board the other until near the end. The probability is that *Richard's* crew looked like such desperate cutthroats that Pearson did not dare board except as a last expedient; and that Jones, with his keen tactical sense, felt that his men could do more execution with firearms than with boarding pikes and cutlasses. It is also strange that both commanding officers, although in full view on deck throughout the action, and conspicuous by their uniforms, escaped without a scratch. Jones probably ordered his sharpshooters to spare Pearson so that he could have the honor of capturing a Captain, RN; and Pearson may have given similar orders in the hope of taking the "pirate."

Jones would either strike or sink, for there were already five feet of water in the hold.

At this moment — five or ten minutes after ten — the situation of *Bonhomme Richard* seemed hopeless to almost every officer except the captain. A sinking ship, on fire, all cannon silenced except three nine-pounders while the enemy's eighteens are still blazing away; prisoners at large; officers losing heart; and chiefs bellowing, "Quarters!" — all that, which to almost any other commanding officer would have added up to the ultimate in desperate circumstances, failed to break Paul Jones's will to victory. And victory was very near. A few minutes before 10:30, when the mainmast of *Serapis*, which Jones had been pelting with double-headed shot, began to tremble, Captain Pearson lost his nerve. Four of his eighteen-pounders were still firing, but he decided that it was time for him to strike. The Red Ensign, which he had caused to be nailed to its staff, he had to tear down with his own hands, since no man near him was able to move.

With the commodore's permission, Lieutenant Dale swung himself on board *Serapis* to take possession, followed by a boarding party in which Midshipman Mayrant was wounded by a pike wielded by a British seaman who had not heard that his captain had struck. Nor had the first lieutenant of *Serapis;* he had to have the fact confirmed by Captain Pearson.

Lieutenant Dale now conducts Captain Pearson on board *Richard* and formally introduces him to Commodore Jones. At this point the tottering mainmast of *Serapis* cracks and falls overboard, carrying with it her mizzen topmast. The defeated captain hands his sword to Jones, who promptly returns it with a few gracious words about his gallant fight, and invites him below into his wrecked cabin to drink a glass of wine. Such were the ceremonial manners of eighteenth-century warfare.

This deadly duel was not the whole of the Battle off Flamborough Head. *Countess of Scarborough*, several cable lengths ahead of *Serapis* when the action opened, was pursued and closely engaged a few minutes later by *Pallas*, commanded by Captain Cottineau. They exchanged broadsides for about twenty minutes, when *Pallas*, for reasons unexplained, dropped astern out of range. Captain Piercy, of *Scarborough*, feeling that he had got off easily since he was greatly outgunned, sailed over to support *Serapis*, but decided not to get involved in that murderous mêlée. Cottineau then forced him to renew action a mile or more to leeward of the other antagonists. Captain Landais looked in briefly on them at this state of the battle, received a few random shots, and fired at the wrong ship, but otherwise did not participate. Captain Cottineau, whom Jones considered the ablest of the French officers under his command, followed standard French tactics of aiming at the enemy's spars and rigging, and to such good purpose that at the end of two hours the *Countess* was disabled, although she had lost only four men. Captain Piercy then surrendered, and his ship made a valuable prize. This brought up the total bag of prisoners made by Jones's squadron to 504, including 26 officers of the Royal Navy and 18 masters and mates of merchant ships.

The fight between *Bonhomme Richard* and *Serapis* had lasted between three and three-and-a-half hours. The British frigate was in a deplorable condition: her spars, sails, and rigging were cut away, and dead and dying men lay about her decks. But the state of *Richard* was even more frightful. Her rudder was hanging by one pintle; her stern frames and transoms were almost entirely shot away; the quarterdeck was about to fall into the gunroom; at least five feet of water were in the hold and it was gaining from holes below the waterline (some of them made by *Alliance*); and her topsides were open to the moonlight. The timbers of her lower deck from the mainmast aft, "being greatly decayed with age, were mangled beyond my power of description," observed Jones in his *Narrative* of the battle, "and a person must have been an Eye Witness to form a Just idea of this tremendous scene of Carneg, Wreck and ruin that Every Where appeared. Humanity cannot but recoil from the prospect of such finished horror, and Lament that War should be capable of producing such fatal Consequences."

This last statement was perfectly sincere. Paul Jones, like many of the greatest admirals and generals of the English-speaking nations, loved fighting but hated war. He shared the belief of eighteenth-century philosophers that war was an outmoded and barbarous method of settling international disputes, and hoped that the particular conflict in which he happened to be engaged would be the last.

The gods willed otherwise.

4

Oh! California, 1844—1850

From THE MARITIME HISTORY OF MASSACHUSETTS (Boston: Houghton Mifflin, 1921).

This was my first "successful" book; that is, the first that sold an appreciable number of copies, and that proved that I could fuse hobby and profession in a manner to please the public. It occurred almost by accident. Upon returning to Harvard from the Peace Conference in 1919, I took up a project released to me before World War I by my generous patron, Professor Edward Channing. This was a short history of my native state, Massachusetts. Not long after, I found myself concentrating on the maritime aspects of that history; and one day it occurred to me to separate these aspects into a book by itself. Ferris Greenslet, of Houghton Mifflin, agreed, and I was off. The book was written at Concord (amid sundry jokes about an asparagus farmer going to sea!), with frequent trips by Model T Ford to the North Shore, the South Shore, Cape Cod, and sailing offshore.

It was written in an atmosphere of euphoria. If inspiration lagged, I would take one of my books of printed sea chanteys to the piano, where Bessie vigorously banged out the tune while I bawled "Blow the Man Down," or one of the other deep-sea classics. Fortunately, too, Captain Arthur H. Clark, author of THE CLIPPER SHIP ERA, *had retired to Boston, and amiably told me both facts and stories, and even corrected parts of my prose. My enthusiasm was such that the whole book, from Ferris Greenslet's "Go ahead, Sam," to my bringing him the completed copy, took only eleven months, during half of which I was actually teaching at Harvard. The first edition, on large paper with extra illustrations, came out in 1921 and is still in print in 1977.*

So, here are three of the chapters from THE MARITIME HISTORY *that the public liked best.*

Oh! Susannah, darling, take your ease,
For we have beat the clipper fleet —
The Sovereign of the Seas.

THUS ROARED in lusty chorus 100 seamen on the Boston clipper ship *Sovereign of the Seas*, as she sailed through the Golden Gate, on November 15, 1852. Before her, behind a hedge of spars and rigging, swarmed a hill of human ants, building a great city where ten years before the only signs of human life were a mission village and a Boston hide-drogher. The refrain of that old popular song, the anthem of the Argonauts, resounds through the clipper ship era of maritime Massachusetts.

Imagine a Yankee Rip Van Winkle who had slept out his twenty years within hailing distance of the State House dome. As he looked about him in 1853 the most astonishing sight would be — not the railroad, not the telegraph, not the steamship — but the clipper ship. During the last half of his sleep there had taken place the greatest revolution in naval architecture since the days of Hawkins and Drake. Below, in Boston Harbor and setting sail for a port whose name he had never heard, were vessels four and five times as large as any he had ever seen, with canvas five and six times the utmost area that the old Boston East Indiamen dared spread to the lightest air.

Now, before we relate this revolution, a paragraph of definitions. A *ship*, as old-time sailors use the word, meant a full-rigged ship, a three-masted vessel with square sails on all three masts. A *clipper ship*, as distinguished from other ships, was built and rigged with a view to speed, rather than carrying capacity or economy. Although larger, in general, than the older sailing vessels, it was the model and the rig of clipper ships that made them such, not their size. They were sharper in the ends, longer in proportion to their breadth, and more heavily sparred than the full-bodied, bluff-bowed ships of previous, and even later, generations. For the clipper ship came all at once, and fled as quickly as she came. There had been clipper *schooners* and clipper *brigs* since 1812, the term "clipper" connoting speed and smartness; but only six or eight clipper *ships* had been built before 1850. Then were brought forth, like so many Cythereas arising from the sea, the fairest vessels that ever sailed, to meet a special need — speed to California at any price or risk.

About 1840 the rate of increase in the American merchant marine began to accelerate. The basic cause was the ability of American shipbuilders and ship-owners to keep pace with the growing wealth, prosperity, and population of America. In 1849 Parliament repealed the Navigation Acts, thereby throwing open the British market to the products of New England shipyards. At the same time, the China trade was prospering; and competition, among the ships of Russell & Co., the New York firms, and the great British houses, to market the new teas stimulated shipbuilders.

These conditions created a demand for more ships, speedier ships, and bigger ships. Samuel Hall, of East Boston, built for the Forbes's China fleet in 1839 an unusually fast ship, *Akbar*, 650 tons, the last word of the Medford type of 1830. New York builders knew how to construct the larger vessels through their experience with the North Atlantic packets; but the merchants wanted something more than size. Baltimore builders had the reputation for speed, through their clipper schooners and brigs of the long, low, rakish type beloved by slavers, pirates, and novelists. Samuel Hall had successfully copied or adapted their lines for pilot schooners, fishing schooners, and small opium clippers. But the Baltimore clipper model was as unsuitable for a vessel of 1000 tons as would be a cat-boat model for a fishing schooner. For centuries, shipbuilders had maintained that you could have either speed or burthen, not both; but New York and Boston wanted both, and they got it.

Although Boston carried the clipper ship to its ultimate perfection, New York invented the type. John W. Griffeths, chief draftsman of Smith & Dimon, produced in 1845 *Rainbow*, 750 tons, the first extreme clipper ship. Her long, fine ends and cross-section like a flattened V came from the Baltimore clipper; but the concave lines of her bow above the waterline, a characteristic feature of the clipper ships, were suggested by the model of a Singapore sampan that Captain Bob Waterman brought home. After some remarkable passages to China, *Rainbow*'s model was imitated in five or six clipper ships of moderate burthen, built at New York between 1844 and 1848. As yet not a single vessel of this type had been launched from a Massachusetts yard. But the way was being prepared.

Donald McKay, born of Scots stock at Shelburne, Nova Scotia, in 1810, played about the local yards as a boy, and built a fishing boat with his brother in their early teens. Stimulated, perhaps, by a wandering Sam Slick, this youthful "blue-nose" emigrated to New York, obtained employment at the shipyard of Isaac Webb, and quickly mastered the profession. Luckily for Massachusetts, he turned eastward again at the age of thirty, when he was ready to launch out as a master builder. At first working under John Currier, Jr., a leading shipbuilder of Newburyport, he became his partner in 1841, and produced for New York order two ships that proved wonders for finish, appearance, and speed.

In 1843 Enoch Train, a Boston merchant in the South American and Baltic trades, decided that his city must have a line of Liverpool sailing packets. He doubted whether any New England yard was capable of turning one out. Meeting by chance the New York owner of Donald McKay's first ship, he heard such praise of the young master builder of Newburyport as to give him the contract for his first packet. When he saw *Joshua Bates,* this pioneer ship of his new line, glide gracefully into the Merrimac, Enoch Train recognized the genius of her builder. At his persuasion, and backed by his financial influence, McKay established a new shipyard at East Boston. There he built in rapid succession *Ocean Monarch, Daniel Webster,* and other famous packet ships for the Train Line, and (in 1846) *New World,* 1404 tons, a record in size, for a New York firm. These ships were not clippers, but they established the reputation of Donald McKay, and gave him the practice and equipment to astonish the world when another event created a demand for clipper ships of 1500 tons upward.

On January 24, 1848, a workman at Sutter's Mill, California, discovered a gold nugget in the raceway. When the news reached the Atlantic coast, it was received with incredulity, but by the end of the year, when reports were accompanied by actual nuggets, the gold fever of '49 swept through Massachusetts. Farmers mortgaged their farms, workmen downed tools, clerks left counting-rooms, and even ministers abandoned their pulpits in order to seek wealth in this land of Havilah. Few Yankee Argonauts took the usual overland trail. True to type, they chose the ocean route. But like most of the "forty-niners," many of them went organized in semicommunistic brotherhoods. How this idea originated no one seems to know. Whether Fourierism had any influence is doubtful, and *The Commu-*

nist Manifesto could hardly have inspired a movement the sole object of which was money-getting. A few companies were financed by local capitalists in return for a guaranteed percentage of the winnings, precisely as the Merchant Adventurers of Old England "grub-staked" the Pilgrim Fathers. But for the most part the gold-seekers of Massachusetts journeyed west in organized groups, each member of which was pledged to serve his fellows to the best of his particular ability, and entitled to receive an equal share in the common gold production.

These emigrant companies varied in number from 10 to 150 young men, of all trades and professions. There was the Bunker Hill Mining & Trading Company, composed of thirty mechanics from Charlestown, Cambridge, and Somerville, paying $500 each; the New Bedford Company, commanded by Rotches and Delanos; the El Dorado Association of Roxbury; the Hampshire & Holyoke Mining & Trading Company; the Sagamore & Sacramento Company of Lynn; the Cotuit Port Association; the Winnigahee Mining Company of Edgartown; the Hyannis Gold Company; the Cape Ann Pioneers; and at least a hundred and fifty others from all parts of the state.

A few of these emigrant companies followed the transcontinental route. The Overland Company, of fifty young Roxbury men, marched in gray and gold uniforms, with seven wagons, thirty-one mules, four horses, six dogs, two black servants, and four musicians. They arrived in Sacramento after intense sufferings, and heavy casualties among the mules. A few took the Panama route, but suffered great hardships crossing the Isthmus, and were charged from $200 to $600 each for passage thence to San Francisco. But the great majority took sail around the Horn. Not clipper ships; far from it! There were few companies like the exclusive North Western of Boston, composed of Adamses, Dorrs, and Whipples paying $1000 each, that could afford a crack clipper brig. Few shipowners would charter. The oldest, slowest, and most decrepit vessels were purchased, because they were cheap. Many companies, especially those recruited on Cape Cod and Nantucket, handled their own vessels. Twelve out of one company of sixteen that left the island on February 1, 1849, were whaling captains, as familiar with the route to 'Frisco as with "Marm Hackett's garden." The gold fever drained Nantucket of one quarter of its voting population in nine months. In the same period, 800 men left New Bedford for the mines. There were 150 clearances from Boston to California in 1849, 166 in 1850, and many more from the smaller ports.

The Mexican War had hardly disturbed Massachusetts; but all through '49 the Bay State presented the spectacle of a community preparing for war on a large scale. Prudent companies took two years' provision, and stories of 'Frisco lawlessness made every emigrant a walking arsenal. Beef-packing establishments, ship-biscuit bakeries, and firearm manufactories were running full blast; and the Ames plow works turned from agricultural machinery to picks and shovels. "The members of a society could be told by their slouched hats, high boots, careless attire and general appearance of reckless daring and potential wealth," wrote Dr. Octavius T. Howe. On the Sabbath preceding departure each company marched in a body to hear a farewell sermon (Genesis 2:12 being the favorite text), and to receive one or more Bibles each from sympathetic and envious neighbors. Most companies took care to admit only men of good character, and their by-laws usually contain prohibitions of drunkenness, gambling, and swearing, which, like all their regulations, were well enough observed until they reached California. The Boston *Journal* published a special California edition for circulation on the coast.

When the Salem barque *Eliza* cast off from Derby Wharf for California, late in '48, one of the passengers sang the following words to the popular tune of "Oh! Susannah":

> I came from Salem City,
>   With my washbowl on my knee,
> I'm going to California,
>   The gold dust for to see.
> It rained all night the day I left,
>   The weather it was dry,
> The sun so hot I froze to death,
>   Oh! brothers, don't you cry.
>   *Oh! California,*
>   *That's the land for me!*
>   *I'm going to Sacramento*
>   *With my washbowl on my knee.*
>
> I jumped aboard the 'Liza ship,
>   And traveled on the sea,

And every time I thought of home
I wished it was n't me!
Oh! California,
That's the land for me!
I'm off for Californi-a
With my washbowl on my knee.

This song in countless versions, but with the same washbowl chorus, became the anthem of the forty-niners.

Deep-sea sailormen have always insisted that the discipline and safety of a ship can be maintained only by despotic power in the master. But democracy ruled on the forty-niner vessels. Each company, although composed in good part of master mariners, was a miniature soviet. The captain was elected, and sometimes deposed, by majority vote; and the same method determined ports of call and whether the Strait of Magellan or the Cape Horn was chosen. One night off the River Plate on the little schooner *Roanoke,* belonging to the Boston Marine Mining Company, all the watch were below playing whist with the skipper, except a man at the wheel and another on the lookout. The latter, seeing a squall approach, called repeatedly to his captain to send up the watch, but the game was too interesting to interrupt. Finally he sang out, "Say, Captain, if you don't send that watch up to take in the flying jib, you can take it in yourself, I'll be damned if *I'm* going to get wet!"

In spite of these soviet methods (or because of them, some will say) it seems that every one of these small and often superannuated vessels arrived safely at San Francisco. But ship fever (typhus) took a heavy toll of their passengers, on the five- to eight-month voyage.

On arrival, each member's part was provided in the by-laws. Some were to stick to the ship, guard the stores, or cook; the majority wash for gold; but all share alike what the mining members produced. What actually happened is well told in a doggerel poem by Isaac W. Baker, in his manuscript "Journal of Proceedings on board the barque *San Francisco,* of and from Beverly for California":

The San Francisco Company, of which I've often told,
At Sacramento has arrived in search of glittering gold,
The bark hauled in, the cargo out, and that is not the worst
The Company, like all the rest, have had a talk and burst.
For 'twas, talk, talk, growl, growl, talk, talk away,
The devil's a bit of comfort here in Californi-a.

While on the passage all was well, and every thing was nice,
And if there was a civil growl, 't was settled in a trice,
But here example had been set by companies before,
Who'd all dissolved and nothing less, so we did nothing more.
   But talk, talk, etc.

Now carpenters can take a job and work for what they please,
And those who do not like to work can loaf and take their ease
And squads can form for travelling, or any thing they choose,
And if they don't a fortune make, they'll not have it to lose.
   And can chat, chat, sing, sing, chat, chat away,
   And take all comfort that they can in Californi-a.

Within three weeks of landing on California soil, every emigrant company dissolved into its separate, individual elements. For a treasure-seeking enterprise like that of '49, in a setting of pioneer individualism, communism was about as well suited as to the New York Stock Exchange or the Supreme Council of the League of Nations.

The Massachusetts forty-niners did not go to California to settle. The average man's intention was to make his pile and return home rich. A few did come back to dazzle the natives, and a few became California millionaires; but the greater part went broke. It was not the miners who made the big money in 1849–50, but the men who exploited the miners.

Of the many stories of fortunes lost and won by emigrating Yankees, that of Dr. Samuel Merritt, of Plymouth, is typical. Liquidating his property, he purchased a brig and loaded her with merchandise and passengers. At the last moment he decided to invest in tacks for the California market, and started on horseback for the Duxbury tack factory. On the way he was overtaken by a messenger, who recalled him to attend an accident, immediately after which he had to sail, without the tacks. They were selling for five dollars a paper at San Francisco when he arrived. At Valparaiso, on the way, he missed another fortune by failing to fill up a hole in the cargo with potatoes, of which the San Francisco market was totally denuded. But the bottom had fallen out of the market for every other article in his cargo. However, within a year, his medical practice at San Francisco brought him $40,000.

Hoping to become the Frederic Tudor of the coast, Dr. Merritt chartered a Maine brig to load ice at Puget Sound and bring it to San

Francisco in time for summer. His captain discovered that Puget Sound was not Maine, but returned with a load of piles in lieu of ice. Piles happened to be much wanted then for wharves, and the venture proved profitable, as did a second of the same nature. Vessels began to flock northward for piles, so the doctor wisely decided he had had the cream and would let them take the skim milk. He directed his shipmaster to take Puget Sound timber to Australia, to exchange for coal. Again the captain used good judgment. Instead of coal, he returned with a load of oranges from the Society Islands, and made another killing. Dr. Merritt then closed his office, purchased a large tract of land across the bay, created the city of Oakland, and in due course became a multimillionaire, mayor of the city, and owner of the finest yacht on the coast.

A stranger fate was that of John Higgins, of Brewster, a forty-niner who never reached California. Working his way out on a steamer, he was wrecked on the Australian coast, shipped as second mate on a brig, was shipwrecked again, and drifted to the Wellington Islands, where the natives received him with open arms. He married the chief's daughter, established a trading business with the whalers, and left two sons to continue his work of civilization, which even the missionaries acknowledged to be more successful than any black-coated brother possibly could have done.

Many Massachusetts shipowners sent their vessels with full cargoes to San Francisco in time to obtain the prices of '49, which seem fabulous even today — $44 a barrel for flour, $16 a bushel for potatoes, $10 a dozen for eggs that had been around the Horn, 1000 percent profit on lumber. Freights rose to such figures that the ship *Argonaut*, built at Medford in 1849 for John E. Lodge, paid for herself before casting off her lines for her maiden voyage. When reports of these prices reached the merchant-shipowners, they rushed cargoes of every sort and description around the Horn, until in 1851 the market became glutted and unopened cases of dry goods were used for sidewalks in the muddy streets of San Francisco. Between June 26 and July 28, 1850, there entered the Golden Gate seventeen vessels from New York and sixteen from Boston, whose average passage was 159 days. Yet on July 24 there arrived at San Francisco the little New York clipper ship *Sea Witch*, just ninety-seven days out. Every mercantile agency in San Francisco began clamoring for goods to be shipped by clipper, and the shipyards responded to their demand.

5

The Clipper Ship, 1850–1854

From THE MARITIME HISTORY OF MASSACHUSETTS (Boston: Houghton Mifflin, 1921).

THE GOLDEN SANDS of California were a quickening force to the shipyards of Massachusetts. For four years they teemed with the noblest fleet of sailing vessels that man has ever seen or is likely to see.

Massachusetts launched her first clipper ships in 1850, from the yard of Samuel Hall; *Surprise* (1261 tons) for the Salem Lows, then of New York; and *Game-Cock* (1392 tons) for Daniel C. Bacon, of Boston.

Samuel Hall, now fifty years old, was the most eminent shipbuilder in the commonwealth. Of an old Marshfield family, he served his apprenticeship on the North River, and at his majority left for Medford with a capital consisting of a broad-ax and twenty-five cents. After pursuing his trade on the Mystic, the Penobscot, and at Duxbury, he became, as we have seen, the pioneer master builder of East Boston. *Game-Cock* and *Surprise* were designed by a twenty-three-year-old Bostonian named Samuel H. Pook,* the first independent architect of merchant vessels in New England.

Well did Sam Hall choose the name of his first clipper ship. One surprise of her launching was a banquet, not for owners and bankers and all bumbledom, but for the mothers, wives, and sweethearts of the workingmen who built the ship. The next sensation came when she was launched fully rigged, with her gear rove off, all three skysail yards crossed, and colors flying. Waterfront pessimists expected her

---

* Samuel Hartt Pook (1827–1901) designed three of the eighteen California clippers that made a voyage of less than 100 days from an Atlantic port to San Francisco before 1861 — the *Surprise*, *Witchcraft*, and *Herald of the Morning*; and the *Northern Light*, which has the record from San Francisco to Boston. An early advocate of ironclads, he became, like his father, Samuel Moore Pook (1804–1878), a naval constructor, USN, and remained in the service until 1889.

to capsize with such heavy top-hamper. Others said she would slide into the harbor mud and stick there. But with half Boston cheering, and the bells of every church and meetinghouse jangling out a welcome, *Surprise* clave the water with her sharp stern, shot out into the harbor, swayed gently to get her balance, and paused, erect, with the air of a young and insolent queen.

She was the first clipper ship commanded by Philip Dumaresq. He came of a long line of merchant-captains. His mother belonged to the Gardiner-Hallowell family, and Philip was born on one of their great Kennebec estates in 1809. But like his only peers on clipper quarterdecks, Captains "Bully" Waterman, of New York, "Nat" Palmer, of Stonington, and "Perk" Cressy, of Marblehead, Captain Dumaresq had followed the sea since his teens, and worked his way aft from before the mast. At twenty-two he received his first command, and in Russell & Co.'s China fleet became noted for his expert navigation, for quiet, effective discipline, and for getting the utmost speed out of a vessel. *Surprise,* under Captain Dumaresq, again fulfilled the promise of her name. On her maiden voyage she knocked a day off *Sea Witch's* record to San Francisco, which conservatives had ascribed to Waterman's luck. But the new mark of ninety-six days did not last long.

On a bitterly cold December afternoon in 1850, Donald McKay launched *Stag-Hound,* his first clipper. Pioneer of a new 1500-ton class, *Stag-Hound* both by her appearance and her performance* placed Donald McKay at the head of his profession. Before many months passed, the head of the New York firm of Grinnell, Minturn & Co. visited McKay's yard, and took a fancy to a ship that was being built for Enoch Train. He offered double the contract price to the owner, who could not afford to refuse. It was a good bargain for Grinnell, Minturn; for this was *Flying Cloud.*

McKay built faster clippers and larger clippers; but for perfection and beauty of design, weatherliness and consistent speed under every condition, neither he nor any one else surpassed *Flying Cloud.* She was the fastest vessel on long voyages that ever sailed under the American flag.

---

* The *Stag-Hound* (209′ × 39′ 8″ × 21′, 1534 tons) holds the record of thirteen days from Boston Light to the equator, no other ship having come within three days of it, whether from Boston or Sandy Hook. She has second-best record, eight days, twenty hours, from San Francisco to Honolulu.

Her dimensions were 229 feet length on deck, 40 feet 8 inches breadth, and 21 feet 6 inches depth; registered tonnage 1783. Her figurehead was a winged angel blowing a trumpet just under the bowsprit. Captain Josiah Perkins Cressy, of Marblehead, thirty-seven years old but fourteen years a shipmaster, was her commander. On her maiden voyage in the summer of 1851, *Flying Cloud* made a day's run of 374 miles, logged 1256 miles in four consecutive days, and arrived at San Francisco eighty-nine days out of New York. This run was only twice equaled, by herself in 1854, and by *Andrew Jackson* in 1860. On her return passage, having crossed the Pacific to Canton for a cargo of tea, *Flying Cloud* made the 2000 miles from that port to Java Head in six days, almost halving the previous record. In addition, she had the best average for three, four, and five voyages from an Atlantic port to San Francisco.

Donald McKay was an unusual combination of artist and scientist, of idealist and practical man of business. With dark hair curling back from a high, intellectual forehead, powerful Roman nose, inscrutable brown eyes, and firm lips, he was as fair to look upon as his ships. His serene and beautiful character won him the respect and the affection of his employees, and made the atmosphere of his shipbuilding yard that of a happy, loyal family. His ships were alive to him, and when permitted to name them himself by a wise owner, he invariably chose something fitting and beautiful. *Stag-Hound* and *Mastiff* for two powerful, determined clippers that could grapple with every element but fire; *Flying Cloud* — her rivals knew what that meant, when she tore by them at sea; *Flying Fish* and *Westward Ho!* — both of the California fleet; *Romance of the Seas* for a ship whose sleek, slender beauty reminded the old salts of their youthful visits to Nukahiva; *Sovereign of the Seas* for a stately clipper that made a marvelous record against head winds and hurricanes; *Great Republic* for the ship of ships; *Lightning* for the fastest sailing vessel every built; and *Glory of the Seas* for his last, and in some respects his best, creation.

Experience, character, and mathematics self-taught were the firm soil from which the genius of Donald McKay blossomed. He designed every vessel built in his yard, and personally attended to every detail of her construction.

> . . . First with nicest skill and art,
> Perfect and finished in every part,

A little model the Master wrought,
Which should be to the larger plan
What the child is to the man,
Its counterpart in miniature.

From the model the lines were taken off, enlarged to their proper dimensions, and laid down in the mold-loft. When the great frames were in place, Donald McKay would inspect the ship's skeleton from every angle, clothing it in imagination with skin of oak; and if anything looked wrong by perhaps an eighth of an inch, he chalked a frame for shaving off or filling out. By such methods were designed these great clipper ships that moved faster through the water, laden down as they were with heavy cargoes, than any sailing yacht or fancy racing machine designed by the scientific architects of today.* Eight knots an hour is considered good speed for an America's Cup race of thirty miles. *Red Jacket* logged an average of 14.7 for six consecutive days in the Western Ocean; *Lightning* did 15.5 for ten days, covering 3722 miles, and averaged 11 for an entire passage from Australia to England. A speed of 12.5 knots on a broad reach in smooth waters, by *Resolute* or *Shamrock*, excites the yachting reporters. *Lightning* logged 18.2 for twenty-four hours in 1854, and *James Baines*, on an Australian voyage in 1856, attained a speed of 21 knots.

The records show conclusively Donald McKay's supremacy over any other builder, and the supremacy of Massachusetts builders over those of any other state. Only twenty-two passages from an Atlantic port around Cape Horn to San Francisco, in less than 100 days, are on record. Of these, seven were made by McKay ships — *Flying Cloud* and *Flying Fish*, two each; *Great Republic, Romance of the Seas*, and *Glory of the Seas*, one each. Only two other builders, Samuel Hall, of Boston, with *John Gilpin* and *Surprise*, and Westervelt, of New York, have even two voyages in this honor list. Including *Witchcraft*, built by Paul Curtis at Chelsea, and *Herald of the Morning*, built by Hayden & Cudworth at Medford, we have one half of these record voyages over the longest race course in the world, to

---

* No disparagement of modern naval architects is intended; they have progressed far beyond the designs of the 1850's in fishing schooners and yachts. Yet, I was informed by one of the most eminent among them, no one today could make an essential improvement over the McKay clippers for a sailing ship of their size.

the credit of Massachusetts-built vessels. Of the rest, four belong to the other New England states, and seven to New York.*

There were a dozen or more Massachusetts builders besides Donald McKay and Samuel Hall who built clipper ships that were a credit to the commonwealth. Edwin and Harrison O. Briggs, of South Boston, grandsons of the North River builder of *Columbia*, specialized in medium clipper ships, a class somewhat underbred in appearance compared with *Flying Cloud* and *Surprise*, but with carefully designed waterlines and small displacement, which often produced remarkable speed. Their *Northern Light* (1021 tons), under the command of Captain Hatch, completed a round voyage from Boston to San Francisco in exactly seven months. On the homeward passage, off Cape Horn, she passed the New York clipper ship *Contest*, which had sailed a day earlier; and with skysails, ringtail, and studdingsails set on both sides, alow and aloft, she slipped into the Narrows of Boston Harbor on the evening of May 27, 1853, just seventy-six days, five hours, from San Francisco. That record remains good to this day.†

Other bright lights of Briggs Brothers were *Boston Light, Starlight,* and the ill-fated *Golden Light,* which, ten days out on her first voyage, was set afire by lightning and abandoned at sea.

Robert E. Jackson, of East Boston, built *Winged Racer, John Bertram, Blue Jacket,* and *Queen of Clippers* (2360 tons), "one of the finest and largest of these ships," wrote Frank Marryat, the English traveler, from San Francisco. "She is extremely sharp at either end, and, 'bows on,' she has the appearance of a wedge. Her accommodations are as perfect as those of a first-class ocean steamer, and are as handsomely decorated; and, as it is worthy of remark that great atten-

---

* The list of all California outward passages between 1850 and 1861 made in 110 days or better (in Captain Clark's *Clipper Ship Era,* Appendix II) gives the same result. Nineteen are by McKay ships. His nearest competitor, Webb, of New York, has fifteen. All the other Boston builders together have twenty-two, all the other New York builders, twenty-three. Medford builders have seventeen; other Massachusetts builders, seven. Yet out of 171 California clipper ships and barques listed by Captain Clark, McKay built only ten; Samuel Hall and Briggs Brothers, of Boston, and Webb, of New York, each built eleven. In addition, McKay built the great Australian clippers, which do not figure in this list, and which no builder, American or foreign, equaled.

† In San Francisco voyages, the homeward passage was much easier than the outward owing to prevailing westerly winds. Consequently, the outward passage is always selected as a test of a vessel's performance, and *Northern Light*'s feat by no means equals *Flying Cloud*'s record of eighty-nine days to San Francisco. But she made Manila in eighty-nine days from Boston in 1856.

tion has been paid to the comfort of the crew." Paul Curtis's *Witch-craft* was a fast and handsome clipper, with a grim Salem witch for her figurehead. Medford builders like J. O. Curtis, Hayden & Cudworth, and S. Lapham have more fast California passages to their credit, considering the number they built, than those of any other place. Several smaller clipper ships were built by the Shivericks, at East Dennis; by J. M. Hood & Co., at Somerset; and by the experienced builders of Newburyport, who surpassed all others for careful work and finish. *Dreadnought* (1400 tons), built by Currier and Townsend, became the most famous Liverpool packet ship, and was the only clipper to have a chantey composed in her special honor. Captain Samuel Samuels, of New York, unexcelled as a driver of men and vessels, commanded this "saucy, wild packet" for almost seventy passages across the Atlantic, in which she made several eastward runs under fourteen days.*

One finds many new names in the list of Massachusetts owners of clipper ships. Their great initial cost and maintenance expense brought about a separation of shipowner and merchant. The clippers were really large packet ships, whose owners depended for profit on freight and passage money, not on speculative cargoes of their own. And profit they certainly did make, in the flush days of 1850–53, for the glut of 1851 at San Francisco did not last long. Freight ranged as high as $60 per ton, and it was an unlucky ship that did not pay for herself by her first round voyage to California. *Surprise* did so, and made $50,000, to boot.

Many of the most famous Massachusetts-built clippers were owned by New York or British firms, and never saw Boston after their first departure. Others, owned by Boston or Salem firms, were operated out of New York. But there were still a goodly number that plied regularly from Boston to San Francisco, and then crossed the Pacific to bring tea, hemp, and sugar to England and America. Several clip-

---

* Captain Clark (*Clipper Ship Era*, 246), by printing her actual log as given in three Liverpool papers, has definitely exploded the myth of *Dreadnought*'s nine-day, seventeen-hour passage from Sandy Hook to Queenstown in March 1859, which Captain Samuels never claimed until the twentieth century. For evidence on the other side of this famous controversy, see F. B. C. Bradlee, *The Dreadnought* (ed., 1920). Mr. Bradlee has discovered a second "nine-day passage" in the *Illustrated London News*, July 9, 1859, which states that *Dreadnought* "arrived off Cape Clear on the 27th ult., in nine days from New York." But the New York *Herald* of June 17, p. 8e, reported by telegraph from "Sandy Hook, June 16, sunset . . . the ship Dreadnaught, for Liverpool, passed the bar at 12½ P.M. Wind SW, light." On July 19, p. 8c, it reported her arrival at Liverpool on July 2.

per ships were owned on shares, like the old-timers, but operated by regular packet lines. Such a one was *Wild Ranger* (1044 tons), built by J. O. Curtis at Medford in 1853 for various Searses and Thachers of Cape Cod, and commanded on two California voyages by one of their number, twenty-four-year-old J. Henry Sears, of Brewster.

In May 1853, an intending passenger for San Francisco, perusing the shipping columns of the Boston *Daily Advertiser*, would be embarrassed to make a choice. Winsor's Regular Line offers the "first-class clipper ships" *Belle of the West* and *Bonita*, and the "half-clipper barque" *Cochituate*. Timothy Davis & Co.'s Line advertises the "half clipper ship *Sabine*" and the "new and beautiful clipper ship *Juniper*."* Glidden & Williams makes the bravest display with the "magnificent first-class clipper ship *White Swallow*," to be followed by *Wild Ranger* and *John Bertram;* the "new and beautiful half clipper ship *West Wind*" and the "first-class and well-known packet-ship *Western Star*." This was the greatest of the Boston firms operating clipper ships. Its San Francisco line also contained, at one time or another, *Witch of the Wave, Golden West, Queen of the Seas, Westward Ho!, Morning Light,* and *Sierra Nevada*. Sampson & Tappan owned the *Flying Fish, Winged Racer,* and *Nightingale*, a supremely beautiful extreme clipper built in Portsmouth, New Hampshire, and named for Jenny Lind. George Bruce Upton owned *Stag-Hound, Reindeer, Bald Eagle,* and *Romance of the Seas*. James Huckins & Sons had most of the Briggs Brothers' "Lights." Baker & Morrill owned *Starlight* and *Southern Cross;* and John E. Lodge (father of Senator Henry Cabot Lodge), *Argonaut, Don Quixote,* and *Storm King;* William Lincoln & Co., *Golden Eagle, Kingfisher,* and *White Swallow;* Curtis & Peabody, *Meteor, Cyclone, Saracen,* and *Mameluke*. *Fearless, Galatea,* and two named *Golden Fleece* carried the black racehorse flag of William F. Weld & Co., a house that outlasted most of the merchant-shipowners of Boston, and after the Civil War owned the largest sailing fleet in America.

Two famous Boston firms of Cape Cod origin were Howes & Crowell, which owned *Climax, Ringleader,* and *Robin Hood,* and

---

* One will search in vain for several of these "clippers" in authoritative lists like Captain Clark's and Dr. O. T. Howe's , for when the clipper ships became popular, every new vessel of a certain size was advertised at least as "half-clipper." A rigid distinction is made in the early American Lloyds' Registers between clipper ships and sharp ships, medium ships and full-bodied ships, only the extremest of clippers falling in the first class.

D. G. & W. B. Bacon, which owned *Game-Cock*, *Hoogly*, and *Oriental*. Daniel C. Bacon was a link between the Federalist and the clipper periods, having been mate under William Sturgis in the old Northwest fur trade. In 1852 he was elected president of the American Navigation Club, an association of Boston shipowners and merchants, which offered to back an American against a British clipper for a race from England to China and back, £10,000 a side. Although the stakes were subsequently doubled, no acceptance was received.

There was no veneer or sham about the beauty of the Massachusetts clippers. They were all well and solidly built of the best oak, southern pine, and hackmatack, copper-fastened and sheathed with Taunton yellow metal. Scamping or skimping never occurred to a clipper ship builder, and if it had, no Yankee workman would have stayed in his yard. In finish the clipper ships surpassed anything previously attempted in marine art. Those built in Newburyport, in particular, were noted for the evenness of their seams and the perfection of their joiner-work. The topsides, planed and sandpapered smooth as a mackerel, were painted a dull black that brought out their lines like a black velvet dress on a beautiful woman. The pine decks were holystoned cream-white. Stanchions, fife-rails, and houses shone with mahogany, rosewood, and brass. Many had sumptuous staterooms, cabins, and bathrooms for passengers that put the old-time stuffy Cunarders to shame. *Mastiff* had a library costing $1200. Constant improvements were made in gear and rigging. Patent blocks, trusses, and steering gear saved time and labor. The Howes' double-topsail rig (an improvement on Captain R. B. Forbes's invention) was generally adopted by the later clippers, spread to the ships of all nations, and is still in use. No detail was omitted that might increase speed, and no expense spared to make the Massachusetts clippers invulnerable to the most critical nautical eye.

Boston Harbor never presented a more animated spectacle than during the clipper ship era. One April day in 1854, wrote F. O. Dabney, no fewer than six large new clippers, undergoing the process of rigging, could be seen from his counting-room windows on Central Wharf. Across the harbor, the East Boston shore from Jeffries' Point to Chelsea Bridge was almost a continuous line of vessels in various stages of construction. Twenty ships of 1100 tons upward were built there that year.

*

The men who handled these great vessels were a class by themselves. The officers, mostly of New England stock and many from Cape Cod, had followed the sea since boyhood, and were steeped in experience. No others could be trusted to drive these saucy, wild clippers against Cape Horn howlers, when the slightest misjudgment meant the loss of a spar, or loss of one hour — which was more important. They were devoted to the rigid traditions of the quarterdeck. The captain gave all his orders through the first officer, except for putting the ship about; and lived in a more dignified seclusion than the colonel of a regiment in a frontier garrison. No one spoke to him unless spoken to; the weather side of the quarterdeck was his private walk; whole voyages passed without a scrap of conversation between master and officers, except in line of duty. Men at the head of the profession, like Captain Dumaresq, were paid $3000 for an outward passage to San Francisco, and $5000 if they made it in under a hundred days.

Occasionally, clipper ship commanders took their wives with them. Mrs. Cressy was the constant companion of her husband on *Flying Cloud.* The wife of Captain Charles H. Brown gave birth to a son during a North Pacific gale, when *Black Prince* was flying under close-reefed topsails. Immediately after, a heavy sea burst in the after cabin deadlight, shooting clear over the box in which the newborn babe was lying. But most remarkable of these brave women of the sea was Mrs. Captain Patten, of *Neptune's Car.* In the midst of a Cape Horn gale, Captain Patten came down with brain fever. The first mate was in irons for insubordination; the second mate was ignorant of navigation. But Mrs. Patten had made herself mistress of the art during a previous voyage. Without question, she took command. For fifty-two days this frail little Boston woman of *nineteen years* navigated a great clipper of 1800 tons, tending her husband the while; and took both safely into San Francisco.

The clipper ships were built by Yankee workmen, but they were not manned by Americans. The Yankee mariner, with his neat clothes and perfect seamanship, had passed into history by 1850. Few Americans could then be found in the forecastles of merchantmen on deep waters. When did this change take place? Why did New Englanders abandon the sea?

In part, no doubt, it was a question of status. The seaman was not

as free as other workmen. His personal liberty was suspended until
the end of the voyage. Discipline was more severe, brutality more
common, and redress more difficult to obtain than in other callings.
Laws forbidding such practices as flogging, and humane judges such
as Peleg Sprague, of the District Court at Boston, could do little to
alter the tradition of centuries. In one of his notable decisions,*
Judge Sprague remarked:

> Seamen, in general, have little confidence in the justice of those whom
> circumstances have placed above them, and there is too much ground for
> this feeling. If a seaman is wronged by a subordinate officer, and makes a
> complaint to the master, it too often happens that he not only can obtain no
> hearing or redress, but brings upon himself further and greater ill treatment;
> and an appeal to an American consul against a master is oftentimes no more
> successful, preoccupied, as that officer is likely to be, by the representations
> and influence of the master. Upon his return home, he finds those whom he
> has served, the owners of the ship, generally take part, at once, with the of-
> ficer, in every controversy with the seamen, and not infrequently exerting
> themselves to intercept that justice which the law would give him. And if to
> all this be added peculiar severity, even by the law of his country . . . he
> may well be excused for feeling little confidence in the justice of superior
> powers. This feeling enters into his character, adds to his recklessness,
> weakens the ties that bind him to his country, and tends to make him a
> vagrant citizen of the world.

Our clipper ships were, in fact, manned by an international proletariat of the sea, vagrants with an attitude curiously similar to that of the
casual workers in the West today.

Low wages, even more than low status, were responsible for this
condition. In Federalist days an able seaman received $18 a month
on Pacific voyages, and even more in neutral trading. In comparison
with shore wages, and in lack of other opportunities, this was sufficient to attract Yankee youngsters to sea, though not to keep them
there. During the slack period that followed the War of 1812, $12
became the standard wage. An increase of tonnage in the thirties
required more seamen. Instead of raising wages, to compete with
the machine shops and railroads and Western pioneering that were
attracting young Yankees, the shipowners maintained or even depressed them, until ordinary and able seamen on California clippers

* *Swain* v. *Howland* (1858), 1 Sprague, 427.

received from $8 to $12 a month.*   In the New Orleans cotton trade and other lines of commerce out of Boston, as high as $18 was paid for able seamen, and the Liverpool "packet rats" got even more for their short and stormy runs.   But in a period of rising costs and wages, the seaman's wage remained stationary, or declined.   He had "no Sunday off soundings," and his calling was the most dangerous in the world. It took strength, skill, and courage to furl topsails on a great clipper ship, with its masts and 80-foot yards bending like whalebone in a River Plate *pampero*, great blocks beating about like flails, and the No. O. Lowell duck sails slatting with enough force to crush a man's ribs.

Americans would not willingly accept such wages for such work. Coasting vessels, paying $18 a month, absorbed the Yankee boys with a craving for the sea.   The shipowners could have obtained American crews had they been willing to pay for them; but they were not.   Like the factory owners, they preferred cheap foreign labor.

A law of 1817 required two thirds of an American crew to be American citizens.   But this law was disregarded, as soon as it became the shipowners' interest to do so; and by the clipper period it was a dead letter.   Captain Clark once had a Chinese cook who shipped as "George Harrison of Charlestown, Mass."   When applicants for foremast berths became fewer, the shipowner had recourse to shipping agencies, which turned to the sailors' boarding-house keepers, making it their interest to rob and drug seamen in order to sign them on, and pocket their three months' advance wages.   Thus began the system of crimping, or shanghaiing.   The percentage of foreigners and incompetents increased.   Men of all nations,† and of the most depraved and criminal classes, some of them sailors, but many not, were hoisted, literally dead to the world, aboard the clippers.   Habitual drunkards formed the only considerable native element in this human hash.   "It is perfectly well known that sailors do get intoxicated," said Judge Sprague, when a pious captain discharged a seaman

---

* Yet in 1856 Boston ship carpenters and caulkers received $3 for a 6¾-hour day; longshoremen, $2 per tide; stevedores, twenty-five cents per hour.

† A sample crew is that of the ship *Reindeer*, Canton to Boston: two Frenchmen, one Portuguese, one Cape Verde Islander, one Azores man, one Italian, one Dutchman, one mulatto, two Kanakas, one Welshman, one Swede, two Chinese, and two Americans (Boston *Atlas*, July 22, 1851). *Black Prince* even had foreign officers.   Captain Brown was a Portuguese by birth; the chief mate was Danish, the second mate British, the third mate German, and out of twenty-four able seamen there were but two Americans; one from Newburyport and one from Boston.

for a drunken frolic. "Masters hire them with this knowledge . . . owners get their services at a less price for these very habits; year after year they serve at a mere pittance because of them." Many a landsman, as well, imbibed too much liquor on the Boston waterfront, and awoke in the forecastle of a clipper ship bound round the world.

Whenever a Yankee boy had the nerve to go to sea under these conditions, and the pluck to stick it out in such company, he was assured of quick promotion. Arthur H. Clark, the historian of the clipper ship era, was the son of a Boston Mediterranean merchant and yachtsman. Instead of going to Harvard, he went to sea before the mast in the clipper ship *Black Prince*, returned around the globe, over two years later, as her third mate, and then shipped as second mate of *Northern Light*. A few more voyages, and he became a shipmaster. Henry Jackson Sargent, Jr., of the Gloucester family that produced eminent writers and artists, shipped before the mast at the age of seventeen on Donald McKay's *Flying Fish* (1506 tons), the only ship except *Flying Cloud* that made two California voyages under 100 days. Within a few years he was not only the youngest, but one of the most accomplished clipper ship commanders. The Medford-built clipper *Phantom*, under his command but through no fault of his own, ran onto the Prates Shoal in thick, heavy weather on July 12, 1862. All hands were saved in the boats, although not all escaped a plundering by Chinese pirates. Obtaining another command in China, at the age of twenty-nine, Captain Sargent sailed from Shanghai, and was never heard from again. To this day, the Pacific holds the secret of his fate and that of his vessel.

If a mate found one or two boys such as these beside the twoscore drugged and drunken bums, loafers, and rare seamen of all nations and colors delivered him by the crimp, he thanked his stars for it, and gave them separate quarters. For this system did not even deliver sailors, except by accident. Of his crew in *Flying Cloud*'s race with the *N. B. Palmer*, Captain Cressy said: "They worked like one man, and that man a hero." But in every crew shipped under the shanghai method there were bound to be men fit only "to keep the bread from moulding." Resenting their involuntary servitude, many did their best to "soger"; to be "yardarm furlers" and "buntline reefers" — in other words, malingerers. Others watched their chance to start a mutiny; and yet others, who tried to do their duty, seemed shirkers because of their ignorance of English. Hence the brutality for which Yankee mates and masters became notorious. There were clipper ships like *Northern Light,* where no hand was ever raised against the men, but aboard most of them, after Congress forbade sailors to be "triced up" and "introduced to the gunner's daughter," or cat-o'-nine-tails, discipline was kept only by heavy and full portions of "belaying-pin soup" and "handspike hash."

As the men were usually stripped of all they had by the crimps, they were forced to buy clothing on board from the slop chest; and as the crimp had pocketed their three months' advance wages, they usually ended the voyage destitute or in debt. Then began another segment of the vicious circle, Jack pawning his body for food, shelter, and drink, and awakening with an aching head on board another ship, outward bound.

Various were the remedies proposed. A committee of the Boston Marine Society, consisting of Boston's most respected shipowners, petitioned Congress in 1852 to restore flogging — as if the "cat" would attract Americans to sea! Captains John Codman and R. B. Forbes wanted an apprentice or schoolship system, which the same Marine Society had rejected many years before. Improvements were made in food and housing; the clipper ships had a deckhouse for their foremast hands, instead of the dark, stuffy forecastle of older vessels; and comparatively good food, with hot tea and coffee. But no one suggested the experiment of attracting Americans to sea by decent wages and freemen's status. New Englanders may have more maritime aptitude than other Americans; but they are not a maritime people like the British or Scandinavians or Greeks, content to serve a lifetime before the mast for a mere pittance. The days were long past when Massachusetts boys had to choose between farming at home and seafaring abroad. In 1850 the workshops of New England needed men, and the great West was calling.

"The California passage is the longest and most tedious within the domains of Commerce; many are the vicissitudes that attend it," wrote Lieutenant Maury. "It tries the patience of the navigator, and taxes his energies to the very utmost . . . It is a great race-course, upon which some of the most beautiful trials of speed the world ever saw have come off."

Every passage from New York or Boston to San Francisco was a race against time, on which the builder's and master's reputations depended; and there were some remarkable ship-to-ship contests of this 15,000-mile course. One of the best took place in 1854, between *Romance of the Seas* (1782 tons), Captain Dumaresq, and *David Brown* (1715 tons), Captain George Brewster. *Romance,* sailing from Boston two days after her New York rival passed Sandy Hook, caught up with her off the coast of Brazil, and kept her in sight a good part of the passage to the Golden Gate, which both entered side by side on March 23, respectively ninety-six and ninety-eight days out. After discharging, they passed out in company, set skysails and royal studdingsails, and kept them set for forty-five days, when *Romance* entered Hong Kong one hour in the lead.

As California afforded no outward lading in the early fifties, the clipper ships generally returned around the world, by way of China. There they came into competition with British vessels, and the result gave John Bull a worse shock than the yacht *America's* victory. So vastly superior was the speed of the American clippers, that British firms in Hong Kong paid them seventy-five cents per cubic foot freight on teas to London, as against twenty-eight cents to their own ships.

Crack British East Indiamen humbly awaited a cargo in the treaty ports for weeks on end, while one American clipper after another sailed proudly in, and secured a return freight almost before her topsails were furled. When the Yankee beauties arrived in the Thames, their decks were thronged with sightseers, their records were written up in the leading papers, and naval draftsman took off their lines while in drydock.

By the time the British builders were learning the first rudiments of clipper-designing, the Americans had made still further progress. As to a cathedral builder of the thirteenth century, so to Donald McKay came visions transcending human experiences, with the power to transmute them into reality. The public believed he had reached perfection with *Flying Cloud;* but in 1852 he created *Sovereign of the Seas* (2421 tons). She had the longest and sharpest ends of any vessel yet built. Her widest point was 20 feet forward of amidships, and her figurehead showed a bronze mer-king, blowing a conch shell. No merchant-shipowner, even in that era of adventure, dared order such a vessel. Her building was financed by McKay's loyal friends. But so convincing was her appearance, that immediately after launching she was sold for the record price of $150,000, almost all of which she earned in freight on her first round voyage.

Lauchlan McKay, who, thirty-four years before had helped his brother Donald build their first boat in Nova Scotia, commanded this great vessel on her maiden voyage to San Francisco. Starting in the unfavorable month of August, *Sovereign of the Seas* encountered southwest gales from the Falklands to Cape Horn. Topmasts bent like whips to the fearful snow squalls, yet nothing carried away, and the noble ship never wore or missed stays once in the long beat to windward. Around the Horn she found no better weather, and in the course of a heavy gale, owing to the main topmast trestle-trees settling, her main topmast, mizzen topgallantmast, and foretopsail yard went over the side. Luckily, the captain was an expert rigger, and had an unusually large crew. Within thirty hours he had *Sovereign* under jury rig, doing 12 knots. And in twelve days' time, by working day and night, she was almost as well rigged as when she left Boston. In spite of the mishaps she "beat the clipper fleet" that sailed with her, and entered San Francisco 103 days out of New York; the fastest passage ever made by a ship leaving the Atlantic coast in August.

On the homeward passage from Honolulu, with a cargo of oil and whalebone, a short crew, a foretopmast sprung in two places, and a tender main topmast, Captain McKay "passed through a part of the Great South Sea, which has been seldom traversed by traders." In the forties and fifties south latitude, a long, rolling swell and the northwest trade winds hurled *Sovereign of the Seas* one quarter of the distance around the world — 5391 nautical miles — in twenty-two days. One sea day (March 17–18, 1853) was memorable above all others. Sun and moon appeared only in brief glimpses. Heavy rain squalls tore down the wind, whipping to a white froth the crests of enormous seas that went roaring southward — but not much faster than their *Sovereign*. When struck by a squall she would send spray masthead high, fly up a point or two, and, heeling over, try to take her helm and shoot along a deep valley between two towering rollers. Brought to her course again, she would righten with the poise of a thoroughbred, and leap forward as if taking a fresh start. On that day *Sovereign of the Seas* made 411 nautical miles: an average of 17.7 knots, and a day's run surpassed only by *Red Jacket* and by three later creations of Donald McKay.

For the year 1853, Donald McKay made another sensation with

Great Republic.   To appreciate her size, recall that any vessel over 130 feet long and 500 tons' burthen was considered large before 1840; that *Stag-Hound*, 1534 tons, was the first sailing ship built over 200 feet long; that *Flying Cloud* was 229 feet long and registered 1793 tons, and *Sovereign of the Seas*, 258 feet and 2421 tons. *Great Republic* was 334 feet 6 inches long and registered 4556 tons. Fifty-three feet 6 inches broad and 38 feet deep, she was as sharp and shapely a clipper ship as any ever built. No vessel, before or since, has had such enormous spars and sail area. Her main yard was 120 feet long; her fore skysail yard, 40 feet. In addition to her three square-rigged masts she carried a spanker-mast with gaff-topsail and gaff-topgallant-sail. The leech- and bolt-ropes of the topsails were 8½ inches, and the fore and main standing rigging, 12½-inch four-stranded Russia hemp.

Great Republic's sails, which would have covered over one and a half acres if laid out flat, were never set. She was towed to New York, where, on the eve of her maiden voyage, she caught fire, and had to be scuttled to prevent total loss. Salvaged, razeed to 3357 tons, and under greatly reduced rig, she made a voyage of ninety-two days to San Francisco. What wonders of speed might this ship of ships have performed, as Donald McKay built and rigged her!

Great Republic had been destined for the Australian trade, whither British adventure and emigration were now tending, following a discovery of gold. *Sovereign of the Seas*, appearing in Liverpool in July 1853, was immediately chartered by James Baines & Co.'s Australian Black Ball Line, which charged £7 a ton freight in her to Melbourne, and offered to return £2 of it if she did not beat every steamer on the route. Baines kept the money. The White Star Line, not to be outdone, chartered three great clipper ships — McKay's *Chariot of Fame,* Jackson's *Blue Jacket,* and *Red Jacket,* designed by Samuel H. Pook and built by George Thomas at Rockland, Maine. On her passage from New York to Liverpool, *Red Jacket,* Asa Eldridge master, broke the record for that route, with rain, hail, or snow falling throughout the entire trip; and made a day's run of 413 nautical miles. Her first Australian voyage was so remarkable that she was purchased by her British charterers for £30,000. James Baines & Co. then went one better, and contracted with Donald McKay for four great clipper ships over 2000 tons, which he completed in the year between February 1854 and February 1855.

With this group, *Lightning,* (2084 tons), *Champion of the Seas* (2448 tons), *James Baines* (2515 tons), and *Donald McKay* (2595 tons), American wooden shipbuilding reached its apogee. *James Baines,* on her way across, made the record transatlantic passage for sailing vessels, twelve days, six hours from Boston Light to Rock Light, Liverpool. "She is so strongly built, so finely finished, and is of so beautiful a model," wrote a contemporary from Liverpool, "that even envy cannot prompt a fault against her. On all hands she has been praised as the most perfect sailing ship that ever entered the river Mersey." Her enormous rig was second only to *Great Republic*'s. In addition to three skysails, she carried skysail studdingsails and a main moonsail.

Owing to Matthew F. Maury's discoveries, vessels en route to Australia now made 48° south latitude before running their easting down, and let the brave west winds sweep them around the world. *James Baines* in 1855 went from Liverpool to Liverpool in 132 days, omitting her stay at Melbourne. No sailing vessel ever equaled this record.

Donald McKay, on her maiden voyage to Liverpool, made a day's run of 421 miles, mostly under topsails and foresail. But this record had already been surpassed by *Lightning.* Built long and low, with the most daringly fine bow ever constructed, *Lightning* looked her name. With mingled pride and regret, Boston watched her glide down the harbor, making scarce a ripple in the water as her topsails caught a light land breeze. On her maiden passage to Liverpool on March 1–2, 1854, she made the remarkable day's run of 436 miles, until recently accepted as the world's record. Later research has uncovered two better ones. *Marco Polo,* built in 1851 at St. John, New Brunswick, made a day's run of 438 miles in January 1854, when running her easting down from the Cape of Good Hope to Australia. But, if Donald McKay lost the blue ribbon to that "Queen of the Blue Noses," he won it back before the year was out. His *Champion of the Seas,* a ship that combined the stately port of a frigate with the airy grace of a yacht, on an outward passage from Liverpool to Melbourne, in the roaring forties south latitude, made 465 nautical miles, noon to noon, on December 11–12.

To realize what these records mean, remember that for almost forty years afterward no steamer could make such a day's run, and that only the fastest express steamers equaled it in the early decades of the twentieth century. No run of 400 miles has ever been made by a modern sailing yacht, though these vessels are built for speed and carry no cargo. *Lightning*, when she made her wonderful record, was laden with 2000 tons of cargo and drew 21 feet of water; the other two were less heavily laden, and *Champion*, larger than *Lightning*, was drawing four feet less than her marks, which helped. Both runs, being on easterly courses, were made in about 23½ hours elapsed time, and this means that *Lightning* logged an average of 18.1 knots and *Champion*, the amazing average of 19.78 knots. Obviously they must have hit it up to 22 or 23 knots in squalls.

6

The Passing of the Clipper

From THE MARITIME HISTORY OF MASSACHUSETTS (Boston: Houghton Mifflin, 1921).

THE CLIPPER SHIPS, costly to build and to operate for their burthen, proved prodigal ventures on routes that paid normal freights. David Snow, of Boston, tried his clipper ship *Reporter* in the Boston–New Orleans–Liverpool trade in 1853; but, as Captain Octavius Howe wrote, she was a "thousand-ton ship in capacity and a two thousand-ton ship to keep in repair." The pleasure of having the smartest vessel on that route did not compensate for losing voyages, and the *Reporter* was shifted to the California trade.

By 1854 that path of riches yielded but normal profits, and 1855 brought the end of the clipper ship era in shipbuilding; although American thoroughbreds won the sweepstakes in the world's carrying trade until the Civil War. Donald McKay, after completing his Australian Black Ball liners, wisely concluded that the limit had been reached; and the three or four clipper ships that he built in 1855–56 were of the medium class. Nevertheless the era left its impress on naval architecture. No more bluff-bowed vessels of the ancient model were built, except for whaling. A type of full-bodied ship, like McKay's *Glory of the Seas,* was evolved; fuller and beamier than the clipper ship, less boldly rigged, yet with that clean appearance, round stern, and beautiful rake to the bow that made it difficult to distinguish from the genuine clipper.

Throughout the clipper ship era, nearly all the traditional lines of Massachusetts maritime commerce continued to expand and new ones were created; cod-fishing and whaling attained their apogee, and the commercial prosperity of Boston, in 1857, reached its highwater mark for the antebellum period. The coffee trade with South America declined, owing to the establishment of steamship lines between Europe and Brazil; the Russia trade declined, as Russia's staple exports were being produced to a great extent in the United States; the China trade continued its migration to New York; but all others increased greatly, and Boston continued to hold her ancient supremacy in the East India, Smyrna, Mediterranean, and South American wool trades, and in such Russian trade as remained profitable. Her exports of ice more than doubled between 1847 and 1856, rum rose from four hundred thousand to over one million gallons, and three times as many boots and shoes left the port as ten years previously. The Boston dry goods trade with the West, the bulk of which still went by water, had doubled since 1854, and increased twentyfold over 1847. Arrivals from foreign ports at Boston increased 50 percent between 1845 and 1856, and their tonnage, 120 percent. Even Newburyport and Salem showed an increase, owing to the new Canadian trade.

The Canadian Reciprocity Treaty of 1854 was of more benefit to Massachusetts commerce than any treaty before or since, for it wiped out the artificial barrier that limited her market and source of supply to the northward and eastward. The trade was conducted almost exclusively in Canadian bottoms, which somewhat obscured its benefits, and gave that increase to the statistics of foreign sail in our ports that has been made so much of by ship subsidy pamphlets masquerading as histories of the American merchant marine. As a matter of fact, if the "Geordies" and "Johnny wood-boats," as the Yankees called the clumsy Down East schooners, had not been permitted free access to our ports, the Canadians would have made Liverpool their *entrepôt* instead of Boston, or developed their own direct export trade — as they afterward did, when the reciprocity treaty was abrogated. From Nova Scotia and New Brunswick flowed a constant and increasing stream of firewood, coal, fish, flour, provisions, grain, and dairy products to Boston and the Essex County ports, where the "blue nose" merchants made their purchases of East and West India goods, manufactures, whaling products, and hides.

Boston now had the facilities and the materials for an export trade to the newer countries, to California, Australia, and South Africa. New England manufactures, though less in value, were then much more diversified than nowadays, when lines such as beef-packing, furniture, and vehicles have been forced to move nearer the raw materials. Whatever was lacking came from other parts of the world to Boston wharves. A merchant could make up at short notice, within

half a mile of State Street, an export cargo containing the entire apparatus of civilized life, from cradles and teething rings to coffins and
tombstones. Of such nature were the outward ladings to California,
Australia, and Cape Town in the 1850's. Plows and printing presses,
picks and shovels, absinthe and rum, house frames and grindstones,
clocks and dictionaries, melodeons and cabinet organs, fancy biscuits
and canned salmon, oysters and lobsters — in fact everything one can
imagine went through Boston on its way to the miners and ranchers
of the white man's new empires. Henry W. Peabody and others
operated lines of Australian packets, which brought back wool and
hides. Benjamin S. Pray and others kept a fleet of barques plying between Boston and Cape Town, Port Elizabeth, and East London,
where fifty years before the only American trade had been a little
smuggling of East India goods on homeward passages. From South
Africa were brought wool, goatskins, ostrich feathers, and, after 1870,
diamonds. The California trade entered a new phase in 1855, when
the Somerset-built clipper barque *Greenfield* took the first consignment of grain from San Francisco, and the Newburyport-built clipper
ship *Charmer* of Boston took a full cargo of California wheat to New
York, receiving $28 a ton freight.

In September 1857 came a great financial crisis, which, unlike that
of twenty years previous, affected Boston most grievously. The East
India merchants, anticipating a stoppage of trade by the Sepoy Mutiny, had glutted the Boston market with Calcutta goods. Prices of all
sorts of merchandise fell one-quarter to one-half, and freights sunk
until it paid a shipowner to let his vessels rot.

For two years ocean freights were dull and business depressed.
The Canadian trade alone showed conspicuous progress. By 1860
conditions were getting back to normal. Of the world's fleet en route
to Australia in January of that year, thirteen ships were from Boston,
as against twelve ships and seven barques from New York, and none
from any other American port save San Francisco. The merchants,
tardily appreciating the importance of steam navigation, built four
splendid iron screw steamers over 200 feet long, for two new lines to
Charleston and New Orleans. The sailing fleet found better employment than in any year since 1857. Then came the firing on Fort
Sumter; and for four years the best energies of Massachusetts, maritime and interior, were devoted to preserving the Union.

*

Every great war has brought an upheaval in Massachusetts commerce, some for the better, but the Civil War conspicuously for the worse. Not that the Confederate cruisers were responsible. The American merchant marine had increased and prospered during the earlier wars, in spite of depredations infinitely greater than those of *Alabama* and her consorts. So prospered, of late, the British marine, despite German undersea boats. I agree with John R. Spears that the decadence of American shipping "was wholly due to natural causes — to conditions of national development . . . that were unavoidable." The Civil War merely hastened a process that had already begun, the substitution of steam for sail. It was the ostrichlike attitude of maritime Massachusetts toward this process, more than the war, by which she lost her ancient pre-eminence. Far better had the brains and energy that produced the clipper ships been put into the iron screw steamer (in the same sense that Phidias had been better employed in sanitation, and Euripides in discovering the printing press). After Appomattox, national expansion and the protective tariff killed or atrophied many lines of commerce in which Massachusetts merchants had specialized; and the transatlantic cable made merchants, in the old sense, anachronisms. Several firms continued the carrying trade profitably in sailing vessels for some years; and many seamen remained faithful to sail for the rest of their lives. But it was Maine rather than Massachusetts that kept the flag afloat at the spanker-gaff of sailing ships. The era of tramp steamers and 4 or 5 percent profit had little attraction for merchants who could gain 6 to 10 percent by exploiting the great West. Many an old shipowner's ledger that begins with tea and indigo and sixteenth shares of the ship *Canton Packet* and brig *Owhyhee* ends up by recording large blocks of C. B. & Q. and Calumet & Hecla.

The maritime history of Massachusetts, then, as distinct from that of America, ends with the passing of the clipper. 'Twas a glorious ending! Never, in these United States, has the brain of man conceived, or the hand of man fashioned, so perfect a thing as the clipper ship. In her, the long-suppressed artistic impulse of a practical, hardworked race burst into flower. *Flying Cloud* was our Rheims, *Sovereign of the Seas* our Parthenon, *Lightning* our Amiens; but they were monuments carved from snow. For a brief moment of time they flashed their splendor around the world, then disappeared with the sudden completeness of the wild pigeon. One by one they sailed out of Boston, to return no more. A tragic or mysterious end was the privilege of many ships favored by the gods. Others, with lofty rig cut down to cautious dimensions, with glistening decks and topsides scarred and neglected, limped about the seas under foreign flags, like faded beauties forced upon the street.

The master builders, reluctant to raise barnyard fowls where once they had reared eagles, dropped off one by one. Donald McKay, dying almost in poverty after a career that should have brought him wealth and honor, sleeps at Newburyport among the comrades of his young manhood. Boston has erected a noble monument to him and his ship, designed by William T. Aldrich and Philip Sears, on Castle Island facing the old ship channel. And in the elm branches over McKay's grave the brave west winds, which he loved so well, murmur soft versions of the tunes they once played on the shrouds of his glorious ships.

Now he has been joined by the last of the men he knew and loved, the shipbuilders and

> Sea-captains young or old, and the mates, and . . . intrepid sailors
> Pick'd sparingly without noise by thee, old ocean, chosen by thee . . .
> Suckled by thee, old husky nurse, embodying thee,
> Indomitable, untamed as thee.

The seaports of Massachusetts have turned their backs to the element that made them great, save for play and for fishing; Boston alone is still in the deep-sea game. But all her modern docks and terminals and dredged channels will avail nothing, if the spirit perish that led her founders to "trye all ports."

Sicut patribus . . . We can ask no more here. But in that unknown harbor toward which we all are scudding, may our eyes behold some vision like that vouchsafed our fathers, when a California clipper ship made port after a voyage around the world.

A summer day with a sea turn in the wind. The Grand Banks fog, rolling in wave after wave, is dissolved by the perfumed breath of

New England hayfields into a gentle haze that turns the State House dome to old gold, films brick walls with a soft patina, and sifts blue shadows among the foliage of the Common elms. Out of the mist in Massachusetts Bay comes riding a clipper ship, with the effortless speed of an albatross. Her proud commander keeps skysails and studdingsails set past Boston Light. After the long voyage she is in the pink of condition. Paintwork is spotless, decks holystoned cream-white, shrouds freshly tarred, ratlines square. Viewed through a powerful glass, her seizings, flemish-eyes, splices, and pointings are the perfection of the old-time art of rigging. The chafing-gear has just been removed, leaving spars and shrouds immaculate. The boys touched up her skysail poles with white paint, as she crossed the bay. Boom-ending her studdingsails and hauling a few points on the wind to shoot the Narrows, between Georges and Gallups and Lovells islands, she pays off again through President Road, and comes booming up the stream, a sight so beautiful that even the lounging soldiers at the Castle, persistent baiters of passing crews, are dumb with wonder and admiration.

Colored pennants on Telegraph Hill have announced her coming to all who know the code. Topliff's News Room breaks into a buzz of conversation, comparing records and guessing at freight money; owners and agents walk briskly down State Street; counting-room clerks hang out of windows to watch her strike skysails and royals; the crimps and hussies of Ann Street foregather, to offer Jack a few days' scabrous pleasure before selling him to a new master. By the time the ship has reached the inner harbor, thousands of critical eyes are watching her every movement, quick to note if in any respect the mate has failed to make sailormen out of her crew of broken Argonauts, beachcombers, Kanakas, and Lascars.

The "old man" stalks the quarterdeck in top hat and frock coat, with the proper air of detachment; but the first mate is as busy as the devil in a gale of wind. Off India Wharf the ship rounds into the wind with a graceful curve, crew leaping into the rigging to furl topgallant sails as if shot upward by the blast of profanity from the mate's bull-like throat. With backed topsails her way is checked, and the cable rattles out of the chain lockers for the first time since Shanghai. Sails are clewed up. Yards are braced to a perfect parallel, and running-gear neatly coiled down. A warp is passed from capstan to stringer, and all hands on the capstan bars walk her up to the wharf with the closing chantey of a deep-sea voyage:

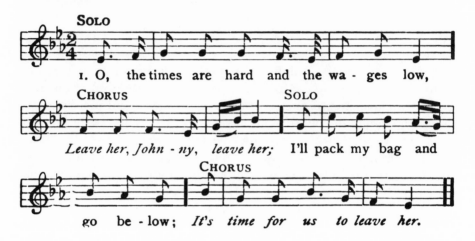

SOLO

1. O, the times are hard and the wa - ges low,

CHORUS   SOLO

Leave her, John - ny, leave her; I'll pack my bag and

CHORUS

go be - low; *It's time for us to leave her.*

7

The *Somers* Mutiny, 1842–1843

From "OLD BRUIN": COMMODORE MATTHEW C. PERRY (Boston: Atlantic–Little, Brown, 1967) *pages 144–62.*

My first visit to Japan, in 1950, to obtain material for my HISTORY OF U.S. NAVAL OPERATIONS, *first opened the possibility of my writing a biography of the eminent seaman and diplomat Matthew C. Perry. On a second visit to Japan, in 1966, accompanied by my wife, Priscilla, and Captain Roger Pineau, USNR, as friend, guide, researcher, and Japanese interpreter, I completed it.*

Perry's attitude toward the United States Navy, in which he served for a few months less than half a century, may best be described by the word "commitment." From an early age he was committed, not only to a naval career, but to making the United States Navy the most efficient fighting force on the oceans, although he could never hope to see it the strongest. He was well called "father" of the steam navy; he promoted the shell gun; he worked for twenty years to establish the Naval Academy at Annapolis. And if his plans for the education and improved status of the bluejacket did not reach fruition, it was largely the fault of a tragic mutiny — the Somers *affair. The account of this mutiny I have chosen as a sampling of my biographical writing.*

DURING THE SUMMER of 1842, Commodore Perry concerned himself with finishing, equipping, and manning a smart new man-of-war brig, U.S.S. *Somers*. Designed by Samuel Humphreys and built under his and the commodore's supervision at the Brooklyn Navy Yard, she was an exquisite example of marine architecture. One hundred and three feet long on deck and 25-foot beam, she was no bigger than many sailing yachts of today or fishing schooners of yesterday; but she carried a press of square sail. Four yards crossed each of her two tall, raking masts. In addition to her square sails, three or four jibs could be set on her monstrous long bowsprit;

spencer and spanker were bent on foremast and mainmast, and there were ample light sails. She carried a complement of 120 officers and men, and ten guns peered out of square ports on her spar deck. Together with her sister ship *Bainbridge* and the three slightly larger brigs, *Truxtun, Lawrence,* and *Perry,* built almost simultaneously, she was designed along Baltimore clipper lines — wineglass-shaped cross-section and sharp ends — primarily for speed. These were the fastest ships in the United States or perhaps in any navy, but badly overrigged; two of the four capsized in squalls, with heavy loss of life. Withe the sloops-of-war built about the same time, they were the last of our war vessels designed with no other view than wind power.

Commodore Perry had *Somers* assigned for an experimental school-ship cruise by naval apprentices. He took particular pains in selecting the officers. To command her, he chose his brother-in-law Master Commandant Alexander Slidell Mackenzie. At the age of thirty-nine, Mackenzie, already an old hand in the Navy, had managed to educate himself and establish a literary reputation. When pursuing pirates with the West Indies Squadron, he suffered two attacks of yellow fever, obtained a furlough to recover his health, traveled in Europe, and wrote *A Year in Spain.* This book earned him the friendship of Longfellow and of Washington Irving, for whose *Life of Columbus* he plotted the discoverer's courses. In 1830–32 he was attached to *Brandywine,* Commander Biddle's flagship in the Mediterranean. After that he took a two-year furlough, again traveled in Europe, published three more books, and in 1835 married Catherine Robinson. Returning to active duty in 1837, he visited Russia and Brazil as first lieutenant of U.S.S. *Independence,* and in Brazil was made commanding officer of the new man-of-war brig *Dolphin.* After a year or two in her, chasing slavers along "the Brazils," he took another long furlough to repair his health, bought an estate at Tarrytown, and wrote a biography of John Paul Jones and a life of Oliver Hazard Perry that stirred up J. Fenimore Cooper. Returning again to active duty in 1841, he was assigned to the new war steamer *Missouri,* and from her transferred to the command of brig *Somers.* As Commodore Perry's shipmate since 1816, close collaborator at the Brooklyn Navy Yard, and sharer in his ideas for naval improvement, he was the natural choice.

Despite the Navy's congenital suspicion of officers who write books, Mackenzie had won golden opinions from the captains and commodores under whom he served, and his attractive personality made friends for him elsewhere. "Mackenzie is one of the . . . kindest, plainest men I know," wrote Francis Lieber the publicist; "very quiet, yet so kind and mild, so true and unaffected, that one cannot help liking, nay, cherishing him." Professor Felton, a Greek scholar who later became president of Harvard College, remarked on Mackenzie's "calmness, gentleness and refinement." Such was the man whose resolute action to preserve the lives of his men and the honor of his flag has been presented by the malignant and the sentimental as that of a savage martinet, a sadist, or a coward who preferred hanging innocent men to taking risks.

Four other members of the Perry-Rodgers clan were on board *Somers*. Lieutenant Matthew C. Perry, Jr., twenty-one years old but already eight years in the Navy, served as acting master, officer next junior to first lieutenant. Calbraith, as the family called him, was a rather stolid young man, brave and loyal, like all the Perrys, but relatively undistinguished during a long naval career. Oliver H. Perry II, the commodore's seventeen-year-old son, was on the roll as captain's clerk. His father had failed to get him a midshipman's billet, since the Navy then had a superfluity of reefers, but once the cruise started, Mackenzie created him acting midshipman. Young Oliver, too, showed that he had the guts to help quell a mutiny, but the experience left him somewhat shaken. Henry Rodgers, younger son of the old commodore, was another *Somers* midshipman, and Adrien Deslonde, of Louisiana, a brother of Mrs. John Slidell's, who had lived in the Perry household as a young lad and been recommended for a midshipman's warrant by his uncle Calbraith, was also on board. All four proved towers of strength to Mackenzie in time of trouble, as did the first lieutenant, Guert Gansevoort. That member of an old Knickerbocker family, thirty years old, had already served nineteen years in the Navy.

Perry and Mackenzie hoped that the prospect of a foreign cruise in a smart new brig would persuade respectable parents in country towns to send their best; but the reputation of naval ratings was such that the commander could not procure many boys of that class. Even so, he selected 74 out of the 166 apprentices on the receiving ship and got rid of some of the worst after the shakedown cruise. Whether the Navy Department or Mackenzie selected the able seamen and petty officers to season *Somers*'s crew and teach raw boys the ropes is uncertain; but someone made two very bad choices. Samuel Cromwell, a great brute of a man, about thirty-five years old, bearded and whiskered, became boatswain's mate and senior petty officer; Elisha Small, of about thirty, a shifty little fellow but an excellent sailor, was captain of the main top. Both had served in slavers before entering the Navy; and Cromwell, if not at one time a pirate, had acquired an intimate knowledge of piratical procedure. But the worst assignment, the fatal one, came from the Navy Department and Commodore Matthew C. Perry. That was the appointment of Midshipman Philip Spencer, aged nineteen.

This youth belonged to one of the first families of New York. His paternal grandfather, Ambrose Spencer, had been chief justice of the state supreme court. His father, John Canfield Spencer, one of the ablest lawyers of the Albany bar, was secretary of war in President Tyler's cabinet. Philip was young in years but old in vice. At Hobart College, whence he had been dropped or expelled, he was chiefly remembered for his favorite reading, *The Pirate's Own Book,* and for having boasted that he would become a pirate. He spent a few months at Union College and dropped out there. Now obtaining an acting midshipman's warrant through his father's influence, he was first assigned to U.S.S. *North Carolina,* receiving ship for the Brooklyn Navy Yard. Passed Midshipman William Craney, to whose cabin and care he was assigned, could do nothing with Spencer, who twice struck him — a serious offense, which, when reported to the Navy Department and Commodore Perry, was ignored. The commodore then assigned Spencer to U.S.S. *John Adams,* bound for Brazil. At Rio, where the ship spent a month, Spencer (as one of his shipmates recalled) passed most of his shore liberty in "the reeky bagnios" of the Rua Sabôa, and on one occasion became so obstreperously drunk as to be reported to Commodore Charles Morris of the Brazil Squadron. That commodore, like Perry, evidently fearing that proper punishment of the lad would get him in wrong with the administration, had Spencer transferred to the frigate *Potomac* for return to the United States, "there to receive the decision of the Secretary of the Navy." On board both her and *John Adams* (so he later confessed to Lieutenant Gansevoort) he had plotted mutiny. Secretary Upshur, after perusing "with pain" the correspondence transmitted by Commodore Morris, and too easily believing in Spencer's penitence, ordered him, in August 1842, to report to Commodore Perry for duty in U.S.S. *Somers*, then fitting out at Brooklyn.

Commander Mackenzie, who knew Spencer's record, refused to accept him, but offered to transfer him to another ship. Spencer then went over Mackenzie's head to Commodore Perry, who made the fatal mistake of having him reinstated as a midshipman in *Somers* — his second intervention in the young rascal's favor. One can only guess at the commodore's reasons. Among other arguments for the apprentice system, he claimed that it would cure juvenile delinquency; here was a chance to prove it. And, one may surmise, Perry wished to please the Tyler administration, since he and his kin had been conspicuous in the Jackson camp. However you look at Spencer, he was a prototype of what nowadays is called a "young punk," and Commodore Perry's giving him another chance was a singular instance of very bad judgment.

One striking thing about this cruise of the *Somers* was the youthfulness of her crew — 70 percent of its members under the age of nineteen. Commander Mackenzie at thirty-nine was the oldest man on board, and only three others — Quartermaster Charles Rogers, Boatswain's Mate Cromwell, and Carpenter's Mate Thomas Dickerson — were over thirty. She had five senior officers, including the commander, the purser, and the surgeon, and seven midshipmen. Three of the middies were twenty years old and up, the other four between sixteen and nineteen years of age. She had eight petty officers, nineteen enlisted seamen (only five of whom were aged twenty or up), and eight cooks and stewards, mostly American Negroes. All seventy-four apprentice boys were minors, twenty-two of them under sixteen years of age. Most of them had never been to sea before. With a total of 121 on board, *Somers* was badly overcrowded; her sister ship *Bainbridge* carried only one hundred officers and men including sixteen Marines; and when sunk later in the Mexican War, *Somers* had a total complement of seventy-six.

In June–July 1842, prior to Spencer's assignment, *Somers* made a shakedown cruise, under Commander Mackenzie, to Puerto Rico and back, in which everything went well. She now made a gala departure from New York on September 13, 1842, officers' and apprentices' relatives flocking to see her off as if she had been a flash packet ship on a pleasure cruise. In order to give her a mission, the Navy had asked her to carry dispatches for U.S.S. *Vandalia*, then cruising on the

West African coast looking for slavers. Prosperous winds attended *Somers* on the outward passage. As far as Madeira, where she arrived on October 5, she was a happy ship. Since naval mutinies fresh in the public mind, such as the one on H.M.S. *Bounty* and those at the Nore and Spithead, had been caused by "cruel hard treatment of every degree," as the old chantey puts it, there was an effort at the subsequent inquiry and court-martial to prove that Commander Mackenzie had been another Captain Bligh. Every one of the enlisted men and boys interrogated testified that they had enjoyed good usage; that Mackenzie showed unusual interest in their welfare, sending delicacies to seasick boys from his own table, buying fresh fruit and vegetables for them in the islands, giving plenty of liberty, and never losing his temper. Only a few of the boys had to be punished, and they with the comparatively mild "colt" rather than the "cat." Boatswain's Mate Cromwell, however, cuffed the boys so frequently that Mackenzie had to reprove him more than once, and even threatened that if he continued he would lose his rating, to which Cromwell made an insolent reply. The only odd feature of the outward passage was the conduct of Midshipman Spencer, who neglected his duties, shunned his messmates, but chatted endlessly with the boys and enlisted men on deck, gave them cigars and tobacco, and even put up a steward to filch brandy from the wardroom to distribute among his cronies. There was no grog ration in the *Somers*, and the boys were not supposed to use tobacco; but Spencer got around that with his gifts.

After calling at Tenerife (October 8) and Porto Praia (October 21), *Somers* sailed to Monrovia in search of *Vandalia*, arriving on November 10. The frigate having already sailed for home, Mackenzie decided, as his orders allowed, to follow. He departed next day, shaping a course for St. Thomas, where he hoped to encounter *Vandalia,* and intending to reach New York before Christmas.

On this return passage, and especially after the departure from Africa, the atmosphere of the ship changed. Orders were obeyed grumblingly, or after repetition, rather than cheerfully and with alacrity. "The elder portion of the crew," testified Matthew C. Perry, Jr., "were surly and morose in their manner." And this manner "daily grew worse until the execution." Spencer was observed holding extended conversations with Cromwell and redoubling his efforts to curry favor with the crew; whilst the big boatswain's mate laid off cuffing the apprentices, became playful and palsy with the older boys, and threw coins on the deck to be scrambled for by the young ones. There was nothing you could put a finger on, as Mackenzie later admitted; hardly anything you could express in words; but the sum total of attitudes told any man who knew sailors that something sinister was cooking.

On November 25 things began to happen. Spencer took James W. Wales, the purser's steward, to the booms. That was the place amidships where the brig's boats were lashed down and the spare yards and studdingsail booms were stored. Here, partly in the presence of Small, the renegade midshipman unfolded a plan startling for ingenuity as well as its utter criminality. He would kill the officers, capture *Somers*, and turn her into a pirate ship. The key members of this conspiracy were Spencer himself, Cromwell, Small, and Wales if willing. Spencer had a list of the "certain" and "doubtful" and those "to be kept *nolens volens*" concealed in his neckerchief. The rest, unwilling sailors and useless boys, the majority of the crew, were to be "disposed of." The mutiny would be sparked off before the ship reached St. Thomas, during the midwatch, when the captain was below, Spencer on duty, Midshipman Rodgers officer of the deck, McKinley (one of the "certain" conspirators) at the arms chest, and McKee (one of the "doubtful") at the wheel. Cromwell and Small would start a mock fight with some of their pals on the forecastle head. Rodgers, on Spencer's appeal, would come forward to stop the fight and, when he reached the gangway, be overpowered and pitched overboard. McKinley would distribute firearms (Spencer having given him the key to the chest), Spencer would dive into Mackenzie's cabin and murder the sleeping captain "with the least noise possible," and then, with Cromwell and Small assisting, penetrate wardroom and steerage and cut the throats of Lieutenant Gansevoort, Master Perry, Purser Heiskell, and a few midshipmen for good measure. Spencer would then call all hands on deck, select "such as would suit his purposes," and cause the rest to be tossed overboard. The brig, now in possession of mutineers, would proceed to Cape St. Antonio or the Isle of Pines off Cuba, where Cromwell had friends among the pirate fraternity. With professional cutthroats added to her complement, she would scour the North Atlantic trade routes as a pirate ship, plundering and sinking defenseless merchantmen and murdering all hands, except that any "females" on board would be taken to the brig "for the use of the officers and men, using them as long as they saw fit; after that, to make way with them." The pirates, after gorging themselves with lust and plunder, would put in at a Cuban port, sell the brig, and live in luxury.

Fantastic as this scheme may now appear, it was practicable. *Somers* could outsail anything afloat except her sister ships, overhaul any merchantman, and overpower any vessel smaller than a frigate. And she would have been far more difficult to catch than C.S.S. *Alabama* in the Civil War or the German raiders of the two world wars.

Spencer picked on Wales to join the gang because he had had an altercation with Commander Mackenzie on the shakedown cruise and, Spencer assumed, cherished resentment. Wales, however, was a loyal man, and decided at first opportunity to get word of the plot to his captain. That was easier said than done.

At this point we must glance at the deck and cabin arrangements of *Somers,* to appreciate what Mackenzie was up against. A flush-decker, her quarterdeck was merely that part of the gun or spar deck abaft the mainmast, not raised above it as on sloops, frigates, and 74's, so not easily defensible against mutineers. Along the midships fore-and-aft section of the quarterdeck rose a rectangular house, like the cabin trunk of a modern yacht, affording light and air to the captain's cabin, the wardroom, and the steerage. At the after end of the cabin trunk, and only two feet four inches forward of the binnacles, a booby hatch led down to the captain's cabin; and at the forward end of the trunk a companionway and ladder led to the steerage, where the midshipmen slung their hammocks and ate their meals. Sole access to the tiny wardroom (eight by ten feet) where four officers slept, ate, and worked out their navigational problems, was by a door from the steerage, a compartment only eight feet long and fourteen wide. Forward of the steerage, separated from it by a flimsy bulkhead and sliding door, lay the berth deck, where the seamen, petty officers, and apprentices lived. Its headroom measured only four feet ten inches. Normal access to berth deck from spar deck was through a hatch just abaft the galley, which snuggled close to the foremast. The brig could not have been better planned for a surprise attack. Even if the afterguard managed to rally, they would find it almost impossible to defend quarterdeck and three cabins against determined mutineers.

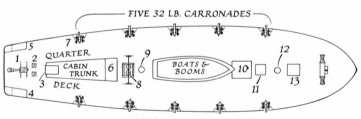

— FIVE 32 LB. CARRONADES —

SPAR DECK OF SOMERS

1. Wheel
2. Binnacles
3. Entrance to captain's cabin
4. Starboard arms chest where Spencer was chained

5. Port arms chest where Cromwell was chained
6. Entrance to steerage
7. After port gun, where Small was chained
8. Pump

9. Mainmast
10. Fore hatch
11. Galley scuttle
12. Foremast
13. Fore scuttle

SCALE 0 5 10 15 20 25 Ft.

BERTH DECK OF SOMERS

1. Captain's cabin
2. Wardroom
3. Exit to spar deck, pantry under
4. Wardroom mess locker
5. Hatch to magazine

6. Sliding doors to steerage & wardroom
7. Steerage - midshipmen's cabin
8. Pump

9. Mainmast
10. Exit from steerage to spar deck
11. Galley stove
12. Foremast

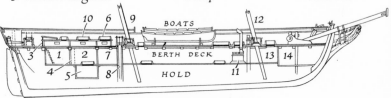

PROFILE OF SOMERS

1. Captain's cabin, 8' × 8' × 4'
2. Wardroom, 6' × 10'
3. Entrance to captain's cabin
4. Wardroom mess locker
5. Powder magazine

6. Sliding doors to steerage and wardroom
7. Steerage, 4' square
8. Pump
9. Mainmast

10. Exit from steerage to spar deck
11. Galley stove
12. Foremast
13, 14. Storerooms

NOTE: Headroom of berth deck was 4'10"

Sam¹ H. Bryant   FROM The History of the American Sailing Navy, BY HOWARD I. CHAPELLE

It took some time for Wales to get his startling news into the right ears, for in a crowded vessel like the *Somers* privacy was a rare commodity. Not until next day, Saturday, November 26, was he able to confide the portentous secret to Purser Heiskell, who carried it to Lieutenant Gansevoort, who told the captain. Mackenzie at first refused to believe the story; he did not want to believe it. But Lieutenant Gansevoort did, and made it his business to find evidence. He was told about Spencer's lengthy conferences with Cromwell and Small, and about his having been seen examining a chart of the Isle of Pines. At evening quarters, acting on Gansevoort's advice, Commander Mackenzie summoned Spencer to the quarterdeck, ordered Master Perry to take the wheel, and confronted the midshipman with Wales's story. Spencer admitted that the steward had reported him correctly, but insisted it was all a joke. "This, sir, is joking on a forbidden subject," said Mackenzie. "This joke may cost you your life . . . You must have been aware that you could only have compassed your designs by passing over my dead body, and, after that, the bodies of all the officers; it will be necessary for me to confine you, sir."

At the captain's command, Gansevoort arrested Spencer, took away his sword, seated him on the starboard arms chest close to the wheel, chained him to the bulwarks, and handcuffed him as an additional precaution. Each successive officer of the deck was ordered to put Spencer to death immediately if he tried to communicate with the crew, but in the meantime to see that he was properly fed and that his other necessities were taken care of. Gansevoort covered him with his own cloak during rain squalls.

Shortly after this arrest, Midshipman Rodgers, searching Spencer's sea chest in the steerage, found in his razor case the paper of which he had spoken to Wales, listing five "certain," ten "doubtful," and eighteen "to be kept *nolens volens*," and assigning posts at wheel, arms chest, cabin, wardroom, and steerage during the mutiny. Spencer, thinking to conceal his sinister design, had used the transparent schoolboy device of writing names and directions in Greek letters. The forms of many letters were wrong, but it was not difficult for Rodgers, who knew some Greek, to decipher them. He brought the result to the captain. There were only thirty-three names on the list, leaving more than eighty to be murdered or thrown to the sharks. Spencer did not even contemplate the humanity of the *Bounty* mutineers, who allowed officers and loyal men to depart in a well-provisioned boat.

Armed with this evidence of who was or might be in the plot, and pondering his next move, Mackenzie decided, largely on the basis of an incident that happened next afternoon (Sunday, the 27th), to arrest Cromwell and Small. The trade wind had moderated; *Somers* was making only 7.5 knots (she was capable of 12). The captain, eager to make best speed, ordered main skysail and royal studdingsails to be set, and sent a boy to the main royal yard to help. Cromwell, Wilson, and others high on Spencer's Greek list went to the main top, which was not their proper station but, owing to the rake of the mainmast, lay directly over the quarterdeck. Midshipman Hays, officer of the deck, ordered the weather royal yard brace to be let go. Small, who was at that station, instead of obeying the order, hauled in the brace "very violently" with the aid of a boy, and belayed it "very hard."* Consequently, the topgallant mast and royal yard, with the sails bent onto them, came tumbling down on deck, and the boy on the yard narrowly escaped going overboard by grabbing the lee royal shrouds. It looked as if this was a plan by Cromwell and his cronies to rescue Spencer by taking advantage of the confusion, especially if a boat had to be lowered to pick up the boy. Fortunately, Lieutenant Gansevoort rushed on deck and efficiently took charge of clearing up the mess of spars, sails, and lines. After dark the same day, when the topgallant mast was about to be swayed up into place, and Rodgers ordered four or five men to help on the quarterdeck, some twenty men and boys rushed aft, stamping their feet in a way unusual and unallowable on a man-of-war. Gansevoort jumped onto the cabin trunk and, pointing his pistol at the tallest man, threatened to shoot anyone who put his foot on the quarterdeck. This, again, looked very much like a rescue attempt.

Mackenzie now decided to arrest Cromwell and Small. The boatswain's mate was seated on the port arms chest of the quarterdeck, facing Spencer and ironed to the rail; Small forward of him next the after gun.

* Much of the discussion turns on whether this was accidental or not. Every yachtsman knows that if you tauten a vang and let out the main sheet you risk breaking the gaff, and that shrouds too taut may break a wooden mast. It is inconceivable that an old seaman like Small could have hauled in and belayed the weather brace accidentally, especially when ordered to do the contrary, and when the ship was rolling to leeward.

Somers was rolling along, sailing large with the trade wind on her starboard quarter; but the wind appeared to be diminishing, an additional anxiety to Mackenzie. Unless he encountered *Vandalia* at St. Thomas and turned the prisoners over to her, he would have to go on to New York and have them tried there. But could he safely make even St. Thomas, at least a week's sail distant? Discipline was disintegrating. *Somers* had no brig where prisoners could be confined, and no Marines to guard them. After the event, shoreside critics of Mackenzie asked why he could not have confined them to the hold or chained them to pad-eyes in his own cabin — a trapezoidal-shaped cubbyhole eight feet long, eight feet broad forward, and two feet broad aft. And the bulkheads between captain's cabin and wardroom, as between wardroom and steerage, were so flimsy that a strong push could have breached them. The hold was full of ballast, water casks, and stores to within a few inches of the berth deck; anyone confined there would have suffocated. What was Mackenzie to do, with this sinister plot simmering, and no possible help from anyone outside the ship? What might not happen in a sudden squall at night? Mackenzie knew perfectly well a stern fact that Admiral Chester W. Nimitz recalled to the Pacific Fleet a century later: "The time for taking all measures for a ship's safety is while still able to do so. Nothing is more dangerous than for a seaman to be grudging in taking precautions lest they turn out to have been unnecessary. Safety at sea for a thousand years has depended on exactly the opposite philosophy."

Let us pause a moment to consider the dramatic contrast between the brightly illuminated setting with the dark designs of the plotters and dismal apprehensions of the intended victims. Sailing west to "the Indies" in the winter northeast trades is perhaps the most beautiful sailing in any ocean; and *Somers*, rolling and dipping in the long swells, had the wind just where she wanted it, on the quarter, to make best time over a sapphire ocean flecked with whitecaps. Flying fish flashed silver past the foam at her bow. Puffy trade wind clouds raced her overhead, and occasionally one lashed her with rain. No throb of engines assaulted the ear; there were no sounds but the striking of the ship's bell, the creaking of spars and timbers, lines slatting against the sails, and the rush and gurgle of great waters. Every few hours the square sails changed color: golden gossamer when the last-quarter moon rose, polished silver just before dawn, ruddy at sunrise, and cream-white at high noon. But the fatigued, harassed, and anxious officers, and the conspirators guessing whether or not they were found out, had neither taste nor time for aesthetic appreciation. Sailors collected in knots to exchange gossip. Officers, divided "watch and watch" (eight hours on and eight off), armed themselves with two pistols and a cutlass each, and even in their watch below kept continually moving about the vessel, to break up any attempt at rescue. Thus Monday passed, and Tuesday, with increasing tension and fatigue on the part of the loyal officers and increasing insubordination on the part of the crew. Orders were obeyed sullenly after repetition; the men "would go growling along as though they did not care," said Wales. Knives and other lethal weapons were discovered in handy spots. Four suspects failed to appear at muster, and it was always they who brought food to the prisoners, hoping perhaps to communicate with them. On the night of the 29th there was another ominous rush aft when the spanker-boom preventer tackle carried away, and young Calbraith Perry had some difficulty chasing unwanted hands off the quarterdeck.

On Wednesday morning, November 30, Mackenzie arrested four suspects whose names were high on Spencer's Greek list: Sailmaker's Mate Wilson, Landsman Daniel McKinley, and Apprentices McKee and Green. Seven prisoners were now chained to the bulwarks of the quarterdeck, their presence interfering with the proper handling of the ship.

The commander's next action was to order the four wardroom officers (Lieutenant Gansevoort, Purser Heiskell, Surgeon Leacock, and Master Perry) and the three senior midshipmen (Rodgers, Thompson, and Hays) to deliberate, take evidence, and give him their collective advice. They met in the little wardroom the rest of that day and most of the night, thirteen to fourteen hours in all, discussing the affair and questioning several older members of the crew. All oral evidence strengthened the case against Spencer, Cromwell, and Small. The witnesses agreed that Cromwell was the most dangerous man on board, the brains of the conspiracy. Spencer's piratical ambitions might have remained the mere fantasies of a depraved youngster's mind, had not Cromwell showed him how to make the dream come true. But Cromwell, who was very "cagey" —

using an alias on Spencer's Greek list — would hardly have conspired without Spencer, the son of a cabinet member whose influence could be counted on to get them off if anything slipped.

At nine in the morning of Thursday, December 1, five days since Wales had communicated the mutiny plot to Mackenzie, the seven officers reported in writing that they had "come to a cool, decided, and unanimous opinion" that Spencer, Cromwell, and Small were "guilty of a full and determined intention to commit a mutiny," and that the uncertainty as to who was in their gang, and "the impossibility of guarding against the contingencies which 'a day or an hour may bring forth,' " had convinced them "that it would be impossible to carry them to the United States; and that the safety of the public property, the lives of ourselves and of those committed to our charge, require that . . . they should be put to death, in a manner best calculated . . . to make a beneficial impression upon the disaffected."

Mackenzie had already reached the same conclusion — that the three ringleaders be put to death. His authority he found in an act of Congress passed in 1800: "If any person in the navy shall make or attempt to make any mutinous assembly, he shall on conviction thereof by a Court Martial, suffer death." The council of officers was not a court-martial, and Mackenzie had no authority to call one; but it was the best substitute at hand. He felt that since Spencer, Cromwell, and Small were the only three men, other than the loyal officers, capable of navigating a ship, their removal would discourage any attempt to carry out Spencer's diabolical plan. But could not Mackenzie have waited until his ship reached Danish St. Thomas, which she did on December 5, or squared away for a nearer island? There the prisoners could have been incarcerated ashore, to await safe transportation to New York for trial. Mackenzie, however, considered "that a naval commander can never be justified in invoking foreign aid in reducing an insubordinate crew to obedience." He had hoped to encounter U.S.S. *Vandalia* in St. Thomas and turn over the prisoners to her; but, owing to "the daily and hourly increasing insubordination of the crew," he dared no longer delay the execution of the ringleaders.

Once the decision was made, Mackenzie proceeded to the execution. All three men were informed that they were about to die, and had better make their peace with God. Spencer, who hitherto had been sneeringly confident, counting no doubt on a big public trial in New York and his father's engaging the best legal talent to get him off, now fell on his knees, blubbering, and confessed his guilt. But he exonerated Cromwell. The boatswain's mate also knelt and begged for mercy, but protested his innocence. Small kept a stiff upper lip but freely confessed his guilt.

Three whips, as the tackles used for hoisting in stores were called, were now rigged to the main yardarm, two on the starboard arm for Cromwell and Small, one on the port arm for Spencer. The condemned men were given time to read the Bible and pray. Spencer said, "There are few crimes that I have not committed; I feel sincerely penitent." All three asked the loyal officers and men to forgive them; Cromwell begging Lieutenant Gansevoort to forgive him was the nearest he came to confession, and he tried to shake off his guard and jump overboard. Little Elisha Small died a manly death. He admitted that the captain was doing his duty, told him, "I honor you for it; God bless that flag!" He made a dying speech to the ship's company, warning them against mutinous intendments and against slaving: " 'Twas going in a Guineaman that brought me to this." He concluded, "Now, fellow topmen, give me a quick death." The nooses were put in place, one around Spencer's neck as he stood on the quarterdeck under the port yardarm, one around each of the others as they stood on the bulwarks under the starboard yardarm. Spencer's face was covered with a black handkerchief, the faces of Cromwell and Small by sailors' blouses. Two men were detailed to haul on each whip, and officers were stationed beside them, with cutlasses drawn and orders to cut down anyone who faltered. Spencer was offered the privilege of giving the word for the execution signal gun to be fired, but his nerve failed him and he asked the captain to do so. Mackenzie called, "Stand by, Fire!" A boy applied a live coal from the galley to a touch-hole, the cannon roared, the men at the whips hauled away, and within a minute three dead men were dangling from the main yard.

Mackenzie now called the crew aft and delivered a sermon on truth, honor, and fidelity. He concluded by calling for three cheers for the flag. "They gave three hearty ones," and this seemed to relieve the minds of all from the prevailing gloom. The crew were now piped to dinner. Mackenzie was shocked that some of the boys, as they went below, pointed at the dead bodies and laughed. But was that not natural? They were now safe from mutineers who had planned to throw them to the sharks.

Dinner is eaten. The bodies are lowered and prepared for proper burial at sea. Mackenzie, a stickler for doing everything properly, orders Spencer, as an officer, to be buried in uniform in a coffin, and "Chips" claps together two sea chests to make one, weighted and bored with holes for a quick sinking. The enlisted men were sewed up by messmates in their own hammocks, the last stitch being taken, according to ancient sea custom, through the nose, and a cannon ball placed at each man's head and feet for quick sinking. During these preparations a black squall passes over *Somers,* as if a last salute by the powers of darkness. There is a delay while the three bodies, laid out in order of rank, are decently covered with tarpaulins.

By the time the squall is over, the short tropical twilight has faded, the new moon has set, and battle lanterns are broken out to light a solemn scene on the spar deck. Prayer books are handed around. While *Somers* sails slowly through the velvety tropical night under the star-studded firmament of heaven, with no other music than the swish of parting waters, Captain Mackenzie reads from the Book of Common Prayer the office for burial of the dead at sea. Bearded men and smooth-faced boys, gathering on the booms and in the gangways, speak the responses reverently, and the four men in irons whisper what they can remember of the service:

We therefore commit their bodies to the deep, to be turned into corruption, looking for the resurrection of the body (when the Sea shall give up her dead), and the life of the world to come, through our Lord Jesus Christ.

There are three loud splashes as the corpses drop into a 3000-fathom deep. Ensign and pendant, half-masted for the burial, are now two-blocked, and *Somers* continues on her course — west and by north — from which she had never deviated during these five days of fear and tension.

There was no further trouble about discipline on board. The arrested men were kept below deck during most of the passage to New York, and took their meals with the others. The crew obeyed orders cheerfully, apparently greatly relieved, although the presence of four enlisted men in irons reminded them that justice was not yet satisfied. After calling a few hours at St. Thomas on December 5, the brig proceeded to New York. She had a quick passage, nine days later anchoring off Brooklyn Navy Yard. No visitors were allowed on board, and nobody was granted leave or liberty.   Mackenzie dispatched Acting Midshipman O. H. Perry II to Washington with his report, then took his entire crew ashore and marched them to the nearest church to give thanks for the preservation of ship and company from capture and murder.   The officers were so fagged out with their extra duties and lack of sleep that when they crossed the lawn to the commandant's quarters, they reeled and staggered like drunken men.

For Commodore Perry, father of two officers in *Somers,* uncle by marriage to a third, and brother-in-law of the commander, this affair provided the most severe trial of his life.   Rightly anticipating that Secretary Spencer would clamp down on Mackenzie, he wrote to his congressman in Washington, General Aaron Ward, trusting he would stand up for *Somers*'s commander.   Ward answered not too hopefully that Secretary Spencer was trying to get Mackenzie tried for murder by a civilian jury, and that he had won over Secretary Upshur to that view.   Perry then sent Ward this stout letter:

> Navy Yard
> Brooklyn Dec. 27 1842

Confidential
My Dear Genl.

I write a line to ask you in the name of our friend McKenzie who you know is like myself a constituent of yours that you will watch after his interest at Washington.

I fear that there is some influence at work which may do him harm unless it is checked.   You know the character of McKenzie well & you know that he would not hurt the hair of a man's head unless from stern necessity.

His conduct is borne out by every one in this quarter.   The Clergy, Judges, Lawyers, Women & Children all praise him & his officers for having crushed in the bud a most diabolical scheme of rapine and murder.

He asks nothing but fair and open justice and he conceives that there should be no influence exerted by persons in power to prejudice the case. He has done what he would do again under like circumstances and what every honorable officer placed under the same responsibility ought to do but there are few who would have sufficient firmness to meet the contingency.

So far as my two sons have been concerned in this melancholy affair they have my unmeasured approbation and they would have been spurned by me if they had acted otherwise. *No man is fit for the Navy if he is not ready at all times to interpose his life in the preservation of the integrity of the American Flag and the Safety of the vessel entrusted to his and their Charge* . . .

With great Regard
I am, D. Genl., Truly Yours

M. C. PERRY

First procedure after the arrival of *Somers* in New York waters, a naval court of inquiry convened on December 28, 1842, aboard Perry's old ship, *North Carolina,* moored off Brooklyn Navy Yard. The court consisted of three commodores on active duty, veterans of the War of 1812, with Charles Stewart as president. Ogden Hoffman, Esq., federal attorney general for New York, also a naval veteran of the last war, served as judge advocate. Commodore Perry's son-in-law John Hone acted as Mackenzie's secretary, and there was a heavy attendance by officers of the Army, Navy, and Marine Corps. Every officer of *Somers*, twenty-two enlisted men (including six black cooks and stewards), and sixty-eight of the seventy-four apprentices were questioned. The court sat until January 19, 1843, and next day Commodore Stewart announced its findings: "The immediate execution of the prisoners was demanded by duty and justified by necessity." The conduct of Mackenzie and his officers "was prudent, calm and firm, and he and they honestly performed their duty to the service of their country."

That did not end the matter. Even before the court of inquiry adjourned, Secretary Upshur, at Commander Mackenzie's earnest request, took the unusual step of ordering him to be tried by court-martial. Mackenzie felt that only thus could he properly be cleared, and that otherwise he might have been indicted for murder in a civil court, for which Secretary Spencer and Cromwell's widow were working. Tried he was, on five counts — murder, oppression, illegal punishment, conduct unbecoming an officer, and cruelty.

The court-martial, consisting of eleven naval captains and two commanders, with Captain John Downes as president, met on board *North Carolina* on February 2, and shortly after adjourned to the chapel in the navy yard. The judge advocate, William H. Norris, Esq., was a relative of Spencer's. Principal counsel for the defendant was his friend Theodore Sedgwick, Esq., third of that name, a famous lawyer and publicist. Sessions were public, and freely commented on by the press. Most of the evidence merely repeated what had come out in the inquiry, but cross-examination brought out some new facts in Mackenzie's favor, which was not what the judge advocate wanted. Cromwell had threatened, in the presence of several members of the crew, to pitch Mackenzie overboard when he was sitting on the taffrail. Two apprentice boys had overheard Spencer and Cromwell discussing a piratical cruise. Two others had heard Spencer ask Cromwell if he could disguise the brig and Cromwell's reply that he could easily do so. Cromwell acted "beside himself" when Spencer was arrested. Seaman Neville had seen Spencer and Cromwell discussing a paper in "not English writing," and Spencer invited him to sail on "his" ship. Cromwell and Small had been overheard exchanging data on the notorious pirate rendezvous, the Isle of Pines, where, Cromwell said, soon they would be.

Lieutenant Gansevoort, stalwart witness for the defense, stood up under vigorous cross-examination, reiterating his belief that the brig could never have been brought into port but for the executions, and that "Spencer or Small had made his plot known to at least twenty of the crew." Asked a member of the court, "Did you see in Commander Mackenzie any traces of unmanly fear, of a despotic temper, or any conduct unbecoming an American officer?" "I did not," replied the first lieutenant. "His course was that of a brave man and a good officer — such as to inspire us with high respect for him as an officer and warm friendship for him as a man."

On April 1, 1843, the verdict was issued. The last two charges were dropped. On every other charge the verdict was "not proved." On the most important one, of murder, it was said in the newspapers that three of the twelve members then sitting dissented. But the entire court voted, *nem. con.*, to "acquit Commander Alexander Slidell Mackenzie of the charges and specifications preferred by the secretary of the navy against him." Secretary Upshur confirmed the verdict.

During the nearly four months of inquiry and trial, the *Somers* affair was discussed all over the country. No case of the century, prior to the assassination of President Lincoln, aroused as much interest and passion. Naval opinion was not unanimous; Captain Robert F. Stockton even refused to serve on the court, alleging that he had already made up his mind, and would have voted to hang Mackenzie. Several hundred merchants of New York and Boston signed memorials to Mackenzie, praising his conduct; they knew very well what damage the *Somers* might have done under the black flag. Charles Sumner, the rising young Boston lawyer, published an account of the case in *The North American Review*, highly praising Mackenzie: "We thank him, and the country thanks him, that he did not hesitate." And Sumner made an excellent legal case for the commander by pointing out that the planned mutiny placed *Somers*, "for the time being, in a state of war." Strong support for the commander also came from a series of letters to the press by Richard Henry Dana, author of *Two Years Before the Mast*, who knew life at sea from the common sailor's point of view. Dana was answered by Captain William Sturgis of Boston, an old China hand. He argued that as shipmaster in the China trade, he had kept discipline among characters more desperate than those on board *Somers* without hanging any, and he believed that Cromwell was innocent. Mackenzie was both vigorously defended and viciously attacked in the press; some even attempted to make political capital out of the affair. It was probably fortunate that the brig reached port after the November elections.

A strong anonymous attack on Mackenzie, probably by a Whig journalist, was a 102-page pamphlet *Cruise of the Somers: Illustration of the Despotism of the Quarter Deck and of the Unmanly Conduct of Commander Mackenzie* (New York, 1844). Far more powerful, from the pen of the leading naval historian, was the attack by J. Fenimore Cooper, still nursing his wounds from the Battle of Lake Erie controversy. Cooper, like "the last of the Mohicans," never forgave an injury. Here was a perfect opportunity for revenge, and he made the most of it. In his 81-page *Review of the Proceedings of the Naval Court Martial* (New York, 1844), he used every argument good or bad to prove Mackenzie to be a jittery, incompetent martinet. He sneered that *Somers* was more of a "family yacht" than a man-of-war, and boasted how he himself could have handled the situation better. Cooper flattered himself that his tract would "finish" Mackenzie as a naval officer, which it certainly did not. It should have finished Cooper as a competent authority on naval affairs.

Every few years there appears an article or book on the *Somers* case exonerating Spencer and his accomplices. Arguments and innuendoes of the sort that have become familiar in discussions of Pearl Harbor and the assassination of President Kennedy are freely used: Why was not so-and-so examined? Everyone available testified, except some of the younger boys. Why was Wales's story of the plot accepted by Mackenzie without corroboration? There was plenty of corroboration, especially from Sergeant Garty, whom Spencer tried to suborn, Boatswain's Mate Browning, Carpenter's Mate Dickerson, and others. Why were the four men whom Mackenzie brought to New York in irons, as accessories, not proceeded against? Because the judge advocate found insufficient evidence against them, and Mackenzie felt that there had been enough punishment. And, did not the skipper provoke a mutiny by cruel treatment? There is abundant evidence that Mackenzie had been a mild and indulgent commander, slow to take offense.

Although Commodore Perry was pleased that his brother-in-law, in whom he never lost faith, had been exonerated, he was deeply grieved by the effect of the *Somers* affair on the apprentice system. All boys who had served in the brig were discharged, and no more wanted to sign on. The plan was quietly dropped, and not revived until 1864, when a freshly recruited group made a successful start. Yet some good came of the attempted mutiny. The principal culprit offered a perfect illustration of the effect of appointing midshipmen haphazardly and by favor. Navy and public were now convinced that a school must be established for the education of naval officers. The final fillip that brought it about was President Polk's appointment of historian George Bancroft as secretary of the navy in 1845. Commodore Perry was a member of the board of examiners of midshipmen which met that year at the Philadelphia Naval Asylum and was asked by the secretary to prepare a plan for "a more efficient system of instruction for the young naval officers." They complied promptly, drafted a table of organization and plan of studies, and Secretary Bancroft cannily got a bill for it through Congress by persuading the Army to give up obsolete Fort Severn, Annapolis, thus avoiding the expense of a new building. On October 10, 1845, the academy opened, with Perry's close friend Commander Franklin Buchanan as superintendent.

On December 1, three years from the day that Philip Spencer's body swung from the *Somers*'s yardarm, Secretary Bancroft made a notable prediction in his annual report. The Naval Academy, by affording midshipmen preliminary instruction before their first cruise, by extending "an affectionate but firm supervision" over them and providing "suitable culture" thereafter, and "by rejecting from the service all who fail in capacity or in good disposition to use their time well," would "renovate and improve" the Navy.

No prophecy about the Navy has been more amply fulfilled. The Naval Academy's course has kept pace with changing conditions of naval warfare, and its discipline is such that nobody even remotely resembling Philip Spencer has since obtained a naval commission.

So much for the *Somers* mutiny. There will always remain the teasing thought that Mackenzie might have risked a rescue attempt for four more days, when he could have had his prisoners confined at St. Thomas, to be tried later in New York. Opposed to that concept is the hard fact that every man on board with maritime experience and proved loyalty believed that execution was necessary. They felt that matters had reached a boiling point on December 1, 1842, and that Mackenzie was justified morally, if not legally, in putting Spencer, Cromwell, and Small to death.

On that conclusion, the present writer rests.

8

The Landing at Fedhala, Morocco, November 8, 1942

From THE AMERICAN FOREIGN SERVICE JOURNAL, March 1943, *pages 113–16, 156–57.*

We now jump a century of naval history to November 1942, Operation Torch for the liberation of North Africa from the German-controlled Vichy government. In this operation I took part personally as a temporary member of the staff of Captain Francis C. Denebrink, commanding officer of U.S.S. Brooklyn, a new light cruiser with a main battery of 6-inch guns. We were in the Western Task Force, with the mission of securing French Morocco. I was the oldest man on board except for the chief medical officer, and we two were the only ones who had been under fire before; but every man was eager to fight. After it was all over, I asked a mess attendant what he had done during the fight. He replied, "I mostly kept out of people's way, sir; but I did a lot of that!"

As this article was published in midwar, I had to alter the names of ships and officers; that has been straightened out in this reprinting.

OUR TASK FORCE departed from several different American bases at different times, and made rendezvous in midocean; when all together, we covered a space of ocean many miles wide and many more long. The Germans had a few score U-boats out looking for us, but we successfully eluded the lot, and thus conserved the element of surprise, which was one of our outstanding assets. Cynics have doubted whether military and naval men are capable of keeping a secret; but in this instance the several hundred officers and civilian officials, in this country and England, who had to know what was going on actually did keep silence, so the Axis powers were completely mystified as to where this great fleet was going. If one of these men had tattled, the resistance might easily have been tenfold as serious as we found it, and our task might have taken sixty days' fighting instead of three.

On our way over, the weather was magnificent and not so rough as to disturb the stomachs of tough, hardened young men. We knew we were going into battle on a certain day, and, as we were also told of the great importance and significance of our enterprise, high were the expectations. Yet our vast force of many thousand sailors, soldiers, and aviators was far from being overconfident, or puffed up with that hubris which brings down the wrath of the gods. With the attack plan there was circulated a list of a dozen "assumptions" — things that might happen to us: night attacks on transports by enemy subs, light surface craft, or motor torpedo boats (and we knew the French navy had ample forces in Casablanca); surf so heavy that we couldn't land troops, and would have to run out to sea again to avoid U-boats and then perhaps run out of fuel; or surf heavy enough to drown a large number of men if we tried to land them. Spain might come in on the Axis side. Almost anything might happen. Yet, all in all, we feared our own mistakes, the thousand and one ways the landing might be botched, more than we feared the enemy; and we feared the weather, and being late, more than either. Morocco is an iron-bound coast, with very few beaches suitable for landing troops on; and those beaches are so exposed to the ocean swells that breaking waves ten to fifteen feet high are not uncommon in November. Most of these beaches were under the protection of strong shore batteries. Hence the landings must be made at night, when surf is most dangerous to boats. Indeed, so many chances were taken that if the breaks had gone against us, or, as one admiral stated in his report, if Divine Providence had not been on our side, those who planned the West African expedition would by now have been branded as incompetents, lunatics, and murderers.

On Wednesday, November 4, with the landing day only a few days off, the wind rises to gale force and seas run so high that the mighty cruiser on which I sail is rolling 30 degrees. Our weatherman's face is as long as his chart, for the Washington weather predictions are pessimistic. It looks as though we are in for a heavy swell and a hard norther. By Friday, the 6th, things look much better; the wind has moderated and the sea is going down. This morning we see the last of the old moon. Saturday, the 7th, our last full day at sea, breaks fair. The sea has gone down still more, the sky is clouding up — a good sign, for we want it dark tonight.

Our mighty fleet begins to split up. The Southern Attack Group, destined for Safi, peels off, the commander sending us this greeting: "Keep your eyes on the sky and your ears on the sea." The Escort Aircraft Carrier Group lingers behind to act as air base over the horizon; the Support Group, made up of big, powerful ships, hovers offshore, ready to rush in and bomb Casablanca or perform whatever mission the task force commander may assign. Finally, we part with the Northern Attack Group, destined for Port Lyautey; and our Center Attack Group, destined for Fedhala, assumes its final approach formation.

A squadron of minesweepers leads us into glory or disaster, only the gods know which. Then comes the outer screen of destroyers, patrolling vigilantly around the entire fleet. Next the guide, the queenly heavy cruiser *Augusta,* and, parallel to her, on the other flank, the scrappy light cruiser *Brooklyn,* my ship. We lead the columns of transports, whose names read like a roll of American history, called as they are after Founding Fathers and famous generals. Finally, far in the rear steams the little minelayer *Contessa.* A modest steamboat before the war, she carries her cargo of TNT mines very ill at ease, rolling heavily. The transport commander called her "Leila the Lethal," and cheerfully cautioned her to keep a good distance from his transports lest she blow them all up.

Sunset at 5:45; enough stars to fix our position. We are right on top of our destination, and a due south course should bring us off Cape Fedhala by midnight.

Several hours later, "Shady" Lane, the incomparable navigator of *Brooklyn,* announces that we are nearing the African coast. The critical hour is drawing near. Captain Denebrink summons the chaplain to the blacked-out bridge and says, "Padre, I think we ought to have a prayer before we go in and fight. Now, I'm not a praying man myself, but here's the sentiment I want to put into language appropriate for the Almighty: 'O Lord, gangway for a fighting ship and a fighting crew!' "

"Aye, aye, sir!" says Father O'Leary, and offers a sailorman's prayer while we stand by with bared heads.

Two hours later: The hoarse alarm of General Quarters summons everyone to his battle station, where he is destined to remain, on our ship, for fifteen hours.

Nearly midnight: The flagship signals STOP, and the transports coast into their predetermined unloading positions off Cape Fedhala, eight minutes in advance of schedule. Before eight bells usher in November 8, we can hear a faint clank and clash from the transports as the first steel landing boats are lowered into the ocean.

South of us but invisible is the coast of "High Barbaree," and beyond that the Atlas, the Sahara, Egypt. Africa was never so dark and mysterious to ancient sea rovers as she seems tonight, veiled in clouds and hushed in slumber. Not a light gleams, not a dog barks, but the wind is offshore and the smell of the land comes out to us, a scent of charcoal smoke and parched dry grass. "Africa! there's Africa!" we say to each other. So long and anxiously have we been looking forward to this landfall that the very word makes us tingle down the spine.

Our objective, the beaches of Fedhala, are twelve nautical miles by sea and fifteen miles by land from Casablanca; and in Casablanca there are known to be the French battleship *Jean Bart,* a cruiser, eight or ten destroyers, thirteen submarines, and sundry small naval craft. Cape Fedhala itself has a battery of 100-mm and one of 75-mm guns, which are able to sweep the beaches and their approaches; and at the other end of the beaches is the Pont Blondin battery of four 138-mm guns — "Sherki," we call it, from misreading an Arabic name on the map. Besides these there are numerous machine-gun nests on the cape, near the beaches, and around the town. Our orders are to put several thousand troops ashore on these beaches before sunrise. Those assault troops are to capture the town, the harbor, and whatever batteries the Navy has not silenced. Then, reinforced by many thousand more troops landed in daylight, they are to establish a beachhead running well back into the country, and prepare to advance overland against Casablanca. The French are known to have several hundred fighter and bomber planes within reach of Fedhala; but our carrier-based planes will be launched before sunrise and should catch them grounded, if they are smart. They are.

The transport unloading area is several miles offshore. As soon as the landing boats are in the water, they come up under rope-net ladders, down which the soldiers scramble with heavy equipment on their backs, while cranes lower the tanks and armored vehicles into tank lighters. The landing boats and lighters are organized in "waves" alongside the transports that are nearest the beach. Four destroyers, one for each transport, conduct these waves of landing boats to the "line of departure," and anchor. At the predetermined hour, the first wave leaves the line of departure for the beaches, followed at short intervals by other waves. As soon as a boat is unloaded on the beach, her naval crew must make every effort to retract her and return to this transport to get another load.

You can see how vulnerable the whole operation is, and how necessary it is to surprise the enemy. Apart from all chances of weather and heavy surf, the boats and the men on the beaches may encounter enemy fire from the ground and from the air. That's where our ship comes in.

While the boats are being loaded from the transports, our task in *Brooklyn* is to patrol eastward and northward of the transport area. That gives plenty of time for reflection. It is the dark of the moon, but the sky clears up, revealing Orion in all his splendor flung across the zenith. Cassiopeia sets, the Great Bear rises right up on his tail, and the Guards of Polaris, the mariner's eternal clock hand, move slowly up from the horizon. What countless stratagems of this sort — land in the dark to conquer before dawn — have been practiced on this very coast since remotest antiquity! We might be caravels of Prince Henry the Navigator in 1442, with sails furled and yards on deck, waiting for the Pole Star clock to register two hours before dawn to move in and rush the town. It has always been the same technique. You want a couple of hours' darkness to get ashore and surprise 'em, and then daybreak, so that you can tell friend from foe, and gold from brass, and wench from wife.

A destroyer signals jubilantly, over voice radio, "The Yanks are coming!" That means the four destroyers are leaving the first line of transports with the boat waves. It will take them at least an hour to reach the beaches. A new chapter in African history is about to open. Maybe a new chapter in American history, too.

The men must be leaping ashore now, rifles in hand, running up the beach, and striking for their first shore objectives. That's exactly what they are doing, but we hear nothing of their activities for another tense hour.

Morning twilight is just beginning as *Brooklyn* moves majestically toward her fire-control position, where she can take care of Battery

Sherki if it gets mean. It does. Firing is now heard on the beach. A searchlight shoots from Sherki and another from Fedhala, looking for planes — the defenders heard the humming of motors and thought that's what we were. Then the searchlights drop and move nervously about, pricking holes in the darkness about the bay and beaches, revealing what must have seemed to the French, at first, a mere commando raid. The shore batteries open fire. Over voice radio we hear the captain of destroyer *Wilkes* asking his commodore, "Can I open fire?" The answer comes, "Go ahead!" and the commodore telephones the prearranged word that resistance has begun. A few minutes later there comes over the air the long-anticipated signal for a general engagement.

FLASH from Battery Sherki, FLASH from destroyer *Wilkes*, and then the sullen BOOM! — BOOM! as the sound catches up. It is still so dark that the shore is invisible, and we first know Sherki is firing at us by seeing red-hot shells hurtling through the air in our direction. Inshore, and at half our range, bold *Wilkes* is blazing away at the battery. Guns on Cape Fedhala join the chorus; cruiser *Augusta* and two destroyers return their fire. Our little corner of the world, so hushed and dark and silent for five long hours, is now split by blinding gun flashes, shattered by machine-gun fire, shaken by the crash of heavy ordnance.

Now *Brooklyn* comes in and contributes to this uproar her own hoarse bray of 6-inch guns. First, however, she must catapult a spotting plane. Sharp rattle of the plane's motors, blue fire snorting from her twin exhausts, the hand signal, a swift rush on the catapult; CRACK goes the explosive charge, and a handsome young lieutenant is shot into space. Three minutes later he's over the target, and our fire-control officer down in the plot room can hear his cheery spot on our first salvo: "Up one hundred; no change in deflection."

It's high time we did get into it, for destroyer *Wilkes* is taking a hot fire at close range. Her fighting skipper telephones about Sherki: "This damn Turkey has got my range. I've got to get the hell out!" She does, with one shot in her innards and one engine room dead — but she performs antisubmarine patrol around the transports even while she licks her wounds.

We, the *Brooklyn*, steam back and forth from Sherki; and how we do pour out the stuff! At 6:32 we're firing the salvos of all our 6-inch guns at once, and a minute later Captain Denebrink orders continuous fire — approximately 150 shots a minute, rapid as a machine gun but unevenly spaced and a thousandfold as loud. For us on board, the scene is magnificent; for those we were protecting it was sublime: "Most beautiful thing I ever saw," said a transport commander when we talked it over afterward. In the gray morning twilight and against a smoky horizon, the hot bright puffs of fire, surrounded by clouds of luminous orange-colored smoke, make the *Brooklyn* stand out like a vicious flame-belching monster of mythology.

Now you can see what we're there for — to draw the fire of Fedhala's powerful batteries away from our men and boats. The coast batteries, manned by French navy personnel, know that if they can't drive off our fighting ships, their goose is cooked, but that if they can dispose of our fighting ships, the transports will be easy meat. So they concentrate on us and pay no attention to the landing boats. Until after sunrise, when hostile plains appear and enemy machine guns can see their targets, our landings are almost unopposed in this Fedhala area, which had the greatest means of resistance, because we plastered the defense with aggressive naval gunfire.

Brooklyn, at the western end of her fire-support area, steamed right into the boat waves plying to and fro between the easternmost transport and beach. My most vivid mental picture of the battle was one such moment in the morning twilight when we executed a 180-degree turn, right among the boats, firing over their heads; and as I looked over the side I could see the soldiers' faces, lighted by our gun flashes and turned up toward us, open-mouthed with amazement at our furious shooting. One of the naval petty officers who steered a landing boat was asked after the battle how the soldiers "took it." "Those fellows were kind of solemn going ashore," he said; "didn't seem to want to talk." Don't blame them, do you?

However, we got them ashore, all right, and guess what the first wave of assault troops did, in black darkness? Bagged a fleet of German cars in one of which Colonel (now General) Wilbur made his famous dash into Casablanca, hoping to persuade the commander, an old friend of his at the Ecole de Guerre, not to fight us. He did not succeed, and the French navy put up a tough battle, which was ended only when Admiral Darlan ordered hostilities to cease on November 11, at seven in the morning.

This three-day war was our first fight with the French since 1798. Let us hope it will be the last!

9

The Battle off Samar, October 25, 1944

*We now skip two years to an action that I still consider the most val-
iant of the entire war, an escort carrier battle with a far more power-
ful Japanese fleet. This action formed part of the three-part Battle for
Leyte Gulf, the greatest sea battle, judged by the number of ships and
men engaged, of all time. The other two parts were the surface night
Battle of Surigao Strait and the surface and air Battle off Cape
Engaño. Both are covered in great detail in my* LEYTE, *Volume XII
of my* HISTORY OF U. S. NAVAL OPERATIONS IN WORLD WAR II
(Boston: Little, Brown, 1958). This version is a shorter one, from my
VISTAS OF HISTORY *(New York: Alfred A. Knopf, 1964), pages
159–72.*

ONE OF THE strangest incidents in this or any other modern war occurred on October 25, 1944, forty miles off the Philippine island of
Samar, about fifteen minutes after sunrise. An escort carrier group
known by its code name, "Taffy 3," under Rear Admiral Clifton A. F.
Sprague in U.S.S. *Fanshaw Bay*, having launched routine patrols to
cover the ships in Leyte Gulf, had secured from Battle Quarters.
The deck crews were eating breakfast. At 0645, lookouts observed
antiaircraft fire to the northward. What could that possibly be? At
0646, the flagship's radar screen showed something odd. One minute
later the pilot of a plane on antisubmarine patrol reported that he was
being fired upon by a force of battleships, cruisers, and destroyers at
a position some twenty miles distant. "Check identification!" yelled
Admiral Sprague to air plot. But before verification of this astonishing contact could be obtained, sailors on lookout sighted the un-
mistakable tall masts of Japanese battleships and cruisers pricking up
over the northwestern horizon. At 0648, these ships opened fire, and
a minute later splashes from their shells began rising all around Taffy 3.
It was Admiral Kurita's powerful Center Force of the Japanese
Combined Fleet. He was every bit as surprised as Sprague. He

thought he had run smack into Mitscher's Task Force 38, the big fleet carriers.

How could this formidable fleet have covered 125 to 150 miles from inside San Bernardino Strait, down along the ocean shore of Samar, in the last seven hours, undetected by ship, search plane, or coast watcher?

Admiral Halsey had been informed by a night-search plane from *Independence* that Kurita's Center Force would sortie from San Bernardino Strait. Sightings on it heading that way reached the admiral as late as 2120, October 24. But he simply did not care. Estimating that his carrier pilots' exaggerated reports of their sinkings in the Battle of the Sibuyan Sea that day were correct, he assumed that Center Force "could no longer be considered a serious menace to Seventh Fleet," in or outside Leyte Gulf, and did not even warn Admiral Kinkaid, the commander of that fleet, to watch out. By the time Halsey received the night-sighting reports, his Third Fleet — less McCain's task group, which he had sent south to fuel — was hightailing north, hellbent after Ozawa's Northern Force. That was exactly what the Japanese wanted it to do. Halsey might have spared one carrier group and Admiral Lee's battle line (*New Jersey, Iowa, Washington, Massachusetts, Alabama*) to guard San Bernardino Strait; but he left not even a picket destroyer. That is why Kurita's Center Force was able to debouch unseen into the Philippine Sea at 0030, October 25, and steam south unseen off the Samar shore, until intercepted by Clifton Sprague's escort carriers. And that is why Taffy 3, composed of six escort carriers with no guns bigger than 5-inch, screened by three destroyers and four destroyer escorts, had to fight Kurita's four battleships, six heavy cruisers, and numerous destroyers.

Taffy 3 was supported by the aircraft of two other groups of nearly the same strength: Rear Admiral Thomas L. Sprague's Taffy 1, which was operating well to the south, off Mindanao; and Rear Admiral Felix B. Stump's Taffy 2, then off the entrance to Leyte Gulf. The total plane complement of these sixteen carriers was 235 fighter planes (Hellcats and Wildcats) and 143 Avenger torpedo planes; and it was they, in addition to Clifton Sprague's skillful tactics, and the intrepid attacks by his screen, that enabled him to win this battle against an overwhelming surface and gunfire superiority. But few of these planes were available at the moment of surprise. Taffy 1 had already launched a strike group to pursue Japanese ships fleeing down Surigao Strait; all carriers had launched planes for routine patrol, or for odd jobs such as delivering cans of fresh water to the troops on Leyte.

The Battle off Samar, thus unexpectedly joined at 0648, was the most remarkable of the Pacific war, since the tactics had to be improvised. Prewar training had prepared the United States Navy to fight battles such as Surigao Strait; but there was no preparation, no doctrine, for a force of "baby flattops" fighting a battle fleet such as Kurita's. The training was all for supporting amphibious operations by strikes and combat air and antisubmarine patrols, not for bearing the brunt of a major battle. Rear Admiral Sprague, known as "Ziggy" in the Navy, an able and conscientious officer forty-eight years old, had commanded fleet carrier *Wasp* in the Battle of the Philippine Sea, but now he faced a unique challenge.

Weather gave the escort carriers their first break. Wind blew from the eastern quadrant, permitting them to steer away from the enemy while launching planes, and rain squalls afforded occasional cover. Admiral Sprague, knowing very well what a pickle he was in, acted with cool and correct decision. He turned Taffy 3 due east, upped speed to the flattop maximum of 17.5 knots, ordered every plane to be launched and to attack, and broadcast an urgent plea for assistance. Admirals Tom Sprague and Felix Stump responded quickly; but Taffy 1 lay 130 miles distant; could its planes get there in time?

Kurita fumbled from the moment the battle joined. His staff told him that the escort carriers were fleet carriers, the destroyers were cruisers, and the destroyer escorts destroyers. At the moment of impact, he was changing the disposition of his force from cruising to anti-aircraft formation. He should promptly have formed battle line with his fast, powerful ships, and committed light forces to torpedo attack. Instead, he ordered General Attack — every ship for itself — which threw his force into confusion and made the battle a helter-skelter affair, ships committed piecemeal and defeated piecemeal, just as the Japanese army was wont to do ashore.

Admiral Sprague formed his six carriers into a ragged circle 2500 yards in diameter, his screen patrolling outside the engaged sector, as Japanese salvos edged closer and closer. At 0706, to quote his action report: "The enemy was closing with disconcerting rapidity and the volume and accuracy of fire was increasing. At this point it did not appear that any of our ships could survive another five minutes of the heavy-caliber fire being received." His task unit being faced by "the ultimate in desperate circumstances," he saw that counteraction was urgently required. He ordered all his escorts to make a torpedo attack. And, also at 0706, compassionate Providence sent a rain squall, under which the carriers, in conjunction with the smoke that they and the escorts were making, were protected for about fifteen minutes. During this respite the admiral decided to bear around to the south and southwest, in order to bring his disposition nearer to hoped-for help from Leyte Gulf. But no help appeared. Admiral Oldendorf, his ammunition depleted by the previous night's battle in Surigao Strait, had to replenish from supply ships in Leyte Gulf; and by the time he was ready to sortie, it was too late to reach the flattops. Sprague's tactics were risky, since they invited the enemy to take the inside track, but they proved to be correct. Kurita was so obsessed with keeping the weather gauge that, instead of cutting corners, he maintained course until he was due north of the carriers, and then bore down. And most of his ships, repeatedly dodging air and torpedo attacks, could not catch up. The Japanese admiral was bewildered by the way everything we had afloat or airborne went baldheaded for his capital ships.

At 0716, after the escort carriers had entered the rain squall, Clifton Sprague ordered his screen to counterattack the Japanese heavy ships. His three destroyers were *Hoel*, flying the pennant of Commander W. D. Thomas, and *Heermann* and *Johnston*, all 2100-tonners of the *Fletcher* class. *Johnston* was already counterattacking. Her skipper, Commander Ernest E. Evans, a fighting Cherokee Indian, short, barrel-chested, loud of voice, was a born leader. As soon as the Japanese ships were sighted, he ordered all boilers to be lighted, called all hands to General Quarters, and passed the word: "Prepare to attack major portion of Japanese Fleet." As *Johnston* sheered out to lay a smoke screen, she commenced firing at a range of 18,000 yards. Closing to within 10,000 yards of a heavy-cruiser column, she launched torpedoes and made one hit on *Kumano*. The Japanese flag officer on board shifted to *Suzuya*, which had already been slowed down by air bombing, and both cruisers dropped astern and out of the battle.

About 0730, *Johnston* took three 14-inch and three 6-inch shell hits. "It was like a puppy being smacked by a truck," recalled her senior surviving officer. The after fireroom and engine room were knocked out; all power to the after 5-inch guns was lost. A rain squall gave her ten minutes to repair damage. At this stage of the battle, confusion reigned supreme. *Johnston,* having expended all torpedoes, used manually controlled 5-inch guns against battleship *Kongo;* and, as if this were not enough, she played the major part in frustrating Kurita's destroyer attack on the carriers. After that, said the survivor, "we were in a position where all the gallantry and guts in the world could not save us." Three cruisers and several destroyers, overtaking her when slowed down, poured in an avalanche of shells. She went dead in the water. Commander Evans ordered Abandon Ship at 0950. The same Japanese destroyer squadron whose attack on the carriers she had just thwarted now made a running circle around her, shooting rapidly. At 1010 she rolled over and began to sink. A destroyer closed to give her the coup de grâce. One of her sailors, swimming, saw the Japanese skipper on his bridge salute as *Johnston* took the final plunge.

Hoel and *Heermann* were fighting just as vigorously, their skippers' one object being to inflict maximum damage on the enemy in the hope of diverting major-caliber fire from the carriers. *Heermann* (Commander A. T. Hathaway) at one point was engaging four battleships. She was too nimble for them to hit, but her spread of six torpedoes caused the mighty *Yamato* to reverse course for ten minutes, which took those 18.1-inch guns out of the fight. *Hoel* (Commander L. S. Kintberger), with one engine and three 5-inch guns knocked out, was not so lucky. She took over forty hits, even 16-inch, which went right through her hull without exploding, but knocked her so full of holes that at 0855 she rolled over and sank. Her crew, wrote her commander, "performed their duties coolly and efficiently until their ship was shot from under them."

In the second torpedo attack that Clifton Sprague ordered, at 0742, the three destroyer escorts of his screen also took part. *Samuel B. Roberts* was sunk, after exchanging gunfire with several heavy cruisers. Here is the tribute of her skipper, Lieutenant Commander R. W. Copeland, USNR, to his men, one that may apply equally well to the entire screen:

To witness the conduct of the average enlisted man on board this vessel . . . with an average of less than one year's service, would make any man proud to be an average American. The crew were informed over the loudspeaker system at the beginning of the action of the C.O.'s estimate of the situation: i.e., a fight against overwhelming odds from which survival could not be expected, during which time we would do what damage we could. In the face of this knowledge the men zealously manned their stations . . . and fought and worked with such calmness, courage, and efficiency that no higher honor could be conceived than to command such a group.

For two hours after 0743, when they emerged from the rain squall, the six escort carriers of Taffy 3 were making best speed of 17.5 knots around an irregular arc, subtended by a chord almost parallel to the coast of Samar. Their own planes, helped by many from Taffy 2 and Taffy 1, were continually attacking the Japanese with bombs, torpedoes, and machine-gun bullets, and making "dry runs" when they ran out of ammunition. Kurita's ships were capable of twice the speed of Sprague's, but their frequent evasive maneuvers to escape torpedoes and bombing attacks canceled the advantage; while the American carriers plodded steadily along. Hence the enemy's main body never appreciably closed range. The three Japanese battleships still advancing at 0820 were astern of the carriers, slowly firing salvos with armor-piercing projectiles that, if they hit, failed to detonate on the thin-skinned flattops. The heavy cruisers were much more deadly: they made thirteen 8-inch hits on *Kalinin Bay*, and she was the only carrier to be hit by a battleship; heroic efforts of damage control kept her in formation. Boatswains' crews worked in five feet of water to plug holes below the waterline. The "black gang" worked knee-deep in oil, choked by the stench of burning rubber and threatened by scalding steam, to repair ruptures in the power plant. Main steering control conked out, and quartermasters steered the ship by hand from far down in her bowels, like helmsmen in the ancient Spanish galleons.

Aircraft for the most part made individual attacks, as they had been too hastily armed and launched to be coordinated. Avengers first used torpedoes, then bombs, even little 100-pounders; and when these gave out they made "dry runs" — buzzing without bombing — to divert the Japanese gunners. Lieutenant Commander Edward J. Huxtable, air group commander in *Gambier Bay*, guided his Avenger for two hours through the flak to make dry runs, once flying down a line of heavy cruisers to divert them from their course and throw off their gunfire for a few precious minutes. The Wildcat pilots strafed topsides or ran interference for an Avenger; and they too made dry runs. Lieutenant Paul G. Garrison, USNR, made ten such out of a total of twenty. Since the American carriers were now scudding downwind and could not afford to luff up to recover planes, aircraft that ran out of fuel had to land on a carrier of Felix Stump's Taffy 2 about twenty-five miles away, or on the more distant Tacloban Field, Leyte, which army engineers had providentially made usable. There they refueled, picked up 500-pound bombs, and flew out to sea to fight again.

The battle reached a crisis when Kurita's four remaining heavy cruisers, *Chikuma, Tone, Haguro,* and *Chokai,* more enterprising than his battlewagons, pulled ahead on the port quarter of the carriers and closed range. *Chikuma* began a steady pounding of *Gambier Bay,* from which even attacks by the intrepid *Johnston* and *Heermann* did not divert her. The escort carrier, after a salvo-chasing snake dance lasting twenty-five minutes, began to take 8-inch hits, and dropped astern. The other three Japanese heavies, light cruiser *Noshiro,* and a destroyer, concentrated on *Gambier Bay.* As she began to sink, Captain Vieweg gave the order Abandon Ship. *Chikuma* continued to pound her at short range, and at 0907 she capsized and went down.

On to the southwest plunged the other five American flattops. *White Plains* fired her single 5-inch guns at each cruiser that closed within 18,000 yards, and made at least six hits on *Chokai.* "Hold on a little longer, boys," sang out Chief Gunner's Mate Jenkins. "We're sucking 'em into forty-millimeter range!" And they almost did, or would have, but for an attack on that heavy cruiser by four Avengers led by Commander R. L. Fowler of *Kitkun Bay's* air group. These planes scored ten hits and had the satisfaction of seeing *Chokai* go down. Next, *Chikuma* was sunk by a well-coordinated Wildcat-Avenger attack from Stump's Taffy 2; and down she went. Sprague's harried and beset carriers, now threatened by high-caliber battleship fire as well as by *Haguro* and *Tone,* saw to their amazement both heavy cruisers break off their pursuit. A moment later a signalman on the bridge of *Fanshaw Bay* yelled: "Goddammit, boys, they're getting away!" The entire Center Force was retiring.

Kurita had ordered the breakoff at 0911. The air and destroyer attacks had cost his force three heavy cruisers. His communications were so bad that he never knew how near *Tone* and *Haguro* had closed the flattops. At that time he intended merely to reassemble his dispersed and disorganized force, ascertain damage, and resume the march to Leyte Gulf. But the more he thought it over, the less he liked the prospect, and the better he relished the idea of going home the way he came. Center Force had been battered for three days — by submarines on the 23rd, fast carrier aircraft on the 24th, and in the battle just over. Kurita and his staff were so muddled as to estimate that the escort carriers were making 30 knots (instead of their maximum of 17.5), so it would be impossible to catch them. "I knew you were scared," said another admiral to Clifton Sprague after reading this postwar statement by Kurita, "but I didn't know you were *that* scared!"

Kurita had already received a radio signal from Admiral Shima indicating that Southern Force, in Surigao Strait, with which he was expected to cooperate, was all washed up. So he figured that his prospects in Leyte Gulf were both thin and grim. American transports and amphibious craft would have departed by the time he could get there; he feared massive land-based air attacks from Tacloban Field and heavy air attacks from Mitscher's fleet carriers. Nor did he care to fight Oldendorf's victorious gunfire force (which lay outside the entrance to Leyte Gulf waiting for him until 1300), in order to sink maybe a few LST's and sprinkle shellfire on American troops ashore. A fresh air attack by seventy Wildcats and Avengers from Taffy 2 and Taffy 3, which came in on Center Force at 1230, and made hits on battleship *Nagato* and heavy cruiser *Tone*, helped Kurita to make up his mind to retire. At 1236 he signaled the Commander in Chief of the Combined Fleet at Tokyo that he was heading for San Bernardino Strait.

Kurita's retirement did not end this day's battle for the escort carriers. While Clifton Sprague's Taffy 3 was fighting to the north, Tom Sprague's Taffy 1 was receiving the dubious honor of first target of the Kamikaze Corps, that formidable suicide club. *Santee* was crashed by a member at 0740, and hit by a torpedo from submarine *I–56* at 0756; but these converted-tanker flattops were tough, and by eight bells *Santee* was making over 16 knots. Sister *Suwannee* received a second kamikaze shortly after, but was able to resume flight operations at 1009. Taffy 3's turn came at 1050, when she hoped that the battle was over. One crashed Rear Admiral Ofstie's flagship, *Kitkun Bay*, but bounced into the sea; two that made for *Fanshaw Bay* were shot down; two were exploded by antiaircraft fire when diving at *White Plains* and *Kitkun Bay*; two crashed *Kalinin Bay* but inflicted comparatively little damage. But one broke through the flight deck of *St. Lo,* burst into flames, exploded the bombs and torpedoes on the hangar deck, and sank her.

An hour later Kurita's Center Force was attacked by aircraft from Admiral McCain's task group of the big fleet carriers. Admiral Halsey, at Kinkaid's urgent request, had ordered this. McCain, fueling when he got the word, turned up flank speed and commenced launching at 1030 when 335 distant miles from Kurita. This was one of the longest-range carrier plane attacks of the war; too long, for Avengers could not carry heavy bombs or torpedoes that far, and they suffered considerable loss without inflicting additional damage.

By noon the Battle off Samar was over. It had been a glorious but expensive victory: two escort carriers, two destroyers, and a destroyer escort sunk; several other ships badly damaged; and heavy casualties:

	Killed & Missing	Wounded
Taffy 1 ships' crews	283	136
Taffy 3 ships' crews	792	768
Aviators, all escort carriers	43	9
Aviators, McCain's task group	12	0
TOTAL	1130	913

Kurita's successful retirement was small consolation for the complete failure of his mission. His defeat was due, in last analysis, to the indomitable spirit of the escort carriers, their screen, and their aviators. It was they who stopped the most powerful gunfire force that Japan had sent to sea since the Battle of Midway.

The Battle for Leyte Gulf did not end the war, but it was decisive. And it should be an imperishable part of our national memory. The night action in Surigao Strait is an inspiring example of perfect timing, coordination, and almost faultless execution. But the Battle off Samar had no compeer. The story of that action — with its dramatic surprise, the quick thinking and resolute decisions of Clifton Sprague; the little screening vessels feeling for each other through the rain and smoke, and, courting annihilation, making individual attacks on battleships and heavy cruisers; naval aviators making dry runs on enemy ships to divert gunfire from their own; the defiant humor and indomitable courage of bluejackets caught in the "ultimate of desperate circumstances" — will make the fight of the "Taffys" with Kurita's Center Force forever memorable, forever glorious.

10

Conclusion to the War in the Pacific

This is my concluding chapter in THE TWO-OCEAN WAR, *pages 578–86. That is my one-volume digest of American naval operations in the entire war, written in 1962 and published by Atlantic–Little, Brown in the following year. Since then, more than another decade has gone by, and many excellent books have been published on the naval war and read by me; but a careful rereading has not caused me to correct any of my conclusions here reprinted.*

IN CONCLUSION, your historian may be allowed a few estimates and remarks on how the United States Navy conducted itself in this, the greatest of all wars in which it has ever been engaged.

On the whole, gloriously. But certain faults and lapses must be remembered, if we are to maintain high standards and meet the challenge of the atomic age. The Navy was caught unprepared mentally for the attack on Pearl Harbor, largely owing to routine and lack of imagination in the higher echelons. It was caught unprepared, both materially and technically, to cope with the U-boat menace — despite benefit of British experience in over two years of antisubmarine war. The Navy's fighter planes and torpedo-bombers were inferior to those of the Japanese, whose night-fighting tactics were superior to ours until mid-1943. Although certain strategists in the United States Navy anticipated the use of aircraft carriers to project striking power deep into enemy-held waters, too many envisaged this war as a succession of Jutlands, to be decided by big guns on battleships. Consequently our gunfire became highly effective, but warships greater than destroyers had no torpedo tubes. Torpedoes themselves underwent no development between wars, and the testing of those we had was so inefficient and misleading that United States submarines long had the mortification of making hit after hit with no explosion to follow. The destroyers, fortunately, retained their torpedoes, but the tactical employment of destroyers for surface action was inferior to that of the Japanese prior to the Battle of Vella Gulf in 1943.

Although the *Iowa*-class battleships never had a chance at a long-range gunfire battle (and what a beauty there would have been off San Bernardino Strait had Halsey released Lee in time!), the accuracy and efficiency of our naval gunfire was a great asset in the war. Gunfire support almost opened a new dimension to amphibious operations. Antiaircraft fire, helped by the proximity-fused shell, became so deadly that the Japanese were forced to adopt suicide tactics. Although aircraft bombing tolled the bell for long-range battleship action, naval gunfire will always be wanted to cover amphibious landings, which are likely to be necessary as long as there is war.

The United States Navy quickly adopted and developed the English invention of radar; but it was not until well into 1943 that officers generally appreciated its capabilities and limitations, and made best use of it. Nevertheless, the prior possession of radar turned out to be a great asset.

In antisubmarine warfare, it was long before the United States Navy caught up with its teacher, the Royal Navy of Great Britain. But we made full use both of British experience and the contributions of American scientists and mathematicians. This was only the second war that the Navy fought as part of a coalition, and its relations with the British and Royal Canadian navies were far closer and more effective than in World War I. In the Pacific the United States Navy, owing to its overwhelming strength, called the tune, but was loyally followed by the smaller navies of three British Commonwealth nations.

Admiral Ernest J. King was the Navy's principal architect of victory. A stern sailor of commanding presence, vast sea knowledge, and keen strategic sense, he was so insistent on maintaining the independence of the Navy, not only from our great Ally but from the Army, that he seemed at times to be anti-British and anti-Army. Neither was true; but King's one mistaken idea was his steady opposition to "mixed groups" from different navies in the same task force, an idea strengthened by the unfortunate experience of the ABDA command. Mixed groups were of necessity adopted on the convoy routes, with American, Canadian, and even an occasional Free French or Polish destroyer in the same escort unit, and they worked well; whilst in the Pacific, ships of the Royal Australian and New

Zealand navies operated perfectly with those of the United States. All three services of the same country worked well on one team in forward areas where the real fighting went on. The in-fighting between services and the disputes between British and American representatives were largely confined to Washington, London, or wherever the Combined Chiefs of Staff met.

We may, however, concede to Admiral King a few prejudices, for he was undoubtedly the best naval strategist and organizer in our history. His insistence on limited offensives in the Pacific to keep the Japanese off balance, his successful efforts to provide more and more escorts for convoys, his promotion of the escort carrier antisubmarine groups, his constant backing of General George C. Marshall to produce a firm date for Operation Overlord from the reluctant British, his insistence on the dual approach to Japan are but a few of the many decisions that prove his genius. King's strategy for the final defeat of Japan — the Formosa and China coast approach, rather than the Luzon-Okinawa route — was overruled; but may well, in the long run, have been better than MacArthur's, which was adopted. King was also defeated in his many attempts to interest the Royal Navy in a Southeast Asia comeback; and in this he was right. The liberation of Malaya before the war's end would have spared the British Empire a long battle with local communists and would have provided at least a more orderly transfer of sovereignty in the Netherlands East Indies.

After King, Chester W. Nimitz was our greatest naval strategist and leader, and, as CINCPAC-CINCPOA, he had, after King, the biggest responsibility. Nimitz engineered, as it were, the Battles of the Coral Sea and Midway; patiently but stubbornly he held out for the dual approach to Japan. He proposed the bold plan to go right into Kwajalein after securing the Gilberts, and he put it across, contrary to the advice of others. He made only two possible mistakes in the war — detaching Admiral Thomas C. Kinkaid prematurely from his South Pacific Task Force, and rejecting Admiral William B. Halsey's proposal that Peleliu be by-passed. Nimitz probably inspired a greater personal loyalty than did any other admiral in the war. Every commanding officer, when his ship, no matter how small, put in at Pearl Harbor, was encouraged to call on Nimitz at the CINCPAC-CINCPOA headquarters in Makalapa and express his views. Knowing that the finest test of a commanding officer is, in Churchill's words, "the quality of his effort," and that mistakes in battle are inevitable, Nimitz was slow to relieve any commanding officer who failed; he believed in the adage that every dog should be allowed two bites. It may be conceded that he allowed one bite too many to certain task force commanders before he relieved them; but it was fortunate for the cause that he allowed two bites to Kelly Turner, who turned out to be a practitioner of amphibious warfare second to none.

In the same web-footed class with Turner were Wilkinson and Barbey in the Pacific, and Hewitt and Kirk in the Atlantic and the Mediterranean. The last two, having to deal with high officers of the Royal Navy who were more used to ordering subordinates than conferring with equals, had to double as diplomats. Ingersoll and Ingram became very competent commanders of the Atlantic Fleet. There was an immense amount of talent in the lower echelons of flag rank. Rear Admirals Hall, Deyo, Conolly, Joy, Fechteler, Blandy, Low, McMorris, Merrill, Denebrink, DuBose, to mention only a few, were fully equal to exercising even higher commands, which seniority denied to them. Of those who were killed in action or as a result of it, we remember Kidd, Scott, Callaghan, Mullinnix, Chandler, and Royal.

When we come to the admirals who commanded at sea, and who directed a great battle, there was no one to equal Raymond A. Spruance. Always calm, always at peace with himself, Spruance had that ability, which marks the great captain, to make correct estimates and the right decisions in a fluid battle situation. He was bold and aggressive when the occasion demanded offensive tactics; cautious when pushing his luck too far might have lost the fruits of victory. Spruance in the Battle of Midway, with his instinct for the enemy's jugular vein — his carriers — deciding to launch planes at the right moment, retiring at night when further persistence would have risked an encounter with Yamamoto's massed gunfire, was superb; there is no other word for it. Spruance in the Battle of the Philippine Sea, overriding Mitscher, the carrier expert, in letting the enemy planes come at him instead of going in search of them, won the second most decisive battle of the Pacific war. And, off Okinawa, Spruance never faltered in face of the destruction wrought by the kamikazes. It is regrettable that, owing to Spruance's innate modesty and his refusal to create an image of himself in the public eye, he was never properly appreciated.

Halsey, the public's favorite in the Navy, will always remain a controversial figure, but none can deny that he was a great leader; one with the true "Nelson touch." His appointment as Commander South Pacific Force at the darkest moment of the Guadalcanal campaign lifted the hearts of every officer and bluejacket. He hated the enemy with an unholy wrath, and turned that feeling into a grim determination by all hands to hit hard, again and again, and win. His proposal to step up the Leyte operation by two months was a stroke of strategic genius that undoubtedly shortened the Pacific war. Unfortunately, in his efforts to build public morale in America and Australia, Halsey did what Spruance refused to do — built up an image of himself as an exponent of Danton's famous principle, "Audacity, more audacity, always audacity." That was the real reason for his fumble in the Battle for Leyte Gulf. For his inspiring leadership in 1942–43, his generosity to others, his capacity for choosing the right men for his staff, Halsey well earned his five stars and his place among the Navy's immortals.

Admiral Kinkaid, after being allowed one "bite" — the loss of *Hornet* in the Battle of the Santa Cruz Islands — rose to be one of our greatest seamen as Commander Seventh Fleet. He had a difficult role to play as head of "MacArthur's Navy," since that great general, for all his genius, at first imperfectly understood the limitations and capabilities of sea power. But he learned from Kinkaid. In the Battle for Leyte Gulf Kinkaid had an unfortunate position in the chain of command: under MacArthur but unable to control Halsey. Within these limitations he acquitted himself very well, and is entitled to no small part of the glory reaped by Oldendorf in Surigao Strait and Clifton Sprague off Samar.

In a special category of excellence are the flag officers of fleet carriers, with Mitscher *facile princeps*. Under him, McCain, Reeves, Bogan, Clark, Frederick Sherman, and Radford showed qualities of greatness; and the Battle off Samar proved that the escort carrier admirals, the two Spragues (Clifton and Thomas) and Felix Stump, were in no way inferior. And we must not forget two great chiefs of staff, Burke and Carney.

Above all these sailors was the commander in chief, Franklin D. Roosevelt — a remarkable leader indeed. Unlike Winston Churchill, Roosevelt never imagined himself to be a strategist. In general, he followed the advice of the Joint Chiefs of Staff, which included King, Marshall, and his own chief of staff, wise old Admiral Leahy. Thrice at least he went over their heads — refusing to redeploy American forces into the Pacific in 1942, insisting that Guadalcanal must be reinforced and held at all costs, and inviting a British fleet to participate in the Okinawa campaign. He also threw his influence in favor of MacArthur's desire to liberate Leyte and Luzon against the Navy's wish to by-pass them. He was a tower of strength to Marshall, King, and Eisenhower against insistent British pressure to postpone Overlord and shift Dragoon from Marseilles to Trieste. The Navy was his favorite service — I heard him once, in true regal style, refer to it as "my Navy" — and he did his utmost to build it up and improve its efficiency both before and during the war.

In operations, there were several things that the Navy did superlatively well. Instigated by the Marines, it studied and developed the technique of amphibious warfare well before 1939. In this important branch the United States Navy was behind the Japanese but ahead of the Royal Navy when war broke; but the Japanese, thrown on the defensive, had no chance to practice amphibious warfare after the Java campaign, and the Royal Navy, thanks largely to Mountbatten's combined operations unit, caught up with us in Sicily and Normandy. In carrier warfare the United States Navy was supreme, because it successfully resisted (as the Royal Navy had not) the efforts of the Army to obtain control over all combatant planes, and because admirals like Mitscher and McCain made constant efforts to improve carrier tactics and profited by early mistakes. In order to service the fast carrier forces and enable them to keep the sea, fighting, for many weeks on end, the Navy devised the at-sea logistics system, one of the principal instruments of victory. For this, credit is primarily due to Admirals Calhoun and Beary, and Commodores Gray and Carter.

The planning of operations, too, was very well done, even though it often had to be done in a hurry. The supreme planning job of the war was that for Operation Neptune-Overlord, in which British and Americans both took part; but for purely United States Navy operations, the top planners — "Savvy" Cooke on King's staff and Forrest Sherman on Nimitz's — deserve a special accolade. Kelly Turner was an amazingly meticulous, thorough, and accurate planner for his own amphibious operations, and oversaw every detail himself. Once Turner gave the word "Land the landing force!" everything went like clockwork; one felt that anybody could have done it, not knowing the immense amount of skill and thought that had gone into the plan. Wilkinson was Turner's peer in the Central, as Barbey was in the

Southwest Pacific. Foul-ups (which the Navy called by a harsher word) had always been expected in amphibious operations, even when uncontested, and it was a tribute to our new tactics that the Japanese finally decided not to contest these operations, but to hole up and sell their lives dear.

One feels particular admiration for the officers of the destroyers, the "tin cans," which operated in every theater of the war. They not only had to be first-rate seamen and ship handlers, but men of science who could assimilate the new techniques of antisubmarine warfare and air defense. Although overwhelmed with paperwork, these young officers maintained something of the port and swagger of the old-time frigate skippers; they were as good for a lark ashore as for a fight at sea. In every theater and every kind of operation, as we have abundantly seen, destroyers were the indispensable component. Whether in convoy duty or in a hunter-killer group in the Atlantic, or supporting amphibious operations, delivering torpedo attacks in a night battle, or taking the rap from kamikazes off Okinawa, the men who manned these ships proved themselves to be the most versatile and courageous of sea warriors. It is no wonder that so many have risen to high command in the new Navy.

Equally admirable were the submariners, an even more scientific and specialized branch of the Navy, and their great leaders, Admirals Lockwood, Christie, and Fife. Owing to wartime secrecy, they seldom received public credit; this was the true "silent service." The submarines not only dogged the Japanese merchant navy to its death and sank more than their share of warships, in both oceans they scouted in advance of amphibious landings, and in the Pacific they maintained contact with Philippine patriots. The submarines lost an even greater proportion of their numbers than did the brave naval aviators. And the "boats" named after fishes were immediate ancestors of the nuclear-powered, Polaris-armed underwater warships that have become the prime protectors of the free world.

Let us also remember the "small boys" — the gunboats, minecraft, destroyer escorts, PT's, beaching and other lettered craft, even the lowly "yard-birds" and small cutters. These, largely commanded by reservists, were forced to perform functions and make long voyages for which they had not been designed. The production of thousands of these in wartime, the training of them at special schools set up for that purpose, the operation of them under the most hazardous conditions are beyond praise; but we may not forget that when the war involved us the Navy was woefully deficient in escorts and small craft, and should resolve never to be caught short again.

On July 1, 1940, the Navy had only 13,162 officers and 744,824 enlisted men; on August 31, 1945, it had 316,675 officers and 2,935,695 enlisted men. Analogous figures for the Marine Corps are 1819 officers and 26,545 enlisted men in 1940; 36,851 officers and 427,017 enlisted men at the end of the war.* In spite of this immense dilution of all ranks and ratings, the Navy did a superlative job in making fighting sailors out of young Americans fresh out of school, farm, or minor shore jobs, teaching them the manifold skills necessary to operate and fight a modern warship, pride in their ships, and courage to face the most hideous form of death, by burning.

The vastly expanded American merchant marine, too, deserves high praise for its worldwide operations, which were indispensable to support of the Navy, the Army, and our Allies. Merchant mariners and the Naval Armed Guards on the ships showed exemplary courage in convoy duty, in actions with German raiders and U-boats, and in replenishing the fleet off Okinawa under constant threat of kamikaze attack. We must never forget that since one of the main functions of a navy is to protect trade and communications both in peace and in war, it can never function properly without a strong and efficient merchant marine, or without the know-how of master mariners and seamen.

So, thanks to all; and, no matter what the atomic age brings, America will always need sailors and ships and shipborne aircraft to preserve her liberty, her communications with the free world, even her existence. If the deadly missiles with their apocalyptic warheads are ever launched at America, the Navy will still be out on blue water fighting for her, and the nation or alliance that survives will be the one that retains command of the oceans.

* To these should be added 8399 women officers and 73,685 enlisted women (the Waves); 813 officers and 17,350 enlisted women Marines, and 10,968 nurses, all at the end of the war.

III

Studies in American History

1

William Bradford

From the Introduction to my edition of William Bradford's OF PLYMOUTH PLANTATION (New York: Alfred A. Knopf, 1952), *pages xxiii–xxvii.*

The manuscript of Bradford's classic story of the Pilgrim Fathers and their Colony of New Plymouth, stolen from Boston's Old South Church during the War of Independence, finally turned up in the episcopal library at Fulham Palace, London, in 1844. From the manuscript, a scribe made a longhand copy, which went to a Boston printer, and became the editio princeps, *in 1856. Forty years later, the British government returned the Bradford manuscript to Massachusetts, where it rests in what I hope is a burglar-proof safe in the State Library. Since that time, several editions have been printed, the best being the one issued by the Massachusetts Historical Society in two volumes, edited by Worthington C. Ford in 1912. But all these were more or less replicas of the original manuscript, with Bradford's erratic spelling and punctuation, or lack of it. Now, what I wanted was an edition that respected Bradford's style, diction, and wording but revised his spelling and punctuation so as to gain him more readers. So I turned to, with the aid of my secretary, Antha E. Card; and for some five years, immediately after World War II, we spent all the time we could save from the naval history, collating our revised text with the original manuscript in the State Library.*

I cannot be so presumptuous as to include a few pages of Bradford in a Morison reader; but we have decided to include a few pages of my Introduction, on Bradford himself.

WILLIAM BRADFORD, the author of this History, was born at Austerfield, Yorkshire, in the early spring of 1590.* He was the third

---

* Baptized March 19; the date of his birth, presumably not earlier than March 15, was not recorded.

child and only son of William Bradford, a yeoman farmer of the parish, and Alice Hanson, daughter of the village shopkeeper. His father died when William was only a year old, his mother married again, and his grandfather and uncles then took him in hand to train him as a farmer. At the age of twelve he became a constant reader of the Bible — the Geneva version that he generally quotes — and, when still a lad, he was so moved by the Word as to join a group of Puritans who met for prayer and discussion at the house of William Brewster, in the nearby village of Scrooby. When this group, inspired by the Reverend Richard Clyfton, organized itself as a separate Congregational Church in 1606, Bradford joined it despite "the wrath of his uncles" and the "scoff of his neighbors."

From that date until his death half a century later, Bradford's life revolved around that of this church, or congregation, first in Scrooby, next in the Low Countries, and finally in New England. In his own words one may read of the members' escape to the Netherlands, their short sojourn at Amsterdam, and their long one at Leyden, under a remarkable pastor, the Reverend John Robinson. Bradford, upon coming of age in 1611, received an inheritance from his parents, which apparently he expended in some sort of mercantile venture; but he saved enough to buy a house in Leyden, where he followed the trade of weaver. He learned Dutch and a certain amount of Latin and Hebrew, and acquired a wide knowledge of general literature and a fair-sized library, which he brought with him to the New World.

In 1617, when the preparations began for the removal of this band of brothers to America, Bradford was twenty-seven years old; but his ability had evidently so impressed the elders of the congregation that he was chosen one of the committee to make the practical arrangements. He sailed in the *Mayflower* with his first wife, Dorothy May, whom he had married at Amsterdam in 1613. He took part in the boat expedition that explored Cape Cod, including the one that scudded into Plymouth Bay before a snowstorm and landed, as tradition has it, on Plymouth Rock, on December 11, 1620. On returning to the *Mayflower* at Cape Cod (now Provincetown) Harbor, he learned that his "dearest consort, accidentally falling overboard, was drowned in the harbor." His failure to mention this in the History is consistent with his modest reticence about his own rôle of leadership in the colony; but it may be that he suspected (as do we) that Dorothy Bradford took her own life, after gazing for six weeks at the barren sand dunes of Cape Cod. For we have it from other tenderhearted women who came to New England among the pioneers that their hearts grew faint and sick when they first beheld that wild-looking northern land, so different from the green and cultivated England they had left. Three years later, when a former member of the Leyden church, the widow Alice Southworth, came out to Plymouth with her two small boys, Bradford married her, and she bore him three children.

In May 1621, after the death of Governor John Carver, William Bradford, just turned thirty-one, was unanimously chosen to that office, "the dificulties whereof were such that, if he had not been a person of more than ordinary piety, wisdom and courage, he must have sunk under them." And he was re-elected to the same office no less than thirty times, for a total term of thirty-three years — every year from 1622.* In other words, he was governor of Plymouth Colony continuously from 1627 to 1656 inclusive, except for five years when he "by importunity gat off," according to Governor Winthrop; and in those years he was chosen an assistant to Governor Winslow or Governor Prence.

So, from 1621 to his death, Bradford was the principal leader of the Pilgrim Fathers. William Brewster, who had had a university education, was elder of the church; Edward Winslow, more a man of the world than Bradford, did the Pilgrims' diplomatic business; Myles Standish provided the power to their politics. But Bradford, who never left New England after he had once landed there, was the man who made the major decisions. He exercised more plenary authority than any governor of an English colony in his day, with the possible exception of Sir William Berkeley, in Virginia.

If Bradford had been moved by love of power or ambition for wealth, he had an opportunity in 1630 when the Warwick Patent from the Council for New England was made out in his name. He might then, had he wished, have become the sole lord and proprietor of Plymouth Colony, like Lord Baltimore, in Maryland. Instead, he promptly shared his proprietary right with the "Old Comers," as the Pilgrim Fathers were called in their own day; and in 1640 he persuaded these Old Comers to surrender the patent to the whole body

---

* An apparent error in this count is due to the fact that in two years, 1646 and 1649, no election was held; the governor simply carried on. Checked from W. H. Whitmore, *The Massachusetts Civil List*, pages 35–40.

of Freemen. He was one of a small group known as the Undertakers, who were given by the Freemen a monopoly of offshore fishing and fur-trading in order to pay off their debt to the Merchant Adventurers who financed the *Mayflower*'s voyage. It is true that we have never heard the Adventurers' side of the story, except in their own letters that Bradford incorporated in his History; but even on their showing, they treated the Pilgrims much as a loan shark treats a man in financial difficulties; the more beaver and other commodities they sent to England, the more the debt grew. Finally it was paid off in 1648, after Bradford, Alden, Standish, Winslow, and Prence had sold houses and large parcels of land to make up the balance.

Thereafter, Bradford continued the Indian trade on his own account, through trading posts on Buzzard's Bay and the Kennebec. At his death, at the age of sixty-seven, on May 9, 1657, he owned a house in Plymouth valued only at £45, an orchard and several parcels of land at Plymouth, a "great beer bowle" and two smaller ones, six leather chairs, three "carved chairs," a "great chair" and a court cupboard, ten and a half pairs of sheets, a large quantity of table linen, about five dozen pewter dishes and vessels, a red Turkey grogram suit of clothes, a red waistcoat and a "sad colored" suit, a "stuff suit with silver buttons," an "old violet colored cloak," and "two hats — a black one and a colored one."

"He was a person for study as well as action," records Cotton Mather; and this may be seen not only by his literary skill, but by the fact that he had at his death a library of about 400 volumes, including John Speed's *Prospect of the Most Famous Part of the World*, Peter Martyr's *De Orbe Novo*, Jean Bodin's *De Republica*, Pierre de la Primaudaye's *French Academy*, and "divers Dutch books."

It is a pity that the governor did not continue his History through 1650, for we would like to know his opinion of Father Gabriel Druillettes, a Jesuit from Canada who visited him at the end of the year in order to come to some arrangement about the Abnaki Indians on the Kennebec. The governor (whom Druillettes called "Jehan Brentford") received him with courtesy and invited him to dine, taking care to serve a fish dinner because it was Friday, although Puritans made rather a point of not eating fish on Fridays.

In his later years, the governor wrote out three "Dialogues" between "Ancient Men" of Plymouth, explaining to "Young Men born in New England" the principles of their religion and their church organization. He wrote a good deal of indifferent verse, some of which is appealing for its very simplicity and sincerity:

> From my years young in days of youth,
> God did make known to me his truth,
> And call'd me from my native place
> For to enjoy the means of grace.
>
> In wilderness he did me guide,
> And in strange lands for me provide.
> In fears and wants, through weal and woe,
> A Pilgrim passed I to and fro.

In his later years, the governor felt that the glory had departed from Plymouth; the town declining in numbers, population dispersed, young people indifferent to religion and heedless of their fathers' sacrifices, luxury coming in with prosperity, Indians growing insolent.

Unfortunately we have no contemporary biographical sketch of Bradford; not even a portrait or description of his person. But it will not be difficult for anyone to infer his character from this History; as fair a permanent monument as any man could wish.

2

The Conservative
American Revolution

Address given to the Society of the Cincinnati in Washington, D.C., April 22, 1975. Now published as a book by the Society, it has footnotes and more material on the last decades of the century.

The reason I chose this subject was that I thought it needed to be said. Everyone else who has written or spoken during the Bicentennial celebration has emphasized its radical or "left-wing" features. That is right; but nobody has pointed out that a strong injection of conservatism was necessary to make our revolution's achievement stick, and not go "down the drain" like those of later revolutions.

TO CALL our American Revolution a Conservative Revolution will be a shock to many, probably most, Americans, since we have been accustomed to look on our Revolution as a torch-bearer for Liberty and the Rights of Man, herald and precursor of the French Revolution and the revolutions of Spanish America. But the mere mention of the French and Latin-American revolutions shows how fundamentally ours differed from those. In our case, the Revolution may be said to have begun with Washington and Jefferson in Virginia and the "brace of Adamses" in Massachusetts; and the Revolution ended with Washington, John Adams, and Jefferson the first three Presidents under a new federal Constitution, with Sam Adams governor under a conservative state constitution (still in force in 1976), written by his cousin John. By contrast, in no other important revolution of modern times did the leaders who started the revolution end it. In France, Mirabeau died and Lafayette and Lameth disappeared; the first constitution lasted but a year; a reign of terror was succeeded by an oligarchic *directoire*, and this by a military despot and emperor, Napoleon Bonaparte. In Russia, the moderate republic of Kerensky was overthrown by the communists, and committees of autocrats have governed the Soviet Union to this day. In China, the moderate republican government founded by Sun Yat-sen in 1912 fell before the thorough-going communist régime of Mao Tse-tung. And the end is not yet.

One reason that historians have generally played down the conservative nature of the American Revolution is that, in comparison with *previous* revolutions, it *was* radical. As Lord Acton wrote, "It was from America that the plain ideas that men ought to mind their own business, and that the nation is responsible to Heaven for the acts of the State — ideas long locked in the breast of solitary thinkers and hidden among Latin folios — burst forth like a conqueror upon the world they were destined to transform, under the title of The Rights of Man." All Western countries were astonished, almost stupefied, by the apparent ease with which Americans threw off their old "shackles" and made themselves new constitutions. But they knew little of the constant struggle during the war to keep innovation within reasonable bounds, to avoid anarchy, and to steer clear of the rocks of dissolution.

One can venture to formulate a law of revolution from the events of the last two centuries. The new régime starts on a euphoria of optimism. A new day has dawned; liberty is in the air. The new rulers, generous with utopian promises that cannot be kept, predict peace and plenty for all; but instead, the people suffer privation and defeat and become disillusioned; a left-wing faction undermines the early leaders, cries out upon them as traitors to the revolution, and sets up a dreary despotism of the left. New strong men take charge, and the much-vaunted republic of liberty ends in a military despotism. We can see this process going on now in Portugal and Africa. But our Revolution stopped short of going into a tailspin.

And why did it happen so? First, because the American Revolution began as a defensive movement to maintain the rights and liberties that the English colonists had always enjoyed and to which they felt they were entitled. Our leaders had no wish to scramble the existing social structure and restructure it on some new basis. "The abilities of a child might have governed this country," wrote Oliver Wolcott, of Connecticut, on May 16, 1776, "so strong has been their attachment to Britain."

That attachment had been strengthened by the last of the colonial wars, but weakened since 1763 by successive, stupid efforts of the English Parliament to tax the nonrepresented colonies. The government's attempt to punish the Boston Tea Party by blockading Boston Harbor was so resented and feared throughout the continent that it produced the first working colonial union, the Continental Congress. What had been originally a Massachusetts Bay revolution became the American Revolution when Congress adopted as its own army the local militia that was trying to contain the British garrison in Boston, and appointed George Washington commander in chief. Second, "revolution" was a respectable word in 1775, with a very different connotation from what it has today. It recalled the Glorious Revolution of 1688 in England, which, without bloodshed yet with parliamentary sanction, threw out James II and set up William and Mary.

Independence was another matter. Everyone in Anglo-America had been brought up to "fear God and honor the King"; hence it was a terrible wrench to repudiate George III. That is why the Continental Congress took fifteen months to face and decide the question of independence. First bloodshed occurred on April 19, 1775; the Continental Army, Navy, and Marine Corps were established; fighting spread both north and south; and Congress mounted two offensive operations — Benedict Arnold's to Canada and Commodore Abraham Whipple's to Jamaica. Yet all this time the colonists claimed to be loyal subjects of George III, fighting a "Ministerial Army," as they designated the British legions. General Washington even toasted the king nightly at his headquarters mess in Cambridge until January 1776, when, after reading Tom Paine's tract *Common Sense*, he decided that George III was the real villain, and was converted to the belief that complete independence of Great Britain was the only solution to preserve liberty in America.

John Adams wrote from Philadelphia on April 22, 1776, to James Warren, in Boston:

After all, my friend, I do not at all wonder that so much reluctance has been shewn to the measure of independency. All great changes are irksome to the human mind, especially those which are attended with great dangers and uncertain effects. No man living can foresee the consequences of such a measure, and therefore I think it ought not to have been undertaken untill the design of Providence by a series of great events had so plainly marked out the necessity of it, that he who runs might read.

We may please ourselves with the prospect of free and popular governments, but there is great danger that these governments will not make us happy. God grant they may! But I fear that in every Assembly members will obtain an influence by noise, not sense; by meanness, not greatness; by ignorance, not learning; by contracted hearts, not large souls. I fear, too, that it will be impossible to convince and persuade people to establish wise regulations.

Adams, back home in the fall of 1775, encountered a "horse jockey"* whose conversation gave him some qualms about the wild forces that even that early had been let loose:

As soon as he saw me, he came up to me, and his first Salutation to me was, "Oh! Mr. Adams what great Things have you and your Colleagues done for Us! We can never be gratefull enough to you. There are no Courts of Justice now in this Province, and I hope there never will be another!" Is this the Object for which I have been contending? said I to myself, for I rode along without any answer to this Wretch. Are these the Sentiments of such People? And how many of them are there in the Country? Half the Nation for what I know: for half the Nation are Debtors if not more, and these have been in all Countries, the Sentiments of Debtors. If the Power of the Country should get into such hands, and there is great danger that it will, to what purpose have We sacrificed our Time, health and every Thing else? Surely We must guard against this Spirit and these Principles or We shall repent of all our Conduct. However the good Sense and Integrity of the great Body of the People, came in to my thoughts for my relief, and the last resource was after all in a good Providence.

And in a later letter John confessed that at any time during the war he would gladly have given up American independence, could the colonies but return to their happy situation in 1763, before the successive British ministers began, with singular maladroitness, to push first one, then another, scheme of American taxation.

John was right. Despite the fundamental conservatism and loyalty to the Crown, there was an underlying strain of radicalism in the American Revolution; and the question is why it did not break out, discredit the leadership of Washington in war, of Robert Morris in finance, of Franklin in diplomacy, and bring into power a group of demagogues who certainly would have lost the war?

A very respectable lot of demagogues, too. Arthur Lee of the diplomatic mission in Paris, his brother Richard Henry Lee in Virginia,

* Meaning, in those days, a horse-trader.

James Lovell of Massachusetts in the Congress, and even, to some extent, Samuel Adams regarded Franklin as a corrupt old lecher, John Paul Jones merely a rough-and-ready sailor looking for prize money, and Washington an incompetent general. This conspiracy never really came to a head, owing to the popularity and character of Franklin and Washington. But it weakened their position at the darkest point of the war, 1779–80, when Washington lost battle after battle, and the enemy occupied eastern Maine and set up a Loyalist government in Georgia. But for the French alliance, the army of Rochambeau, and the fleet of de Grasse, there is no telling what would have happened. For the British government in 1778–79 was ready to make peace with the thirteen states on the basis of dominion home rule; the Carlisle Mission to Philadelphia in 1779 was authorized to conclude a cease-fire, to promise repeal of all acts of Parliament to which the Continental Congress had voiced objection, and to concede any other American demands "short of open and avowed Independence" from the Crown. And these terms were to be secured by treaty like the one that in our time recognized the independence of Ireland, less Ulster. Had this plan been accepted by the thirteen states, they would have returned to their British allegiance, leaving only war and foreign relations to the government in London.

Although several members of Congress were in favor at least of discussing these amazingly favorable terms of reconciliation, General Washington emphatically advised against even considering them, and others pointed out that to accept them would be a breach of the French alliance. So nothing was done. I believe that, given our bad military situation, the reluctance of the states to supply Washington's army with recruits or even food, and the fall of paper money to a point where no respectable farmer would accept it, there would have been a collapse of independence at this time but for General Washington's steadfast loyalty to the American cause, and Franklin's securing of the French alliance.

The expropriated Loyalists, who lost their land, their homes, and everything, would have been the first to deny that the American Revolution was conservative. Whilst treatment of the Loyalists is not one of the things that we view with pride, it was not nearly so severe as the treatment, in other countries, of counterrevolutionary groups in the great revolutions of our time. Thousands in France, hundreds of thousands in Russia, and millions in China were arbitrarily killed by revolutionaries for no other reason than that they were opposed to the new régimes or owned property that the new régimes wanted. The highest estimate of those leaving the United States during or after the war, out of loyalty to England and the Crown, is 80,000, but this emigration was almost wholly voluntary. There were no mass expulsions, much less executions, and the great majority of American Loyalists never left the states, but eventually became good American citizens. Also, a surprisingly large number who did leave drifted back. Cadwallader Colden returned from self-imposed exile and was elected mayor of New York City. Henry Cruger, a member of Parliament during the war, came back and was elected to the New York State senate. Dr. John Jeffries, of Boston, a surgeon in the British army during the war, made the pioneer crossing of the English Channel by balloon, then returned to Boston and built up a large practice. Philip B. Key, uncle of the author of "The Star Spangled Banner," served as an officer in a Maryland Loyalist regiment, but after the war was admitted to the Maryland bar and received an appointment to the federal bench while still receiving his British pension. Isaac Coffin, of Boston, an officer of the Royal Navy when the war began, remained in the king's senior service and rose to be Admiral Sir Isaac Coffin; but he founded a school at his ancestral home, Nantucket, and exported English thoroughbreds to improve the breed of horses in New England. In general, the only Loyalists who were not allowed to return to their homes after the war were those who had indulged in partisan warfare and Indian raids or who, like Governor Hutchinson of Massachusetts, had been open and notorious enemies of the American cause.

In Connecticut, immediately after the war, we find something unique in the history of revolutions: self-exiled Loyalists being invited to return and having their confiscated estates restored. This was done first by the towns on Long Island Sound, scene of wartime depredations by British raids that had been largely manned by the Loyalists, then by the state legislature. For Connecticut realized that if her seaports were to compete with New York and Newport, the capital and know-how of the former Loyalists would be highly desirable assets.

Connecticut is the best example of a state that fully pulled her weight in the War of Independence, yet remained steadfastly loyal to the ways of the past, not only during the war, but for thirty-five years after. Young Thomas Jefferson wrote to Thomas Nelson in 1776, six weeks before his Declaration of Independence was adopted, that the making of new constitutions "is the whole subject of the present controversy, for should a bad government be instituted for us in future, it had been as well to have accepted . . . the bad one offered to us from beyond the water, without the risk and expense of conflict." Most of the thirteen colonies followed his advice; but Connecticut and Rhode Island had enjoyed charters from Charles II, which gave them complete autonomy within the empire, so they saw no reason to change. Both Washington and Jefferson were puzzled by the irrefragable conservatism of Connecticut, the most democratic of all the states, socially. The key to the Connecticut system was its method of electing the state council through a series of winnowings based on the principle that unless a councilor died or resigned during his term, creating a vacancy, no new member could be nominated.*

Theodore Dwight, one of the "Hartford Wits" who flourished immediately after the War of Independence, succumbed to the muse of poetry when he viewed the politics of his "Land of Steady Habits," as Connecticut used to be called:

> Connecticut, thou wondrous State!
> Forever firm, forever great!
> Oft Faction here her tools employs,
> And oft we hear a mighty noise,
> That Government is full of evil,
> The Nation running to the Devil —
> The blindest eyes begin to wink,
> The thickest skulls begin to think.
> The little-ones are growing big,
> "The tail has got on t'other pig" —
> But when the hour of trial's o'er,
> Those short-lived tempests cease to roar;
> Sedition's vermin sneak from day,
> And all goes on the good old way!
> Still the old Council keep their seats,
> Still Wisdom there with Honor meets. †

* James Clarke Welling, in "Connecticut Federation, Aristocratic Politics in a Social Democracy," Chapter ix of his *Addresses . . . and Other Papers* (Riverside Press, 1903), has made the most perceptive analysis of this system.

† Dwight's effusion is in the *Connecticut Courant* of January 5, 1801.

While the conservative leaders of Connecticut and Rhode Island found their seventeenth-century charters adequate as constitutions of independent states, the left wing in Pennsylvania "put over" — I use this phrase designedly — a left-wing, logical, "enlightened" constitution, which proved in action to be a complete flop.

The history of how this constitution was brought about, and of how the state of Pennsylvania fared under it, well illustrates the value of conservatism to the American Revolution. It was put over by a discontented radical faction, mostly Philadelphia working class, and inspired by recent arrivals — Tom Paine from England, and Dr. Thomas Young from Boston, where he had been a leader of Samuel Adams's mobsters. Other local leaders were Thomas McKean, who had been in politics for twenty of his forty-two years, and James Cannon, Sam Adams's equal as a master of demagogic appeal. Paine's political ideas were those of the Enlightenment in France. All special privileges, such as property qualifications for voting or office-holding, must be abolished. To be responsive to the will of the people, the main organs of government should be a one-chamber legislature — no upper house, no senate — and a multiple executive — not a single head of state. These radicals in Pennsylvania manipulated sentiment, by printed and oral propaganda and by political finagling worthy of the most machine-ridden municipalities, into overriding the conservative Pennsylvania Assembly, led by John Dickinson, the "Pennsylvania Farmer," and calling a specially elected convention.

James Cannon, a leader in promoting and drafting this Pennsylvania constitution of 1776, managed to embalm in it the new and radical idea that eventually, in President Jackson's time, overthrew élitism in American politics. He believed that the common people should not only support a government, but should take part in it; this constitution must make certain that the people get control of politics in fact, and must also set up obstacles to the élite's ever recovering control. Property qualifications for voting were abolished, though not sexual qualifications. There was no senate or upper house of the legislature. The twelve members of the plural executive could serve for only three years and were ineligible for re-election for four years after their terms. The chairman of this council was president of Pennsylvania. Judges, appointed by the council, held their offices for seven years only. Imprisonment for debt was abolished. No game laws were to be passed. Cannon was disappointed because he could not get adopted a new article to the bill of rights declaring that large estates were "dangerous to the Rights, and destructive of the Common Happiness, of mankind." Nevertheless, the radical leaders of Pennsylvania — and Ben Franklin, too — declared that this was a "scientific" constitution; the framers were determined to see how "experimental philosophy" (like Franklin's experiments with electricity) would "succeed in politics." "You learned fellows," wrote Thomas Smith, one of the Pennsylvania radical leaders, to a friend, "who have warped your understanding by poring over musty old books, will perhaps laugh at us; but, know ye, that we despise you!"

This Pennsylvania constitution of 1776 established the nearest thing to a dictatorship of the proletariat that we have had in North America; a real "popular front" government. The legislature managed to disfranchise Quakers and some of the German sects by a loyalty-test oath, to which Quakers and others could not conscientiously subscribe; and the assembly, controlled by the leather-aproned artisans and rough frontiersmen, expended more energy during the war in plundering Loyalists, jailing profiteers, and persecuting conscientious objectors than in supporting the war. Notable was the case of the so-called Virginia Exiles. When the British army was approaching Philadelphia, in August 1777, some twenty Quakers were chosen arbitrarily and, without any trial, were declared to be "mischievous people" and shipped off to Virginia by wagon. In the session of 1779–80, in which an obscure local politician named George Brian was the leader, a constructive measure was passed looking toward the abolition of black slavery. Yet, at the same time, Franklin's Philadelphia College, pride of the colony and indeed the continent, was abolished, mainly because the members of the assembly disliked the political complexion of its board of trustees. In the realm of finance, the assembly in 1781 issued a flood of paper money, nominally worth £800,000; but within two months these bills became worthless.

The mob element gradually got control. An extralegal court, like the French Committee of Public Safety, started trying unpopular Philadelphians, and an armed mob tried to drive opponents out of the city. Speculators, not Tories, were now the scapegoats, for the common people were really suffering from the rise of prices. It was just such an explosive situation that led to the Reign of Terror in France.

The fourth day of October 1779 marked a highwater of radical control in Pennsylvania. The radicals were planning to seize all women and children of citizens who had gone Loyalist and fled the state, and ship them to New York City; and, at the same time, drive out leading citizens, like James Wilson, who had offended them. Local militia, demonstrating before the assembly hall to demand more money for doing nothing, assisted by a working-class mob, seized three unpopular citizens and paraded them through the streets while playing the "Rogue's March" and crying, "Get Wilson!"

James Wilson, having heard the day before that the mob was after him, appealed to the assembly for protection, but did not get it. He then gathered about twenty of his friends, armed them, and, while waiting for the mob to arrive, formed an informal defense company and drilled on Walnut Street. The militia mob arrived, armed with muskets and two field pieces, to find the defenders of "Fort Wilson" ready; both sides fired, the mob broke down Wilson's front door and surged into the house, where they were met by a volley of gunfire. Help then arrived: Philadelphia City Troop to the rescue! The appearance of these gallant horsemen, "composed of gentlemen of fortune" (as General Washington wrote in a thank-you letter for their aid at Princeton), dashing at the mob with swords drawn put a damper on the attack. A cease-fire was then agreed upon so that all hands could go to dinner. Dinner hour over, the City Troop galloped back to Walnut and Third, to find that the militia and mob also had gone to eat and that the defenders of Fort Wilson were loading their weapons against a second attack. But this never occurred; the "Battle of Fort Wilson" ended that afternoon.

Had James Wilson and his friends not defended themselves, this brawl of October 4, 1779, would have been to the American Revolution what the capture of the Bastille on July 14, 1789, was to the French Revolution. Joseph Reed, president of Pennsylvania under the radical constitution, played the role of mediator, dissuaded the militia from making a revenge attack next day, explained to the assembly that the Fort Wilson incident was just "casual overflowings of liberty," and asked for an act of oblivion, which was granted.

The vital stumbling block of the radical régime in Pennsylvania was not so much mob rule as the helplessness of the state government before inflation. The radicals, of course, blamed inflation on wealthy merchants and bankers. The assembly canceled the charter of the Bank of North America, and conditions became intolerable. In 1780, the outstanding merchants and financiers of Philadelphia, led by Robert Morris, whom the radicals regarded as an archvillain, raised £300,000 in real money to create a fund that would supply and transport three million rations and 300 hogsheads of rum to the Army, and eventually be reimbursed by Congress. This was done, and the lesson was not lost on the Pennsylvania public. In the election of October 1780, conservatives like Robert Morris made outstanding gains, even in Philadelphia; and in 1782 John Dickinson, the most prominent leader in the conservative ranks, was elected president of the council, and, consequently, of Pennsylvania. The newspaper war at this election was so vicious, even obscene, in its accusations, that Ben Franklin wrote he could not lend the papers to his French friends, hitherto so enthusiastic for the "scientific" Pennsylvania constitution.

For the French intelligentsia admired the Pennsylvania constitution of 1776 for its supposed scientific basis. Brissot de Warville, "l'ami des noirs," praised the Pennsylvanians' concern for "the happiness of the individual." The Abbé de Mably, in his printed book on the new Republic overseas,* was especially fond of Georgia, which

---

*L'Abbé Gabriel Bonnot de Mably, *Observations sur le Gouvernement et les Loix des États-Unis d'Amèrique* (Paris, 1784), p. 65; *Observations on the Government and Laws of the U.S.A.*, translated from the French (Amsterdam, 1784) pp. 46–47. He imagines himself addressing the Georgians, and the entire speech is delicious:

"I observe with chagrin," would I have added, "that you have ordered an *elegant mansion* to be engraved on the Seal of the Republic. I would prefer that it showed a plain, simple house, which might remind posterity of those manners void of luxury and splendour, which prevailed at the foundation of this state, and which they ought to imitate. I should view with pleasure on the design of this seal, *a field of wheat, a meadow covered with cattle, a river running through the same,* but why, to these images, which paint your character, will you add *a ship under full sail?* Let us remember that to us this will be Pandora's box; let us dread becoming familiar with these ideas of a false prosperity, which we shall too easily impress on the yet uninformed minds of our children. Would to God, no ship might ever arrive, which, by importing pleasures and wants hitherto unknown, would render us disgusted with a simplicity that is sufficient for our happiness! Would to God we were retired far into the country, and had nothing to fear on any side except the neighbouring savages, less dangerous than the seas that bathe our coasts! Why should we be so partial to the ports of Savannah and Sunbury, as to allow the one to send four representatives to the house of the assembly, and the other, two members to represent its trade? Let us avoid following the example of Europe, wretched from the attempt to found her strength, her power, and her happiness upon a wealth that must weaken and impoverish her. From the moment that we look upon commerce as the object and end of a flourishing State, we must renounce all the principles of sound policy, or if we have established them, we must expect to see them speedily overturned. If we would encourage the virtues that are necessary to us, let us confer honours, rewards, distinctions on those cultivators who are most able and industrious, and who, that they may learn to defend their possessions, practice the honourable exercises of the militia, as a relaxation from the labours of the plough. Let us not think of inviting a great multitude to reside among us; a handful of worthy citizens of spirit and virtue, will be of infinitely greater value."

had set up a constitution like Pennsylvania's; but he also took occasion to scold Georgia for adopting a state coat of arms on which "an elegant house" and a "ship under full sail" were represented. "Pure republicanism," he admonished the Georgians, should emulate not a mansion, but a humble farmer's dwelling, surrounded by fields of wheat and cattle pastures; and instead of promoting prosperity by an emblem of commerce, they should remember that foreign trade is a Pandora's box corrupting society with luxuries; the soil is the only real base for wealth; and the savages on the frontier are "less dangerous than the seas that bathe our coasts!" But the Georgians persisted in aiming at better housing and on seaborne trade for their cotton. Thomas Jefferson, incidentally, picked up in Paris this idea that "foreign commerce corrupts," and that merchants were natural enemies to republics, and promoted it, when President of the United States, by his embargo on foreign commerce. The French finance minister Turgot, who in a then-famous letter of 1778 to Richard Price, wrote, "The Americans are the Hope of this World. They may become the models," also wrote a treatise attacking the American state constitutions for compromising with custom and privilege; but he gave the constitution of Pennsylvania a clean bill of health. John Adams replied in a lengthy treatise, defending the bicameral system as necessary to protect the people against unwise, hasty, and proscriptive legislation, and defending a strong executive as necessary to enforce the laws and give the government leadership. The events of the American Revolution period showed unmistakably that John Adams was right and Turgot wrong; yet, in 1791, the French Constituent Assembly adopted a unicameral constitution for France. It, too, went down the drain, very quickly.

The claim that this Pennsylvania constitution was "scientific" is interesting, as it recalls the years immediately after World War II when many eminent British, French, and American men of science plumped for communism on the same grounds — that communism was a "scientific" reorganization of human society from which everything antiquated, privileged, or useless had been eliminated. Very few of those naïve men of science still so believe today. They have found that, in practice, communist régimes, after calling on their citizens to sacrifice liberty to gain security, have given their people a very poor substitute for liberty. Their predecessors of the eighteenth century discovered that — in the excesses of the French Revolution.

Franklin, elected president of Pennsylvania in 1785, found his much-admired constitution to be somewhat wanting, but guided the assembly into moderate channels, and it repealed the obnoxious test oaths, which had effectively disfranchised between 40 and 50 percent of the male population. This resulted in conservatives' capturing the state government. The assembly restored the Philadelphia College and set up again Robert Morris's Bank of North America, which had saved Congress and the state from complete bankruptcy. It appointed conservatives, including James Wilson and Gouverneur Morris, to the Federal Convention of 1787, won over the radicals in the state ratifying convention by a two-to-one majority. In 1789 the conservatives, in a supreme effort, managed to call a state constitutional convention, which adopted a conservative constitution on the New York and Massachusetts model. By this time, so strong was sentiment for a new government that the convention declared this new constitution in force on September 2, 1790.

Thus, the only really "scientific" radical state constitution, so admired by the French intelligentsia, disappeared, unregretted and soon forgotten. For this radical constitution of 1776 had notably failed to secure "life, liberty and the pursuit of happiness."

All this was part of a conservative reaction that set in throughout the United States around 1780. Notorious radicals were dropped from the Continental Congress, which gave greater authority to General Washington over the Army, and to Franklin in France; appointed Robert Morris superintendent of finance; and created the office of secretary of foreign affairs. This reaction was reflected in the constitution of Massachusetts.

This most conservative of state constitutions was adopted through a completely democratic process. A constitutional convention, elected by manhood suffrage, met in the fall of 1779, appointed a committee to prepare a draft, and adjourned. The committee wisely let John Adams draw up the draft. It was submitted to the convention in 1780, amended, and then tossed back to the town meetings. A surprising popular interest was shown; many town meetings debated the constitution clause by clause, stated their objections, and some made original proposals, such as the popular initiative and referendum, which were adopted many years later. And, most amazing, they consented to a small property qualification for voting. But they did ratify the constitution as a whole, and declared it in force on June 15, 1780.

John Adams's Massachusetts constitution was based on Polybius' theory of "mixed government," which by Adams's time had been renamed "checks and balances." The theory was this: any "pure" governmental form degenerated into something else — pure democracy into class tyranny or anarchy, pure aristocracy into a selfish oligarchy, pure monarchy into despotism. Hence, to secure the happiness of the people, a government must be a mixture of all three: a strong chief executive to represent the principle of authority, a senate to represent property, and a lower house to represent the multitude. These "mutually keep each other from exceeding their proper limits," as Blackstone wrote in his *Commentaries*. Finally — John Adams's own contribution — you wanted an independent judiciary as a balance wheel, the judges appointed "during good behavior." And that is what Massachusetts got: the most durable of the revolutionary constitutions, still in force today, although severely amended in a democratic direction.

The Revolutionary state constitutions of New York and Maryland were also on the conservative side, and worked very well.

John Adams concluded the bill of rights in his Massachusetts constitution with the statement that the three powers, executive, legislative, and judicial, must never encroach on each other, "to the end it may be a government of laws and not of men." That concept — "a government of laws and not of men" — which Adams was the first to state, is central to the Anglo-American system of government. President Gerald Ford, in his inaugural address in 1974, exulted that the presidential crisis had been solved peaceably, and that once more we had a government of laws and not of men. Let us hope he was right.

J. Franklin Jameson, in 1924, published a book called *The American Revolution Considered As a Social Movement*, which tried to prove the contrary. It has become a sort of Bible to our left-wing historians since World War II. But, on leafing through this book, one asks, *what* social reforms were enacted by the states during and immediately after the Revolution? The confiscation and dividing up of the Loyalists' land; but that merely substituted new and patriotic owners for the Tories; and, before long, these new proprietors became just as conservative on property issues as the old ones. Not until the 1840's, after a local revolution in New York, the "antirent war," were land titles derived from the old Dutch patroons of that colony relieved of their antiquated feudal dues. Another social revolution alleged by Dr. Jameson was the abolition of primogeniture (the inheritance of parents' entire property by the eldest son) and entails (making it illegal for an heir to sell his estate) in Virginia and other states. In reality, this abolition amounted to very little. Primogeniture was abolished only for the heirs of people who died intestate (without a will); and entails, in a country expanding westward with wide economic opportunities, were a burden to heirs rather than a privilege.

The separation of Church and State was indeed accomplished in Virginia, of which Jefferson's famous Statute of Religious Liberty is proof; but all that meant was that the poor parsons, who had been robbed already in the Two-Penny Act, which brought Patrick Henry into prominence, henceforth had to depend for their support on their parishioners' Sunday contributions in the plate. And the Congregational Church continued to enjoy state support until 1818 in Connecticut and until 1834 in Massachusetts.

The one reform that might have entitled our Revolution to be called a real thoroughgoing social revolution would have been the abolition of slavery.* There a beginning was made in states where slavery was not considered essential to the economy. Massachusetts went antislavery in 1781 by judicial process, the state supreme court declaring that the state bill of rights — "All men are born free and equal" — was incompatible with holding people in bondage. The other New England states and Pennsylvania did not immediately free the slaves, fearing lest their support fall on the taxpayer, but gave freedom to all children thenceforward born of slave parents — the *post nati* system.

South of Mason and Dixon's line, the efforts of leaders such as Jefferson and George Mason to put slavery on the way to extinction were defeated, precisely because this would have meant a social revolution. They and other Southern leaders declared publicly that slavery was morally wrong and contrary to Revolutionary principles; but they could not convert the voters. In 1785, when Methodists petitioned the Virginia Assembly to begin a general emancipation on the ground that slavery was "contrary to the fundamental principles of the Christian religion" and a violation of the Declaration of Rights, their

* The most recent thorough discussion of this subject is in David Brion Davis, *The Problem of Slavery in the Age of Revolution,* Cornell University Press, 1975.

petition was unanimously rejected. Had it been acted upon, there might have been no American Civil War.

George Washington's dilemma is well described by his latest biographer, James T. Flexner. Even before the war, he adopted the principle of never selling a slave without the slave's consent or that of his parents; but as the blacks enjoyed working for "the Gineral," their consent to go elsewhere was seldom forthcoming. Thus, at Mount Vernon slaves proliferated to the extent that they ate up almost all the plantation products. At one point Washington considered selling the lot, consenting or not, and putting the money into bank stock; but he was too humane to throw hundreds of blacks, good and bad, into the market like cattle. Finally, he decided to live with the problem; but only a year before his death he told an English visitor that "nothing but the rooting out of slavery can perpetuate the existence of our union." And in his last will and testament he declared the emancipation of all his slaves by will, at the death of his widow, Martha. He made careful provision for the blacks' future, and there were about 150 of them. The old and infirm were to stay put and be supported by his heirs. The children were to be taught their letters, to serve to the age of twenty-five, and, if they wished, then to be set free, and bound to some trade like any white apprentice. All this was done, and his heirs made their last pension payment in 1833. Had 500 other Virginia planters done likewise, slavery would have disappeared in the pivotal state; but none did. Thomas Jefferson, by contrast, despite his earlier fulminations against slavery, sold about fifty of his blacks in the first ten years after the war, and in his will of 1826 freed only five favorite household slaves and left some 260 in bondage to his heirs.

New York and New Jersey, where slavery was more of an economic factor than in New England and Pennsylvania, did not even adopt the *post nati* system until 1799 and 1804, respectively. A real gain was made in the Northwest or Territorial Ordinance, which Congress passed in 1787, because the Ohio Company proposed to purchase 1.5 million acres of that great western territory, covering four future states, for the same number of dollars. The ordinance, drafted by Nathan Dane, included a bill of rights that stated, "There shall be neither Slavery nor involuntary servitude in said territory." And that promise was kept. But in the western territory, and in all states south of the Mason-Dixon line, where black slavery was basic to the economic and social system, every effort to get rid of it, or to put it in the way of eventual extinction, was thwarted because in those states emancipation would have meant a social revolution.

This Revolutionary period proved to be the last chance, short of war, to erase this blot from the body politic; it was the one conservative measure of the Revolution that, from our present-day outlook, was bad. The number of slaves was so small in 1790 (less than 700,000 in a population under four million) that most of the blacks could have been absorbed into the body politic without too much friction, and a large number of them might have accepted repatriation to Africa.

Our Declaration of Independence, and the necessity to fight for it, released hidden energies and abilities in the United States, and as a consequence the American Revolution became one of the most creative periods in our history, especially for its political achievements: the Virginia Bill of Rights and Statute of Religious Liberty, the state constitutions, the Articles of Confederation, and the federal Constitution. The Federal Convention of 1787, presided over by General George Washington, was the capstone on the edifice, and its nature and adoption proves that our Revolution was essentially conservative. A final and convincing proof of the political maturity of America in 1788 was the quiet acceptance by the anti-Federalists of their defeat. They were good losers. Patrick Henry struck the keynote on the final day of the Virginia ratifying convention, when he knew that he was licked: "I will be a peaceable citizen. My head, my hand, and my heart shall be at liberty to . . . remove the defects of that [new] system *in a constitutional way.* I wish not to go to violence . . . I shall . . . patiently wait." Not long, nor in vain, did he wait. The adoption by constitutional amendment of the federal Bill of Rights in 1791 satisfied Patrick Henry, and he died a good Federalist.

I have no intention of denigrating the radical achievements of the Revolution. My thesis is that the conservative element was necessary to preserve these gains for posterity. And one of the main forces of conservatism was George Washington. His strength, his wisdom, and his skill drilled the raw, undisciplined levies of militia, in 1775, into a national army. His character more than once stood between that Army and total defeat of the Revolutionary cause. His support of the federal Constitution meant more for the acceptance of that predominantly conservative charter than all the writings of Hamilton and Madison. As an English admirer said after his death, "Tranquil and firm he moved with one pace in one path, and neither vaulted nor tottered . . . He had no vain conceit of being himself all, and did those things only which he only could do."*

And I protest against the conservatives of the Revolution being called counterrevolutionaries. They believed in all the fundamental things of our Revolution — independence, the abolition of hereditary elements, starting with monarchy; and the rights of man. Alexander Hamilton, the particular target of our young left-wingers, wrote the following: "I consider civil liberty . . . as the greatest of terrestrial blessings. I am convinced that the whole human race is entitled to it, and that it can be wrested from no part of them without the blackest and most aggravated guilt." And again: "Real liberty is neither found in despotism, or the extremes of democracy, but in moderate [that is, "mixt"] governments."

The leaders in the 1780's, then, were predominantly conservative but they, too, were proud of having established a new order, as the action of the second Continental Congress in adopting a Great Seal of the Republic proves. *Novus ordo seclorum* on the Great Seal of the United States, adopted by the Continental Congress in 1782, was felt to be literally true; and so were the other lines of Virgil that Americans of the 1780's liked to think meant them:

> *Magnus ab integro saeclorum nascitur ordo,*
> *Iam redit et Virgo, redeunt Saturnia regna;*
> *Iam nova progenies caelo demittitur alto.*
>
> A great cycle of centuries now is born anew;
> Now Justice returns, and the rule of Saturn;
> And from High Heaven descends a new generation of men.†

Thus, the American Revolution differed from most of the other great revolutions because it stopped just about where those who started it wanted it to stop. In 1789 we had the same leaders as in 1775, except that some of the early agitators, like Tom Paine, had gone to France, and obscure Sons of Liberty in Boston and Philadelphia had disappeared. They were not, like the Girondins in France

---

* Samuel T. Coleridge, after Washington's death; quoted in Morison, *Oxford History of the American People* (1965), page 347.
† Virgil, *Eclogues* (or *Bucolics*), IV:5, 7.

and the Mensheviks in Russia, destroyed by purges and terror; they merely slipped into oblivion because they had nothing constructive to offer, and the people simply forgot their existence. There are no statues to the obscure men who dominated the state of Pennsylvania for almost a decade.

Your typical revolutionary leader is an idealist or a fanatic, or both; a man like Robespierre or Trotsky, who has strong emotional impulses, vast energy, and great driving power. These are men who hate injustice, corruption, tyranny, and violence, which, they believe, characterize the existing régime; but they are willing to use the most violent, arbitrary, and cruel methods to bring about the millennium at which they are aiming.

None of this type got control of the American Revolution. Tom Paine had the characteristics more than anyone else, but he never reached a position of power in the American Revolution, and he had to go to France to blow off steam. Jefferson had a touch of it, but he was too cultivated and well rounded a man to be a fanatic. Until after the fighting started in 1775, our patriot leaders in the American Revolution had no program, no blueprints for the future, other than to sever their connection with Britain and set up a republican government; and up to 1776 they wanted not even that, only a redress of grievances within the British Empire. Only in 1776, with great reluctance, did they venture to "dissolve the political bands which have connected them with another, and to assume among the powers of the earth the separate and equal station to which the Laws of Nature and of Nature's God entitle them."

"The Laws of Nature and of Nature's God." This happy reference in the great Declaration rings a bell for the right of civil disobedience to unjust laws, a right that goes back to remotest antiquity. "The Laws of Nature and of Nature's God" echoes that eloquent speech of Antigone to the tyrant Creon in Sophocles' drama *Antigone** two millennia before Jefferson appealed America's cause to these same

---

* *Antigone*, lines 452–57, Loeb edition of Sophocles, F. Storr, translator, I, 349. A recent application is this: Mary Peabody, whom I am proud to call my friend, widow of Bishop Malcolm Peabody and mother of Governor Endicott Peabody of Massachusetts, went to jail briefly in Florida for having broken that state's Jim Crow laws. She was asked where her primary allegiance lay — country, family, or faith? She answered, "I believe that my highest allegiance is to a Christian sense of what is right and just. If I disobey a law of my country I must do it openly and be ready to take the consequences." Boston *Sunday Globe*, April 13, 1975, supplement on "The Unfinished Revolution," page 9.

natural laws. Antigone had defied Creon's edict that the body of her brother, killed in battle, be left where it fell, for the wild beasts and vultures to devour, a thing impious and horrible to the ancient Greeks. The young woman, haled before Creon for breaking his laws by giving her brother's corpse a decent burial, says:

> Nor did I deem that thou, a mortal man,
> Could'st by a breath annul and override
> The immutable, unwritten laws of Heaven.
> They were not born today nor yesterday:
> They die not; and none knoweth whence they sprang.

3

The Young Man Washington

I was fortunate to be brought up in the house of my grandfather Samuel Eliot, an historian himself, old enough to remember sitting on Lafayette's lap when that hero was entertained by his father at Boston in 1824. And my grandfather had the leisure to answer the questions of an inquisitive small boy. One day, around 1897, I said, "Grandpa, who was the greatest man in the world?" "Why, George Washington, of course!" was the immediate reply. I told this anecdote to Douglas Freeman when he visited me in the same library in 1949, and the great biographer of Washington and Lee answered, "Grandpa was right!"

The occasion for this essay was the bicentenary of Washington's birth, for the commemoration of which President Lowell of Harvard ordered me to organize a meeting and give the address. With the aid of a program of songs and ballads of the Revolutionary era, sung by the Harvard Glee Club and conducted by Dr. Archibald Davidson, we managed to fill Sanders Theater on February 22, 1932. My address, with footnotes and appendices to back up some of my controversial statements, was printed by the Harvard University Press in 1932. It has been revised, following correspondence on several points with the late Fairfax Harrison and John Fitzpatrick, and also after checking with Douglas Freeman's incomparable biography of George Washington.

WASHINGTON is the last person you would ever suspect of having been a young man, with all the bright hopes and black despairs to which youth is subject. In American folklore he is known only as a child or a general or an old, old man: priggish hero of the cherry-tree episode, commander in chief, or the Father of his Country, writing a farewell address. By some freak of fate, Stuart's Athenaeum portrait of an ideal and imposing, but solemn and weary Washington at the age of sixty-four has become the most popular. This year it has been reproduced as the "official" portrait, and placed in every school in the country; so we may expect that new generations of American school-children will be brought up with the idea that Washington was a solemn old bore. If only Charles Willson Peale's portrait of him as a handsome and gallant young soldier could have been used instead! His older biographers, too, have conspired to create the legend; and the recent efforts to "popularize" Washington have taken the unfortunate line of trying to make him out something that he was not: a churchman, politician, engineer, businessman, or realtor. These attempts to degrade a hero to a go-getter, an aristocrat to a vulgarian, remind one of the epitaph that Aristotle wished to have carved on the tomb of Plato: *"Hic jacet homo, quem non licet, non decet, impiis vel ignorantibus laudare"* (Here lies a man whom it is neither permissible nor proper for the irreverent or the ignorant to praise).

Perhaps it is not the fault of the painters and biographers that we think of Washington as an old man, but because his outstanding qualities — wisdom, poise, and serenity — are not those commonly associated with youth. He seemed to have absorbed, wrote Emerson, "all the serenity of America, and left none for his restless, rickety, hysterical countrymen." The comte de Chastellux, one of the French officers in the war, said that Washington's most characteristic feature was balance, "the perfect harmony existing between the physical and moral attributes of which he is made up." Yet Gilbert Stuart, after painting his first portrait of Washington, said that "all his features were indicative of the most ungovernable passions, and had he been born in the forests, it was his opinion that he would have been the fiercest man among the savage tribes." Both men were right. Washington's qualities were so balanced that his talents, which were great but nothing extraordinary, were more effective in the long run than those of greater generals like Napoleon, or of bolder and more original statesmen like Hamilton and Jefferson. Yet as a young man Washington was impatient and passionate, eager for glory in war, wealth in land, and success in love. Even in maturity his fierce temper would sometimes get the better of him. Here in Cambridge, at his headquarters in the Craigie House, he once became so exasperated at the squabbling of drunken soldiers in the front yard that, forgetting the dignity of a general, he rushed forth and laid out a few of the brawlers with his own fists; and then, much relieved, returned to his office. Under great provocation he would break out with a torrent of Olympian oaths that terrified the younger men on his staff. Tobias Lear, the smooth young Harvard graduate who became Washington's private secretary, admitted that the most dreadful experience in his life was hearing the general swear!

It was only through the severest self-discipline that Washington attained his characteristic poise and serenity. Discipline is not a popular word nowadays, for we associate it with schoolmasters, drill sergeants, and dictators; and it was certainly not discipline of that sort that made the passionate young Washington into an effective man. His discipline came in a very small part from parents, masters, or superiors; and in no respect from institutions. It came from environment, from a philosophy of life that he imbibed at an impressionable age; but most of all from his own will. He apprehended the great truth that man can only be free through mastery of himself. Instead of allowing his passions to spend themselves, he restrained them. Instead of indulging himself in a life of pleasure — for which he had ample means at the age of twenty — he placed duty first. In fact, he followed exactly that course of conduct which, according to the secondhand popularizers of Freud, make a person "thwarted," "inhibited," and "repressed." Yet Washington became a liberated, successful, and serene man. The process can hardly fail to interest young men who are struggling with the same difficulties as Washington — although, I am bound to say, under the far more difficult circumstances of the depression, machinery, and jazz.

Whence came this impulse to self-discipline? We can find nothing to account for it in the little we know of Washington's heredity. His family was gentle but undistinguished. George knew little of his forebears and cared less, although he used the family coat of arms. Lawrence Washington, sometime Fellow of Brasenose College, Oxford, was ejected from his living by the Roundheads as a "malignant Royalist." His son John came to Virginia by way of Barbados as mate of a tobacco ship, and settled there. As an Indian fighter, John Washington was so undisciplined as to embarrass the governor of Virginia almost as much as did the Indians. His son Lawrence, father of Augustine and grandfather of George, earned a competence in the merchant marine and settled down to planting. Love of the land was a trait that all Washingtons had in common: they might seek wealth at sea or glory in war, but happiness they found only in the work and sport that came from owning and cultivating land.

Usually the Washingtons married their social betters, but the second marriage of George's father, Augustine, was an exception. Mary Ball, the mother of Washington, has been the object of much sentimental writing; but the cold record of her own and her sons' letters shows her to have been grasping, querulous, and vulgar. She was a selfish and exacting mother whom most of her children avoided as early as they could; to whom they did their duty, but rendered little love. It was this sainted mother of Washington who opposed almost everything that he did for the public good, who wished his sense of duty to end with his duty to her, who pestered him in his campaigns by complaining letters, and who at a dark moment of the Revolutionary War increased his anxieties by strident complaints of neglect and starvation. Yet for one thing Americans may well be grateful to Mary Ball: her selfishness lost George an opportunity to become midshipman in the Royal Navy, a school whence few Americans emerged other than as loyal subjects of the king.

There is only one other subject connected with Washington upon which there has been more false sentiment, misrepresentation, and mendacity than on that of his mother, and that is his religion. Washington's religion was that of an eighteenth-century gentleman. Baptized in the Church of England, he attended service occasionally as a young man, and more regularly in middle age, as one of the duties of his station. He believed in God: the eighteenth-century Supreme Being, a Divine Philosopher who ruled all things for the best. He was certain of a Providence in the affairs of men. By the same token, he was completely tolerant of other people's beliefs, more so than the American democracy of today; for in a letter to the Swedenborgian Church of Baltimore he wrote: "In this enlightened age and in the land of equal liberty it is our boast that a man's religious tenets will not forfeit the protection of the law, nor deprive him of the right of attaining and holding the highest offices that are known in the United States." But Washington never became an active member of any church. Even after his marriage to a devout churchwoman, and when as President of the United States the eyes of all men were upon him, he never joined Martha in the beautiful and comforting sacrament of the body and blood of Christ. Considering the pressure always placed on a man to conform by a religious wife, this abstention from Holy Communion is very significant. Christianity had little or no part in that discipline which made Washington more humble and gentle than any of the great captains, less proud and ambitious than most of the statesmen who have proclaimed themselves disciples of the Nazarene. His inspiration, as we shall see, came from an entirely different source.

Washington gained little discipline from book-learning; but like all Virginian gentlemen of the day he led an active outdoor life, which gave him a magnificent physique. When fully grown, he stood a little over six feet, and weighed between 175 and 200 pounds. Broad-shouldered and straight-backed, he carried his head erect and his chin up, and showed a good leg on horseback. There is no reason to doubt the tradition of his prowess at running, leaping, wrestling, and horsemanship. The handling of horses, in which Washington was skilled at an early age, is one of the finest means of discipline that a youngster can have; for he who cannot control himself can never handle a spirited horse. And for the same reason fox-hunting, which was Washington's favorite sport, is the making — or the breaking — of a courageous and considerate gentleman. His amazing physical vitality is proved by an incident of his reconnaissance to the Ohio. At the close of December 1753, he and the scout Christopher Gist attempted to cross the river just above the site of Pittsburgh, on a raft of their own making. The river was full of floating ice, and George, while trying to shove the raft away from an ice floe with his setting-pole, fell overboard, but managed to climb aboard again. They were forced to land on an island and spend the night there without fire or dry clothing. Gist, the professional woodsman, who had not been in the water, froze all his fingers and some of his toes; but Washington suffered no ill effects from the exposure. For that, his healthy Virginia boyhood may be thanked.

His formal education was scanty. The colonial colleges provided a classical discipline more severe and selective than that of their successors, but George had none of these "advantages." There were no means to prepare him for William and Mary, the college of the Virginia gentry; his father died when he was eleven years old, and as a younger son in a land-poor family, his only schoolmasters were chosen haphazardly. Endowed with the blood and the instincts of a gentleman, he was not given a gentleman's education, as he became painfully aware when at adolescence he went to live with his half brother at Mount Vernon.

In modern phrase, George was "parked" on the estate that would one day be his. Evidently there had been some sort of family consultation about what to do with him; and Lawrence good-naturedly offered to take his young brother in hand, if only to get him away from the termagant mother. Lawrence Washington, Augustine's favorite son and fondest hope, had been sent to England for his schooling, had served under Admiral Vernon in the war with Spain, and had inherited the bulk of his father's property, to the exclusion of George and the four younger brothers and sisters. The proximity of Mount Vernon to the vast estates of the Fairfax family in the Northern Neck of Virginia gave Lawrence his opportunity. He married a Fairfax, and was admitted to the gay, charmed circle of the First Families of Virginia. He was already a well-established gentleman of thirty when the hobbledehoy half brother came to stay.

George was then a tall, gangling lad of sixteen years, with enormous hands and feet that were continually getting in his way. Young girls giggled when he entered a room, and burst out laughing at his awkward attempts to court them. He was conscious that he did not "belong," and made every effort to improve his manners. About three years before, a schoolmaster had made him copy out 110 rules of civility from a famous handbook by one Hawkins — a popular guide to good manners already a century and a half old; and George was probably glad to have this manuscript manual of social etiquette ready to consult. One of the most touching and human pictures of Washington is that of the overgrown schoolboy solemnly conning old Hawkins's warnings against scratching oneself at table, picking one's teeth with a fork, or cracking fleas in company, lest he commit serious breaks in the houses of the great.

These problems of social behavior no doubt occupied much space in Washington's adolescent thoughts. But he was also preparing to be a man of action. At school he had cared only for mathematics. He procured more books, progressed further than his schoolmaster could take him, and so qualified to be surveyor to Lord Fairfax. This great gentleman and landowner required an immense amount of surveying in the Shenandoah Valley, and found it difficult to obtain men with enough mathematics to qualify as surveyors, or sufficient sobriety to run a line straight and see a job through. So George at sixteen earned as Lord Fairfax's surveyor the high salary of a doubloon (about $7.50) a day, most of which he saved up and invested in land. For he had early decided that in the fresh lands of the Virginia Valley and the West lay the road to position, competence, and happiness. His personality as well as his excellent surveying earned him the friendship of the Fairfaxes, liberal and intelligent gentlemen; and this, as we shall see, was of first importance in Washington's moral and intellectual development.

That friendship, not the doubloon a day, was the first and most fortunate gain from this surveying job; the second was the contact it gave young Washington with frontiersmen, with Indians, and with that great teacher of self-reliance, the wilderness. He had the advantage of a discipline that few of us can obtain today. We are born in crowded cities, and attend crowded schools and colleges; we take our pleasure along crowded highways and in crowded places of amusement; we are tempted to assert ourselves by voice rather than deed, to advertise, to watch the clock, escape responsibility, and leave decisions to others. But a hungry woodsman could not afford to lose patience with a deer he was trying to shoot, or with a trout he was trying to catch; and it did not help him much to bawl out an Indian. If you cannot discipline yourself to quiet and caution in the wilderness, you won't get far; and if you make the wrong decision in woods infested with savages, you will probably have no opportunity to make another. What our New England forebears learned from the sea, Washington learned from the wilderness.

His life from sixteen to twenty was not all spent on forest trails. This was the golden age of the Old Dominion, the fifteen years from 1740 to the French and Indian War. The old roughness and crudeness were passing away. Peace reigned over the land, high prices ruled for tobacco, immigrants were pouring into the back country; the traditional Virginia of Thackeray and Vachel Lindsay — "Land of the gauntlet and the glove" — came into being. Living in Virginia at that time was like riding on the sparkling crest of a great wave just before it breaks and spreads into dull, shallow pools. At Mount Vernon, on the verge of the wilderness, one felt the zest of sharp contrasts, and one received the discipline that comes from life. On the one side were mansion houses where young Washington could learn manners and philosophy from gentlefolk. He took part in all the sports and pastimes of his social equals: dancing and card-playing and flirting with the girls. When visiting a town like Williamsburg he never missed a show; and later as President he was a patron of the new American drama. He loved shooting, fox-hunting, horse-racing, and all the gentlemen's field sports of the day; he bet small sums at cards, and larger sums on the ponies, and was a good loser. He liked to make an impression by fine new clothes, and by riding unruly steeds when girls were looking on; for though ungainly afoot, he was a graceful figure on horseback. He belonged to clubs of men who dined at taverns and drank like gentlemen; that is to say, they drank as much wine as they could hold without getting drunk. Tobacco, curiously enough, made George's head swim; but he learned to smoke the peace pipe with Indians when necessary without disgracing himself.

On the other side of Mount Vernon were log cabins, and all the crude elements of American life: Scots-Irish, Pennsylvania German pioneers, and other poor whites, who, as insubordinate soldiers, would prove the severest test of Washington's indefatigable patience. The incidents of roughing it, such as the "one thread-bear blanket with double its weight of vermin, such as lice, fleas, etc." that he records in the journal of his first surveying trip, were not very pleasant, but he took it all with good humor and good sportsmanship. A little town called Alexandria sprang up about a tobacco warehouse and wharf, and young Washington made the first survey of it. There was a Masonic lodge at Fredericksburg, and George, always a good "joiner," became brother to all the rising journalists and lawyers of the northern colonies. The deep Potomac flowed past Mount Vernon, bearing ships of heavy burthen to the Chesapeake and overseas; you sent your orders to England every year with your tobacco, and ships returned with the latest modes and manners, books and gazettes, and letters full of coffee-house gossip. London did not seem very far away, and young George confessed in a letter that he hoped to visit that "gay Matrapolis" before long.

It was probably just as well that he did not visit London, for he had the best and purest English tradition in Virginia. When Washington was in his later teens, just when a young man is fumbling for a philosophy of life, he came into intimate contact with several members of the Fairfax family. They were of that eighteenth-century Whig gentry who conformed outwardly to Christianity, but derived their real inspiration from Marcus Aurelius, Plutarch, and the Stoic philosophers. Thomas, sixth Lord Fairfax, was a nobleman devoted to "Revolution Principles" — the Glorious Revolution of 1688, in which his father had taken an active part. Of the same line was that General Lord Fairfax, commander in chief of the New Model Army, who of all great soldiers in English history most resembles Washington. The ideal of this family was a noble simplicity of living and a calm acceptance of life: duty to the commonwealth, generosity to fellow men, unfaltering courage, and enduring virtue; in a word, the Stoic philosophy that overlaps Christian ethics more than any other discipline of the ancients. A Stoic never evaded life: he faced it. A Stoic never avoided responsibility: he accepted it. A Stoic not only believed in liberty: he practiced it.

It is not necessary to suppose that young Washington read much Stoic philosophy, for he was no great reader at any time; but he must have absorbed it from constant social intercourse with the Fairfaxes of Belvoir, neighbors whom he saw constantly. At Belvoir lived George William Fairfax, eight years Washington's senior, and his companion in surveying expeditions. Anne, the widow of Lawrence Washington, was Fairfax's sister, and Sally, the lady with whom George Washington was so happy (and so miserable) as to fall in love, was his wife. Books were there, if he wanted them. North's Plutarch was in every gentleman's library, and it was Plutarch who wrote the popular life of Cato, Washington's favorite character in history — not crabbed Cato the Censor, but Cato of pent-up Utica. At the age of seventeen, Washington himself owned an outline, in English, of the principal dialogues of Seneca the younger, "sharpest of all the Stoics." The mere chapter headings are the moral axioms that Washington followed through life:

An Honest Man can never be outdone in Courtesy.
A Good man can never be Miserable, nor a Wicked man Happy.
A Sensual Life is a Miserable Life.
Hope and Fear are the Bane of Human Life.
The Contempt of Death makes all the Miseries of Life Easy to us.

And of the many passages that young Washington evidently took to heart, one may select this:

No man is born wise: but Wisdom and Virtue require a Tutor; though we can easily learn to be Vicious without a Master. It is Philosophy that gives us a Veneration for God; a Charity for our Neighbor; that teaches us our Duty to Heaven, and Exhorts us to an Agreement one with another. It unmasks things that are terrible to us, asswages our Lusts, refutes our Errors, restrains our Luxury, Reproves our avarice, and works strangely on tender Natures.

Washington read Addison's tragedy *Cato* in company with his beloved; and if they did not act it together in private theatricals, George expressed the wish that they might. At Valley Forge, when the morale of the Army needed a stimulus, Washington caused *Cato* to be performed, and attended the performance. It was his favorite play, written, as Pope's prologue says,

> To make mankind in conscious virtue bold,
> Live o'er each scene, and be what they behold.

Portius, Cato's son, whose "steddy temper"

> Can look on guilt, rebellion, fraud, and Caesar
> In the calm lights of mild Philosophy

declares (I, ii, 40–5):

> I'll animate the soldiers' drooping courage
> With love of freedom, and contempt of Life:
> I'll thunder in their ears their country's cause
> And try to rouse up all that's Roman in 'em.
> 'Tis not in Mortals to Command Success
> But we'll do more, Sempronius, we'll Deserve it.

These last two lines sound the note that runs through all Washington's correspondence in the dark hours of the Revolutionary struggle; and these same lines are almost the only literary quotations found in the vast body of Washington's writings. Many years after, when perplexed and wearied by the political squabbles of his presidency and longing to retire to Mount Vernon, Washington quoted the last lines of Cato's advice to Portius (IV, iv, 14–54):

> Let me advise thee to retreat betimes
> To thy paternal seat, the Sabine field,
> Where the great Censor toil'd with his own hands,
> And all our frugal Ancestors were blest
> In humble virtues, and a rural life.
> There live retired, pray for the peace of Rome:
> Content thy self to be obscurely good.
> When vice prevails, and impious men bear sway,
> The post of honour is a private station.

From his camp with General Forbes's army in the wilderness, Washington wrote to Sally Fairfax on September 25, 1758: "I should think our time more agreeably spent, believe me, in playing a part in Cato with the Company you mention, and myself doubly happy in being the Juba to such a Marcia as you must make." Marcia was the worthy daughter of Cato, and Juba her lover, the young Numidian prince to whom Syphax says:

> You have not read mankind, your youth admires
> The throws and swellings of a Roman soul,
> Cato's bold flights, th' extravagance of Virtue.

And Juba had earlier said (I, iv, 49–58):

> Turn up thy eyes to Cato!
> There may'st thou see to what a godlike height
> The Roman virtues lift up mortal man.
> While good, and just, and anxious for his friends,
> He's still severely bent against himself;
> Renouncing sleep, and rest, and food, and ease,
> He strives with thirst and hunger, toil and heat;
> And when his fortune sets before him all
> The pomps and pleasures that his soul can wish,
> His rigid virtue will accept of none.

So, here we have a young man of innate noble qualities, seeking a philosophy of life, thrown in contact during his most impressionable years with a great gentleman whom he admired, a young gentleman who was his best friend, and a young lady whom he loved, all three steeped in the Stoic tradition. What would you expect? Can it be a mere coincidence that this characterization of the emperor Antoninus Pius by his adopted son Marcus Aurelius, the imperial Stoic, so perfectly fits the character of Washington?

Take heed lest thou become a Caesar indeed; lest the purple stain thy soul. For such things have been. Then keep thyself simple, good, pure, and serious; a friend to justice and the fear of God; kindly, affectionate, and strong to do the right. Reverence Heaven and succour man. Life is short; and earthly existence yields but one harvest, holiness of character and altruism of action. Be in everything a true disciple of Antoninus. Emulate his constancy in all rational activity, his unvarying equability, his purity, his cheerfulness of countenance, his sweetness, his contempt for notoriety, and his eagerness to come at the root of the matter.

Remember how he would never dismiss any subject until he had gained a clear insight into it and grasped it thoroughly; how he bore with the injustice of his detractors and never retorted in kind; how he did nothing in haste, turned a deaf ear to the professional tale-bearers, and showed himself an acute judge of characters and actions, devoid of all reproachfulness, timidity, suspiciousness, and sophistry; how easily he was satisfied — for instance, with lodging, bed, clothing, food, and servants — how fond of work and how patient; capable, thanks to his frugal diet, of remaining at his post from morning till night, having apparently subjected even the operations of nature to his will; firm and constant in friendship, tolerant of the most outspoken criticism of his opinions, delighted if any one could make a better suggestion than himself, and, finally, deeply religious without any trace of superstition.

When Washington was twenty years old, his brother Lawrence died. George, next heir by their father's will, stepped into his place as proprietor of Mount Vernon. At this stage of his life, George did not greatly enjoy the exacting task of running a great plantation; he thirsted for glory in war. But he soon began to enlarge and improve his holdings, and in the end came to love the land as nothing else. Late in life, when the First Citizen of the World, he wrote: "How much more delightful is the task of making improvements on the earth than all the vain-glory which can be acquired from ravaging it by the most uninterrupted career of conquests." And again: "To see plants rise from the earth and flourish by the superior skill and bounty of the laborer fills a contemplative mind with ideas which are more easy to be conceived than expressed." That was the way with all Washington's ideas: they were more easily conceived and executed than expressed on paper. Ideas did not interest him, nor was he interested in himself. Hence the matter-of-fact objectiveness of his letters and diaries.

Nevertheless, it is clear from Washington's diaries that farming was a great factor in his discipline. For the lot of a Virginia planter was not as romance has colored it. Slaves had to be driven, or they ate out your substance; overseers had to be watched, or they slacked and stole; accounts had to be balanced, or you became poorer every year. There were droughts, and insect pests, and strange maladies among the cattle. Washington's life at Mount Vernon was one of constant experiment, unremitting labor, unwearying patience. It was a continual war against human error, insect enemies, and tradition. He might provide improved flails and a clean threshing floor in his new barn; when his back was turned the overseer would have the wheat out in the yard, to be trod into the muck by the cattle. His books prove that he was an eager and bold experimenter in that "new husbandry" of which Coke of Norfolk was the great exponent. There were slave blacksmiths, carpenters, and bricklayers; a cider press and a stillhouse, where excellent corn and rye whiskeys were made, and sold in barrels made by the slaves from plantation oak. Herring and shad fisheries in the Potomac provided food for the slaves; a grist mill turned Washington's improved strain of wheat into flour, which was taken to market in his own schooner, which he could handle like any Down East skipper. Indeed, it is in his husbandry that we can earliest discern those qualities that made Washington the first soldier and statesman of America. As landed proprietor no less than as commander in chief, he showed executive ability, the power of planning for a distant end, and a capacity for taking infinite pains. Neither drought nor defeat could turn him from a course that he discerned to be proper and right; but in farming as in war he learned from failure, and grew in stature from loss and adversity.

Not long after inheriting Mount Vernon, Washington had an opportunity to test what his brother had taught him of military tactics and the practice of arms. Drilling and tactics, like surveying, were a projection of Washington's mathematical mind; like every born strategist he could see moving troops in his mind's eye, march and deploy them and calculate the time to a minute. He devoured accounts of Frederick's campaigns, and doubtless dreamt of directing a great battle on a grassy plain, a terrain he was destined never to fight on in this shaggy country. As one of the first landowners in the county, at twenty he was commissioned a major of militia. He then asked for, and obtained, the post of adjutant of militia for the county. The settlement of his brother's affairs brought him into contact with Governor Dinwiddie, a shrewd Scot who knew a dependable young man when he saw one; and from this came his first great opportunity.

At twenty-one he was sent on a highly confidential and difficult 1000-mile reconnaissance through the back country from western Virginia to the Ohio, and almost to the shores of Lake Erie. This young man just past his majority showed a caution in wilderness work, a diplomatic skill in dealing with Indians, and a courteous firmness in dealing with French commanders that would have done credit to a man twice his age. But on his next mission, one notes with a feeling of relief, youthful impetuosity prevailed. Unmindful that one must always let the enemy make the first aggression, our young lieutenant colonel fired the shot that began the Seven Years' War.

A phrase of the young soldier's blithe letter to his younger brother, "I heard the bullets whistle, and believe me, there is something charming in the sound," got into the papers, and gave sophisticated London a good laugh. Even King George II heard it and remarked, "He would not say so, if he had been used to hear many!" That time would come soon enough. Washington's shot in the silent wilderness brought the French and Indians buzzing about his ears. He retired to Fort Necessity, which he had caused to be built in a large meadow, hoping to tempt the enemy to a pitched battle. But the enemy was very inconsiderate. He swarmed about the fort in such numbers that Washington was lucky to be allowed to capitulate and go home; for this was one of those wars that was not yet a war; it was not declared till two years after the fighting began. The enemy was so superior in numbers that nobody blamed Washington; and when General Braddock arrived with an army of regulars, he invited the young frontier leader to accompany his expedition into the wilderness.

There is no need for me to repeat the tale of Braddock's defeat, except to say that the general's stupidity and the colonel's part in saving what could be saved have both been exaggerated. Parkman wrote in his classic *Montcalm and Wolfe:* "Braddock has been charged with marching blindly into an ambuscade; but it was not so. There was no ambuscade; and had there been one, he would have found it." That is the truth of the matter; and whilst Washington's behavior was creditable in every respect, he did not save Braddock's army; the French and Indians were simply too busy despoiling the dead and wounded to pursue.

Shortly after Washington reached Alexandria, the annual electoral campaign began for members of the Virginia Assembly. In a political dispute the colonel said something insulting to a quick-tempered little fellow named Payne, who promptly knocked him down with a hickory stick. Soldiers rushed up to avenge Washington, who recovered just in time to tell them he was not hurt, and could take care of himself, thank you! The next day he wrote to Payne requesting an interview at a tavern. The little man arrived, expecting a demand for an apology, or a challenge. Instead, Washington apologized for the insult that had provoked the blow, hoped that Payne was satisfied, and offered his hand. Some of Washington's biographers cannot imagine or understand such conduct. One of them brackets this episode with the cherry-tree yarn as "stories so silly and so foolishly impossible that they do not deserve an instant's consideration." Another explains Washington's conduct as a result of his defeat at Fort Necessity: "Washington was crushed into such meekness at this time that . . . instead of retaliating or challenging the fellow to a duel, he apologized." But the incident, which has been well substantiated, occurred after Braddock's defeat, not Washington's; and it was due to Stoical magnanimity, not Christian meekness. "It is the Part of a Great Mind to despise Injuries," says Seneca the Younger, in the L'Estrange translation that Washington owned. The Payne affair was merely an early instance of what Washington was doing all his life: admitting he was wrong when he was convinced he was in the wrong, and doing the handsome thing in a gentlemanly manner. A man who took that attitude became impregnable to attack by politicians or anyone else. For a young man of twenty-three to take it meant that he had firm hold of a great philosophy.

During the next two years Washington had charge of the frontier defenses of Virginia, and a chain of thirty garrisoned stockades that followed the Shenandoah Valley and its outer bulwarks from Winchester to the North Carolina line. In the execution of this command he showed a prodigious physical activity, often riding thirty miles a day for several days over wilderness trails. His letters show a youthful touchiness about rank and recognition; he sorely tried the patience of Governor Dinwiddie, who, to Washington's evident surprise, accepted a proffered resignation; but he was soon reappointed and took a leading part in General Forbes's expedition against Fort Duquesne. It was merely to settle a question of precedence that Washington undertook a long journey to interview Governor Shirley, the commander in chief, at Boston. Two aides, and two servants clad in new London liveries of the Washington colors and mounted on horses with the Washington arms embroidered on their housings, accompanied their colonel; for George had a young man's natural desire to make an impressive appearance. He stopped with great folk at Philadelphia and New York and gave generous tips to their servants. At New London the exhausted horses had to be left behind, and the colonel and suite proceeded by sea to Boston, where George ordered a new hat and uniform, a mass of silver lace, and two pair of gloves. But Washington never made the mistake of wearing splendid clothes on the wrong occasion. In the French and Indian War he wore a plain, neutral-colored uniform instead of royal scarlet, and dressed his soldiers as frontiersmen, in buckskin and moccasins, so that they carried no superfluous weight and offered no mark to the Indians.

As a young officer he often became impatient with the frontier folk — their shortsighted selfishness in refusing to unite under his command, their lack of discipline and liability to panic, and the American militiaman's propensity to offer unwanted advice and sulk if it was not taken. But he found something to like in them as he did in all men, and learned to work with and through them. Militiamen deserted Washington as they deserted other officers, despite the flogging of sundry and the hanging of a few to encourage the rest. Here is plenty of material for a disparaging biographer to describe Washington as a military martinet who had not even the merit of a notable victory; and some of the "debunkers," who have never known what it is to command troops, have said just that. A sufficient reply to them, as well as striking proof of the amazing confidence, even veneration, that Washington inspired at an early age, is the "Humble Address" of the twenty-seven officers of his regiment, beseeching him to withdraw his resignation:

SIR,

We your most obedient and affectionate Officers, beg leave to express our great Concern, at the disagreeable News we have received of your Determination to resign the Command of that Corps, in which we have under you long served . . .

In our earliest Infancy you took us under your Tuition, train'd us up in the Practice of that Discipline, which alone can constitute good Troops, from the punctual Observance of which you never suffer'd the least Deviation.

Your steady adherence to impartial Justice, your quick Discernment and invariable Regard to Merit . . . first heighten'd our natural Emulation, and, our Desire to excel . . .

Judge then, how sensibly we must be Affected with the loss of such an excellent Commander, such a sincere Friend, and so affable a Companion . . .

It gives us an additional Sorrow, when we reflect, to find, our unhappy

Country will receive a loss, no less irreparable, than ourselves. Where will it meet a Man so experienc'd in military Affairs? One so renown'd for Patriotism, Courage and Conduct? Who has so great knowledge of the Enemy we have to deal with? Who so well acquainted with their Situation and Strength? Who so much respected by the Soldiery? Who in short so able to support the military Character of Virginia? . . .

We with the greatest Deference, presume to entreat you to suspend those Thoughts [of resigning] for another Year . . . In you we place the most implicit Confidence. Your Presence only will cause a steady Firmness and Vigor to actuate in every Breast, despising the greatest Dangers, and thinking light of Toils and Hardships, while lead on by the Man we know and Love . . .

Fully persuaded of this, we beg Leave to assure you, that as you have hitherto been the actuating Soul of the whole Corps, we shall at all times pay the most invariable Regard to your Will and Pleasure, and will always be happy to demonstrate by our Actions, with how much Respect and Esteem we are,

Sir,

Fort Loudoun   Your most affectionate
Decr 31st 1758   and most obedient humble Servants

[Followed by twenty-seven signatures]

There stands the young man Washington, reflected in the hearts of his fellows. As one reads this youthfully sincere composition of the officers' mess at Fort Loudoun, one imagines it addressed to a white-whiskered colonel of fifty. Washington was just twenty-six.

A farewell to arms Washington was determined it must be. Fort Duquesne was won, and his presence at the front was no longer needed. Virginia, the colony that had received the first shock of the war, could justly count on British regulars and the northern colonies to carry it to a glorious conclusion on the Plains of Abraham.

In four years Washington had learned much from war. He found it necessary to discipline himself before he could handle men. He had learned that the interminable boredom of drill, arguing about supplies, and begging for transportation was ill rewarded by the music of whistling bullets; that war was simply hard, beastly work. The sufferings of the border people, the bloody shambles on the Monongahela, the frozen evidence of torture on the road to Fort Duquesne cured his youthful appetite for glory, completely. When Washington again drew his sword, in 1775, it was with great reluctance, and only because he believed, like Cato (II, v, 85), that:

The hand of fate is over us, and Heaven
Exacts severity from all our thoughts.
It is not now a time to talk of aught
But chains, or conquest; liberty, or death.

From one woman he learned perhaps as much as from war. Sally Cary, his fair tutor in Stoicism and the love of his youth, was eighteen and married to his friend and neighbor George William Fairfax, when, at sixteen, he first met her. Beautiful, intelligent, and of gentle birth, Mrs. Fairfax took a more than sisterly interest in the callow young surveyor; and as near neighbors they saw much of each other. Cryptic jottings in his diary for 1748 show that he was already far gone in love. His pathetic letter to her from Fort Cumberland in 1755, begging for a reply to "make me happier than the day is long," strikes a human note in the midst of his businesslike military correspondence. No letters from her to him have been preserved, but from the tone of his replies I gather that Sally was somewhat more of a tease than befitted Cato's daughter. Whatever her sentiments may have been toward him, Washington's letters leave no doubt that he was passionately in love with her; yet gentlemanly standards were then such that while her husband lived she could never be Washington's wife, much less his mistress. What anguish he must have suffered, any young man can imagine. It was a situation that schooled the young soldier-lover in manners, moderation, and restraint — a test cast of his Stoical philosophy. His solution was notable for its common sense: when on a hurried visit to Williamsburg in the spring of 1758, to procure clothes for his ragged soldiers, he met, wooed, and won a housewifely little widow of twenty-seven named Martha Custis. She wanted a manager for her property and a stepfather for her children; he needed a housekeeper for Mount Vernon. It was a *mariage de convenance* that developed into a marriage of affection. But Martha well knew that she was not George's first or greatest love, nor was he hers.

Thirty years later, when Mrs. Fairfax was a poor and childless widow in London, crushing the memories of a Virginia springtime in her heart, there came a letter from Washington. The First Citizen of the World writes that the crowded events of the more than a quarter-century since they parted have not "been able to eradicate from my mind the recollection of those happy moments, the happiest in my life, which I have enjoyed in your company." Martha Washington enclosed a letter under the same cover, in order to show that she, too, understood.

Let us neither distort nor exaggerate this relation, the most beautiful thing in Washington's life. Washington saw no visions of Sally Fairfax in the battle smoke. He did not regard himself as her knightly champion, or any such romantic nonsense; Walter Scott had not yet revived the age of chivalry. Women occupied a small part in Washington's thoughts, as in those of most men of action. No more than Cato did he indulge in worry or bitter thoughts about his ill fortune in love. Suppose, however, Washington had turned out a failure or shown some fault of character at a critical moment, instead of superbly meeting every test. Every yapping biographer of the last decade would have blamed the three members of this blameless triangle. Since he turned out otherwise, we can hardly fail to credit both women with an important share in the formation of Washington's character. And who will deny that Washington attained his nearly perfect balance and serenity, not through self-indulgence but through restraint?

What of other women? — a subject that cannot be shirked in any honest account of the young man Washington. Many of you must have heard the story of that so-called letter of Washington's inviting someone to Mount Vernon, and setting forth the charms of a certain slave girl. No investigator has ever managed to see this letter, or even found a person who has seen it. The nearest we get is to the man who knows a man who has seen it — but that man for some peculiar reason is always sick, dead, or nonexistent when you look for him, or else he refers you to another man, who knows the man who knows the man that has it. John C. Fitzpatrick, who has spent much time on the trail of the seductive if mythical octoroon of Mount Vernon, believes that all stories of this sort were started by a spurious sentence in a letter from Benjamin Harrison to Washington, during the war, that was intercepted by the British and printed in England. Fortunately, the original, a plain letter of military information, has been preserved. But when it was given out for publication to *The Gentleman's Magazine* (of all places), the editor interpolated a jocularly bawdy description of "pretty little Kate the washerwoman's daughter," whose charms the commander in chief was invited to share. Of similar origin are the stories of Washington's illegitimate children. Of course one cannot prove a negative to every rumor. I can only state my opinion that, in view of the fact that Washington fell deeply in love at sixteen, and remained in love with the same lady until his marriage; in view of his reputation under pitiless publicity, he led a clean life, in every sense of the word.

Plutarch wrote of Cato: "He had not taken to public life, like some others, casually or automatically or for the sake of fame or personal advantage. He chose it because it was the function proper to a good man." That was why Washington allowed himself to be elected, in 1758, a representative to the Virginia Assembly, an office proper to a gentleman of his station. He had no gift for speaking or for wire-pulling; he showed no talent or desire for political leadership. But he learned at first hand the strange behavior of *homo sapiens* in legislative assemblies. Everyone marvels at the long-suffering patience shown by Washington in his dealings with the Continental Congress during the war; few remember that he had been for many years a burgess of Virginia, and for several months a member of the very Congress to which he was responsible.

So at twenty-seven George Washington was not only a veteran colonel who had won the confidence and affection of his men, but a member of the Virginia Assembly, a great landowner, and a husband. His youth was over, and he had the means for a life of ease and competence; but the high example of antique virtue would not let him ignore another call to duty. When it came, his unruly nature had been disciplined by the land and the wilderness, by philosophy and a noble woman, and by his own indomitable will to become a fit instrument for a great cause. There were other colonial soldiers in 1775 who from better opportunity had gained more glory in the last war than he; but there was none who inspired so much confidence as this silent, capable man of forty-three. So when the political need of the moment required a Virginian, there was no question but that Colonel Washington should be commander in chief.

If he had failed, historians would have blamed the Continental Congress for a political appointment of a provincial colonel with an indifferent war record. If he had failed, the American Revolution would have been something worse than futile — a Rebellion of '98 that would have soured the American character, made us another Ireland, with a long and distressful struggle for freedom ahead. If, like so many leaders of revolutions, he had achieved merely a personal triumph, or inoculated his country with ambition for glory, the world would have suffered from his success. His country could and almost did fail Washington; but Washington could not fail his country, or disappoint the expectations of his kind. A simple gentleman of Virginia with no extraordinary talents had so disciplined himself that he could lead an insubordinate and divided people into ordered liberty and enduring union.

4

The Wisdom of Benjamin Franklin

From THE SATURDAY EVENING POST, *January 21, 1961; also in* VISTAS
OF HISTORY (New York: Alfred A. Knopf, 1964).

Benjamin Franklin has long been my favorite Revolutionary charac-
ter, after Washington; the first American statesman of that era of
which Washington was the first general. The opportunity to do some-
thing about old Ben came in 1961. The first two volumes of the
definitive PAPERS OF BENJAMIN FRANKLIN, *edited by my friend*
Leonard W. Labaree, had just been published; a celebration was in
order, and Yale generously invited a professor from the university
that gave Franklin his first honorary degree to give the address and,
with his wife, Priscilla, to receive the hospitality for which New
Haven is justly famous. The date was January 17, 1961. And here it
is.

MANY GREAT MEN in history have had little or no sense of humor,
and George Washington was one of them; but Benjamin Franklin, the
most versatile genius in American history, not only had a sense of
humor, but was one of the few people who could get a laugh out of
George. The story he liked best was Ben's reply to the stuffy Englishman who, in 1775, protested that it was foul ball for the Yankee
Minutemen to fire at British redcoats from behind stone walls.
"Why," said Ben, "didn't those walls have two sides?" George relished this so well that when he visited Lexington, fourteen years
later, he told it to his guides, astonishing them with roars of laughter.
And, like most of Franklin's jokes, this had a moral to it — don't
be mad at your enemy if he is smarter than you, but try to be
smarter yourself.

Franklin's humor, as revealed in his *Poor Richard's Almanack*, is
always kindly, often earthy to the point of coarseness, but never bitter. He makes fun of pretense and stuffiness, but never sneers at

poverty or ignorance. He is whimsical, as in his "Drinker's Dictionary," where he gives more than 100 terms for drunkenness — some of which, like "fuddled," "stew'd," and "half seas over," have endured; but most, like "cherry merry," "as dizzy as a goose," and "loose in the hilts," have disappeared. He was a master of political satire, as in that fake edict of a German king proposing to tax England because the Anglo-Saxons originally came from Germany, and he excelled in the typically American humor of exaggeration. For instance, he warns passengers sailing down Delaware Bay in August not to be alarmed at hearing "a confus'd rattling noise, like a shower of hail on a cake of ice." It is the season of fevers and agues in the "lower counties" — the present state of Delaware — and the noise is the chattering of the inhabitants' teeth!

Born in Boston in 1706, missing the Puritan century by only six years, Ben Franklin was three years older than Dr. Samuel Johnson and ten years older than Thomas Gray. Every other leader of the American Revolution belonged to a generation later than his: Washington was twenty-six years younger; Jefferson, thirty-seven years younger; Hamilton might have been Ben's grandson and was, in fact, only five years older than his grandson William Temple Franklin. Benjamin Franklin was old enough to have called on the Reverend Cotton Mather, who, when approaching a low-hanging beam in his parsonage between the living room and the library, gave young Ben a piece of advice he always remembered and acted upon: "You are young and have the world before you; stoop as you go through it, and you will miss many hard bumps." Expediency; or, accept the second best if you cannot get the best, might have been Franklin's motto. He was always advising it in his almanacs, as, "Write with the learned, pronounce with the vulgar," and "Keep your eyes wide open before marriage, half shut afterwards."

Ben Franklin set the pattern of the American success story. Withdrawn from Boston Latin School within a year because his father, a tallow chandler, could not afford the small tuition fee for Ben, the tenth son and fifteenth child. Yet he became, by his own efforts, one of the most learned men of his age. He would have enjoyed enduring fame as a scientist and philosopher had he never dabbled in politics. "Doctor Franklin" he was called, because of honorary degrees from Harvard, Yale, St. Andrews, and Oxford; he could put "FRS" after his name as a Fellow of the Royal Society of London, and was elected corresponding member of most of the learned societies of Europe. At home he was the only American leader except Washington who commanded respect and confidence throughout the Thirteen Colonies, four of which, New Jersey, Massachusetts, Pennsylvania, and Georgia, appointed him their agent, or official lobbyist, in England. And his popularity went deep; he had the confidence of all classes. Robert Morris, Philip Livingston, and Cadwallader Colden were proud to have him to dinner; yet the frontiersmen of North Carolina proposed that he "represent the unhappy state of this Province to His Majesty."

Ben was as American as clam chowder and johnnycake, but equally at home in England, where he spent almost twenty years prior to 1776; and in France, where he had popular renown and great influence. A pioneer in experimental physics, especially in the new branch of electricity, he was in touch with everything else that went on in the scientific world; yet he could also make practical inventions, such as the lightning rod and the Franklin stove. Incidentally, the so-called Franklin stoves now found in antique shops are much less effective than the original "Pennsylvanian Fire-Places," which Franklin invented in 1740. This metal fireplace included an air box over which the hot combustion gases passed on their way to the chimney. Outside air was drawn in through a duct, circulated through the air box around baffles, and passed out into the room.

When he crossed the Atlantic he studied winds and currents to such good purpose that he could instruct Yankee skippers how to work the Gulf Stream to best advantage. A conservative until the very eve of the Revolution and an advocate of compromise with Britain, Franklin became, in 1775, one of the strongest exponents of American independence; and although seventy years old when American independence was declared, he was one of the more radical Revolutionary leaders.

Franklin never made much money, but was generous with what he had, and was a public benefactor. He refused to have his inventions patented; everyone could profit from them. One of his legacies, operated under sagacious principles that he laid down, still provides the Franklin Medals for top scholars in the Boston schools; another still contributes income to the Franklin Institute of Philadelphia. His many private charities were unobtrusive; most touching were his efforts to preserve the self-respect of his sister, Jane Mecom, by setting her up in business with the old family recipe for crown soap. And he was a most accomplished man. He could fix anything around the house and tell others, in his annual almanac, how to fix things. He could play the violin, guitar, and harp, and he invented a new musical instrument, which he called "the armonica," on the principle of the musical glasses. Mozart and Beethoven composed music for the armonica, and Queen Marie Antoinette, among others, learned to play it.

A great man by any standard, Franklin was a universal genius, great in a variety of ways — as printer, philanthropist, statesman, man of science; as naturalist, and humanist, and writer whose *Autobiography* and *Poor Richard's Almanack* had an international vogue. Nor was Franklin content to write literature; he organized it, as he did everything else. He organized the Philadelphia Library, the first important semipublic library in the colonies; Philadelphia College, which became the University of Pennsylvania, and a "Junto," or discussion club, which eventually became the American Philosophical Society, our senior learned society.

Franklin's secret, the thing that "made him tick" and pulled every aspect of his mind together, was his love of people. Not people in the abstract, like Karl Marx, Henry George, and other dreary prophets of progress, but people in particular, and of all kinds. He liked intellectuals, businessmen, workingmen, children, and Negroes; not only Americans but Englishmen, Frenchmen, and Europeans of a dozen other nations. Not that he had any illusions about people. He knew them at their worst as well as their best, but he accepted them. Note this remarkable prophecy written in 1780:

The rapid progress *true* science now makes, occasions my regretting sometimes that I was born so soon. It is impossible to imagine the height to which may be carried, in a thousand years, the power of man over matter. We may perhaps learn to deprive large masses of their gravity, and give them absolute levity . . . Agriculture may diminish its labor and double its produce; all diseases may by sure means be prevented or cured . . . O that *moral science* were in as fair a way of improvement, that men would cease to be *wolves* to one another and that human beings would at length learn what they now improperly call humanity!

He talked with English and French statesmen as an equal; yet he was as homely and comfortable as an old shoe. If you had been a young man in 1776 calling on the great ones of the day, you would have been overawed by George Washington; and Sam Adams you would have found rather grim. Alexander Hamilton would have made you feel very small and stupid; Patrick Henry would have made you a speech; and John Adams would have talked your head off. But Ben would have made you at home. He would have asked after your parents, and probably have known them, or at least about them; he would then have asked you about yourself, drawn you out, and sent you away with some good advice, a warm handclasp, and a smile you would have remembered all your life. The same would be true if the visitor were a young and pretty girl. "Caty" Ray, a lively lass of twenty-three who happened to meet Franklin at his brother's house in Boston when he was forty-eight, became his friend for life. For more than thirty years they maintained an intimate correspondence, charming on both sides though rather illiterate on hers; and Ben's last letter, written shortly before his death, ended: "Among the felicities of my life I reckon your friendship, which I shall remember with pleasure as long as that life lasts."

It was because he loved people so much that he hated war profoundly. After peace had been concluded, in 1783, largely owing to his efforts, he wrote: "At length we are in peace, God be praised, and long, very long, may it continue. All wars are follies, very expensive, and very mischievous ones. When will mankind be convinced of this, and agree to settle their differences by arbitration?" Yet Franklin hated cruelty and injustice even more than he hated war. Outrages on humanity, such as those perpetrated by the Pennsylvania frontiersmen on the Moravian Indians, evoked savage indignation from his usually serene and tolerant mind. His last public paper, in 1790, was written in favor of the abolition of Negro slavery; and for it he was bitterly attacked in the United States Senate. No doctrinaire pacifist, he supported the three principal wars of his time. He used the wisdom of the serpent to get around the pacifism of Pennsylvania Quakers and persuade them to cooperate in the French and Indian War.

Hopeless of abolishing war in his day, Franklin made every effort, through treaties and international agreements, to render war less horrible by safeguarding the rights of neutrals and of noncombatants; by obtaining agreements that farmers, fishermen, and other civilians would not be molested by armies and fleets. He hoped to confine war to professional forces and to make it less frequent by recourse to arbitration. The United States followed this policy until the present century; but between the Second Hague Conference of 1907 and the London Naval Conference of 1909 there came a turning point, and we joined other nations on the road to total war and, possibly, total destruction.

Franklin's life passed through many phases — the poor boy of a large family, the Boston journeyman printer, the young man making his way in Philadelphia. Following one of his favorite quotations from the Bible, "It is better to marry than to burn," Ben married his landlady's daughter Deborah. "Debby," almost illiterate, already married to a sailor who had simply disappeared, shared few of Franklin's interests and prevented his being accepted by the polite society of his adopted city. How the scum rises!" remarked a Philadelphia matron when Franklin's grandson moved uptown. But that sort of thing didn't bother Ben. He was no status seeker; he accepted every social contact that came his way; and in all his vast correspondence that has been preserved there is not one complaint of being slighted or snubbed. No man ever born had less class consciousness. He never attempted to conceal his working-class origin; in his last will and testament he described himself as "Benjamin Franklin, printer." He was not ashamed of his poor relations, who were both numerous and importunate. Many people, when he rose to fame, became his enemies and did their best to pull him down; but he never retaliated, and in his thousands of letters I have found no unkind word about anyone.

Poor Richard's Almanack, from 1733 on, is full of epigrams and mottoes that we still use in common speech, often forgetting whence they came, such as:

Time is money.
Snug as a bug in a rug.
Keep one's nose to the grindstone.
Necessity never made a good bargain.
Three may keep a secret if two of them are dead.
Experience keeps a dear school, but fools will learn in no other.

And these, now forgotten, deserve a revival:

Fish and visitors smell in three days.

There are no fools so troublesome as those that have wit.

There are three faithful friends, an old wife, an old dog, and ready money.

None but the well-bred man knows how to confess a fault, or acknowledge himself in error.

Ten or twelve years after he started the almanac, Franklin began his electrical and scientific work. In 1748 he retired from active printing and bookselling, which gave him leisure for writing and science. His *Experiments and Observations on Electricity,* printed at London in 1751, was translated into French, Italian, and German. The book earned its author several honorary degrees and the Copley medal of the Royal Society of London, and made him a leading figure in the world of science. These experiments, of which the one with kite and key was the best known but not the most important, were a notable contribution to knowledge. Franklin was responsible for the concept of positive and negative electricity; he made the first electric battery and armature; he explained how the Leyden jar, the first electrical condenser, worked. He would have liked to devote his entire life to science, but was too public-spirited to confine himself to that. He served as deputy postmaster general for the English colonies for twenty-one years, and very efficiently. He entered Pennsylvania politics early, and became a member of the assembly. He organized logistic support for British armies in the interior during the old French and Indian War, and he represented Pennsylvania at the Albany Congress of 1754. Three years later the assembly sent him to England to try to persuade the Penn family to allow their millions of acres of wild land to pay a small tax to the province.

In England Franklin remained for seventeen years, most of the time as agent for the assemblies of several colonies. He made a host of friends among scientists, men of letters, economists, and politicians; he promoted the scheme for a new Vandalia colony on the Ohio; he met Dr. Johnson as member of a charitable society, the Associates of Doctor Bray, which set up schools for Negro children in colonial towns. He frequently contributed to the London newspapers articles, letters, and squibs supporting the rights of the colonists, the most humorous called "Rules by which a Great Empire may be Reduced to a Small One," which he dedicated to one of the leading

British ministers. At the same time he wrote to his American friends begging them to moderate their demands, to respect law and order, since time was working for them.

This policy got him in wrong with the colonial radicals. He spoke different languages to his English and his American friends, precisely because he was trying to moderate the extreme demands of each side and to find a formula by which American liberty could be preserved within the British Empire. That, of course, exposed him to the charge of hypocrisy. His position as colonial agent became very shaky in 1773. Sam Adams attacked him, partly because of his moderation, but mostly because he regarded Franklin as a wicked old man. Debby refused to cross the ocean, and so never came to London with Ben, who was reported to be leading the life of young Boswell; and in his writings he took an earthy, practical view of sex that outraged Puritanical sentiment. Curiously enough, it was Franklin's realistic attitude toward sex that inspired the vicious attack on his reputation, in *Studies in Classic American Literature* (1923), by D. H. Lawrence, who, though far from a Puritan in sexual matters, seems to have expected everyone else to be one.

Franklin worked hard to prevent a breach with the mother country, but when it became clear that Parliament would not repeal the Coercive Acts, he realized that his mission had failed. In March 1775, he sailed from England for the last time as a subject of King George. The very day after his arrival in Philadelphia he was chosen by the Pennsylvania Assembly a delegate to the Continental Congress.

In Congress or out, Franklin was no great or original political thinker. In politics he was an opportunist, or pragmatist, to give opportunism its modern philosophical term. His one test of a constitution, or of a political arrangement, was, "Will it work?" The British Empire before 1763 worked very well, so he wished to continue it, or restore it as it had been, rather than break off. Similar was his attitude toward religion. As a young man he had been a typical eighteenth-century deist, but be abandoned deism because "this doctrine might be true, but was not very useful." He observed that public morality was essential to good government and that organized Christianity was the best promoter of public morality; so he supported churches and even occasionally attended them.

Franklin placed a high value on conciliation and compromise in politics. He did not like the result of the Federal Convention of 1787, of which he was the oldest and most experienced member, because he disliked checks and balances, and wanted no United States Senate. Yet such was his common sense and his respect for the opinions of others, that he accepted and supported the federal Constitution instead of standing out against it, as did George Mason, Elbridge Gerry, and other members whose vanity had been wounded because their pet ideas had not been adopted. The famous speech he delivered near the end of the convention expresses his attitude perfectly:

I confess that there are several parts of this Constitution which I do not at present approve, but I am not sure I shall never approve them; for having lived long, I have experienced many instances of being obliged, by better information or fuller consideration, to change opinions . . . which I once thought right, but found to be otherwise . . .

Thus I consent, sir, to this Constitution because I expect no better, and because I am not sure that it is not the best. The opinions I have had of its errors I sacrifice to the public good; I have never whispered a syllable of them abroad; within these walls they were born, and here they shall die. If every one of us in returning to our constituents were to report the objections he has had to it, and endeavor to gain partisans in support of them, we might prevent its being generally received . . .

Franklin may therefore be considered one of the Founding Fathers of American democracy, since no democratic government can last long without conciliation and compromise. And the mere knowledge that he was in favor of the Constitution did more to win acceptance from the common people of America than all the learned, close-reasoned articles in *The Federalist*, admirable as they are.

In diplomacy, too, Franklin was a genius. The sending of him to France to represent the Continental Congress was a master stroke; for in France he already had a great reputation as a man of science and as "Bonhomme Richard." The French government, of course, favored him because he represented American resistance to its hereditary enemy; and all who were dreaming of liberty for France revered him as a signer of the Declaration of Independence. His book on electrical experiments, which had been translated, paraphrased, and published more than once, gave him high prestige among scientists and philosophers. An edition of *Oeuvres de M. Franclin* had appeared in 1773; and an enterprising Paris bookseller had translated his *Way to Wealth* and a selection of his proverbs and witty sayings in the almanacs as *La Science de Bonhomme Richard.* This turned out to be even more important than his work on electricity in enhancing Franklin's reputation.

The simple yet witty moral teachings in these maxims made a tremendous appeal. Edition followed edition off the French press; it was even referred to as the "Bible of the Eighteenth Century," and a royal official advised the use of it in connection with the catechism. *Bonhomme Richard* proved that a scientist could be religious and creative, not merely a destructive critic of religion and a puller-down of ancient institutions, as most of the French men of science had been. The maxims were acceptable to the Church, and made Franklin a favorite figure among the people at large. The ancient warfare between science and religion seemed to be ended. It was Franklin, more than any other person, who convinced the average Catholic bourgeois that natural science was not to be feared as impious and anti-Christian, but a good thing that would react in a beneficial way on human life.

Hitherto, little effort had been made to define the limits between science and religion. It was generally supposed to be immoral to assert a scientific cause for phenomena such as earthquakes, shooting stars, thunder, and lightning. Thus, Franklin's proof that lightning is an electrical phenomenon became very significant. It had an impact comparable to that in our time of Einstein's theory of relativity. It took out of the field of religion something earlier classified as a mere act of God, and included it in natural science. Yet nobody could deny that Franklin was a religious man, that he believed in God and called himself a Christian.

Franklin behaved in France with great sagacity. He did not mix with the people or drive through the streets waving his hat and soliciting cheers; he lived aloof in the Hôtel Valentinois at Passy, and appeared seldom in public. The rumor that he was a Quaker seemed to be confirmed because he allowed himself to be presented to the king without a wig or elaborate court dress. That was just an accident — the wig did not come in time — but it was all to the good because Quakers were the only Christian sect favored by the philosophers. Franklin also used his membership in the Masonic fraternity to good effect; the Masonic Lodge of the Nine Sisters, which he joined in Paris, and of which he became grand master, helped to mobilize public opinion in favor of French intervention in the War of Independence.

One of the warmest tributes to Franklin's influence and standing in France came from the pen of John Paul Jones, whose naval efforts he consistently supported, despite countless difficulties. Jones wrote to Robert Morris:

I know the great and good in this kingdom better, perhaps, than any other American who has appeared in Europe since the treaty of alliance, and if my testimony could add anything to Franklin's reputation I would witness the universal veneration and esteem with which his name inspires all ranks, not only at Versailles and all over this kingdom, but also in Spain and Holland. And I can add from the testimony of the first characters of other nations that with them envy is dumb when the name of Franklin is but mentioned.

John Adams, Franklin's colleague at Paris, has left an amusing account of the doctor's working day as a diplomat. Hard-working, conscientious John tried to get the doctor to do business, or at least to sign papers, before breakfast, but seldom with success. He breakfasted late; and as soon as the meal was over, carriages began arriving at the Hôtel Valentinois with all sorts of people, "some philosophers, academicians, and economists," some literary men; "but by far the greater part were women and children, come to have the pleasure of telling stories among their acquaintances about his simplicity, his bald head, and scattering straight hairs." These visitors occupied all his time until the hour to dress for dinner, between one and two o'clock. He was invited to dine out almost every day, and seldom declined. After dinner he sometimes attended the play, sometimes a session of the academy or a lodge meeting, but more often visited one of his lady friends to take tea.

"Some of these ladies," says Adams, "I knew, as Madame Helvétius, Madame Brillon, Madame Chaumont, Madame Le Ray, and others whom I never knew and never enquired for. After tea the evening was spent in hearing the ladies sing and play upon their pianofortes and other instrument of musick, and in various games as cards, chess, backgammon." Franklin, however, never played anything but chess or checkers. "In these agreeable and important occupations and amusements," says Adams, "the afternoon and evening was spent, and he came home at all hours from nine to twelve o'clock at night. This course of life contributed to his pleasure and I believe to his health and longevity."

To one of these ladies, Madame Helvétius, wealthy widow of a noted philosopher, Franklin proposed marriage when he was more than seventy and she was but a few years younger. The young, beautiful, and amiable Madame Brillon de Jouy was willing to sit on Franklin's lap and to let him play chess with her when she was soaking in one of those enormous covered bathtubs of the period, but no other favors beyond that would she allow. Madame Le Ray de Chaumont — she was one person and not two, as John Adams seemed to remember — was the wife of the owner of the Hôtel Valentinois, in a wing of which Franklin lived. Her husband was a practical ship-owner who handled much of the unneutral aid given by France to America before the treaty was signed in 1778. She became the first of a succession of French mistresses to John Paul Jones, when that gallant captain arrived in France as commanding officer of U.S.S. *Ranger*.

For all that John Adams said, Franklin managed to write a surprising number of letters, by dictating them to his secretaries at breakfast or between social engagements. And he did the main work of the American mission, through personal contacts. Far more effective than formal notes were a whispered conversation at the play, a hint to a cabinet minister's mistress, a confidential chat at the Masonic lodge.

Franklin was also keenly interested in aeronautics. He was a friend of the Montgolfier brothers, who made the first balloon ascensions. "We think of nothing here at present but of flying," he wrote from Paris in 1783. "The balloons engross all attention." John Jeffries, who made the first crossing of the English Channel by balloon, brought Franklin from London the world's first airmail letter.

Thus, Benjamin Franklin was a universal genius, more so than any other man of his day, American or European; one from whose writings the student of almost any subject, from orchids to oceanography, or from politics to population growth, can learn something. He was the embodiment of what we like to call the American spirit — idealistic but practical, principled but expedient, optimistic for human betterment and the world's future.

One of his last letters, written on March 9, 1790, was in answer to

President Ezra Stiles of Yale. "You desire to know something of my religion," he says. "It is the first time I have been questioned upon it." (Who but a president of Yale would have dared?) "But I cannot take your curiosity amiss, and shall endeavour in a few words to gratify it." He affirms his belief in God as the creator of the universe, and in immortality. He expresses some doubt of the divinity of Jesus; but with characteristic humor adds that he will not dogmatize on the subject, "having never studied it, and think it needless to busy myself with it now, when I expect soon an opportunity to know the truth with less trouble."

He has less than six weeks to wait.

As "Poor Richard" he had remarked in one of his almanacs:

> If you would not be forgotten
> As soon as you are dead and rotten,
> Either write things worth reading
> Or do things worth the writing.

Benjamin Franklin did both. Everything he wrote is worth reading, and everything he did has become part of the fabric of American history and of Western civilization.

5

Perry's First Visit to Japan, July 8–17, 1853

From "OLD BRUIN": COMMODORE MATTHEW C. PERRY (Boston: Atlantic–Little, Brown, 1967), *Chapter XXIV.*

> We pray God that our present attempt to bring a singular and isolated people into the family of civilized nations may succeed without resort to bloodshed.
> —Perry, *Journal for July 9, 1853*

THE GOVERNMENT AND PEOPLE OF JAPAN seemed to sense that this third day of the sixth month, sixth year of Kaei (July 8, 1853) would be a milestone in their country's history. The sight of the two steam men-of-war — first steamships ever seen in Japan — each towing a sailing vessel, dashing along in a calm at 9 knots, struck the natives with astonishment. On the fiftieth anniversary of this event an old man of Shimoda on the Izu Peninsula described how it felt:

People in the town made such a fuss that I asked what was up and was told that offshore there were burning ships. With two or three men I climbed a hill. There we saw a big crowd of people jabbering about the ships. As they drew gradually closer to shore it became clear that they were not Japanese but foreign. What we had mistaken for a fire was smoke belching forth from these warships and they caused a great commotion . . . When we came down the hill the whole town was astir. Some men rushed to Edo . . . Today it may seem a laughing matter but I later learned that not only in Shimoda but also in Edo it was a matter of great concern. A popular doggerel of the time tells about the reaction in Edo when the ships first approached:

> O what America has done with *jokissen!*
> It took only four to keep the Bakufu awake.*

---

* *Jokissen* is a pun; it can mean either a kind of tea drunk by Buddhist priests to keep themselves awake, or steamships.

All Edo was appalled.   Perry's visit should have been no surprise; in 1852 the Dutch at Nagasaki sent them an official warning that the Americans were coming to Uraga to present a letter from their President to the Emperor, and word had arrived from Okinawa that Perry was on his way.   But, owing to the Bakufu policy of secrecy and procrastination, the recipients discounted the warning as a Dutch ruse to get more business for themselves, and did nothing about it.   Hence, when the American Squadron arrived, nobody knew how to receive it.   Abe Ise no kami, Daimyo of Fukuyama, senior member of the *roju* (the Shogun's Council), had dealt with Biddle successfully; Edo Bay was supposedly so well fortified that no other stranger would dare enter, and so no preparations were made to deal with Perry.   Abe was practically running the government, owing to the Shogun's feeble character and ill heath.   Nobody dared tell His Highness about Perry's arrival — he heard of it only by accident three days later while attending a *noh* play at Edo Castle, and the news threw him into such a tizzy that he went to bed and stayed there.

A parallel situation would be an announcement by astronauts that weird-looking aircraft from outer space were on their way to earth; nobody would know how to receive them.   Baba (Bun'ei), a Japanese historian at the turn of the century, describes the consternation at Edo Castle, seat of the Shogun: "Fresh messages arrived one after the other," and when the *roju* met, the members were "too alarmed to open their mouths," but finally issued orders to the daimyo responsible for defense to mobilize at once to defend Japan from invasion. Dr. Ito, the gossipy court physician, noted that provisions became scarce, that plain suits of armor quadrupled in price, and the tailors were working round the clock to manufacture *jinbaori,* the cloaks worn over armor.

But Perry had not come to invade Japan.   "I have come here as a peacemaker," he said in one of his interviews with Japanese officials — words selected by General Douglas MacArthur to be inscribed on the Opening-of-Japan monument at Shimoda.   This first visit, as the Commodore wrote to his wife, was " a preliminary demonstration," with no immediate object except to deliver the letter. With only four warships available out of the twelve promised before he left home, Perry expected the Bakufu to procrastinate about a treaty.   Best therefore to try the old one-two tactics that he had employed in Naples: state his country's demands, sail away to give the government time to reflect, and return with a more imposing force.

The *kurofune* (black ships), as the Japanese called all foreign vessels, anchored off Uraga in line-of-battle. They were promptly approached and almost surrounded by Japanese guard boats. Each of these craft was rowed by six to eight stalwart oarsmen standing and facing forward. Each displayed a flag bearing the Tokugawa trefoil, together with sundry pendants and streamers, and carried a score of soldiers commanded by two officers. Fastening their painters to the ships, the guard boat people tried to climb on board over the chains or the bobstay. Commodore Biddle had allowed that, to his subsequent undoing, and Commodore Perry was determined to prevent it. By his orders, the sailors cast overboard or cut the guard boats' painters, and repelled would-be boarders with pikes and cutlasses. No foreign ship had ever dared do that. The boats' officers roared angrily, and their crews kept up "an awful pow-wow and noise," hoping no doubt to intimidate the barbarians. What appeared to be the senior guard boat then approached *Susquehanna* near enough to hold up a scroll inscribed in large letters in French (supplied by the Dutch): "Depart immediately and dare not anchor!" A Dutch interpreter in the boat explained through Perry's interpreter that a high personage was on board and wished to be received. He was told that the commander of the American Squadron represented the President personally, and would see nobody under the rank of cabinet minister; but the high personage might board if he wished.

John Contee, Perry's flag lieutenant, interviewed the alleged dignitary, Nakajima (Saburosuke) by name. He, it turned out, was merely a *yoriki*, aide to a vice governor. Contee informed him that Perry's intentions were friendly; that his one object, which had been communicated to the Bakufu in 1852 through the Dutch, was to present the President's letter to the Emperor. Nakajima said that he knew nothing about the Dutch communication, but that, in any case, if Perry wished to send a letter to the Emperor, his squadron must proceed to Nagasaki. That, Perry was determined never to do; it would not only involve him with the Dutch factors at Deshima and the degrading restrictions to which the Netherlanders had submitted, but (as the Russians discovered to their cost) would require three months to receive an answer from Edo. Through Contee he informed the Japanese official that the squadron had come to Uraga because it was near Edo where (he supposed) the Emperor resided; he refused absolutely to go to Nagasaki, and if the guard boats surrounding his ships did not immediately retire, they would be dispersed by force. Nakajima promptly went to the gangway and shouted an order that sent all but a few boats back to shore, and those few were chased away by an armed barge from *Susquehanna*.

Thus three important positions were gained initially: Perry would not talk with "bottle-washers," would not allow sightseers on board, and would not suffer his ships to be surrounded by a cordon of boats. A fourth position, already taken at Okinawa, he again maintained when a messenger from shore offered to supply food, water, and fuel. The Bakufu always gave supplies gratis to intrusive foreign ships, in order to afford them no excuse to tarry for want of necessities; and for that reason Perry gave strict orders to accept nothing except for money or some other quid pro quo. In this instance, a ship's officer told the messenger that the Commodore thanked him, but had plenty of provisions on board; however, as the American presence had apparently interrupted Uraga's usual supply of junk-borne food, "We shall be pleased to let you share our stock of provisions." This unheard-of reply left the Japanese speechless.

In the meantime, to take no chances, Perry kept his ships in top condition of readiness, maintaining every precaution against surprise attack. Himself he kept invisible to the Japanese. Not that he was confined to his cabin; *Susquehanna* had six-foot bulwarks, so the Commodore could walk on deck without any outsider catching sight of his stalwart figure. Perry's unapproachableness was regarded in some quarters as unduly formal, even stuffy. A former biographer accuses him of "playing Mikado," making himself "His High Mighty Mysteriousness, Lord of the Forbidden Interior," etc. Amusing, but beside the point. Perry, far better than most Americans of the twentieth century, knew the value of "face" when dealing with Orientals. He had observed the ill effects of Biddle's palsy-walsy approach. In the official Narrative he thus answered complaints of "un-Americanism":

The Commodore, also, was well aware that the more exclusive he should make himself, and the more unyielding he might be in adhering to his declared intentions, the more respect these people of forms and ceremonies would be disposed to award him; therefore it was that he deliberately resolved to confer personally with no one but a functionary of the highest rank in the empire . . . he felt that it was well to teach the Japanese, in the mode most intelligible to them, *by stately and dignified reserve, joined to perfect equity in all he asked or did,* to respect the country from which he came, and to suspend for a time their accustomed arrogance and incivility toward strangers. The Japanese so well understood him that they learned the lesson at once. It was this feeling, and this only, which prompted him to refuse to see the Vice-Governor of Uraga, and to refer him to his aide for conference. He saw him enough afterward, when matters had been arranged between the governments, on terms of friendship and equality.*

"Stately and dignified reserve" is right. Perry acted imperiously, which the Japanese understood; never arrogantly, which would have offended them.

That night, beacon fires were lighted on the hilltops and along the shore of Edo Bay, placid as a lake. Silence was broken only by the tolling of a great bronze gong ashore, by ships' bells striking the half-hours, and by a lights-out gun from the flagship. Along the bay, shrines and temples were thronged with worshipers supplicating their gods to raise another *kamikaze* (heavenly wind) like the providential typhoon that defeated a Mongol invasion fleet in 1570.† Shortly after eight bells ushered in the ninth day of July, a remarkable meteor appeared to the south and crossed the sky, giving off sparks like a rocket, illuminating the roadstead during the midwatch, and reflecting a bright blue light on the hulls and spars of the American ships. To the Japanese, this seemed a portent, whether for good or ill they knew not; Commodore Perry noted in his Journal that, like the ancients, we should regard it as a favorable omen, "as we pray God that our present attempt to bring a singular and isolated people into the family of civilized nations may succeed without bloodshed."

A bright morning sun dispersed the night mists and revealed a superb panorama of pine-tufted hills, cultivated fields, and villages embowered in groves of trees, with Fuji towering over all. The same scene delights a sea or air traveler of today as he enters Tokyo Wan,

---

   * Dulles, in *Yankees and Samurai*, states, "Perry insisted throughout the negotiations on being called 'Admiral.'" This is not correct. The Japanese had never heard of a commodore but had heard of an admiral; so the Dutch interpreter referred to Perry as "the Admiral." He never assumed the rank himself. Similarly, "The Governor and his interpreter were requested to use the same designation in speaking of the President as by that which distinguished the Emperor [Daïri]." Such details were very important when dealing with a ceremonious nation like Japan.

   † It was this same event of 1570 that gave its name to the famous Japanese Kamikaze Corps of crash-suicide aviators in 1944–45.

although the coast from Kannon Zaki northward has become almost one continuous city. The shore was a scene of bustling activity, as mobilization decreed by the Bakufu began. Every daimyo responsible for the defense of Edo Bay sent a contingent, displaying banners emblazoned with its lord's arms, and great gilt tassels as emblems of his authority; for the Japanese were as keen on heraldry as mediaeval Europeans. There were caracoling cavalry, long-swordsmen, archers with eight-foot bows, musketeers carrying ancient smooth-bores, spearmen with ten-foot pikes: altogether a brave and beautiful spectacle, wholly new to Americans. There were already some twenty forts on the shores of Edo Bay, mostly concentrated on the Uraga narrows, but now additional earthworks were thrown up, partly concealed by canvas screens; ancient smooth-bores were sited, and every other preparation that the Japanese then knew was made for defense, in case these "outer barbarians" were bent on conquest. Commodore Perry and his officers gazed unafraid upon this scene. The screened earthworks, which they called "dungaree forts," were not impressive, and through telescopes and binoculars they ascertained that the Japanese had no weapons that they need fear.

This mobilization, which included 17,000 soldiers exclusive of those at Kurihama, and all able-bodied males to act as labor troops, was the first reaction of the Shogun's government to the black ships. The Bakufu was really on a spot. If it did not get rid of these intruders as it had all earlier ones, it would lose face with the Japanese people; there might even be a revolution to depose the House of Tokugawa. An order was issued that people must not discuss the arrival of the black ships, but it could not be enforced. Perry evidently meant business, and the Bakufu had no means of defense against his weapons if he chose to land and march on Edo, or if he elected to blockade the heavily populated capital, all of whose provisions came by sea. Further, the high councilors of the Bakufu assumed that, if given an excuse, Perry would occupy territory as the British had done in China and set up an American Hong Kong; a useful misconception since it caused strict orders to be issued to withhold gunfire, no matter how insolent the barbarians might be, to avoid an "incident." So the Bakufu decided to accept the President's letter, but in reply to evade and procrastinate, hoping that another *kamikaze* would blow up; and if that did not happen, make as few concessions as possible to get rid of Perry. As a contemporary Japanese historian records:

The city of Edo and the surrounding villages were in great tumult; in anticipation of the war which seemed imminent, the people carried their valuables and furniture in all directions to conceal them in a house of some friend living farther off . . . So at last they decided that it would be best to arrange the affair quietly, to give the foreigners the articles they wanted, and to put off sending an answer to the Letter; to tell the envoy . . . that he had better go away, and that in a short time he should get a definite answer.

The first important event of Saturday, July 9, was a call from Kayama (Eizaemon), accompanied by a suite and two interpreters. The interpreters, possibly misunderstood, introduced him as the governor of Uraga. Actually, Kayama was merely a *yoriki*, or aide to the governor, doubling as chief of police, in which capacity he had dealt with Biddle and other unwanted visitors. He was obviously a shade higher than Nakajima in rank; but Perry, rightly guessing that he was not high enough, turned him over to Commanders Buchanan and Adams, keeping himself in the flag cabin and using his son Oliver as go-between. Kayama again pressed the squadron to sail to Nagasaki. Perry again refused. If President Fillmore's letter was not properly received somewhere in Edo Bay, his only alternative would be to land with an armed force and deliver the letter in person at Edo Castle. Kayama, horrified at the impious suggestion, said he would send to Edo for further instructions but it would take eight days to receive an answer. Perry sent word that he would wait but three or four days before putting his dread alternative into effect. Kayama inquired, with a trace of malice, why four warships were required to deliver a letter to the emperor. "Out of respect for him!" answered Perry, with his customary aplomb. Kayama hastened to the capital the same day and reported to Ido Iwami no kami, the new co-governor of Uraga, who admitted that he had received word from the Dutch of the Americans' coming but had not bothered to tell the other governor of Uraga, who would have to deal with the barbarians! Kayama advised him to receive the President's letter as soon as possible, and where Perry wanted; "so unmistakably did the countenances of not only the Commander but also of all the officers in the wardroom show their resolve to fight."

During this conference, a boat from each American ship, with a white flag at the bow, began to sound and survey Edo Bay. Kayama, observing them, declared that they were breaking Japanese law, to which Commander Buchanan replied that the United States Navy operated under American law wherever it went. An international lawyer would be somewhat put to it to defend that proposition, but the big guns of the squadron, covering the boats, made it valid on this occasion.

On the following day, Sunday, July 10, no visitors were allowed on board; the Commodore insisted on proper keeping of this, their first Sabbath in Japan. The big capstan on *Susquehanna* was covered with a flag, on which the ship's Bible rested. Chaplain Jones read the office of morning prayer with the lesson for the day and preached one of his less lengthy sermons. To the accompaniment of the full band and the familiar tune "Old Hundred," some 300 lusty voices sang Isaac Watts's prophetic hymn:

> Before Jehovah's awful throne
> Ye nations, bow with sacred joy;
> Know that the Lord is God alone —
> He can create and He destroy.

When the sounding parties resumed work on Monday morning, the 11th, there occurred an incident painted by Heine and entitled "Passing the Rubicon." A flotilla of thirty to forty guard boats filled with soldiers, who "presented quite a bristling front with their spears and matchlocks, while their lacquered caps and shields flashed brightly in the sun," confronted the flag launch under charge of Lieutenant Silas Bent, and the senior Japanese officer made minatory gestures with his iron fan and yelled orders that nobody in the American launch understood. The lieutenant, anxious to avoid a rupture, altered his collison course but dispatched another boat to *Mississippi* to ask Captain Lee to move closer. On the steamer's approach the guard boats retired. And Perry well named the nearest point of land "Point Rubicon," because no foreign ship had passed it for three centuries.

Ignoring the Japanese batteries along shore whose guns were trained on them, Silas Bent and his men sounded up to a point off the present Tokyo International Airport, and *Mississippi* towed the boats back to their ships. Perry's purpose was to locate the channel to Edo so that, in case no proper person were sent to receive the President's letter, he could land a delegation near the Shogun's capital under the cover of his guns and deliver it himself. Kayama, sent on board *Mississippi* to protest and inquire the reason for this intrusion, was told by Adams that the Americans were charting the bay in order to fight their way into Edo in case the Bakufu procrastinated too long, or refused to receive the letter. This candor amazed the Japanese. Any Oriental would have given ten different reasons, none of them correct.

Incidentally the Americans indulged in the old discoverers' privilege of naming places — not because Perry claimed them by right of discovery but because he did not know the Japanese names. Thus, Otsu Wan became, on Perry's chart, "Susquehanna Bay," and Negishi Wan, "Mississippi Bay"; Saru Shima, a pretty, well-wooded islet crowned by a three-gun battery, was named after Perry himself, and Natsu Shima called "Webster Island," to commemorate the late senator's interest in the expedition. Other points and headlands acquired temporarily the exotic names of American Presidents and Navy secretaries. One of the surveying parties rowed up Kanazawa Wan, an inlet bordered by villages and gardens, and named it "Goldsborough," after the superintendent of the Naval Academy. Many inhabitants rallied round and offered the men pots of sweet water and ripe peaches; officers of a guard boat invited the foreigners on board and enjoyed a social smoke with them, and the Americans amused their hosts by firing Colt revolvers. During this friendly gathering, "in which the Japanese seemed remarkably genial in manner and expansive in hospitality," a glowering official turned up and shooed off his countrymen like naughty children. All hands were "in raptures" over "the kindly disposition of the Japanese and the beauty of their country." Strange indeed was the contrast between simple popular friendliness and official alarm, confusion, and standoffishness.

Boats rowing and flagship steaming up the bay caused even greater consternation in Edo than their initial appearance, because (according to Dr. Ito), "Since the age of our ancestral gods, it has been firmly believed that the hidden bank of Futtsu would prevent any foreign vessel from entering Edo Bay."* This advance touched off no hostile act, but from Japanese sources we learn that clashes were narrowly avoided. Retainers of two bellicose daimyo, of Aizu and Kumamoto,

* Futtsu Saki sticks far out from the eastern shore, but even in 1853 there was a deep channel between it and the western shore. The ancestral gods were possibly appeased by *Saratoga's* hitting the submerged part of the Futtsu shoal, but she got off with little damage, and Perry named it "Saratoga Spit" after her.

sent messages to their lords asking permission to open fire on the American boats, but were denied. One boat, unidentified, landed in front of a six-gun battery at Hatayama and, according to our Japanese source, "pointed drawn swords at our battery, jeered at us and were very overbearing." When the Japanese commander in a rage dashed forward with a spear pointed at the sailors, they retreated to their boat, laughed, and clapped their hands. "There have been reported instances without number of insolence like this one."

On Tuesday morning, July 12, a decorated barge brought Kayama, suite, and interpreters to *Susquehanna*. Perry sent Commanders Buchanan and Adams to receive them. Kayama promised to have the letter received on shore at Kurihama by high officials in a specially erected building, but said that no answer could be delivered save at Nagasaki, through Dutch or Chinese intermediaries. To this Perry replied, "The Commander in Chief will not go to Nagasaki." Neither will he receive communications through foreigners. "He has a letter from the President of the United States to deliver to the Emperor of Japan, or to his secretary of foreign affairs, and he will deliver the original to none other." If it "is not received and duly replied to, he will consider his country insulted, and will not hold himself accountable for the consequences. He expects a reply of some sort in a few days, and he will receive such reply nowhere but in his neighborhood."

This exchange of views, which in Europe would have barely consumed fifteen minutes, according to Japanese custom lasted three hours; and there was a second of similar length in the afternoon to discuss where the letter would be delivered and whether the high official would be authorized by the Emperor to receive it. Kayama assured Perry that he would, and the Commodore admitted that he expected no immediate reply but would return in a few months to receive it and enter into negotiations. Both parties agreed that there should be no discussion at the presentation, only an exchange of compliments, and the Japanese delegation was piped over the side after partaking freely of liquid refreshments. "During the whole of this interview the bearing of the Japanese was dignified and self-possessed," recorded Dr. Williams, to which the official Narrative adds that they "were disposed to be quite social, and shared freely and gaily in conversation." Perry commented on their "elegance of manners," "amiability of disposition," proficiency in Dutch and Chinese languages, and noted that they were "not unacquainted" with world geography. They knew something of the material progress of the United States, "asking, as they examined the ship's engine, whether it was not a similar machine, although smaller, which was used for travelling on the American roads." One of them recognized, and named, a Paixhans gun. Perry held nothing back from the Japanese; the working of guns, engines, and anything that attracted their interest he had carefully explained to them.

Japanese mobilization to meet the "invader" was now almost complete. Dr. Ito observed that the entire western shore of Edo Bay was crowded with troops, every town and village had a garrison, and the roads were congested with gun carriages, carts hauling arms and provisions, laden pack horses and porters carrying heavy burdens slung on poles. The "state of consternation" among Bakufu officials was "beyond description," according to the doctor; but those who dealt with the Americans put on a good show of imperturbability.

On the following afternoon Kayama returned on board, exhibiting a letter bearing the imperial seal to "His Highness Toda, Prince of Izu, first counsellor of the Empire," and "Prince Ido of Iwami" (as the names and titles were translated), authorizing them to receive the President's letter. A prefabricated wooden building had been erected especially for the presentation in Kurihama, a little village on a beach between the two headlands, about a mile and a half south of Uraga. This quiet spot had been selected because each headland to the harbor was fortified and the area behind the beach (now a baseball field) was level and broad enough for the deployment of thousands of troops. Further, to hold the ceremony there preserved the fiction that Uraga was the ne plus ultra for foreigners. Kayama, before going ashore, had a good look at the President's letter in its casket; and as he left the quarterdeck for his barge, he received a three-gun salute, as if he were the governor of Uraga and not merely chief of police. The intended compliment was lost on Kayama; he thought the Americans were saluting the letter, not him!

At this point one must consider a silly story to the effect that the Shogun dressed up a couple of servants or soldiers in princely garb and palmed them off on Perry as noblemen. Actually, Toda and Ido were men of high birth, the former being Izu no kami and the latter

Iwami no kami;* and each was *bugyo,* or governor of Uraga, a place so important for coastal traffic that two governors were required, one to reside there and the other in Edo. Toda had been resident governor for several years; and Ido, appointed co-governor several months before Perry's arrival, had previously been the Shogun's official in charge of maritime defense, thus enjoying a rank commensurate with an American secretary of the navy or a British First Lord of the Admiralty. His appointment to the Uraga post was a promotion carrying with it the honorable title of *kami,* which perhaps started the story of his being an ad hoc nobleman. Both men were eminently proper officials to receive a presidential missive to the Emperor. Toda set up a camp with three hundred retainers near Kurihama beach, and Ido had a hundred armed men in his headquarters.

Perry summoned his commanding officers to a conference, told them to allot so many bluejackets and so many Marines from each ship, and all the officers who could be spared. At break of day on Thursday, July 14, the two American steamers weighed, proceeded the short distance to Kurihama Wan, and anchored off the beach with springs on their cables so as to bring a full broadside to bear in case of a surprise attack. Kayama and Nakajima, dressed in bright-colored silk brocade turned up with yellow velvet and embroidered with gold lace, came out in official barges and were piped on board the flagship. Everyone on board could see that thousands of Japanese troops surrounded the village, so Perry sent his men ashore heavily armed. They numbered about 250 but were outnumbered by the Japanese at least twenty to one.

Fifteen launches and cutters under Commander Buchanan, filled with sailors and Marines, now approached the beach in single line, flanked by the Japanese aides' barges as guides. The rest of the ships' boats followed, containing more sailors and bands from the two

---

* The Japanese title *no kami,* (literally "of lord"), which Perry's interpreters translated "prince" and later writers, "lord of," has no precise English equivalent. Suffixed to a place name, it meant that the man belonged to the feudal clan of that place; he might be only a remote cousin to the daimyo. The same word, added to a high position, meant something like our "honorable." Thus, Toda Izu no kami means that his family name was Toda, and that he belonged to the same clan as the daimyo of Izu; Hayashi Daigaku no kami means that Hayashi was head of the Daigaku, or university at Tokyo. Similarly the English speak of a "Lord Bishop" or "Lord of the Admiralty," although neither bishop nor Admiralty official belongs to the nobility. The title of *kami,* however, could not be assumed by a cousin who had insufficient status; and to use it one had to have the Shogun's permission.

steamers. The Commodore saluted with thirteen guns by *Susquehanna*, stepped into his barge just as Commander Buchanan, first American to set foot on Japanese soil, jumped ashore; and when the Commodore stepped ashore, the Marines presented arms, sailors in the boats tossed oars, and the bands struck up "Hail! Columbia!" Major Zeilin's Marines, heading the American procession, were followed by a band and a contingent of sailors. Two little ship's boys, bearing the President's letter and the Commodore's letter of credence, came next. They were followed by two seamen of "stalwart proportions," bearing the American ensign and the blue pendant.* After them came the Commodore, marching between two orderlies, both tall and stalwart blacks, since he wished citizens of color to take part. More blue-jackets and the second band fell in behind them. The sailors were dressed in white frocks, or blouses, with blue collar and black necker-chief, blue bell-bottom trousers, and the newly issued blue cloth cap, to which Perry caused to be added a hatband of red, white, and blue horizontal stripes with thirteen blue stars on the white stripe. Marines wore blue jackets crossed by white bandoliers, white trousers, and plumed shakos. The American formation and discipline impressed the Japanese. Kayama recorded, "The adroit maneuvers of the guards in the van as well as the rear, conducted just as if they had been marching into enemy territory, truly left us in amazement."

Drawn up to meet them behind the long *baku*, the canvas screens that were standard equipment for concealing troop movements, were some 5000 Japanese soldiers organized in brigades, each of which comprised a section of infantry armed with ancient muskets, one of pikemen, one of archers, and one of cavalry. The gaily colored banners that they displayed bore the arms of the four daimyo represented at Kurihama. The tall thin banners were the scarlet insignia of Ii Kamon no kami, Daimyo of Hikone, destined to become the *Tairo*, the Shogunate's first prime minister. Boats belonging to Matsudaira Higo no kami, who was responsible for maritime defense, flew blue banners with a character representing his ancestral castle of Aizu. Seven hundred men from Edo wore the livery of Matsudaira Tosa no kami, who, as a member of the Shogunate family, was privileged to display the Tokugawa arms. Also displayed were the "nine

---

* Perry brought the ensign home, and it is now in the Naval Academy Museum at Annapolis. Following a happy suggestion of General MacArthur's, it was displayed on the quarterdeck of the U.S.S. *Missouri* during the surrender ceremony on September 2, 1945.

star" arms (one big one in center and eight circling it) of Hosokawa Etchu no kami. The officers, each a two-sworded samurai, wore the traditional lacquered bamboo or leather-braided corselet, but most had discarded the branching steel helmet that made them look like human crustaceans. A very beautiful and impressive spectacle — "even the ranks of Tuscany could scarce forbear to cheer."

It was a tense moment when the Americans began landing; but not a man of the Japanese host raised hand or weapon to oppose them. Apparently ugly scowls on the faces of Japanese officers were merely the conventional ferocious expressions of the samurai. Excellent discipline on each side prevented an explosion that might have touched off a war instead of a treaty. The Americans never realized what a near thing it was. Many years later, Kashiwagi (Shigefusa), a samurai, recorded that he and about nine other two-sworded gentry were concealed under the floor of the reception hall with orders from Toda that if the visitors attempted any violence, they were to rush out and slay the Commodore and his staff.

Intensely dramatic was this confrontation of the Americans with a muster representing the gallantry and chivalry of mediaeval Japan. There had been nothing like it since Columbus met the caciques of Jamaica; never again could it happen, anywhere. To realize the deep significance of this meeting, imagine an England that had been sealed up by Henry VII and his successors for three centuries, confronting a Napoleonic landing force with armored knights, archers, and foot soldiers bearing the costumes and weapons of Bosworth Field and flaunting banners emblazoned with the arms of Richmond, Stanley, Norfolk, and Northumberland.

The Japanese, too, grasped the meaning of this event, as is proved by their many extant paintings of the landing at Kurihama.

At the end of the short march from the beach, the Commodore and about twenty-five selected officers entered a canvas pavilion that served as vestibule. The main building, hastily constructed of pine, was carpeted and hung with violet-colored silk on which were stamped the Tokugawa arms. Toda Izu no kami and Ido Iwami no kami, seated on camp stools, rose and bowed as the Commodore entered. They preserved an air of statuesque formality during the proceedings, speaking never a word and rising again only when the Commodore left. Had there been any doubt of their rank, it would have been dissolved by the deep prostrations before them of the two aides and all other Japanese present. Opposite them, Perry and suite were seated on priests' thrones borrowed from Buddhist temples. An awkward silence was broken by the Japanese interpreter's declaring that their highnesses were ready to receive the documents, which should be placed in a scarlet dispatch case on a table in the center. Perry beckoned to the letter-bearers and his black bodyguards, who marched up to the dais. The blacks took the boxes from the boys, opened them, displayed the documents with their seals, and placed them, with the rosewood casket, on the lid of the imperial dispatch case. This flaunting of the documents had no visible effect on the Japanese; actually they were more interested in the blacks, the first they had ever seen. The two aides prostrated themselves before Ido and received from his hand a scroll. It turned out to be a grudging receipt of the documents, which the Narrative translates as follows:

The letter of the President of the United States of North America, and copy, are hereby received, and will be delivered to the Emperor. It has been many times intimated that business relating to foreign countries cannot be transacted here in Uraga, but at Nagasaki; nevertheless, as it has been observed that the Admiral, in his quality of ambassador of the President, would feel himself insulted by a refusal to receive the letter at this place, the justice of which has been acknowledged, the above mentioned letter is hereby received, in opposition to Japanese law. As this is not a place wherein to negotiate with foreigners, so neither can conferences nor entertainment be held. Therefore, as the letter has been received you can depart.

Delivery of this missive to the Commodore was followed by another long silence. Perry broke it by informing the Japanese through the interpreter that he expected to leave for Okinawa and Canton within two or three days, and would be pleased to convey any dispatches or messages from the imperial government. No reply. He remarked that he would return in the spring. "With all four vessels?" asked the interpreter. "Probably more," said the Commodore. The interpreter inquired the cause of the Tai-ping rebellion in China. Perry crisply replied, "Discontent of the people with the government." This so smacked of *lèse-majesté* that the interpreter dared not translate it. In Japan, people were not supposed to be discontented with their government.

Kayama and Nakajima fastened the dispatch case, informed Perry that the conference was over, and led the way out of the building.

The procession formed in reverse order and all hands returned to their ships, well satisfied with the day's proceedings, which, as Perry recorded, were conducted in perfect courtesy and decorum, despite the abrupt order to depart and the coldly correct attitude of Ido and Toda.

With justifiable pride, Perry wrote to his wife after returning to Macao: "This achievement of mine I consider an important event in my life. The Pageant was magnificent and I am the only Christian that has ever before landed peacefully on this part of Japan or in any part without submitting to the most humiliating degradation." It was unprecedented, unpredictable, and, in view of the consequences, one of the most important events of modern history. "My next visit may prove still more eventful," continued Perry. It did indeed; but this first one, on July 14, 1853, set a pattern for the next.

Immediately after the ceremony, Perry moved all four ships up Edo Bay in line abreast, running lines of soundings across the bay, and anchoring out of sight of Uraga in a roadstead that the Commodore named "American Anchorage," between Webster Island (Natsu Shima) and Point Fillmore (Koshiba Zaki). The two aides, with suite, bustled on board to inquire why the squadron anchored there. Because it was safer than the Uraga roadstead, said Perry. They forbade him to proceed farther up the bay. Perry ignored the order but entertained the Japanese in the wardroom. "Quite a convivial scene ensued," says the official Narrative, "in the course of which abundant supplies of ham, ship's biscuit, and other stores, washed down by plentiful draughts of whiskey, quickly disappeared. The cheer seemed to be much relished." In accordance with Japanese custom, "substantial mementos of the pleasant feast [were] carried off in their capacious sleeves."

Although Perry decided to make his initial visit to Japan short, he felt obliged to explain his reasons to the Secretary of the Navy, in order to forestall criticism. Nothing was to be gained, and much lost, by hanging around Edo Bay for a month, the extreme limit of his food supply. The Shogun would certainly take longer than that to make up his mind; important presents for the Emperor, such as the train of cars and the telegraph, had not arrived; sailors' morale would suffer if they were given no shore liberty; and "incidents" might occur if they were turned loose. But he wished to show the Japanese that he could not be ordered out, and also to find out whether there was enough water for big ships further up the bay. So, transferring his pendant to *Mississippi* on July 15, he steamed ten miles past American Anchorage to a point off Kawasaki, the southern suburb of Edo; then, at Kayama's earnest plea, turned back. "I might have gone still higher," wrote Perry, "but was apprehensive of causing too much alarm, and thus throwing some obstacle in the way." On Saturday, the 16th, he moved the squadron to a landlocked anchorage in Susquehanna Bay (Otsu Wan). Kayama came on board for a final call, bearing as presents, besides eggs and poultry, forty fans, five pipes, and fifty lacquered soup bowls. Perry, observing that they were all cheap stuff, forwarded them from Hong Kong to President Pierce, trusting that he would receive better presents next year when he had better things to give. In return, the commodore contributed rolls of calico, a bag of sugar, and a case of wine described by the Japanese as "*sanhauen*" (champagne). He asked his officers to contribute any odd items that they could spare — such as a picture of a steamboat, an almanac from China, and a three-volume *History of the United States,* probably Richard Hildreth's. Kayama declared he was forbidden to accept anything, but finally consented, concealing books, bolts, and bottles in his sleeves. After a final libation on board, Kayama shook hands all around and departed with tears in his eyes. He was last observed in his barge, knocking off the neck of a champagne bottle and imbibing its contents.

Kayama showed good judgment in consuming the wine quickly because his boss Ido made a bonfire of the American presents and demoted him as punishment for being too friendly with the Americans. That was after Perry had left, and everyone from the Bakufu down had breathed a sigh of relief.

Dr. Ito, the court physician, noted in his diary that Perry's visit was "good medicine for the entire Japanese nation. The Bakufu for the first time realized how formidable a foreign nation might be." A junior councilor remarked to the doctor: "These Americans are certainly different from the British and others. They seem to be sincere and honest. I hear that their military order is strict and they know the rules of politeness. From now on the Japanese had better stand on friendly relations with them." Ito marveled that any councilor could say as much; he regarded this as a revolution in thought.

*

Plymouth and *Saratoga* having joined *Mississippi* and *Susque-hanna*, the squadron weighed and sortied from Edo Bay on Sunday morning, July 17, steamers towing sailing vessels. Kannon Saki headland, the shores around Uraga, and hundreds of boats were thronged with sightseers to watch the Americans leave. Outside the bay, *Plymouth* and *Saratoga* were cast off and made sail, with orders for Okinawa and Shanghai, respectively. The two steamers made for Naha.

Upon returning to China, Perry wrote to his friend James Watson Webb, editor of the New York *Courier:* "It is up hill work to manage these very intractable people, and I have found it necessary to practice a very novel system of diplomacy with them, which I find works very well so far. I have been tolerably successful and hope to do something more when I again call upon His Imperial Majesty."

It would be difficult to criticize the Commodore's conduct during the eight days of this, his first visit to Japan. One false step, and there would have been no treaty, no opening, but a big fight in which the Americans, despite their superior fire power, might have been overwhelmed by sheer numbers. He had maintained the dignity of his government by insisting on a proper reception of an official document. He had surveyed Edo Bay sufficiently for any future contingency. He had been uniformly friendly and conciliatory, and called forth similar sentiments on the part of his hosts. Through careful organization and strict discipline, no untoward incident had occurred. And not a gun had been fired, except for salutes and morning and evening colors.

IV

American Life

1

The Harvard Man of 1700

From HARVARD COLLEGE IN THE SEVENTEENTH CENTURY, Volume II (Cambridge: Harvard University Press, 1936), *pages 561–65.*

This is the conclusion to my last big volume in the TERCENTENNIAL HISTORY OF HARVARD COLLEGE AND UNIVERSITY, *although a later one,* THREE CENTURIES OF HARVARD (1936), *was published in time for the Harvard Tercentenary, in 1936; and, forty years later, is being "updated" by William Bentinck-Smith to cover the Conant and Pusey administrations.*

ON THE BASIS of statistics, and the biographies in Sibley's *Harvard Graduates,* it will not be difficult to imagine the "typical Harvard man" of the 291 alive in 1700. He is a member of the Class of 1689 or 1690, about thirty years old, pastor of the Church of Christ in a farming community between twenty and thirty miles from Boston. He had taught school, returned to college for his M.A., become a candidate for this pulpit, and, after a satisfactory tryout, had been duly "settled" and ordained. Shortly after, he married the eighteen-year-old daughter of a well-to-do neighbor. By 1700, she has borne him three children, and expects to produce another every eighteen months or two years. On weekdays, our parson dresses in homespun made up by his wife; on Lord's Days and at funerals, he sports a black broadcloth suit, made for his ordination by a Boston tailor and expected to last a lifetime. He still wears the full-bottomed William of Orange wig that cost him a pretty penny at Commencement. His annual salary is £80, paid (seldom on time) half in Massachusetts currency and half in country pay, together with sufficient wood to heat two or three rooms of the parsonage, which was built for him by the parish as part of his "settlement." An apple orchard supplies his table with cider every other year; and the parish glebe is sufficient to grow most of his food and to allow him to pasture a few head of cattle. This

HARVARD ALUMNI LIVING IN 1700

Occupation				Residence		
Classes	1642–89	1690–1700	Total		1642–89	1690–1700	Total
Clergymen	93	57	150	Massachusetts	95	87	182
Physicians	10	8	18	Connecticut*	28	29	57
Public Servants	21	4	25	Long Island, N.Y.	4	5	9
Schoolmasters	6	16	22	New York City	0	1	1
Merchants	7	12	19	Rhode Island†	3	3	6
Planters, etc.	5	6	11	Maine and N.H.	3	6	9
College Tutors	0	3	3	New Jersey	2	3	5
Soldiers and				Pennsylvania	0	1	1
Mariners	3	3	6	South Carolina	0	3	3
Lawyers	1	2	3	West Indies	0	4	4
Students	0	28	28	England	10	3	13
Unknown	0	6	6	Netherlands	1	0	1
Total	146	145	291	Total	146	145	291

* Including Enfield and Woodstock, then in Massachusetts.
† Including Bristol, then in Massachusetts.

estate he farms himself, with the aid of a black slave (presented by his father-in-law) and volunteer help at harvest, which he reciprocates when the neighbors need a hand. By dint of hard work and intelligence, he has made the glebe one of the best farms in town, keeps the fences "hog tight, horse high, and ox strong," and experiments with strange plants, such as potatoes. He keeps one horse, with a saddle for himself and pillion for his wife; but no carriage. The housework is done by the wife and an unmarried sister who lives with them. They are as well off as any in the parish; the financial pinch will come after 1715, when prices rise, money goes down, and there are more children to feed.

Twice every Lord's Day the parson preaches; and although he has given up the public Thursday lecture for want of interest, he presides weekly at private religious societies that meet in different parts of town; and spends considerable time calling on the people and catechizing the children. He knows by name every man, woman, and child, and most of the dogs, in his parish of several hundred souls; and is on friendly terms with all except certain frontier individualists, who wish they had an evangelical exhorter, and some of the stricter Puritans, who disapprove his baptismal tolerance of five-month-old babies. The village schoolmaster is his friend, and every few years sends him an ambitious lad to be fitted for Harvard. Everyone is in awe of his learning, and all except the village elders respect his opinion on a variety of subjects. During the late French and Indian War the parson did watch and ward with the other able-bodied young men. As there is no physician within twenty miles, he personally attends to most of his parishioners' ailments, and keeps on hand a supply of the more common drugs in order to prescribe as directed in Culpeper's *English Physician*. And until the town is large enough to have a justice of the peace, he will draft the legal papers, write wills, and do his best to prevent the parishioners from going to law.

The parson's library, about 200 volumes, largely in the three learned tongues, consists mostly of college textbooks, theology, and devotional works, acquired before he took his second degree. The classics, especially Horace and Ovid, he has worn almost threadbare with repeated readings, for he can save little from his salary to purchase new books; but occasionally books may be borrowed from brother ministers. As yet there is no newspaper in New England for him to read; he is dependent on travelers and chance gossip for news of the great world. A former pupil of John Leverett's, he is friendly toward the Church of England, and inclined to overlook or explain away some of the rigors of Calvinist theology. For that reason he has dropped preaching on fine points of theology, and prefers practical discourses on the divine attributes and human conduct. Strange plants, minerals, two-headed calves, meteors, and the like attract his curiosity, and provide anecdotes to exchange with other provincial virtuosi at Commencement. This annual journey on horseback to Cambridge is his unique vacation and only relaxation, except reading, smoking, and an occasional glass of wine.

To what can such a man look forward? Spiritual serenity and the love of his neighbors; not fame, nor even security. Custom forbids a richer parish to call him from rural duties, and there are no high offices in the Congregational Church. With good luck and a scholarship, one or two of his sons will enter Harvard and become ministers themselves; the others may fulfill their parents' hopes in any respectable occupation.

The loyalties of our typical Harvard man in 1700 are, first, to God, who is as real to him as his own father, but more orderly, scientific, and merciful than his father's God; second, to King William, the savior of England and the Protestant religion; and, third, to New England, his native land and nation. Such notice from her as an invitation to deliver the annual election sermon in Boston would satisfy his highest personal ambition. The rights of the Bay Province and the privileges of the Congregational churches he would maintain with equal jealousy; and while ready to admit that all respectable Protestant sects, such as the Baptists and Quakers, should be tolerated, he hopes to keep such persons out of his parish. The state of morality and the French menace give him considerable concern; privately and publicly he prays that New England, chastened for her sins by these terrible wars, may redeem God's convenant with her founders, and become a pattern for the rest of the world. In the century that is dawning, may the reformed churches reunite on a modified New England platform, which, through its obvious superiority and marks of divine favor, will even convert the French king, and unite all Christendom in bonds of brotherhood!

2

Harry Otis, Friend and Host

From HARRISON GRAY OTIS, 1765–1848: THE URBANE FEDERALIST
(Boston: Houghton Mifflin, 1969), *Chapter X.*

*Boston society around 1800 was quite as class-ridden as that of Phila-
delphia or London. The better people are all aristocrats," wrote John
Singleton Copley, Jr., from Boston in 1796. "My father is too rank a
Jacobin to live among them." Well-to-do professional men like Harrison Gray Otis, Federalist politicians like Josiah Quincy, retired capitalists like Christopher Gore, and wealthy shopkeepers like Samuel
Eliot and David Sears formed as conspicuous a portion of the social
upper crust as merchant-shipowners; and few names were included
that had risen to prominence since the Revolution. Social life was
both formal and informal, with private balls and cotillion parties, and
immense dinners. Several merchants maintained country seats in the
neighborhood, like their colonial forebears; but most of them found
Boston a good enough summer resort. Few traces of Puritanism were
left among the gentry. It was a period of religious tolerance, before
Protestant and Catholic had renewed their quarrels, or orthodox and
Unitarian begun theirs. But political feeling was exceedingly bitter,
and any deviation from Federalist orthodoxy was punished by social
ostracism. East India voyages seemed to mellow manners and Madeira wine, but to sharpen political prejudices.*

*The Federalist Harrison Gray Otis was the subject of my first book,
the two-volume* LIFE AND LETTERS OF HARRISON GRAY OTIS,
*which Houghton Mifflin published in 1913. Over fifty years later, so
many were the requests for a new edition by offset, that we decided
to make a new one-volume edition ourselves. In this new edition I
have greatly reduced the space devoted to political history; for instance, one chapter only instead of seven on the Hartford Convention. And I expanded chapters devoted to personality and social life.
This is one of them.*

Harry and Sally

HARRY OTIS the husband, father, friend, and host is even more interesting than the Honorable Harrison Gray Otis, politician and
statesman. Among citizens of all classes in Federalist Boston no one
was more beloved and respected than he; even in Whig Boston,
Daniel Webster never supplanted him in popularity. He owed this
widespread admiration more to his well-rounded, vigorous personality than to any outstanding qualities as a public figure. Josiah
Quincy, son of Otis's contemporary of the same name, wrote: "Men of
the stamp of William Sullivan and his friend Otis were more conspicuous for what they were, than for what they did. They were predomi-
nant men, and gave the community its quality, shaping, as if by
divine right, its social and political issues." Yet Quincy himself de-
spaired of transmitting Otis's personality by pen and ink. "I wish it
were in my power," he wrote in his diary, "to preserve for posterity
some traces of the wit, brilliancy, eloquence, and urbanity of Harrison Gray Otis; for when he is gone there is no man who can make
good his place in Society."

The relationship between Harry and Sally is the brightest, loveliest
aspect of their lives. Her chief concerns were the happiness of her
husband and the care and education of their children; she followed,
though unconsciously, the pattern of the *haute bourgeoisie* of France.
To their old age, in correspondence and in conversation, this couple
employed the charming, loving formulas of the eighteenth century.
"Dear angel," he wrote to her from Washington shortly before the
turn of the century, "but a few weeks and I come to you; never
(unless forced by necessity), never again to quit your side for distant
& tedious employments. It is my firm resolution not to serve another
Congress . . . If health & inclination should render it eligible for you
to accompany me, & suitable accommodations can be procured . . . I
may take you to Washington for one season; but I certainly will never
go there without you."

He kept his promise; and when elected to the United States Senate
seventeen years later, he took Sally with him. She not only directed
the Otis household, whether in Boston, Philadelphia, or Washington,
not only bore him eleven children; she also understood and encouraged her husband, applied her charm to his friends, read with
him the books that he liked, cared for him in his frequent attacks of

gout or arthritis. She had the quality that the French call *"tendresse,"* a humorous appreciation of people and sympathy with their shortcomings. Although like Harry she abhorred French politics, she loved French culture, manners, and fashion; and like the French she accommodated her dress to advancing age, always retaining a neatness and simplicity that gave her both dignity and elegance.*

Harry appeared at his best in family life. In the early nineteenth century it was usual for parents to impress on their children that an awful gulf existed between them and their elders. "Honored Papa" and "Honored Mamma" were the proper titles by which to address a parent, and the formalities of a court were exacted in the daily life of the household. With the Otis family it was otherwise. Harrison Gray Otis, like Squire Bracebridge, made each child feel that home was the best place on earth. The children in turn adored him; and not one gave his or her parents any unusual trouble or suffered from any incurable malady of mind or body. Except for the drowning of the first Allyne, there were no domestic tragedies at 45 Beacon Street until 1833, and the two youngest boys were born there. These two, the second Allyne and George, were spoiled by their parents, but that cannot be said of their elders.

When absent from home, Harry was apt to send his children presents mingled with parental admonition. Sally and Sophia, aged fourteen and ten, received each a pair of earrings from Philadelphia. In his covering letter, Papa remarked that he would not say that the young ladies of New York and Philadelphia were prettier than those of Boston, but they were very careful *never* to appear with dirty teeth or fingernails!

The life the Otises led differed completely from that of New England country towns so well described in Harriet Beecher Stowe's *Oldtown Folks.* Nor did they fit the "proper Bostonian" cliché. Harry and Sally comprehended the most attractive characteristics of the society into which they were born, holdovers from the courts of the colonial governors; and in that society few puritanic traits survived. Although they abandoned the harsh faith of their fathers, they

---

* When Mrs. Austin Wadsworth, whose family purchased 45 Beacon Street after Otis's death, took me over the house around 1910, there were still in the attic the long, coffin-shaped trunks in which Sally Otis's dresses came from Worth or some other couturier in Paris. My grandmother told me that Mrs. Wharton was quite right in stating in one of her novels that the Boston and New York ladies who imported their clothes from Paris had to wait a year or two before wearing them, as the fashion would seem *outré* if they wore them at once.

never became irreligious or agnostic; many joined the Episcopal Church, but most, under the guidance of liberal Congregational clergymen, became Unitarians. The Otises belonged to the Brattle Street Church, which John Adams described as the "politest" in Boston, under four successive liberal ministers: J. S. Buckminster, Edward Everett, John G. Palfrey, and Samuel K. Lothrop. In taste and manners, the Boston Federalist aristocracy were closer to Southern gentlemen than to their own country neighbors. When William Wirt, the distinguished lawyer and writer of Richmond, visited Boston, he was astonished to find that his preconceived notions of Yankee society must be cast aside. "This is the most hospitable place in the world," he wrote to Judge Cabell. "Otis has been twice with me, pressing me to dine with him . . . I think the people of Boston amongst the most agreeable in the United States . . . I say they are as warm-hearted, as kind, as frank, as truly hospitable as the Virginians themselves. In truth, they are Virginian in all the essentials of character . . . Would to Heaven the people of Virginia and Massachusetts knew each other better!"

Would indeed that they had! If the gentlemen of Virginia had not "gone a-whoring" after strange gods, they and the gentry of New England and New York might have prevented three wars and solved the slavery problem without fratricide.

At the prime of life Harry Otis was slightly above the average height, well proportioned, with dark brown hair, sparkling, dark blue eyes, a rather broad face, a Roman nose, and a florid complexion. His personal appearance, combined with his gracious charm of manner, gave him distinction without stiffness or pomposity. Contemporaries always described his appearance as "elegant" — by which they meant that he dressed with care and fastidiousness at a period when these qualities were not common among American gentlemen. Elder statesmen of New England, refusing any concession to "Jacobin" fashions, continued to wear cocked hats and knee breeches well into the nineteenth century; but Harry always dressed in the latest fashion. Other Federalists were careless and slovenly; Chief Justice Parsons, for instance, returned from a week's circuit wearing, one on top of the other, the seven shirts with which his wife had provided him at the start. Of Otis it is related that he once met on the street a married couple of his acquaintance as the lady was arranging the shirt ruffles of her untidy spouse. "There — look at Mr. Otis's bosom!" said she, pointing to his immaculate linen. "Madam," said Otis with one of his best bows, "if your husband could look within my bosom, he would die of jealousy."

The secret of Otis's popularity lay in his tact, affability, consideration for others, and a natural courtesy that came from the heart. To enumerate his circle of loyal friends would take pages. The fact that he formed as warm friendships among men of the southern and middle states as among his fellow Bostonians was significant. It was impossible for him ever to embrace the extreme brand of New England Federalism affected by the Essex Junto and the "River Gods" of Connecticut. No matter how great the provocation, he could never bring himself to the belief that disunion might be preferable to union.

Enemies Otis had, as any man with a particle of backbone who took part in politics must have had, but he looked on mankind with none of the sour malignity that appears in the writings of puritanical colleagues like Tim Pickering. Considering the political bitterness of that era, his correspondence is remarkably free from illiberal reflections on men and motives. Joseph Story, however, he held suspect for many years on account of his early attachment to Jefferson. After the death of Chief Justice Marshall, someone in conversation said he hoped that President Jackson would say unto this learned judge, as Pharaoh did unto Joseph, "Thou shalt be ruler over my house." "Joseph, indeed! Why, yes, an excellent comparison," snorted Otis. "Pray, was anything said about his coat of many colors?"

The Adams Relationship

It was impossible for Otis, with his sunny nature, to carry on one of those lifelong political feuds that were meat and drink to some of his contemporaries. His relationship with John Quincy Adams came the nearest. No two gentlemen could have been more temperamentally unlike: Otis, warm, tactful, and pleasure-loving; Adams, cold, tactless, conscientious, and, above all, an Adams. "What a queer family!" Otis wrote of them in his old age, apropos of Charles Francis Adams's entry into politics. "I think them *all* (beginning with the grandsire) varieties in a peculiar species of our race exhibiting a combination of talent, & good moral character, with passions and prejudices calculated to defeat their own objects & embarrass their friends, that would puzzle La Bruyère to describe & which has no Prototype in Shakespeare or Molière."

John Quincy Adams seems to have been under the delusion that Otis looked upon him as a rival, and a block to his political advancement — "an adder in his path," as he expressed it in Biblical language. But there is no trace in Otis's writings of any such feeling. The first break between them occurred when Adams voted for Jefferson's embargo and joined the Republican party. Their fathers were old and intimate friends, but during the stormy years that followed, the clans of Otis and Adams ceased personal intercourse. The following letter from Abigail Adams to her son, when he was minister to Great Britain, describes the characteristic manner in which Otis brought about a reconciliation:

Quincy, Aug. 27, 1816

My dear Son . . .

In this still calm, and political pause, I must entertain you with domestic occurrences, one of which is a Family visit, which we received a fortnight since from Mr W Foster, your old neighbor,* (who lost his Lady about two months since,) accompanied by Mrs A Otis† and daughter, Mr H G Otis Lady and daughter and son; who all came in a Body to take tea with us. This visit has been long in contemplation: Mrs A Otis was commissioned to inquire, if your Father would like to receive the visit? to which a candid reply was given that he should be pleased to receive it. Whether the Hartford millstone hung so heavy that it could not be thrown off, or for what other reason I cannot say, the visit was never accomplished untill a fortnight since, when we past a very pleasant and social afternoon together. Upon taking leave Mr Otis in his very civil and polite manner, asked it as a favour that I would dine with him the next week? I replied, that I had long declined all invitations to dinner, as well as all public company, upon which he said it should be only a Family party. I then referred him to your Father who promptly accepted his invitation. Accordingly when the day came, we went, and were most kindly and cordially received by all the assembled families. Mr Mason [and] Mr Tudor were considered former appendages to us, and were a part of the company. All appeared pleased and mutually gratified.

I know not when I have past a pleasanter day, and I could not but regret the hour of separation. All this past off very well. I never expected to hear more of it. But you cannot imagine what a sensation it has created in the Capital. A Gentleman from Town yesterday informed me, that it was a sub-

---

* H.G.O.'s father-in-law.
† Mrs. Samuel Allyne Otis, H.G.O.'s stepmother.

ject of speculation in the public offices. Whether the Stocks have risen or fallen in consequences, I do not pretend to say, but the wise ones cannot comprehend the phenomenon. Some whisper it was to obtain a recommendation for a foreign Mission, — now I do not believe in any such motive I ascribe it to the benevolent desire of extinguishing all party spirit, and to a desire of renewing former friendship, and Family intimacy. As such I received it, and in the same spirit returned it.

John Adams had already written to his son on the same event: "As you live: your Father and Mother & Louisa dined last Tuesday in Boston with Judge Otis* in the neatest Company imaginable; none but Otis's, Lymans, Thorndykes, Minots, Boardmans and Fosters, except Tudor and Mason. I never before knew Mrs. Otis. She has good Understanding. I have seldom if ever passed a more sociable day. Exert all your Witts to draw Inferences from this Phenomenon. Do you ascribe it to the Eclipse of 1806, to the Comet or to the spots in the sun?"

No better description of Otis's social qualities exists than the letter that John Quincy Adams wrote to his father after receiving his account of the reconciliation:

Since beginning this Letter I have received yours of 26 August and 5 September, and am highly gratified by your and my Mother's Account of your social party at Judge Otis's. Among the lights and shades of that worthy Senator's character, there is none which shows him in higher colours than his hospitality. In the course of nearly thirty years that I have known him, and throughout the range of experience that I have had in that time, it has not fallen to my lot to meet a man more skilled in the useful art of entertaining his friends than Otis; and among the many admirable talents that he possesses, there is none that I should have been more frequently and more strongly prompted to Envy; if the natural turn of my disposition had been envious. Of those qualities Otis has many — His Person while in Youth, his graceful Deportment, his sportive wit, his quick intelligence, his eloquent fluency, always made a strong impression upon my Mind; while his warm domestic Affections, his active Friendship, and his Generosity, always commanded my esteem . . . Mrs. Otis is and always has been a charming woman; and I am very glad you have seen them both in the place where of all others they appear to the greatest advantage — their own house.

His son Charles Francis, some twelve years later, could not figure them out. After calling at the Otis house, he wrote in his diary: "Saw

---

* Otis at that time was judge of the Boston court of common pleas.

all the family. There is something about them which I like very much, and yet what it is, is hardly possible to tell. Mrs. Otis scolded [me] well for my not having been before." What an insufferable young prig! He could not see what his father had perceived, that one secret of the Otises' charm was making every visitor feel that it was a pleasure and a privilege to know him, and that he should come more often.

Houses, Hospitality, and Harvard

The seat of this warm hospitality was Number 45 Beacon Street, the third house built by Otis and designed for him by Charles Bulfinch, the architectural genius of Federalist Boston. Otis sold his Cambridge Street house in 1801 and built a second (now 85 Mt. Vernon Street), which in turn he sold to his friend Benjamin Pickman in 1805, and the same year he built for his father a house on the downhill corner of Spruce and Beacon streets. These, and the houses built by Jonathan Mason and others on the south slope of Beacon Hill, helped the Mount Vernon Proprietors to make that part of Boston fashionable. The Otises moved to Number 45 in 1806. It remained Sally's home until her death thirty years later, and Harry's for the rest of his life.

This mansion lay open to Boston Common; from its front windows one could see the Blue Hills across the Back Bay, a broad sheet of water that came within 200 yards of the door. Courtyards and a garden surrounded it on the other three sides. Built to accommodate a large family, it housed seven Otis children when they moved in: Eliza, aged 15; Harry Jr., 14; Sally, 13; Allyne, 10; Sophia, 8; James, 6; William, 4; and two more were born there. There were no fewer than eleven bedchambers, almost every one with an open fireplace.

From the entrance on Beacon Street one entered directly a vestibule, cannily screened from the stair hall to cut off winter blasts. On the left was Otis's library, where he loved to sit, as he could see through the windows everyone who passed along Beacon Street. On the right was an "office" — meaning the room where home accounts and such business were done; and in the rear, a storage room, which eventually became Otis's upstairs "wine room," to supplement the wine cellar in the basement. An ell, extending to the stables, contained the main kitchen, a "wash room" (laundry), and a woodshed.

By a typical Bulfinch spiral stairway one ascended to the *piano nobile*, the main or second floor. Here, in front, were two handsome square rooms, the "dining parlour" and the "saloon." The latter opened into an "oval room," the second drawing room, whose bow extended into the garden. Behind the dining parlor was a china closet; and, behind that, across a landing on the back stairs, the "upstairs kitchen." Three bedrooms were eventually built behind that, making a second floor over the ell.

Passing a beautiful Palladian window on the stairs, one reached the third floor. The sunny Beacon Street side was taken up by two large square chambers, Harry's and Sally's, separated by a charming dressing room finished with carved woodwork. In the rear were two big chambers and a dressing room for the older girls. The fourth floor had seven chambers, three of them in front, for the younger children and five or six maidservants.

These were either New England country girls or girls from the Maritime Provinces. The Otises lived without ostentation; they did not go in for liveried butlers or footmen or French chefs, but always kept a coachman and groom and a stout houseman or two to lug in the fuel, polish boots, and keep the steel knives bright. The menservants lived over the stable and coachhouse at the foot of the cobble-stoned yard. There was no central heating; wood or cannel coal had to be manhandled to keep a dozen fires burning, and the house was not piped for gas in Otis's time; all the lighting came from candles and Argand sperm-oil portable lamps imported from France. Since plumbing did not exist, water had to be carried upstairs, for drinking, bathing, washing, and cooking, from a capacious cistern in the garden. My grandmother, who passed twelve of the first sixteen years of her life at 45 Beacon Street, told me that she and her brother and sister were marched to the Tremont House weekly for hot tub baths — but there was no Tremont House when her father and aunts and uncles were growing up. On the northern end of the ell, reached from the main floor, was a privy for the family; and, below, opening off the shed and the stable, another for the servants. These were pumped out every week or so into a horse-drawn tank truck, to be discharged in Brighton to manure truck gardens. The rumbling of these trucks on the cobblestoned streets accounts for their nickname, the "Brighton Artillery."

Whilst there was a certain amplitude in the Otises' way of living, it was neither extravagant nor aristocratic; for a contemporary parallel, a *hôtel* of the *haute bourgeoisie* in Lyon, Toulouse, or Saint-Malo would be much nearer than anything in England.

The Otises never moved out of Number 45 Beacon Street, but they did acquire a country house. In the winter of 1808–1809 Harry purchased a twelve-acre farm in Watertown, and by extensive additions and improvements to the grounds turned it into a country estate of some thirty-eight acres, named Oakley. On the hilltop, whence one had a beautiful view of the Charles River valley, Bulfinch built for him a stately country house complete with spiral staircase and oval dining room. Otis wrote to John Rutledge at Charleston on May 13, 1809, asking him to lay out "five or ten dollars" on "a little assortment of seeds of any kind of shrubbery or plants which are not indigenous to this cold climate." To which Rutledge replied genially on June 6:

Having settled the affairs of the State, & put Democracy "in a Hole," as that queer gentleman John Adams quaintly said, it seems you have bought a Villa, & are going to indulge in a little rural felicity. This I presume is the *Ton* at Boston, & Mrs. Otis & the President* are at the head of the fashionables, getting this Country seat was, I presume, quite "en regle." But it really seemed to me that having such a House as you have, with the whole Common of Boston as an Apendage, & open & improved grounds all around, might have satisfied any man of ordinary ambition. I will with very great pleasure send you an assortment of Seeds of Shrubs & Plants which may subsist in your frozen region — but this, my good friend, is not the season. I have spoken to a Mr. Champneys who is the President of our Agricultural Society, & has in this neighbourhood a prodigiously fine garden, & he promises to make an assortment of plants for you in the season, which will not [be] before the month of December. He says that altho' you are an Oracle in Politics & in law, that you are in the very horn book of Botany & Gardening in supposing that Plants can be removed at this Season. As Mr. Robert [Rutledge] has determined to make a visit to Boston, I shall have the pleasure of seeing you *deo volente* about the beginning of August . . . I pray of you to present me affectionately to Mrs. Otis, Miss Eliza, Sarah & the young folks. I request you would give my affections to Mason & say to him that I shall be in Boston in August — in the meantime God bless you & yours —

Rutledge did send him some copper beech trees, which were still flourishing in 1968, and some cuttings for Black Hamburg grapes, which reached prodigious size in a greenhouse, long since torn down.

---

* Otis was then president of the state senate.

Yet Oakley was not altogether a success. Both Otises were town bred; Harry knew nothing of horticulture, and Sally (so her grand-daughter told me) used to say, "Better an attic in the city than a pal-ace in the country!" And the children, too, preferred Boston to Watertown. Unable to lease part of the land to farmers, and warned by John Lowell that any attempt to go shares with a gardener would be disastrous, Otis sold the place in 1825 and thereafter spent part of each summer at Nahant, Newport, or Sharon Springs. The estate eventually became the Oakley Country Club, but the Bulfinch-designed mansion burned down in 1961.

The Otises never left Boston for an entire summer because they loved to entertain visitors from other cities. John Rutledge and other Carolinian friends made a practice of spending the summer at New-port and passing a week or two at 45 Beacon Street coming and going, especially at the time of Harvard Commencement — the last Wednesday of August. Harvard families made a point of being in town at that time, not only to enjoy the festival rites at Cambridge, but also to entertain friends from Philadelphia and the South who had sons in college. There was seldom a year after 1805 when Harvard contained no member of the Otis clan, and Harry himself served on one or both of the governing boards from 1810 to 1825. Although not a great benefactor, he subscribed $100 toward the Massachusetts Chair of Natural History, established in 1807, and twenty years later gave $500 toward the founding of the Harvard Divinity School.

Harvard students during the early nineteenth century used to express their disapproval of the college government by the modern methods of strike, boycott, and sabotage. In 1805 occurred the "Bread and Butter Rebellion." As a protest against the quality of food provided, the student body refused for ten successive days to attend commons. The authorities suspended regular exercises and threat-ened to lock out the entire student body. The lads were too spirited to submit. A committee of the Board of Overseers presided over by Levi Lincoln, President Jefferson's former attorney general, reported in favor of a general pardon and promise of improved commons. This led to a prolonged debate in the board (which then included the en-tire state senate) along strict party lines. A majority upheld the Federalist Harvard Corporation and defeated Lincoln's "jacobinical" report by 29 votes to 26. Two distinguished alumni, Samuel Dexter and Harrison Gray Otis, were then called upon to arbitrate. This they did to such good purpose that both sides accepted Lincoln's original proposal and peace was restored to the banks of the Charles.

Many of the Harvard students from outside New England, who came to make up 20 percent of the total under the benign presidency of Dr. Kirkland, were introduced by their parents to Otis. He thus became an unofficial mentor to several young Southern gentlemen in the college. One of these, John Lee, son of Governor Thomas Sim Lee of Maryland, was the first Roman Catholic to enter Harvard. Some of these young Southerners were rather a trial, owing to their casual attitude; they would disappear from college without leave, spend weeks or months away, and cheerfully return when they felt like it, expecting to be received back into their class — and usually were. Thus, John Rutledge's son Robert, in and out of college since 1801, was finally dropped in 1809, "not for any vice or meanness, but for negligence," wrote Otis, who advised the father to put him into business; and John's cousin, Hugh Rutledge, not only dropped out, but went home leaving his last term bill and about $500 in debts for classmate Charles Cotesworth Pinckney II to collect, and Otis to pay. Robert Smith, a younger son of the Bishop of South Carolina and uncle to the Rutledge boys, dropped in and out for years, but made Phi Beta Kappa as well as the Porcellian Club, and graduated in 1805. John Rutledge, Jr., however, was a model student "and conducts himself like a gentleman," said Otis. With Harrison Gray Otis, Jr., he prepared for college at a private school kept by the Reverend John Sylvester John Gardiner, rector of Trinity Church, Boston; and the two boys became "chums" — the old word for roommates — in college. Otis feared they would not get along, "John being of a mild and even temper, and Harry ardent and choleric to a degree that gives me concern, though a fellow of fine heart and as yet addicted to no species of dissipation or excess." But they did become good friends. The elder Rutledge wrote to Otis from Charleston early in 1808 on behalf of John Jr., to "pay him monthly Fifty Dollars, or, if it would be more agreeable to him, one hundred & fifty once in three months. With a due regard to economy (which I hope he will observe) Six hundred Dollars a year will be a sufficient allowance during his residence at Cambridge." That was a generous allowance for those days, assuming that father also paid for board, lodging, and tuition.

On March 26, 1809, Rutledge wrote about both his sons, with a typical parental caution that they typically disregarded:

I enclose a Bill of Exchange for the use of my Boys. Pray my dear friend, discourage as much as possible their visiting Boston, frequenting Taverns, driving carriages &c &c. It is using a great freedom I know to draw upon your Charities in this way — I also know it is not "Othelo's occupation" to be lecturing & ordering Boys. I know how much, & how well, "he serves the state"; but my friend unless you have the goodness & humility to condescend to advise these fellows, &, by your parental attentions, give some correction to their aberations, I fear that the objects of their residence at Cambridge will not be realized. John writes to me of the brilliance of Mrs. Apthorpes Ball, Mrs. Otis's Parties, &c. This is all wrong, & these Boys must not be permitted to have any engagements but with their Books.

Politics and Social Life

Social life in Boston in the first decade of the nineteenth century became more elaborate as a natural result of material prosperity. "Private balls are numerous, and little cotillion parties occur every week," wrote one of the Quincy girls in 1807; and in addition to private parties there were club cotillions at Concert Hall, which continued through the War of 1812. At the Samuel Welles ball in November 1807, music was furnished by a "Turkish band," and the supper, including peaches and melons, served 300 people. "All went off with éclat," noted Miss Quincy, "except the toasts, which were rather flat. The gentlemen were not prepared to be either witty or sentimental, and impromptus suit the genius of the French better than that of the English or their American descendants. Mr. Otis alone was happy on this occasion; his wit is ever ready." Eliza Quincy left a good description of a house dance at the Quincy town house on Summer Street in 1817, which would hold good for any similar party before the war. The 150 or so guests, including the entire Otis clan, "began to appear at 8 o'clock. The ladies were all in full dress, gold and silver muslins, lace & jewels of all descriptions . . . We took care to have plenty of beaux invited; all our Cambridge acquaintances, Josiah and several of his friends, collegians, were of the party, in addition to the Boston gentlemen . . . Anna was much admired as a little girl of 7 years, and danced a cotillion with Mr. H. G. Otis jr. — who took a fancy to the young lady."

It will be observed that all ages from seven to seventy were represented. That was the Old World custom, now unhappily done away with in every eastern city except Baltimore, and replaced by parties of the same age group. "Plenty of beaux" from Harvard now swamp every Boston ball. As Santayana caustically remarked, "The young [in America] were simply young, and the old simply old, as among peasants."

Almost every visitor of distinction to Boston brought a letter of introduction to Harrison Gray Otis and received abundant hospitality. "We have kept tavern for John Bull these thirty years," Harry once wrote; and he loved to relate the answer of his victualer, when pressed to tell whether he had any customer as good as himself. After scratching his head, the tradesman, a noncommittal Yankee, replied that he guessed he sold about as much to the Hotel Albion — the second largest hotel in Boston. Less formal entertainment than the dances for both sexes were so-called tea parties, precursor of cocktail parties, from about 5:00 to 7:00 P.M.; and evening parties, especially Sunday evenings. These were *conversazioni*, followed by a supper of scalloped oysters, many hot and cold dishes, and Madeira wine. Men's clubs, of the London pattern, with their own houses and restaurants, did not appear in Boston before Otis's old age, but in his time there were several men's dinner clubs. These were formed among Harvard classmates and other congenial friends who met weekly or fortnightly at a member's house. Otis, with William Sullivan, Thomas Handasyd Perkins, Benjamin Joy, General David Cobb, President Kirkland of Harvard, and other choice spirits, belonged to one of these coteries known as the Saturday Fish Club, of which little more than the name is known; presumably the excuse for it was to eat an old-fashioned New England salt fish dinner, which the Yankees always consumed on Saturday night in order to be different from the Catholics. When General Cobb, deposed from his agency for the Bingham lands east of the Penobscot in 1822, returned to Gouldsborough for the last time, each member of the club contributed two bottles of Madeira and shipped them to him Down East. Two years later, Sullivan, in a Sunday letter to Otis, told about the club's previous dinner:

The club dined yesterday at Mr. Joy's — *wine* from 20 to 45 years old — and no better for being more than 20. Besides the members we had Mr. Henderson of N. York, Pres. K[irkland], Brother Rufus [King or Amory?], who complained to Mr. J. that the women wear no *pockets* nowadays — that his House keeper takes the keys out of her bosom, when he wants them, and

that they are so *warm* that he likes to let them *cool* before he uses them. —
Joy broke the sober rules of the club, by bringing oysters from the shell, to
give a *gout,* and a market, for his wine; — it certainly needed no such aid.

Until after the end of the second war with Britain, Federalists and
Republicans kept rigidly separate in Boston. Theophilus Parsons tells
us in the memoir of his like-named father, the Chief Justice, that he
never saw a "Jacobin" in their house until 1807, when his Uncle
Cross, a Maine Democrat, came to dinner on a visit to Boston. The
children examined him attentively, as specimen of a new and strange
breed. In the course of the meal the chief justice remarked pleasantly, "Mr. Cross, pray take a glass of wine with me," and handed
him the decanter; when to the consternation of the company young
Theophilus called out, "Why, he is not a Jacobin, after all!" "No, my
young friend, I am not a *Jacobin;* at least, I hope not," said Uncle
Cross; "did you think I was?" "Yes, sir!" said young hopeful, "but I
see you are not, for I have heard father say, again and again, that
nothing on earth would make him drink wine with a Jacobin!" At
which point the conversation was broken off by young Theophilus's
being sent away from the table.

Yet Otis and his friends, who dreaded democracy in theory, were
in some respects more democratic socially than the bloated billion-
aires of today. They lived on terms of friendly intimacy with servants, tradespeople, and country neighbors. J. W. Hale tells us how
"almost any morning might be seen Col. Thos. H. Perkins, Harrison
Gray Otis, William (Billy) Gray, Ben. Bussey, Peter C. Brooks, Israel
Thorndike and other wealthy townsfolk, trudging homeward for their
eight o'clock breakfast with their market baskets containing their one
o'clock dinner." Harry always did just that, when not laid up by arthritis, with this difference: he ate the hearty breakfast first and a
manservant carried the basket.

A story of Theophilus Parsons's may give us the key to this seeming
inconsistency. When a Salem man asked his father why the New-
buryporters were forever quarreling about religion, he replied, "Because we look upon religion as having a real importance. We think it
worth quarreling about; you don't." The situation was the same in
politics. Federalists and Republicans alike, at the period of which we
speak, took their politics with a grim earnestness that the present
generation can hardly comprehend. To a Federalist, a Jacobin was an

anarchist who would pull down the entire political and social structure; Jacobinism was a disease to be avoided and proscribed. Dance
with a Jacobin? Drink wine with a Jacobin? Of course not! Would a
daughter of Jefferson Davis's have danced with Wendell Phillips?
Would Pius IX have invited Cavour to dinner?

Otis once took offense from finding Jeffersonians at a social party in
Washington, but he never allowed political differences to sour family
relations. He always remained intimate with the James Warrens and
with Sally's father, William Foster, ardent Jeffersonians. Presumably, when Aunt Warren or Father Foster dined at Number 45,
Eliza, Harry, Sally, Sophy, Jimmy, and Willie were firmly warned
not to mention the word "Jacobin." Otis loved his Aunt Warren, but
did not approve of her. In sending to John Rutledge in 1805 the
prospectus of her *History of the Rise, Progress and Termination of the
American Revolution,* he warned his Carolina friend that "her political
opinions will exhibit the tincture of democracy. Though well born &
a real lady, and as proud a woman as lives, she is the wife of a disappointed patriot of seventy-five and is too much under his influence
altho' vastly his superior in every sort of literary attainment. She assures me however that she has been strictly impartial, and it is at her
request that I send you the prospectus . . ." The book turned out to
be anything but impartial, containing cracks at John Adams, which
aroused his ire, and afforded the reading public vast amusement.

Otis found his brother-in-law, William Foster, Jr., a bit hard to
take. William, one of the American speculators in Paris in the 1790's,
enlisted in the French republican army, married a cousin of General
Moreau's, and in 1809 returned with her to Boston, there compound-
ing his "Jacobin" villainy by writing pro-French articles for the Democratic press. Nevertheless, Otis promoted Foster's candidacy for the
new Smith Professorship of French and Spanish Literature at Harvard in 1815. Fortunately for Harvard, George Ticknor received the
chair.

Eating, Drinking, and Scandals

Every Thanksgiving there took place a huge family reunion of the
numerous Otis, Foster, Apthorp, Lyman, Ritchie, and Thorndike
connections. In the winter season there were frequent parties of a

hundred or more, and breakfast parties such as the following, related in one of Otis's letters, were not uncommon:

Night before last, Sophia undertook to ask Mrs. I. P. Davis and Miss Lovell to eat buckwheats, and the party swelled to between twenty & thirty, — all the 2nd & 3rd generations of Fosters, my sisters, Thorndikes, Callanders, Holleys, and half a doz Codmans, Grays, Brooks' &c to fill up chinks.

Those old Bostonians unashamedly enjoyed eating and drinking. While the Otis family was in residence at Number 45 Beacon Street, a blue and white Lowestoft punch bowl, with a capacity of over two gallons, sat every afternoon on the landing halfway to the drawing rooms, filled with punch for the benefit of visitors. Otis became famous as a gourmet and connoisseur of wines, although how he managed to indulge in the good things of this world on the scale that he did through forty gouty years is hard to imagine. Family tradition is positive that his usual breakfast dish, even at the age of eighty, was a moderate-sized tureen of pâté de fois gras. After beginning the day in this fashion, Otis would walk to the State House if the general court was in session; and, if not, to his law office on Court Street, or to the courthouse if a case in which he was involved needed his presence. At noon or shortly after, the merchants, lawyers, and other professional men left their offices for " 'Change," which meant strolling up and down State Street in fair weather, or meeting in the Exchange Coffee-House or an insurance office if the weather was cold or inclement. For an hour or so the gentlemen exchanged gossip, made deals, wrote insurance for ships going foreign, and damned the Democrats. At about two o'clock 'Change broke up; everyone walked or drove home for a two-thirty or three o'clock dinner, which lasted until candlelight in winter. At other seasons, dinner ended in time for the family to drive out to the country — maybe to Oakley, or to Tom Perkins's house in Brookline, Jack Lowell's Bromley Vale in Roxbury, or Theodore Lyman's The Vale in Waltham — to take tea. Once home, a hearty supper was enjoyed at eight or nine o'clock, "and so to bed."

The punch bowl on the stairs prevented the male members of the Otis family from becoming thirsty during the afternoon, and tradition assures us that a special ice chest, within easy reach of friends and family, provided jellies, whips, and syllabubs for whoever might be attacked by hunger between meals. At the dinner table there was none of your modern false modesty about looking at food — joints and pies were spread out to regale sight and nostrils; no great variety, to be sure, and no French cooking; but good honest food in unstinted abundance.

There was a fabulous consumption of Madeira in nineteenth-century Boston. Otis's old friend George Harrison, of Philadelphia, became agent for the house of Gordon Duff & Company, and received orders from Harry and his Boston friends for that king of wines. A sample consignment of "choice particular old Madeira" at £46 the pipe (a double hogshead containing 126 gallons) arrived in the schooner *Lark* in 1807, just in time to escape Jefferson's embargo.

In addition to his quota in the aforementioned consignment, Otis procured another pipe direct. The previous year, he had received "2 pipes choice particular Madeira wine in strong iron-bound casks at £45 Stg. p. pipe, mark'd H G O branded I A G," and "1 pipe ditto wine"; but in 1809 (the embargo having lifted) he considered it time to lay in a new stock, for in that year George Harrison writes, "I will order 'H G O — G H' of very superior wine for you, & God grant that I may partake of it when ripe 7 years hence."

Madeira was always imported in the wood, preferably in a vessel that had sailed around the world, which was supposed to have a favorable effect on its flavor and bouquet. After resting a few years in the owner's house — in the attic rather than the cellar if he wished it to mature quickly — the wine was drawn off into bottles and given the name of the ship in which it had been imported, as well as the vintage year. Naval officers commanding ships and frigates made a practice of bringing home pipes of Madeira for their friends, which not only saved them freight money but also gave their wine a peculiar distinction. In my youth in Boston a generous host would open a bottle of "Constitution," "Constellation," or "Macedonian" Madeira; and the last bottle of the "Constitution," owned by Russell Codman, was drunk at my house in 1967. Bostonians never cared much for port wine; claret, Burgundy, hock, and champagne they drank only at mixed parties or on gala occasions. Otis, however, was always ready to give a new wine a try, as this letter to him from A. F. Humphreys of Boston, in 1812, indicates:

Do not be surprized, my dear Mr. Otis should you see a cask of *Bucellas* wine walking into your yard today . . . I wrote to Lisbon for it immediately after I heard you express a wish to try that wine, & behold! it is already here . . . A light white wine, between *Vin de Grave* & *Vin du Rhin*.

A natural consequence of the high living then prevalent was arthritis or gout, with which Otis was afflicted during the last forty years of his life. This irritating disease soured the temper of many an old gentleman, but Otis's temper and constitution were proof against it. Although he lived to the age of eighty-three, he retained until the last his wit, good nature, and every quality that endeared him to his fellow men.

Scandals, especially illicit love affairs, were rare in this close-knit society, which honored the Puritan ethic after moving away from the Puritans' religion. Occasionally, however, they did occur. Otis early in 1803 received a distressing letter from Newport written by his friend Rutledge, who had just discovered the unfaithfulness of his wife, daughter of the Bishop of South Carolina and mother of his three children. Otis offered to place his Boston house at Rutledge's or Mrs. Rutledge's disposition if a physical separation was desirable, and undertook to deny publicly malicious gossip "which I foresaw would be propagated from Newport, that Pandora's box & fertile source of public and private vice." With Otis's approval, Rutledge challenged the lover, also a Southern summer visitor at Newport, to a duel. They fought in Georgia; Rutledge killed the lover and obtained a divorce by special act of the South Carolina legislature.

A similar case occurred about the same time in Boston; and since the only record of it omits the names of the parties, we shall call them Mr. and Mrs. Smith, and Mr. Jones, Smith's partner and lodger. Jones was caught *in flagrante delicto* with Mrs. Smith. Again there was a duel, this time in Canada; the lover fell dead and the injured husband sought a divorce *a vinculo* from the Supreme Judicial Court of Massachusetts. Mrs. Smith's friends persuaded her to resist, and she retained Harrison Gray Otis and William Sullivan as counsel. As our one informant describes it:

Mr. Otis was himself, that day; elegant in his person and carriage; his voice appeared more than usually melodious, as though he had adapted it to that tone of supplication, which seemed to be the only resource for his miserable client; and he poured forth a profluvium of that characteristic eloquence, which was ever so captivating in promiscuous assemblies, and with the softer sex. When he sat down, there were, doubtless in that dense assemblage — for the court room was literally packed with excited and deeply interested listeners — some persons, who had a vague impression that the adultress must be innocent; or, if guilty, that there was nothing, after all, so very terrible in the little slip that she had made!

But the litigant's counsel, the great Samuel Dexter, had not been heard. Evidence against the naughty lady was so complete that he easily disposed of Otis's arguments. Dexter had the reputation of displaying "that kind of eloquence which struts around the heart without ever entering it." But in this case he drew a picture of domestic happiness tarnished by sordid adultery that pulled tears from the same audience that had been almost persuaded by Otis that the lady's sin (if it were a sin) was venial. Smith won his divorce.

The Otis Wit

Otis became famous for that "sportive wit" which Adams mentions among his attractive characteristics. We look in vain for it in his political correspondence and speeches, for politics of the Federalist era were so intense and seemed so vital that to season them with humor was considered almost blasphemous. But Otis, who in private intercourse was always bubbling over with spontaneous fun and good nature, was the life of every assembly of men or women where he appeared. At public and private dinners he was the favorite toastmaster.

Then there were the lawyers' stories. Otis wrote to Hamilton that the 1800 treaty with France, according to which all ships captured by each side were to be returned and nothing done about spoliations, reminded him of the fictitious case of *Bullum* v. *Boatum*. Farmer A owned a bull; Farmer B owned a flatboat. The second farmer's scow, laden with turnips, was moored to the riverbank by a grass rope. Farmer A's bull climbed into the boat to eat the turnips and then, for good measure, ate the rope. The boat floated downstream, hit a rock, the bull was drowned, and the boat smashed. The owner of the boat sued the owner of the bull, and the owner of the bull sued the owner of the boat. After hearing extended arguments by both common and admiralty law, the learned justice nonsuited the parties;

upon paying all costs, they were allowed to begin again *de novo*. As the French spoliation claims consumed time and effort in Congress for over a century, this comparison was very much to the point.

Another story that Otis told illustrated the fact that a big lawyer from a small town might not appear so distinguished in Boston. Squire Waldron of Newburyport, having business to transact with Governor Gore in springtime, procured a Merrimack River salmon as a propitiatory gift, packed it with ice in the boot of his chaise, and started for Boston along the Newburyport turnpike. When he broke the journey at Salem to dine with brother lawyers, a couple of wags removed the salmon from the chaise and substituted a common codfish. The squire innocently continued to Boston, where, after stabling his horse, he was astonished to find a cod in the boot, a fish he dared not offer to a gourmet like Governor "Kitty" Gore. So he left it there; but not wishing to waste it, applied more ice to take it home fresh. Returning next day, he again lunched at Salem, where the same two jokers removed the codfish and put back the salmon. Upon her spouse's returning home, Mrs. Waldron greeted him with, "How did His Excellency like the salmon?" "Why, 'twa'nt no salmon," said the squire; "you made a mistake!" "No mistake at all! That was one of the finest salmon I ever did see, and I packed it in ice myself!" "Well, let's take a look at it." They did. The squire, dumbfounded, burst out with, "Maybe 'tis a salmon in Newburyport, but in Boston 'twas nothin' but a goddam codfish!"

Many surviving examples of Harry Otis's humor consist of puns — a form of witticism now out of fashion. We are told, for instance, how he won a case from a Mr. Gee, who was trying to acquire land to which he had no good title. Since $\gamma\tilde{\eta}$ in Greek means "the earth," Otis played about with geography, geology, geometry, perigee, apogee, until the jury was roaring with laughter and poor Gee was utterly confounded. A more convincing example of his ready wit — although to appreciate it requires some knowledge of Massachusetts topography — was told to me by Frank B. Sanborn, who heard it from Wendell Phillips. It seems that one of the colleagues of Otis and John Phillips in the state senate about the year 1808 rejoiced in the curious name of Salem Towne. On one occasion, when the Democratic minority offered a "joker" resolution, drawn up for the express purpose of trapping unwary Federalists into endorsing Democratic principles, Mr. Towne alone of the Federalists swallowed the bait and voted yea in the roll call. Otis came to him after the vote had been taken and remarked in a solemn tone, "Mr. Towne, your parents were four miles out of the way, more or less, in naming you." "Four miles, Mr. Otis! What do you mean, sir?" "Instead of *Salem Towne*, they should have christened you *Marble Head!*"

3

The Ropemakers of Plymouth

From my book of that name, published by Houghton Mifflin in 1950; pages 1–7.

This little book I wrote directly after World War II, when the Plymouth Cordage Company was about to celebrate its 125th anniversary. Alas, the company is dead, bought up by American Hardware in 1963, when the old ropewalk was closed for the first time since 1824.

This book is the subject of one of my favorite Maine stories, my attempt to extract a compliment from the keeper of a general store on Mount Desert Island. It goes as follows:

Storekeeper to S.E.M.: "Seen your book."
S.E.M.: "What book?"
Storekeeper: "Th' one about rope."
S.E.M.: "How did you get that?"
Storekeeper: "Company sent it to me free — I sell their rope."
S.E.M. (hopefully): "How did you like it?"
Storekeeper: "Didn't read it; wife read it."
S.E.M.: "How did she like it?"
Storekeeper: "Didn't say."

ON SATURDAY, December 9, 1620, a band of ten Pilgrim Fathers in search of a suitable place to pitch their settlement entered Plymouth Harbor in their shallop during a snow squall, and after a wet and miserable night ashore "found themselves to be on an island secure from the Indians, where they might dry their stuff, fix their pieces, and rest themselves; and gave God thanks for His mercies in their manifold deliverances." After resting the Sabbath on Clark's Island, on Monday, December 11, "they sounded the harbor and found it fit for shipping, and marched into the land and found divers cornfields and little running brooks; a place (as they supposed) fit for situation; at least it was the best they could find, and the season and their present necessity made them glad to accept of it."

One of these "little running brooks," later called Nathan's, from the name of an early settler, became the site of the Plymouth Cordage Company about two centuries later. The mouth of Nathan's Brook may well be the exact spot where these exploring Pilgrims first landed; it was certainly the nearest land they could have reached in their shallop without running on mud flats. Anyone who enters Plymouth Harbor in a small boat can see for himself that the "Cordage Wharf" is much easier to reach than the wharves of Plymouth Town. However, we shall leave the Plymouth Rock tradition unchallenged. Wherever the exploring party landed, the Pilgrim band as a whole decided to settle at the mouth of Town Brook, two and a quarter miles to the southward.

When a colonial New England village expanded and a group of houses was built on the outskirts of a township, the new hamlet was often given an informal and humorous name before it acquired an official one. Thus, the few houses that grew up around the water-powered grist mill on Nathan's Brook in colonial days were collectively called "Playne Dealing" in the records, a name that has been "a puzzle to the student of Pilgrim history." The implied compliment to the local inhabitants apparently wore thin in course of time, since we find that around the year 1800 the place was known as "Bungtown." Possibly the inhabitants whittled out barrel bungs in their spare time; perhaps they were noted for extracting the same from full barrels. A later and sentimental age called it "Seaside." Around the turn of the twentieth century the sensible name "North Plymouth" was adopted. That is the present name and address of this section of the ancient Town of Plymouth where the cordage plant and its dependent wharves, sidings, offices, employees' houses, and other buildings are situated.

Bourne Spooner, descendant of several Pilgrim Fathers, was the father of the Plymouth Cordage Company. Born in Plymouth on February 2, 1790, and there educated, he left home as a young man, during or immediately after the War of 1812, for the booming city of New Orleans. There he was employed in a ropewalk that used Kentucky hemp for raw material and Negro slaves, hired from their masters, for labor. Young Spooner was a natural abolitionist. He hated slavery as an institution, and the inefficiency of slave labor disgusted him. Consequently, after learning the ropemaking business, he returned to his home town determined to make a try at manufacturing cordage with free labor.

The time was propitious and the place suitable. New England had recovered from the postwar depression; trade, shipping, and manufacturing were flourishing. Congress, in May 1824, raised the tariff to four cents a pound on tarred, and five cents a pound on untarred cordage. Plymouth Bay was no mean port in 1824, although the three towns (Plymouth, Kingston, and Duxbury) that front on that large body of water inside Saquish and Long Beach were prevented, by deep embayment, intricate harbor channels, and lack of inland communication, from keeping pace with Boston and Salem. Here fishing schooners, coasting sloops, and foreign-going brigs and ships up to 500 tons' burthen were built. In 1820, some 21,000 tons of shipping were registered in the Plymouth customs district, more than in Gloucester or Newburyport and not far behind Nantucket or New Bedford. Plymouth-owned vessels were active in the triangular trade in sugar, iron, and hemp from Boston to Havana, thence to Russia and back to Boston; others traded to the Mediterranean or the West Indies; but most of them were coasters. For this was before the railroad era, when anyone who went anywhere from Plymouth, or sent to Plymouth for anything, generally went or sent by sea. In 1830, when the town still had less than 5000 inhabitants, it employed six sloops of 60 tons each as Boston packets, two schooners of 90 tons each as "constant traders" to Nantucket, New Bedford, and New York, and three other vessels to bring lumber and firewood from Maine.

In addition, the district annually fitted out over a hundred vessels for the cod and mackerel fisheries and even owned a few whaling ships that sailed to the Pacific and back. In the interior of Plymouth County, around Bridgewater, there was a flourishing iron industry, where anchors, shovels, nails, and bolts were made; and the county boasted seven woolen and fourteen cotton mills.

Ships and Rigging

While every factory and home in New England required a certain amount of rope, it was the maritime market that Bourne Spooner dreamed of capturing. The modern sailor or yachtsman can hardly imagine the amount of line that was consumed on a nineteenth-century sailing vessel. Every sail (a full-rigged ship carried at least fifteen sails, a barque twelve, and a brig nine) had to be edged all around with boltrope. The yard to which it was bent — with rope — needed stout lifts, or halyards, to be raised and lowered. Two tacks and two sheets were required to trim each square sail; two bowlines to keep the leeches taut; two clewlines, two buntlines, and two leech-lines for clewing it up to the yard for furling; and the sailors needed a footrope to stand on. The several jibs and triangular staysails be-tween the masts, the fore-and-aft driver on the main and spanker on the mizzen, and the studdingsails, if studdingsails were carried, had their own halyards and sheets, topping lifts, or brails. Most of this running rigging ran up and down masts that might be 50, 60, or 100 feet tall, and those that did the heaviest work had double or triple purchases at the ends for swaying them up taut. In addition there was the standing rigging, the shrouds and backstays that held up the lower masts, topmasts, and topgallant masts, all of heavy tarred rope, neatly wormed, and served with small line, together with the rope lanyards that enabled them to be set up or slacked away; for wire rigging did not come into use until after the Civil War. Chain cable was introduced somewhat earlier, but until 1840, at least, every ship needed several heavy rope anchor cables 120 fathoms in length, and these cables consumed an enormous amount of fiber. Frigates like the *Constitution*, for instance, carried seven cables 21 inches in circum-ference, which is the size of the largest cable ever made by the Plymouth Cordage Company. Then there were the dipsey leadlines, the spare tackles, handy-billys, and cargo hoists; downhauls, painters, flag halyards, and boat ropes; hawsers, jeers, shank painters, and a dozen other lines now obsolete; ratlines to enable seamen to go aloft on the run, and gaskets with which they secured a furled sail; and the one, two, or three rows of short reef points on almost every sail. All of rope.

If you consider the hull as a ship's body and the sails her means of locomotion, the "lines," as seamen called the ropes, were her nerves and tendons. The wind blowing on this intricate network of cordage made a deep humming noise in a fresh gale and a high-pitched whis-tle in a storm; halyards slatting against the spars provided the wood-wind; the sails spilling wind and then filling out with a hollow boom were the percussion instruments; and the rush of great waters the organ accompaniment — in a symphony of sound that was music in a seaman's ear. Even in the lightest air there was music of a sort from spars creaking and the reef points tap-tap-tapping against the duck sails. There's nothing like this to be heard today, even in a modern sailing yacht, whose wire rigging twangs and snaps like a sick piano.

V

History the Craft

1

Prescott, the American Thucydides

From THE ATLANTIC MONTHLY, *November 1957.*

William H. Prescott, author of THE CONQUEST OF MEXICO *and* THE CONQUEST OF PERU, *has always seemed to me one of the greatest American historians. And also, in a way, a great friend, for he was a warm friend to my grandfather Samuel Eliot, whose house I inherited; his library includes presentation copies of Prescott's works. A handsome bust of the historian by one of the Greenoughs, which he gave to my grandfather, looks down on me as I sit at my desk. In 1956 I was invited by Mrs. Helen Macy to edit a new edition of* THE HISTORY OF THE CONQUEST OF PERU *for her Limited Editions Club. That appeared in a sumptuous limited edition in 1957 with illustrations by Everett Gee Jackson (Mexico: Imprenta Nuevo Mundo, 1957), with a trade edition to follow. This gave me the incentive to make a fresh study of Prescott's life and works, which was first printed as the Introduction to the above edition, and to write a shorter account for* THE ATLANTIC MONTHLY, *which was printed in their number for November 1957 as "Prescott, the American Thucydides." Two years later, in 1959, we celebrated the centenary of Prescott's death at 55 Beacon Street, which at the same time was marked by a handsome portrait in bronze by the Boston sculptor Joseph Coletti, and a brass plaque with a Spanish inscription, donated by the Republic of Peru.*

My ATLANTIC *article follows.*

IN 1774 HORACE WALPOLE wrote to Sir Horace Mann: "The next Augustan age will dawn on the other side of the Atlantic. There will perhaps be a Thucydides at Boston."

There was; and three quarters of a century later Walpole's friend Miss Berry, then a venerable vestal of eighty-seven, had the satisfaction of meeting him in London. His name was William Hickling

Prescott, and he was being received by political, social, and literary England in a manner that no American writer has experienced before or since. Macaulay gave him a breakfast party at Albany; the Lyells took him to Royal Ascot; Oxford conferred on him an honorary D.C.L.; and the Earl of Carlisle entertained him together with Queen Victoria at Castle Howard. Prescott sat next but one to her at dinner, and described her in a letter to his wife as "very plain, with fine eyes and teeth, but short and dumpy, with a skin that reddens easily with the heat of the room. I observed that the Queen did great justice to the bread and cheese."

This "American Thucydides," as people were beginning to call him, was then at the height of his fame. His three greatest works, *Ferdinand and Isabella, The Conquest of Mexico,* and *The Conquest of Peru,* had appeared, greeted with enthusiasm by the critics of both continents including even the snooty Scots reviewers, and they had been eagerly bought by the public. Prescott was then a tall, well-built gentleman of fifty-four, with an infectious smile and hearty laugh that charmed everyone. A pair of well-trimmed sideburns, in the fashion of the day, framed a strong, handsome countenance with a fine Roman nose, brown eyes, and a ruddy complexion. He was lively, agile, an excellent horseman, and a fast walker; few except his intimate friends suspected that for long intervals he was racked by rheumatism and that one of his eyes was artificial.

This was in 1850, when Prescott was reaping the fruits of thirty-five years of courageous struggle to overcome a grave physical disability. It is a curious coincidence that the only other American historian, Francis Parkman, to be mentioned in the same breath with Prescott had to undergo a similar experience.

Let us take a look at him at almost the start of the struggle. It is the year 1817. Son of a Federalist lawyer and judge, grandson of Colonel William Prescott of Bunker Hill fame, young William had gone through Harvard College gaily and easily, but lost an eye as a result of a brawl in college commons. The infection had spread to the other eye and acute rheumatism set in. After the local physicians had almost killed him with "copious bleedings and other depletions," he had been sent to Europe in search of better medical aid than could be had in America. First he spent a winter with his maternal grandfather, Thomas Hickling, the United States consul at St. Michael's in the Azores, and there he became sensible of the beauty and mystery

of the Old World. He then made an attenuated grand tour of
Europe, consulted the best eye specialists in Paris, and returned to
live in his parents' house, a big square mansion with a garden on
Pearl Street, Boston. There the old malady returned. We may picture Prescott confined for days, sometimes weeks, to a dark room on
the top story, a devoted sister reading aloud to him by lying on the
floor where she could catch the light that came in over the threshold,
since any stronger light gave the young man excruciating pain.

Yet Prescott refused to admit defeat, and gave careful thought to
what he should do for a profession. And he wooed and won a girl of
his own social circle, Susan Amory. They were married on his
twenty-fourth birthday, and for the next twenty-four years lived with
the elder Prescotts. The Amorys were one of those American Loyalist families — more numerous than is generally supposed — who
managed to retain their property and social position through the tur-
moil of the American Revolution. Susan was a beautiful girl with a
somewhat bovine character. "She didn't go out much — as an
Amory she didn't have to," a granddaughter remarked; she was content to rear a family and to watch tenderly over her husband's health
and interests. He was completely and romantically devoted to her.
She inherited the sword of her grandfather, who had served in the
Royal Navy on board one of the British ships that supported the assault on Bunker Hill, and William inherited that of his grandfather,
who commanded the provincial troops in that battle; so they had the
two mounted and placed on the wall of the Prescott library. These
were the famous "crossed swords," which Thackeray saw on his visit
to Boston and which inspired *The Virginians,* as the opening paragraph of that novel relates.

Even before he married, Prescott decided to fit himself for what he
called "the literary life," although as yet he had little inclination to
any particular branch of that far-spreading tree. It was not really necessary that he do anything, considering his infirmity, his social position, and his father's generosity. But in Boston every young man was
supposed to "make an effort," as the phrase went; Prescott himself
later observed that an American who neither made money nor cultivated letters might "as well go hang himself; for as to a class of idle
gentlemen, there is no such thing here." That was true in general;
but even in Boston there were young men of means who did nothing
in particular, and not too well at that, flitting about between New

York, Newport, and London.   Henry James has immortalized the type of American who rejected his native country as a hopeless Boeotia and moved to Paris or Rome to dabble in the arts or pursue some pallid branch of scholarship.   Prescott was made of stouter stuff.

As a scholar he had to start from scratch, having carried away from Harvard little more than a good knowledge of Latin and Greek.   After many false starts and physical relapses, and with the guidance and advice of his older friend George Ticknor, he settled at the age of twenty-nine on a history of the reign of Ferdinand and Isabella of Spain.

There were two main reasons for this choice.   He wished to show his compatriots that their history had a richer and more varied background than the Virginia colony, the Pilgrim Fathers, and the Protestant Reformation.   He wished to prove to the world that an American could produce a work at once scholarly and literary that would bear comparison with the best of England, France, Germany, and Spain. He was eager for the good opinion of European scholars.   They might brush off anything he could write on United States history as inconsequential; but they would have to listen to a work that was the result of prolonged research, a nice weighing of conflicting authorities, and a thorough knowledge of classical and modern languages; especially if it was well presented.

When Prescott made the great decision for Ferdinand and Isabella in 1826, ten years of almost unremitting labor were ahead of him. The material difficulties that he surmounted were even greater than his physical handicap.   The way to perform the task with the greatest economy would have been to settle in Madrid, as his friend the American minister there advised him to do.   He could have worked there, or in London or Paris, far more effectively than in Boston, and have been nearer to specialists who could have kept his one good eye working.   But Prescott was determined not to be an expatriate, even temporarily.   He felt that he owed it to the memory of Colonel Prescott, and to his family and friends, to prove that an American could produce a literary and scholarly work of the highest quality right in Boston.

Yet how could that be done in Boston?   There were no collections of old Spanish books there or anywhere else in the United States. Ticknor, blessed with ample means, imported the essential books as rapidly as he could find them and gave Prescott the run of his library; but Prescott was not content to "make new books, as apothecaries make new mixtures, by pouring out of one vessel into another," as Tristram Shandy once remarked. He must have the original sources, and with few exceptions these were still in manuscript. In those days there was no multivolumed set of *Documentos Inéditos;* the Las Casas *Historia General de las Indias* had never been printed, nor the better part of Oviedo, nor Andrés Bernáldez's chronicle of the Catholic kings. These and hundreds of other manuscripts had to be copied for him in longhand. The cost was not excessive, since there were plenty of unemployed intellectuals in Europe who were glad to do such work for starvation wages; the trouble was to find responsible scholars to direct research in public and private archives and to supervise the copying. Therein the United States consuls and diplomatic officials gave indispensable aid, and Dr. Friedrich Lembke, a German who had written a history of Spain to the year 800, consented to carry on vicariously for Prescott in return for a modest retainer.

Eventually, books and copies of manuscripts began to pour into the paternal mansion on Pearl Street, where they were placed on shelves in the son's attic study. And he managed to surmount his physical handicap by methodical living, by having most of the material read aloud to him by a secretary who learned to pronounce Spanish, and by a simple device called a noctograph, which had been invented in London to enable the blind to write. This was a sort of slate crossed by a grid of stout brass wires between which, with an ivory-pointed stylus, one could write on carbon paper, which made an indelible impression on another sheet of paper placed underneath.

When, after ten years of work, the manuscript of *Ferdinand and Isabella* was completed, it was set up in type at the author's expense, and four copies were printed for his close friends to criticize. These privately printed copies were hawked about English and American publishing houses for months with slight success. Finally, a short-lived firm called the American Stationers Company of Boston agreed, for $1000, to print 1250 copies of the three-volume set to be retailed at six dollars, if the author would foot the bills for the stereotype plates; and Richard Bentley agreed to publish a small edition in London.

Ferdinand and Isabella appeared in Boston on Christmas Day, 1837, and in London a month or two later. It was an immediate and astounding success on both sides of the water, partly because it came as a complete surprise. The author's name was unknown in Europe; and so well had Prescott kept his secret in Boston, where everyone was supposed to know everyone else's business, and so gay and unrestrained had been his social life that not more than six persons outside the immediate family knew what he had been doing. It was commonly supposed that he was reading for his own amusement. Only a week before *Ferdinand and Isabella* came out, an elderly relative stopped Prescott on the street to upbraid him for frittering away his life, and to tell him it was high time he amounted to something!

Prescott could have boasted, like Lord Byron, "I awoke one morning and found myself famous." To a German who had called it folly to publish Spanish history in the United States, "where the taste was for nothing higher than a periodical," Prescott wrote that 3300 sets of *Ferdinand and Isabella* had been sold in the first sixteen months; "that is pretty well for 'Brother Jonathan,' is it not? . . . The publishers indeed are quite as much surprised as I am."

He gained the favor of the critics by his vivid and spirited narrative style, arresting as that of an historical novel, yet with each detail authenticated in a footnote. I shall not attempt to analyze his style, because it is to be enjoyed and admired, not plucked apart. Certain modern critics regard it as artificial (of course every style, even Hemingway's and Joyce's, is that); and certainly nobody would think of imitating it today. But he was a master of *narrative*, which history essentially is, a fact that too many modern historians have forgotten. And the quality that gave his works permanent value, and that appealed most to the more discriminating critics, was (as Roger B. Merriman wrote) "the scrupulous care and integrity with which he used his materials, and the pains that he took to find the exact truth. All his statements are supported by abundant references; if there is any possible doubt as to the interpretation of his authorities, it is fairly expressed in the footnotes; in short, one may be certain of the source for every fact which Prescott gives, though one may differ with him over the significance of it."

Before his first work appeared, Prescott had decided on the next two, *The Conquest of Mexico* and *The Conquest of Peru*. Washington Irving, who had planned to do a *Mexico* himself, magnanimously dropped it in favor of the younger historian. Prescott's *Conquest of Mexico*, completed in 1843, was an even greater success than his first book, and has remained his best seller. Over 20,000 sets of it were sold during his lifetime; and as he had paid for the plates himself, he collected substantial royalties. But the profits from each book were plowed into preparations for the next; into copying, salaries to secretaries and researchers, purchase of books and manuscripts. Only his inherited and invested income of somewhat over $12,000 a year enabled him to carry on.

Almost everyone who reads his works assumes that Prescott visited the scenes he wrote about, so vivid and convincing are his descriptions of scenery, battlefields, and the like. But, owing to his infirmities, he never went nearer South America than Washington, D.C. His lack of physical contact with these countries was compensated for by an historical imagination, well controlled by the facts as related by Bernal Díaz and the early Spanish chronicles, and developed by correspondence with people who knew these countries at first hand. The most useful to him in that respect was Madame Calderón de la Barca, whose *Life in Mexico* has become a classic. She was Fanny Inglis, a charming and witty Scotswoman who had a private school in Boston and became a close friend of the Prescotts. After her marriage to the Spanish minister to the United States, who was later transferred to Mexico City, she continued to interchange letters with Prescott; and it is probably owing to her devotion that he was able to write his accurate and striking descriptions of Mexico City and Teotihuacan under the Aztecs.

It was also a subject of astonished praise that a Boston Protestant like Prescott could write so understandingly of Catholics and Catholicism, even asserting that there was something to be said for the Inquisition. He was the first English-speaking historian of Spanish lands whom a loyal Spaniard could read without disgust. For, Unitarian though he might be by conviction, Prescott judged historical characters by the standards of their day, not by those of nineteenth-century liberalism. He regarded the Catholic Church as one of the world's great religions, which was here to stay and not on the way out, as many liberals fondly imagined. And like other New Englanders who retained a "pious disbelief" after rejecting the Church, he found anticlericalism distasteful and the raillery of Voltaire disgusting.

Even more gratifying to Prescott than the acclaim of the critics was his popularity among all classes of American readers. When, shortly after the Mexican War, he visited Washington, he was delighted to hear from the secretary of the navy that the bluejackets of the U.S.S. *Delaware* had petitioned him to add *The Conquest of Mexico* to their ship's library; and that the secretary had not only done that, but ordered a set to be placed on board every ship of the United States Navy.

And there was one humble reader whom Prescott obtained many years after his death, whose story would have gratified him immensely. That was Edward E. Ayer, a young Middle Westerner in the First California Cavalry, U.S. Army, who in 1862 was guarding the Cerro Colorado silver mine in Arizona against attacks by the Apache. Colonel Colt, of revolver fame, had given the mine a small library, and in it trooper Ayer discovered *The Conquest of Mexico*. He read it through twice, "and was astonished to find that history could be so interesting." After his discharge from the Army, Ayer was given by his father an interest in a country store in Illinois. On visiting Chicago to lay in a stock of goods, he called at a bookshop and asked if they had a copy of this fascinating history. They had, and *The Conquest of Peru* as well, but the price was $17.50 for the set. Young Ayer — he was still only twenty-three years old — had only $3.50 to spare, but he offered to pay that for Volume I of the *Mexico*, and to buy a volume every month. The proprietor let him pay the $3.50 down and gave him the five volumes to take home. "My return was a triumphal procession," wrote Mr. Ayer almost fifty years later. "I was certainly the happiest boy in the world." And the world knows that Mr. Ayer became one of the greatest of American book collectors, to the ultimate benefit of the Newberry Library of Chicago. The place of honor in that library's Ayer Collection is given to these identical copies, which the owner eventually had sumptuously rebound in London at a cost over tenfold that of his original investment.

Prescott never wholly recovered from his physical disabilities, but he never let them get him down. Fortunately, one of his secretaries recorded in detail his regimen, a Spartan one that would have crushed the life out of a less valiant and buoyant man. The scene of it is the house still numbered 55 Beacon Street, Boston, which the historian bought after the death of his father and where he wrote most of

The Conquest of Peru. His atelier, as he called his study, was on the third floor, rear; one viewing the outside of it today from the little street that runs behind Beacon would suppose that a recent owner had installed a picture window there, but the two large panes of plate glass were put in by Prescott in order to afford his weak eye maximum light.

The historian rose before seven, winter or summer, mounted one of his saddle horses, and rode for an hour and a half, to Jamaica Plain or Cambridge. This he called "winding himself up." After breakfast he shaved, bathed, and changed, while Mrs. Prescott read aloud to him from a novel by Scott, Dickens, or Dumas. Prescott not only enjoyed a good novel; he learned from them how to make his histories tridimensional by including chapters on manners and morals — social history, as it is now called. At ten o'clock he went out for a half-hour walk and at ten-thirty started work in his atelier. After glancing at the headlines of the morning paper, he had the secretary read aloud items that he thought would be interesting — but seldom found them so. Then came the correspondence. The secretary read letters that poured in from all parts of the world, and Prescott dictated the replies. Next came accounts. These were finished by noon, when the historian walked downtown to make purchases or talk to his friends; for all Boston, even the wharves, lay within twenty minutes' walk of his house.

Returning at one, he began the real business of the day. The secretary read aloud from memoirs and other documents pertaining to the book then being written, Prescott interrupting frequently to dictate notes or to discuss the persons and events described. After all sources for the chapter at hand had been gone through, the secretary read aloud repeatedly the notes he had taken, and was often called upon to reread some of the sources. This process went on for days. Prescott was then ready to compose. He outlined the entire chapter in his mind, sometimes while sitting silent in his study, but more often when walking or riding. He wrote the first draft very rapidly, on his noctograph. The secretary numbered each sheet as it was finished and copied it in a large, round hand so that Prescott could read it himself. His memory was so remarkable that he could commit a chapter of forty or fifty printed pages to memory, mull it over on horseback, and decide on alterations and improvements. He would

then dictate to his secretary the changes to be made in the manuscript, and have the whole reread to him. Finally, he dictated the
footnotes.

This same secretary, Robert Carter, wrote after the historian's
death:

> Mr. Prescott's cheerfulness and amiability were truly admirable. He had a
> finely-wrought, sensitive organization; he was high-spirited, courageous, res-
> olute, independent; was free from cant or affectation of any sort . . . He was
> always gay, good-humored and manly; most gentle and affectionate to his
> family, most kind and gracious to all around him . . . Though not at all dif-
> fident, he was singularly modest and unassuming. He had not a particle of
> arrogance or haughtiness . . . Praise did not elate him, nor censure disturb
> him . . . He was totally free from the jealousy and envy so common among
> authors, and was always eager, in conversation, as in print, to point out the
> merits of the great contemporary historians, whom many men in his position
> would look upon as rivals.

Prescott dined at home at two-thirty or, if with friends, at three
o'clock, the then-fashionable hour. He enjoyed good food, well
cooked, and limited himself to exactly two and a half glasses of sherry
or Madeira. At dinner he relaxed, drew out his family and friends in
conversation, and never talked shop. After dinner he smoked one of
the Havana cigars with which he was kept supplied by his Cuban ad-
mirers, while Mrs. Prescott read aloud again. Another half-hour solitary walk followed, and at six o'clock the secretary returned for a
two-hour evening session in the study. At eight the family had
supper, and at ten-thirty the historian retired.

The evening session of work was omitted if Prescott attended one
of his club meetings or went to an evening party with his wife. The
memory of one of these was preserved by President Charles W. Eliot
of Harvard. "Prexy," in his old age, was asked by a young man
whether he had ever heard Daniel Webster speak.

"Yes, once," said Dr. Eliot. "I was six or eight years old. My father was entertaining him at dinner, and I hid in a corner of the hall
on Beacon Street to catch a sight of the great man. In the procession
to the dining room Mr. Webster led in Mrs. Prescott, a remarkably
handsome lady; and just behind them were Mr. Prescott with Mrs.
Webster, who was exceedingly plain. As they passed me, Mr. Webster, who had been talking with great animation to Mrs. Prescott,

turned half around and said in his booming voice, 'Prescott, what do you say to our swapping wives for this evening?' "

Besides the Beacon Street mansion, Prescott maintained two other homes — the ancestral farmhouse at Pepperell and a summer place at Nahant. At Pepperell he spent the spring and fall of each year, drawing strength from the soil that his ancestors had tilled for over a century; here the final chapter of *The Conquest of Peru* was composed. The house was rambling and unpretentious, but Prescott's friends and their children and his children's friends were often entertained there; life was free and easy, with riding, driving, and long walks, and charades and games in the evening. Prescott's favorite spot was a hill behind the house, with a superb view across the Nashua Valley to the rolling country of New Hampshire, dominated by the grand Monadnock. He had a seat built on the hill and used to sit there for hours, meditating and mentally composing; Monadnock had the same fascination for him as for Emerson and Thoreau. This mansion still stands.

The summer place was a flimsy wooden cottage, long since torn down, on the rocky peninsula of Nahant, north of Boston. In the 1830's and 40's Nahant was a leading American summer resort, where many of Prescott's friends, such as Longfellow, Sumner, Eliot, and Appleton, passed the season, together with hundreds of visitors from New York, Philadelphia, and the South. Life at Nahant was no unmixed blessing for Prescott. He was pestered by visitors in working hours. The cottage, which he named "Fitful Head" after the dwelling of Norna in Scott's *Pirate*, lay on a cliff overhanging Swallows' Cave and so near the water that the piazza was sprinkled with spray in every gale. "It is a wild spot," he wrote to his friend Fanny, "and the winds at this moment whistle an accompaniment to the breakers that might fill a poet's cranium with the sublime. But I am no poet. I imagine myself however in some such place as the bold headland in the Algarve, on which Prince Henry of Portugal established his residence when he sent out his voyages of discovery."

The Conquest of Peru was completed by the end of 1846. The reviews were even more favorable than those of *Mexico*. But this historian was not one to rest on his laurels. He started promptly on *Philip the Second*. The work was interrupted by eye trouble and rheumatism, by tours to Albany, New York, and Washington, and by his visit to England in 1850. His English friends had long been urging him to come; but, remembering the rigors of his early voyage to Europe in a sailing vessel, "bumping and thumping over the qualmish billows," he put it off until he could sail in a Cunarder, which made the voyage in only twelve days. One of his sons accompanied him, but Mrs. Prescott could not face an ocean voyage.

Prescott, like Irving and other American writers of his day, has been accused of being too deferential to the English by critics who mistake good manners for obsequiousness and regard a rude arrogance as the mark of sound Americanism. His letters are full of racy Americanisms like "OK," but for publication he tried to write the King's English, since he sought English-speaking readers all over the world. And to an English correspondent who sent him a long list of alleged Americanisms in *The Conquest of Peru* he replied, politely but firmly, that "realize" had become a verb, that "snarl" was a perfectly good noun for a tangle, and that "counterblast," to which his friend objected, had been taken from the famous tract of King James I against tobacco. Prescott was always sturdily American; if anyone doubts that, let him read in his collected *Miscellanies* his gently sarcastic remarks on Englishmen visiting America or his letters describing the scenery of England, which he thought "too tame." He longed to see "a ragged fence, or an old stump," as in his "own, dear, wild America."

In politics he was a steadfast liberal. His father had been a high Federalist, a member of the Hartford Convention; and the son, like almost everyone of his social standing in Boston, started as a Federalist and became a Whig. Boston society then took politics very hard and ostracized anyone who deviated from the accepted doctrine. George Bancroft, for example, was regarded as little better than a traitor after he joined the Democrats and accepted office under Polk; and Charles Sumner, until Brooks's assault made him a martyr, was generally looked upon as the most dangerous sort of radical. But Prescott always maintained an intimate friendship with both men. Instead of becoming a reactionary late in life, in 1856 he voted for the first Republican presidential candidate, John C. Frémont, and for Anson Burlingame for Congress, although his friend and neighbor Nathan Appleton was the Whig candidate. There is no doubt that he would have supported Lincoln in 1860 if he had lived.

The first two volumes of *Philip the Second*, published in 1855, met with the same favorable reception as did Prescott's earlier works. Work on the third volume was interrupted by a stroke, but it was finally published in 1858. He had started on the fourth and last when, on January 27, 1859, he suffered a second stroke in his Beacon Street home and died within a few hours.

The entire community was moved by grief. Memorial meetings in Prescott's honor were held by the historical societies and academies of which he had been a member, as far west as Illinois and as far south as Maryland; all the noted orators, from Edward Everett down, held forth. He died "a man without an enemy; beloved by all and mourned by all," as Longfellow wrote in his diary. And Charles Sumner, writing from France, said, "There is a charm taken from Boston. Its east winds whistle more coldly around Park Street corner."

2

———◇◇◇———

Francis Parkman

From THE PARKMAN READER, *published by Little, Brown in* 1955; *in England the same year, by Faber and Faber, with the title* ENGLAND AND FRANCE IN NORTH AMERICA BY FRANCIS PARKMAN, A SELECTION.

If Prescott deserves to be called "the American Thucydides," Parkman (of a later generation, 1823–1893), I believe, remains America's number one historian. He, too, was a product of "Brahmin" Boston and a friend of my grandfather's. As a boy I might have seen him in his old age painfully hobbling with two canes down Chestnut Street, or at Jamaica Plain; but I cannot claim to remember him. In a sense he never was old. In 1923, at the centenary celebration of his birth, a Canadian archivist, Aegidius Fauteux, happily described him as an historian whose laurels have never faded because he had "the gift of vitality." Parkman's work is forever young, "with the immortal youth of art"; his men and women are alive: they feel, think, and act within the framework of a living nature. Documents are, to be sure, the basis of his history; but to him documents were not facts; rather, the symbols of events, which the historian must re-create for his readers. In Parkman's prose the forests ever murmur, the rapids perpetually foam and roar, the people have parts and passions. Like that "sylvan historian" of Keats's "Ode on a Grecian Urn," he caught the spirit of an age and fixed it for all time, "forever panting and forever young."

So, here is my Introduction to my book of selections from Parkman's own works.

IN HIS INTRODUCTION to *Montcalm and Wolfe* (1884), last volume but one of *France and England in North America* to appear, Parkman wrote:

The plan of the work was formed in early youth; and though various causes have long delayed its execution, it has always been kept in view. Meanwhile, I have visited and examined every spot where events of any impor-

tance in connection with the contest took place, and have observed with attention such scenes and persons as might help to illustrate those I meant to
describe. In short, the subject has been studied as much from life and in
the open air as at the library table.

Early youth is correct! Francis Parkman conceived the plan of
writing the history of the struggle between France and England in
the New World during his sophomore year at Harvard College, when
he was eighteen years old. He prepared for it, not only by the conventional means of reading and research but, as he says, "from life
and in the open air." He persisted in his plan, through long, dark
years of suffering, until some measure of health returned; and he had
the satisfaction to see the last of his volumes in print, forty-one years
after the first had appeared.

To know what manner of man this historian was, and the surround-
ings in which he worked, one can read no better description than that
of his friend the Reverend Henri-Raymond Casgrain, "l'Abbé Casgrain," as he was known throughout French Canada. This account of
his visit to Parkman in 1871, when he was forty-seven years old and
at the height of his strength and achievement, is translated from the
Memoirs that the abbé wrote in 1898–99. It is here printed for the
first time, by the kind permission of his heirs.

In the month of May 1871, I was climbing the steps of the peristyle of the
Revere House in Boston, admiring the two fine couchant lions on each side
of the staircase, when my attention was distracted by a stranger who ad-
vanced toward me, and smilingly bade me welcome. I recognized instantly
my old friend Mr. Francis Parkman. For several years we had corresponded
without having seen one another . . . I begged him to come to my hotel
parlor, where we talked for some time.

"You intend," he said, "to stay several days in Boston. So I shall take you
with me to Jamaica Plain, my summer residence where I have been installed
for some weeks with my family. You will meet my sister who keeps house
for me and takes care of my two children, Grace and Catherine, both in the
flower of their age. My carriage will convey us to my house in a short time.
Jamaica Plain is only four miles from Boston, and not far from Harvard University, which I shall insist that you visit. I shall introduce you to some of
the most celebrated professors, and you will be in the center of the intellectual aristocracy of our country."

Mr. Parkman's phaeton, which he drove himself, was waiting at the door
of the hotel. The route that we followed in leaving Boston is adorned with

luxurious villas, half-concealed at their entrance by richly wooded grounds, with foliage in all the freshness of early spring. One may say that all is artificial; even the soil is so sterile that it has to be covered with good loam, or, literally, with fertilizer, to produce anything. The jest has passed into a proverb that in Massachusetts nature is so ungrateful that the farmers have to carry a file in their pockets to sharpen the teeth of their animals, to give them a chance to crop a bit of grass! You would not believe it in seeing on every side magnificent gardens created by millions of money. That is what Mr. Parkman has done for his property at Jamaica Plain.

The cottage which he then inhabited on the edge of a little pond was modest compared with the princely châteaux which surrounded it. He has since had it rebuilt.* Miss Mary Parkman and her two nieces awaited us on the verandah. Their welcome was both warm and graceful. American politeness has the naturalness and ease of French courtesy, but with less exuberance and marks of demonstration.

The interior of the cottage corresponded to the exterior; everything was comfortable, but no display of luxury. What I most observed, and comes back to me when my thought returns to that American home, was the perfume of flowers spread through all the rooms. Everywhere there were very beautiful bouquets, or rather bunches, composed principally of rhododendrons of the most delicate rose tints.

Mr. Parkman was not only an eminent historian; he was also a horticulturist of high distinction. His favorite flower was the rose; he had collected, they say, a thousand different varieties. At the annual shows in Boston, he often won the first prizes. I have at my hand a charming little volume composed by him, *The Book of Roses,* which he sent me as a souvenir. It is the fruit of several years of study and of personal experience.

He told me himself how he had happened to take up this avocation. During a buffalo hunt in the Rocky Mountains, when he was still young, he had contracted, as a consequence of his exhaustion and the intemperate climate, a malady of which he has never been cured. He explained the nature of it to me in one of his letters, of January 26, 1872:

"According to the 'Medical Faculty' — as the newspapers say — the trouble comes from an abnormal state or partial paralysis of certain arteries of the brain. Whatever it is, it is a nuisance of the first order, and a school of patience by which Job himself might have profited." To which he added pleasantly, "However, Providence permitting, I will spite the devil yet."

During the acute crisis of this malady, the sensation that he felt was that of

* Parkman's cottage on Jamaica Pond was enlarged and practically rebuilt shortly after this visit. After his death the property was purchased by the commonwealth to round out the parkway that extends from Back Bay to Franklin Park. A new road, named the Francis Parkman Drive, has been run through the site of the historian's rose garden, and a monument to his memory, erected by his friends, is on the site of the house.

a weight of several hundred pounds pressing on his head. His sight was extremely affected by it, and he almost lost the use of his eyes. All mental effort was forbidden, he had to look for distractions in the country, and what agreed with him best was the cultivation of his garden, which he first oversaw while remaining seated near his employees. When his strength began to return, he tried to work with his own hands, while seated for the most part of the time in a folding chair. In this position he would cut his plants and the edges of his flower beds, or weed the ground nearby . . .

At the time of my stay at Jamaica Plain, his health had obviously improved. He had for some time resumed his historical work, and was continuing the series of works on Canada which he had begun. After *The Jesuits in North America* came *The Discovery of the Great West,* and next, successively, *The Old Régime; Frontenac; Montcalm and Wolfe;* and *A Half Century of Conflict,* forming, with the *Pioneers* (1865) and *The Conspiracy of Pontiac* (1851), the most learned history of the French régime in Canada that we possess. Many years elapsed before he succeeded in finishing this great work.

When one reflects on the state of health in which he almost always lived, one finds it difficult to conceive the amount of energy and perseverance which he had to employ in order to succeed.

And what of his appearance? He was the ideal type of Yankee, tall, thin, but with big bones. His face was smooth-shaven; its features well sculptured; small, tired eyes under a fine forehead radiating intelligence. His expression, normally serious and meditative, lighted up easily with a fugitive smile. The tone of his voice was nasal, like that of New Englanders; his speech hesitating in conversation; it would seem that he was searching for words.* There was nothing to suggest a writer with the imaginative and brilliant style that one admires in his books. His discourse had quite another charm, that of a high intelligence served by a vast extent of knowledge. His bearing was fairly alert, although one observed that his legs were weak. He did not seem too fatigued in conducting me to see what would interest me most, at Boston, Cambridge, and Harvard . . .

My stay in Boston confirmed my conviction of the immense services that Mr. Parkman has rendered to our country by his historical works. A natural sympathy and interest is connected with this writer, who has so nobly avenged the odious calumnies that had been invented to sully the name and character of our ancestors.

* In his little booklet *Francis Parkman,* of 1872, page 41, the abbé adds: "The features of his face resemble one of those remarkable types that Leonardo da Vinci loved to paint: a harmonious combination of intelligence, *finesse* and energy; large forehead, finely sculptured nose, strong and prominent chin." Bostonians visiting Venice were struck by the resemblance of Verrochio's head of Bartolommeo Colleoni to Parkman, and several friends brought him photographs of the famous equestrian statue. Parkman felt much flattered by the comparison!

With this picture of the active historian in mind, let us go back to the beginning. Francis Parkman was born in Boston on September 16, 1823. The Parkmans, who had come to New England in the early Puritan migration, had risen from obscurity to fame through the familiar means of commerce and the Congregational Church. Frank, as his friends called him, was related to half the families that constituted Boston society in the Federalist era. His grandfather Samuel Parkman, who had become wealthy by shipping and foreign commerce, owned the trapezoid of land stretching back from Bowdoin Square to Staniford Street. Most of it was garden; the three-story mansion house stood on the narrow end, facing the square; and among the nearby smaller houses were two or three inhabited by some of the merchant's many children.

Of these, the Reverend Francis Parkman, minister of the New North Church in Hanover Street,* is the only one who interests us; for his eldest son and namesake was the future historian. Frank had three younger sisters, one of whom, Eliza, acted as his hostess and amanuensis in later life; and a much younger brother, John Eliot, who went to sea and joined the United States Navy in the Civil War.

Frank was so high-strung a child that at the age of eight he was "put out to grass" with his maternal grandfather, Samuel Hall, a merchant who lived in the neighboring town of Medford. The Hall property abutted a rough, rocky, wooded tract of some 3000 acres that even the early Puritans had been unable to farm; it is now a state reservation known as the Middlesex Fells, crisscrossed by trails and bridle paths. There young Parkman spent his holidays, and many other days when he should have been at school, roaming the forest, collecting birds' eggs, trapping squirrels, shooting with bow and arrow, and conjuring up Indians. Here he acquired his lifelong love of the woods and of natural history. Every Saturday, to his great displeasure, his reverend father drove out to fetch him home to keep the Sabbath; but he usually managed to smuggle into the Boston house a few dead birds or a rat or chipmunk, which he stealthily stuffed between services during the tedious hours of the Puritan Sunday.

After four years of rustication, Frank was considered sufficiently robust to stand the rough-and-tumble of a Boston school, the famous Chauncy Hall. There the masters developed their pupils' sense of

---

* Their meetinghouse was eventually purchased by the Catholic Archdiocese of Boston, and as St. Stephen's Church maintains the severe dignity of Bulfinch's architecture.

English style by requiring frequent translations of Virgil and Homer into idiomatic English. There, too, Frank first learned French, which stood him in good stead throughout his life, and he became an enthusiastic reader of Walter Scott and Lord Byron. His parents were now living in the Bowdoin Square mansion built by his grandfather.

In 1840, just before his seventeenth birthday, Francis Parkman entered Harvard College, of which Josiah Quincy was then president. Henry W. Longfellow was lecturing on French and Spanish literature; John W. Webster (who nine years later murdered Frank's uncle George) taught chemistry, and Edward T. Channing headed what would now be called the "English Department"; but "Potty" Channing, as the boys called him, was a completely undepartmentalized character, with a genius for teaching good speaking and writing; among his pupils were Emerson and Thoreau. The studies of Harvard undergraduates were mostly prescribed. Freshmen and sophomores took Latin, Greek, mathematics, natural and ancient history, English rhetoric, chemistry, metaphysics, and one modern language; juniors read Aeschylus, Terence, and Plautus, wrote Greek and Latin prose, went on with their chosen modern language, studied the calculus, and received a few smatterings of philosophy. Juniors also studied the then-famous work by William Smyth, professor at the English Cambridge, called *Lectures on Modern History, from the Irruption of the Northern Nations to the Close of the American Revolution.* They could, if they chose, attend the lectures of Professor Jared Sparks on the American Revolution; and Frank Parkman evidently did, since he received highest honors in history, and dedicated his *Pontiac* to Mr. Sparks. Formidable as this undergraduate curriculum sounds, it actually made very easy demands on a student's time, and boys like Parkman who had outside interests had plenty of opportunity to exercise them.

In the summer of freshman year, Frank made his first journey through the northern New England woods. That seems to have confirmed the love of the wilderness that he had acquired in childhood. "I had a taste for the woods and the Indians," he wrote to Casgrain, over forty years later, "and it was this that turned my attention to forest themes. At one time I thought of writing the history of the Indians, with the Iroquois as a central point; but on reflection I preferred the French colonies as equally suiting my purpose, while offering at once more unity and more variety, as well as more interest to civilized readers." It was early in his sophomore year, when he was only eighteen, that the two influences, academic and outdoors, became "crystallized into a plan of writing the story of what was then known as the 'Old French War,' that is, the war that ended in the conquest of Canada . . . My theme fascinated me, and I was haunted with wilderness images day and night." Before long he "enlarged the plan to include the whole course of the American conflict between France and England, or, in other words, the history of the American forest."

In college with Parkman, although not all in his Class of 1844, were an unusual number of boys who later became famous: Benjamin Apthorp Gould the astronomer (who roomed with him freshman year); Daniel Denison Slade (who went on one of his summer hikes); J. C. Bancroft Davis of the Geneva Tribunal; Colonel Thomas Wentworth Higginson; Stephen H. Phillips, minister of foreign affairs in the Kingdom of Hawaii; William Morris Hunt the painter; William A. Richardson, a future secretary of the treasury; William Crowninshield Endicott, a future secretary of war; Horace Gray, a future justice of the Supreme Court; George F. Hoar, United States Senator from Massachusetts; and three who became great scholars: Francis James Child, Charles Eliot Norton, and George Martin Lane. Frank knew them all and liked most of them. He was distinctly "one of the boys"; member of several short-lived undergraduate clubs, of the then-literary Institute of 1770, and the ever-convivial Hasty Pudding, of which he was president. Handsome and well dressed, he was a favorite with the young ladies at Mr. Papanti's Boston assemblies, but fell in love with an accomplished horsewoman, a high-spirited beauty of Keene, New Hampshire. She resisted his ardent wooing and eventually married someone else.

What distinguished Frank from his fellows in those pre-athletic days was his zest for outdoor life. He would study in the early morning by candlelight in order to spend the sunlit hours out of doors, walking earnestly and briskly with a rifle on his shoulder — and he became a dead shot with the rifle, disdaining, like Westerners, a "scatter-gun." He was the principal patron of the crude college gymnasium, and the admired "strong man" of his class. His pace and endurance on the vacation tours in the northern forest exhausted his companions, few of whom ever went with him twice; he thought nothing of sleeping outdoors without a blanket, harassed by black flies and "no-see-'ems," and living off the country on trout and moose meat. But he kept a journal of each summer's excursion, which proves that, at seventeen or eighteen, he was already well on his way to being a master of English style.

In these excursions, and in his daily regimen, Parkman pushed himself too hard. Late in life he once attributed his accumulation of physical ills to the three days and nights spent in the woods during continual rain, after his spruce-bark canoe fell apart in the rapids of the Magalloway. On another occasion (as Casgrain has already told us) he said that hardships on his Far Western journey of 1846 were responsible. But in his autobiography he admits that his Spartan and ill-advised efforts to cure "conditions of the nervous system abnormal . . . from infancy" were responsible. It is fairly certain that the nervous disorder, which troubled Parkman for at least forty years, was derived, not from one or another accident or overstrain on his outings, but from the relentless driving of his physical powers from his eighteenth until his twenty-seventh year. His symptoms form a now recognizable pattern of neurosis. Consciously or unconsciously, he created a "struggle situation." Given his worship of manliness and contempt for weakness, he could be content with no less than mastery of "the enemy," as he personified the terrible headaches, the insomnia, and the semiblindness.

A comparison with Theodore Roosevelt, born thirty-five years later than Parkman, is relevant. Roosevelt as a boy suffered from poor eyesight and asthma, and endeavored to overcome them by "the strenuous life"; but his weakness was not nearly as serious as Parkman's, and in his day there were physicians who knew what to do about it. So T.R. became in almost every respect a healthy and vigorous man. Parkman either disregarded medical advice, or had none until it was too late; his method of being tough with himself merely made matters worse. Thus, he was denied the balanced sort of life, partly literary, partly of action, that Roosevelt achieved; but by the most severe self-discipline and denial he was able to carry on his writing. It is also worth noting that by the time T.R. entered Harvard, college athletics were going full swing, much as today; it had become "the thing" for college men to play ball games, run, leap and wrestle, row races, go camping, big-game hunting, and all that; whilst in Parkman's youth such activities for a college student were almost unheard-of, and Frank found it difficult to recruit friends for his forest adventures. Consequently, he had to fight the opinions and desires of his parents and older friends; and his urge to justify himself, by proving a success at his chosen tasks, in turn reacted on his health. Roosevelt recognized a certain affinity with Parkman, to whom he dedicated his *Winning of the West;* and Parkman, one may guess, envied the robust health that permitted his young admirer to enter public life and at the same time to shoot, hunt, fight, and write books. But the parallel must not be pushed too far. Parkman was neither egoist or extrovert, but a man dedicated to one pursuit — his history; all else was secondary. Unlike Theodore Roosevelt (and also unlike Henry Adams), Parkman had no quarrel with his education, and he refused to be discouraged when the public refrained from buying his first book of history.

Parkman's first physical breakdown occurred shortly after the beginning of his senior year. His parents then persuaded him to make the grand tour of Europe; but Frank, although well provided with money, made about the most unconventional grand tour possible. In mid-November 1843, just turned twenty, he sailed as the only passenger on board a Mediterranean fruiter barque, the *Nautilus* of Boston. The passage interested him very little, and he was never tempted to write of sea voyages and discoveries. At Gibraltar he left this vessel and made his way by steamer to Malta, Syracuse, Messina, and Palermo. There he procured a guide, three mules, provisions, and a portable stove for a tour of western Sicily. In this manner, spending nights in flea-bitten *alberghi* but catered to by the faithful Luighi, he reversed the course followed by the United States Seventh Army a century later, visiting Agrigento, Selinunte, Marsala, Trapani, and Segesta. His journal of this tour is as fascinating as those of the northern woods. Note these two passages:

The church of the Benedictines [in Messina] is the noblest edifice I have seen. This and others not unlike it have impressed me with new ideas of the Catholic religion. Not exactly, for I reverenced it before as the religion of brave and great men — but now I honor it for itself. They are mistaken who sneer at its ceremonies as a mere mechanical farce: they have a powerful and salutary effect on the mind. Those who have witnessed the services in this Benedictine church, and deny what I say, must either be singularly stupid and insensible by nature, or rendered so by prejudice.

Saturday. I recall what I said of the beauty of the Sicilian women — so far, at least, as concerns those of high rank. This is a holy day. They are all abroad, in carriages and on foot. One passed me in the church of the Capuchin convent, with the black eye, the warm rich cheek, and the bright glance that belong to southern climates, and are beautiful beyond all else.

At Naples, Frank had the good fortune to encounter the Reverend Theodore Parker, then thirty-three years old, a left-wing Unitarian minister but a wise and intelligent cicerone. Together they attended the carnival and the puppet shows, and climbed Vesuvius; with Mrs. Parker they drove by six-horse diligence to Rome, saw all the sights, and were presented to Pope Gregory XVI. Frank's classmate Hunt, the artist, also turned up, and together they wandered over the Alban Hills. In Sicily, as we have seen, Frank had been impressed by the Catholic Church; and as the execution of his life plan required some knowledge of that Church and her ways, he took the original step (which shocked the Reverend Mr. Parker) of joining a retreat in the Passionist Fathers' monastery at Rome. This experience naturally did not afford him a very profound insight into the Catholic mind; but it did help him to understand French Canada, just as his later sojourn among the Sioux helped him to understand Indians; and he used to say with a smile that he found the Sioux more congenial than the monks. They tried to convert him but made not the slightest dent. Young Parkman, brought up a Unitarian, became what he called a "reverent agnostic," and so remained.

After Easter, the youth continued his grand tour as far as Scotland. He returned home by steam packet, just in time to pass his examinations and take part in the festivities of Class Day and Commencement, 1844. As one of the first twenty scholars in his class of sixty-two, he was given a Commencement part — "Romance in America" — and was taken into Phi Beta Kappa.

If Parkman's parents hoped to restore Frank's health by this tour, they were rewarded; but if they expected to woo him from love of the forest to the more reputable fields of scholarship, they were disappointed. Europe fascinated him, but only as a background to America. There was no chance of his becoming an American scholar rooted in Europe, like his college friend Charles Eliot Norton; none whatever of his turning out to be a Miniver Cheevy, or one of those faint and futile expatriates described by Henry James. All his life Parkman had nothing but contempt for "a way of life whose natural fruit is that pallid and emasculate scholarship of which New England has had too many examples."

After another summer tour, in the Berkshires, he entered Harvard Law School at the earnest request of his father, who still hoped that "Frank would settle down." He consoled himself by the thought that knowledge of the law would help him in studying and writing history, and undoubtedly it did. And in the summer of 1845 he extended his travels to the Great Lakes, in order to obtain both visual and documentary material for the first book that he planned to write, *Pontiac's Rebellion*.

It is difficult nowadays to imagine the disappointment among Parkman's friends and well-wishers when he announced that his life work was to be the story of the conflict between France and England in North America. The subject seemed odd for a cultivated gentleman to take up. The proper thing, at that time, was ancient history, or something Spanish. As Barrett Wendell recalled, the New England historians "were generally held by the local public opinion of their time rather more profoundly respectable than anything else on earth." Washington Irving, the senior American historian, had written his *Columbus* and *Conquest of Granada;* Mr. Prescott followed suit with *Ferdinand and Isabella* and *The Conquest of Mexico;* Mr. Ticknor was about to publish his *History of Spanish Literature*, and Mr. Eliot had produced the first volume of his *History of Liberty*, starting with Rome. Those were subjects that proved their authors to be scholars. Mr. Bancroft, to be sure, had already produced three volumes of his *History of the Colonization of the United States*, but he wrote in the Whig tradition, almost as a sequel to Macaulay — and, anyway, he had left literature, temporarily, for Democratic politics. What possible interest could there be for any cultivated reader in the crude struggles of Indians with almost equally barbarous French and English colonists in the wilderness? Nobody, it seems, except Mr. Sparks and the Reverend Mr. Ellis, a local historian, encouraged Parkman's ambition; yet he persisted. And, by the time he was through, there was no question but that North American colonial history was a "respectable" and "scholarly" subject. The trouble was to get young men to write about anything else!

Research for *Pontiac* was begun by Parkman even when he was an undergraduate; most of the available source materials were gathered in his law school years, but he did not follow the life of the typical scholar. "For the student there is, in its season, no better place than the saddle, and no better companion than the rifle or the oar," he wrote late in life. A jockey brought a string of untrained horses to Boston; Parkman and his friends helped to break them, and he perfected his horsemanship by learning to perform circus stunts while riding bareback. That was a form of exercise that stood him in good stead; nobody but an accomplished equestrian could have survived his sojourn with the Sioux.

He had plenty of fun, too. There is extant a letter of his describing a "Class of '44 old-fashioned supper," in the fall of that year, which broke up after 1:00 A.M. with a smashing of empty bottles against the Washington Elm, followed by "a War-dance with scalp-yells in the middle of the Common."

Parkman first broke into print with some blood-and-thunder tales in *The Knickerbocker Magazine* in 1845, based on his own experiences in the northern woods. And then, suddenly, a great opportunity opened. Reading for his law degree, which he took in 1846, had severely strained his eyes. A cousin, Quincy A. Shaw, about to leave on a hunting expedition in the Far West invited Frank to come along. He promptly accepted, since for him it was a heaven-sent opportunity to observe a new frontier and to see Indians in their primitive state. He walked and rode through Pennsylvania, calling on the celebrated Mr. Schoolcraft for Indian lore; then dropped down the Ohio by stern-wheeler and exulted at his first sight of the Father of the Waters, whose descent by La Salle he would chronicle, years later. At St. Louis he presented letters of introduction to the Chouteaus, leaders in that center of the fur industry; and through them he engaged Henry Chatillon, an expert Rocky Mountain trapper, as guide. In May 1846 the young men jumped off from Independence on the Oregon Trail. The story of their adventures is told in Parkman's famous book of that name, and even better in the original journals that Mason Wade has printed.

This journey to the Black Hills had a profound effect, for good and ill, on Parkman's career. Owing to the fortunate circumstance of Chatillon's wife being an Oglala Sioux, the tribe of Sitting Bull and Crazy Horse, Parkman was able to join a roving band of Sioux warriors and to stay with them for weeks. This gave him the unique opportunity of observing Indians who in many respects resembled the

Iroquois, and who were still in the wild and primitive state that Champlain and LaSalle had found their forebears. On the other hand, the experience almost killed him. The burning sun of the high plains injured his eyes; and by sharing the strange diet of the Sioux, prepared in their filthy manner, he suffered a severe attack of dysentery. Nevertheless he kept on, scorning to show any weakness; even participating in mounted buffalo hunts over rough and rocky ground when he was so weak that only firmness of will kept him in the saddle.

The result of this culmination of imprudent overdoing was a complete nervous breakdown — a state that to Parkman, of all people, was intolerable and humiliating. For weeks after returning home, he was deprived of the use of his eyes; he passed sleepless nights in great pain. Yet his determination was such that under these conditions he wrote the account of his Western adventures that has become a classic, *The Oregon Trail*. It was all written literally in the dark, for his eyes could not stand the light. One of his sisters or Quincy Shaw would read the rough notes aloud to the author, who composed while tramping his father's garret in Bowdoin Square; then, with closed eyes, he dictated it to one of these devoted amanuenses; someone else even had to read the proof.

The Oregon Trail and its author have found detractors in recent years because Parkman was not interested in the American westward migration, in the thick of which he found himself; so he has been labeled a "Boston Brahmin," a "Harvard snob," "Federalist oligarch," "Proper Bostonian," and victim of an "Anglo-Saxon superiority complex." Now, although any attempt to label, ticket, or otherwise account for an individual like Francis Parkman is vain, and although nobody properly described by one of the above labels even thought of doing as he did, there is no doubt that he was a gentleman; and, even in the best sense of a much-abused word, an aristocrat. "My political faith," he wrote in 1875, "lies between two vicious extremes, democracy and absolute authority, each of which I detest, the more because it tends to react into the other." Like most gentlemen, he disliked equally the newly rich and democrats of the envious and pushing type; but like a true sportsman he loved primitive people like Indians and trappers and rough-and-ready white folk who were not trying to put on airs.

Although, on his tour of Europe, he had received the cringing obsequiousness then accorded to traveling gentlemen, he much preferred the rude, independent Yankee tavern-keepers whom he encountered in his American travels, and greatly preferred the ordinary run of American country people to the smirking and bowing European peasants. Some of the Western pioneers whom he met he summed up as "a very good set of men, chiefly Missourians"; others as "fine-looking fellows, with an air of frankness, generosity and even courtesy." But others whom he encountered — the ancestors, apparently, of Steinbeck's Okies — he described as "rude and intrusive" and "mean-looking fellows." It is true that Parkman was not interested in the westward movement; it was simply not his dish. He went west to hunt buffalo, view the scenery, and study the Indians — which is what he did. Everyone praises Parkman for seeing through that eighteenth-century myth of the Noble Savage; why, then, scold him for not supporting the nineteenth-century myth of the Noble Democrat, or the twentieth-century myth of the Noble Western Pioneer? His guide, Chatillon, once remarked that "gentlemen of the right sort" could stand hardship better than ordinary people; and if Parkman had not been that kind of gentleman, he could never have surmounted his physical infirmities and we should have had no great history from his pen.

The greater part of 1847–48 was spent by Parkman in search of health at the spa of Brattleboro, Vermont, in New York City, and with a specialist on Staten Island. Under the most trying circumstances — using his eyes for a minute, resting a minute, and not reading for more than an hour a day; hiring a schoolgirl who did not know French to read aloud French documents to him — he managed to finish *Pontiac* early in 1851, and that year it came out. He had to pay for having the book set up and stereotyped, and it was not an immediate success. The reason he published first this, the concluding volume of his series, was that he had already put in a great deal of work on the subject, and feared lest it be his last. But for his indomitable will, it doubtless would have been. "In achievement I expect to fail," he wrote to his cousin and confidante, Mary Eliot Parkman, "but I shall never recoil from endeavor."

In 1850, when he was almost twenty-seven years old, believing that his health was on the way to complete recovery, Parkman wooed and won Catherine Bigelow, daughter of an eminent Boston physician. Of this marriage he wrote in 1853, five years before his wife's death,

"Looking for peace and rest, I found happiness." After the Reverend Francis Parkman's death in 1852, the young couple bought the cottage at Jamaica Pond described by Abbé Casgrain; and for several years they were very happy. Two daughters and a son were born. For several hours a day Mrs. Parkman and her sister Mary Bigelow would read aloud copies of documents from the foreign archives, or take down the historian's dictation for his one novel, *Vassall Morton*. An awful novel it was, and difficult for the young wife to take; since the hero was obviously her husband, and the heroine the high-spirited amazon from Keene who had been his first love. Mrs. Parkman must have been blessed with a sense of humor, and an unusually strong conviction of marital security.

Suddenly darkness descended. The little boy died in 1857, and within a year his mother followed him to the grave. "The enemy," Parkman's malady, moved in on him. He feared lest he go mad. He journeyed to Paris to consult Dr. Brown-Séquard; but that famous eye specialist could do little for him. What he probably needed was a neurologist, but none there was until much later.

To Jamaica Plain he returned in 1859, where his sister Eliza kept house for him and his two little girls in summer, and for him and his widowed mother at 8 Walnut Street, Boston, in winter. His malady was now complicated by arthritis in both knees, so he could no longer walk; reading and writing were out of the question. It was then that he turned to horticulture for solace and an occupation. He could supervise the gardeners, and even do a little raking and weeding himself, from a wheeled chair; and this hobby he turned into a second profession. It used to be a joke in Boston that visiting Englishmen and Frenchmen asked to be presented to Mr. Parkman the historian, while the first person whom visitors from the Netherlands wished to see was Mr. Parkman the horticulturist.

It was not until 1862 that Parkman's "power of mental application was in the smallest degree restored," as he later recalled. Up to then, "several bushels of historical MSS.," copies which he had ordered from European archives, "and fragments of abortive chapters have been packed under lock and key, to bide their time." Now he began to break them out; and when *Pioneers* appeared in 1865, the first volume (except the abortive novel) since *Pontiac*, it was a signal that the harvest was coming in, ripe and full. Indeed, he felt so well in 1863 that he almost screwed up his courage to propose marriage to

Ida, the daughter of Louis Agassiz; but a young cavalry officer, Major Henry Higginson, got ahead of him.

The summer home at Jamaica Plain was kept up; and for a winter residence he moved, in 1864, with his mother, to 50 Chestnut Street, Boston. Although he could have had any of the sunny rooms in the house, he characteristically chose one on the top floor with a northern exposure, toward his beloved Canadian forests. Through the sixty years since his death, in the occupation of his niece Miss Cordner, this room has been kept exactly as he left it.* Souvenirs of the Oregon Trail, photographs of Chatillon and of the Colleoni statue, are on the walls; and the wire frame that he used to guide his pencil when he could not use his eyes is in the desk drawer. In late spring the family, now consisting of Parkman, his sister Eliza, and the two little girls, moved to Jamaica Plain; and after the younger daughter married J. Templeman Coolidge, Jr., who acquired the old Benning Wentworth mansion at Little Harbor, New Hampshire, the historian passed a few weeks of each summer with them; he had a room looking out on the harbor and Leach's Island, which he bought for his daughter. Five times, between 1868 and 1887, he visited France in search of documents; and every other year he made an excursion to the scenes he was writing about, from western Canada to Louisiana and Florida.

It is probable that the extreme difficulties under which Parkman worked, having most of his sources read aloud to him, and either dictating his text or writing it in the dark by means of his wire frame, enhanced the quality of the product. His own impressions of northern woods and western rivers, the data in ancient chronicles and Jesuit relations, the reports of French and English officials were distilled in the crucible of his powerful and creative mind. It can hardly be a coincidence that both leading stylists among American historians, Parkman and Prescott, overcame the handicap of partial blindness; and, out of the semidarkness in which they worked, wove tapestries of brilliant prose.

Although Parkman once wrote that he "loathed the drudgery of historical research," I for one find the statement hard to believe, because he never employed a research assistant, and his relish over the

---

* Miss Cordner died shortly after *The Parkman Reader* appeared, and the contents of the historian's study were then transferred, intact, to a similarly situated room at 87 Mt. Vernon Street, the home of the Colonial Society of Massachusetts.

discovery of new source material, which complicated and lengthened his task, was obvious. He revised his text again and again, and was scrupulously accurate in checking his quotations with the sources.

It was very irksome to Parkman to be a mere spectator of the Civil War, in which several friends and classmates lost their lives, and to be unable to take part in public affairs. The demagoguery and corruption of the postwar era was a grievous disappointment to him, as to Henry Adams. He seems to have expected that war would purge the Republic of its grossness and restore the rule of an educated élite.

Except for an occasional article or review in *The Nation* or *The North American Review* or in horticultural journals, Parkman confined his writing to his history. As each volume rolled from the press — *Pioneers* (1865), *Jesuits* (1867), *Great West* (1869), *Old Régime* (1874), *Frontenac* (1877), *Montcalm and Wolfe* (1884), and, finally, *Half-Century of Conflict* (1892) — his fame increased. Yet his health was never fully restored. Even when his eyes were functioning fairly well, arthritis or water on the knee compelled him to walk with two canes. In 1889, he wrote that he had been getting only two or three hours' sleep in the twenty-four for the last five years. The two last works were the only ones of which he was able to write a part with his own hand.

It must not be supposed that his works had universal acclaim. American, British, and British Canadian reviewers were generally enthusiastic; but many French Canadians, accustomed to view their history through rose-colored glasses as a romantic lost cause, began to attack Parkman after *The Old Régime* appeared, in 1874. He had expected that they would. In the Preface to that work he wrote: "Some of the results here reached are of a character which I regret, since they cannot be agreeable to persons for whom I have a very cordial regard. The conclusions drawn from the facts may be a matter of opinion, but it will be remembered that the facts themselves can be overthrown only by overthrowing the evidence on which they rest, or bringing forward counter-evidence of equal or greater strength; and neither task will be found an easy one." His research in Paris had brought out many incidents of clerical politics in Canada that had long been forgotten, and that the French Canadians thought should have been left in a pious oblivion.

Parkman did not attempt to conceal his indignation at Jesuit intrigues against La Salle and Frontenac. His friend Margry, after reading what he wrote, or was about to write, on the subject, begged him to remember the good that the Jesuits had done in Canada during the infancy of the colony, when it was neglected by the French government; and added this warning: "Watch yourself, my friend; for the honor of the historian is to elevate himself above the preoccupations of his era, of his party, even of his country." Let the reader decide for himself whether or not Parkman followed this good advice.

Moreover, besides the theme of French heroism, piety, and tenacity, of which French Canadians were proud, there was another theme running through his work that they could not be expected to accept. That was the antithesis: English liberty versus French absolutism, Protestant freedom versus Catholic authority, with victory to the forces of light and progress.

Nevertheless, many French Canadians have appreciated Parkman's services to their people, and have been willing to overlook his theories because of the charm of his narrative and his fidelity to historic truth. It was proposed, and apparently decided, that the Université Laval confer on him an honorary degree. The news leaked out in Quebec and provoked such a fury of opposition that the university authorities were frightened and wrote to Parkman that he could not have it. But an honorary degree was conferred on him in the following year (1879) by McGill University.

When *Montcalm and Wolfe* appeared, a new outcry arose because of Parkman's treatment of the expulsion of the Acadians. He did not attempt to justify that unfortunate act, but he did point out that equally to blame with the English were the French priests and other emissaries who kept the Acadians and Indians stirred up to a point where they became a menace to the English settlers, and then let them down. No French Canadian, however, could regard the expulsion as anything but indefensible and wholly abominable. Even Abbé Casgrain entered the lists against Parkman, arguing that he had ignored or suppressed the real reason for removing the Acadians: the greed of New England Yankees for their land. Parkman was not indifferent to these clerical attacks on his integrity; but Stoic that he was, he gave no sign of being wounded; and he answered his critics in kind, by reviewing Casgrain's *Pèlerinage au pays d'Evangeline* in *The Nation*. And friendship outlasted the dispute. Shortly after, their correspondence was resumed, and continued to the day of Parkman's death.

The historian was never a severe and lonely man, detached from time and place, pontifical or sacerdotal, living in a past world of his imagination, as he has sometimes been described. He was no reformer or protagonist of "every good cause," like many Bostonians of his class; but he had plenty of compatriots who were neither liberals nor reformers and who agreed with him in deploring the tendencies of the times. He read Godkin's *Nation*, voted Mugwump, and occasionally reviewed a book or wrote an article pointing out the sins of democracy for *The North American Review*. He liked people, loved to have his friends in to dinner or in the afternoon, and even dined out as much as his health permitted, although he could not stand crowds. Unlike most American men of letters of his generation, he never cultivated the English nobility or the French noblesse, unless they had documents pertaining to his theme. He saw to it that his daughters were properly presented to society, and both were happily married in 1880. He attended his college class functions regularly, belonged to the Saturday Club (that mutual-appreciation society of the New England literati), as well as to the Historical Society and other organizations enjoyed by elderly Bostonians. He helped to organize the convivial St. Botolph Club on the model of London's Savage and New York's Century, served for six years as its president, and took part in its jovial gatherings, from which Edward Everett Hale vainly endeavored to banish alcoholic beverages. He was one of the founders of the Archaeological Institute of America and took a lively interest in its work, directed by the Bandeliers, in the American Southwest. He served faithfully as an Overseer of Harvard College and Fellow of the Corporation for many years, and on numerous committees. One who knew him well said that "there was always about his eyes and mouth an expression of kindly, alert interest in what was doing, which did away with the notion of severity." He was, essentially, a simple, uncomplicated person, with a direct approach to everyone and everything; kindly, with a whimsical sense of humor, and naturally sociable; but he had dedicated his life to a great literary task, and that always came first.

Perhaps the best test of an author's humanity is his attitude toward small children. Parkman loved to have his grandchildren and their friends about him, especially at Little Harbor, where they ran wild, playing and shrieking; but he never complained of the noise, and for their amusement he made up stories about personified animals. A collection of china cats became endowed with life as he and the children handled them together, and letters were produced, supposedly from errant family felines who had gone hunting and never returned.

Want of money never troubled Parkman after his early married life — when it troubled him a good deal, as he and his wife started housekeeping with a total annual income of slightly over $400. From his grandfather and father, who died in 1852, he inherited enough to live according to his simple tastes, until his books began to bring in royalties; but he received very little net from his writings, because the profits from one volume went toward copying documents for the next, or for travel. He regarded his inheritance as a trust, which conferred on him the obligation to make all the return he could to his country, in the form of historical literature. Owing in part to his independent means, and perhaps even more to his frugal manner of living, Parkman was never tempted to teach history, or even to go on the lecture circuit, as almost all the New England literati of his day were forced to do. However, when the Bussey Institution, the agricultural department of Harvard University, was opened in 1871 on one of the country estates adjoining Parkman's Jamaica Pond cottage, he was prevailed upon to accept the appointment of professor of horticulture, with a salary of $2000 a year. The catalogue announced that the following year, after the freshmen had been indoctrinated, he would give a course on plant propagation and the management of hothouses, nurseries, flower and fruit gardens. But even the light duties of the first year, supervising the building of greenhouses and planting in what later became the Arnold Arboretum, so fatigued the historian that he resigned the chair before giving any formal instruction.

A good example of Parkman's practical side is the *affaire Margry*. That crotchety French archivist had under lock and key a mass of documents about La Salle and French exploration of the Far West, and would let nobody see them until and unless he could get funds for publication. The French government was not interested; and Parkman's friends, whom he had solicited for subscriptions, were too badly hit by the fire of 1871 to come through. But he did not despair. By writing dozens of letters a day, stirring up the Wisconsin and other Western historical societies, and playing on the idea that these documents were essential to the history of the Great West, he enlisted the support of several Congressmen, notably the future President James A. Garfield, and actually procured an appropriation of $10,000. That, however, was not the end of it. Mr. Spofford, the librarian of Congress, appointed paymaster, hated to see the money go, and easily persuaded himself that Margry was cheating; the two exchanged furious letters, and Parkman had to calm them down. Eventually the six volumes of Margry's *Découvertes et établissements des français dans l'ouest et dans le sud de l'Amérique* were published. All Parkman got out of them was a few new facts for revising his volume on the discovery of the Mississippi.

In the summer of 1892, with the publication of *Half-Century of Conflict,* the last gap in the series was filled; the last voussoir fell into its planned place in the great arch. Yet, even then, the indefatigable historian carried on. Some new documents on the amusing rivalries between La Tour and d'Aunay in L'Acadie, and the absurd attempts of Governor Winthrop to play international politics, persuaded him to write fifty new pages, "The Feudal Chiefs of Acadia," for a new edition of *The Old Régime,* and this he saw through the press. He was about to begin a complete revision of the entire series when, in 1893, he suffered successive attacks of pleurisy and phlebitis. From both he recovered, and on his seventieth birthday, in September, he received many friends at his cottage. It was a warm and lovely autumn, which tempted him to linger on in the country; but one day in early November, after returning from a short row on Jamaica Pond, he suffered a sudden and severe attack of peritonitis. For three days more the heroic historian struggled to live, but on the 8th he breathed his last.

He was buried from King's Chapel, the Westminster Abbey for unchurched Bostonians. Harvard University held in his honor a commemorative service at which addresses were made by President Eliot, Justin Winsor, and John Fiske. The last-named then well said, "Of all American historians [Parkman was] the most deeply and peculiarly American [yet] at the same time the broadest and most cosmopolitan"; that his history of France and England in the New World was "a book for all mankind and for all time."

3

Sir Winston Churchill: Nobel Prize Winner

From THE SATURDAY REVIEW GALLERY (New York: Simon & Schuster, 1959) *pages 413–18.*

In 1953 I accepted with alacrity an offer by the editor of New York's leading literary weekly to write a piece on Winston Churchill, who had been awarded the Nobel Prize for Literature. It was printed in THE SATURDAY REVIEW *for October 31, 1953, and reprinted in the magazine's* GALLERY *six years later. Here it is.*

THE ENTIRE HISTORICAL PROFESSION is honored in the honor to Sir Winston; for it is the first time in half a century that an historian has won the Nobel Prize for Literature; in 1902 it was bestowed on Theodor Mommsen. Restricted as this prize is to "literature of an idealist tendency," few historians would even qualify, since few are able to apply "idealist" tendencies to the past. Even if we define "idealist" as synonymous with "creative," what historians might have won the prize — assuming, of course, that the prize had always existed? Herodotus certainly, and Thucydides. Gibbon would have rated, and Macaulay and Lord Clarendon, the Winston Churchill of Charles II's day. Our own Parkman and Prescott, certainly. For Italy, Ferrero; for France, Henri Martin; possibly Sorel. And of living historians, George Macaulay Trevelyan. But I cannot for the life of me think of another I would have voted for if I had been a judge.

There is no question but that Churchill is a great historian. He has verve, style, honesty, imagination, and, above all, superb craftsmanship.

How did he learn the craft? The young men and women today who are training to be historians wish to know. Well, my answer is background, innate capacity, experience, and a vigorous course of self-teaching; that each was essential, but no one would have worked without the others.   Sir Winston is a descendant of the great Marlborough, and the son of Lord Randolph Churchill, an important figure in Victorian politics; and, on the distaff side, he is a member of our oldest hereditary society, the Cincinnati.   Thus he absorbed history *through the skin*.   History was in the air during his youth.   People discussed it at his parents' table.   He knew from childhood that he was heir to a great tradition.   And right here is an important lesson for us.   We have plenty of intelligent youths in the United States and Canada with a background similar to Churchill's, but we do not recruit them for Clio.   We choose graduate students from the top-grade college graduates and wonder why they do not do better when it comes to writing history.   The trouble with these lads is that, no matter how bright they may be, they never can catch up with the sort of thing that Winston had from birth.   Call this snobbery if you will; it is the truth.

So we are back at the question, how did Winston become a great historian, the only one to win the Nobel Prize for Literature?   First and foremost, this infiltration of history through the skin.   Second, a prodigious memory, which enables him to repeat verbatim a lecture that has interested him, or a whole Shakespeare play.   Third, Harrow-on-the-Hill.   He has told us about that school in *My Early Life* (1944).   He hated the classical education forced on him, but he had to go through with it.   He hated to translate Caesar, Ovid, Virgil, Horace, and Martial, even with a trot.   And he doubled his work in what we call English composition, because he swapped tasks with a good classicist who did his translations while he wrote the other fellow's English themes.   Most of all, the encouragement of a wise headmaster and the English system of education, which requires every teacher, no matter what his subject, to teach English.   In the United States only the teachers in the English department teach English; the others let their students get by with any old gobbledygook; an aspiring historian has two strikes against him at the start.   Winston hated Latin, but I will wager that when he read Caesar's *Commentaries,* the boy said to himself, "I'll have something like that to write one day, and I'll do it even better."   Which he did.

Winston's school record was so poor that his father refused to let him go on to Oxford or Cambridge; he sent him to Sandhurst for an army career.   That and the Royal Navy were the only respectable alternatives in those days for English boys of his class who did not make good in public school. Winston went through Sandhurst and obtained his commission. Then began his real literary education. It was in the winter of 1896–97, in his twenty-second year, when, as an officer of the Fourth Hussars, he was stationed at Bangalore, in India. He had already "picked up a wide vocabulary . . . and a liking for words, and for the feel of words fitting and falling into their places like pennies in the slot" — a gift that he never lost. Now he wished to find out about things, and concepts. *Ethics.* What did that mean? He had to read Aristotle to find out. *History.* What was that? He had had to read no history at school except a wretched abstract of Hume. So he sent for sets of Gibbon and Macaulay, and devoured them. His cousin and my friend Sir Shane Leslie, to whom he gave one of his volumes of Gibbon, tells me that the margins are covered with Winston's questions, remarks, criticisms. All that was vital for his literary future. He had read critically the two great stylists among modern English historians. He was too sensible to try to imitate their style. But the beauty, the muscular strength, the majestic cadence of their style did something to his mind, and there are distant echoes of Gibbon and Macaulay in his latest volume. Here is another lesson that our American historical students have never learned. Gibbon to them is "old stuff," Macaulay is "old hat," Parkman is "drum and trumpet history," and so on. They never read through an historian who is pre-eminent for his style. Without one inspiring example how can they become first-rate themselves?

Churchill's first serious history, *The River War: An Historic Account of the Reconquest of the Soudan,* which came out fifty-four years ago, was not a great book. It was just the average sort of contemporary history, showing the author's rather unusual flair for vivid description. For instance: "Since they [the Seaforth Highlanders] would not run, their loss was heavy, and it was a strange sight — the last vivid impression of the day — to watch them struggling through the deep sand, with the dust knocked up into clouds by the bullets which struck all around them. Very few escaped, and the bodies of the killed lay thickly dotting the river bed with heaps of dirty-white. Then at 8:25 the 'Cease Fire' sounded and the battle of the Atkara ended."

This is good writing; but any first-class newspaper correspondent could have done as well; and no critic reading *The River War* predicted, "Here is a great historian." Churchill had to work constantly to improve his style. It would be a fascinating study to follow him, book by book; but we have no time for it here. His competence developed with his political experience. Polybius, twenty-one centuries ago, wrote that historians should be men of action; for without a personal knowledge of how things happen, a writer will inevitably distort the true relations and importance of events. Basil Williams quotes a French writer: *"Ecrire l'histoire, c'est agir; et c'est pourquoi il convient que l'historien soit homme d'action."* But most of our men of action today have neither the time nor the capacity to write; Churchill found the time and had the capacity. He wrote when he was out of power about the Duke of Marlborough, and he wrote when he was in power about the events that he observed; and he went right on improving.

Neither of his greater histories, his memories of World War I or his *Second World War*, is impartial, and he never pretended that any of them was; but each is honest. The books describe events as he saw them, and in the most arresting and intriguing prose. Turn, if you will, to *Their Finest Hour* (*Second World War*, Volume II) pages 383 and following, and read the story of how Professor Lindemann (now Lord Cherwell), Winston's *éminence grise*, brought in one of his former pupils to explain what he knew of one of the Germans' secret weapons, the "Knickebein," and how the British dealt with it. Could anything be more fascinating? Turn to *The Hinge of Fate* (Volume IV), on the Battles of the Coral Sea and Midway. He boiled it all down from one of my own volumes — and handsomely acknowledged his debt in the Preface — but I could never have done it so well myself. And the ringing conclusion to these two great naval battles is all Churchill:

The annals of war at sea present no more intense, heart-shaking shock than these two battles, in which the qualities of the United States Navy and Air Force and the American race shone forth in splendour. The novel and hitherto utterly unmeasured conditions which air warfare had created made the speed of action and the twists of fortune more intense than has ever been witnessed before. But the bravery and self-devotion of the American airmen and sailors and the nerve and skill of their leaders was the foundation of all. As the Japanese Fleet withdrew to their far-off home ports their commanders knew not only that their aircraft-carrier struggle was irretrievably broken, but that they were confronted with a will-power and passion in the foe they had challenged worthy of the highest traditions of their Samurai ancestors and backed by a development of power, numbers, and science to which no limit could be set.

Note his use of vibrant words and phrases: "splendour," "twists of fortune," "will-power and passion"; note the reference to history, of which he was always conscious even if, in this case, it was Japanese history; and he even gets in a tribute to American production and science. Not only sentence and paragraph structure, but choice of words — le mot juste — are vital elements in Churchill's craft. Tens of thousands of people, not only English-speaking, but from all parts of the world, read Churchill when they will read no other history of World War II. Churchill was not at Coral Sea or Midway; he had little time to know what went on in the Pacific; but he recognizes brave deeds and the effect of great decisions when he hears of them; and he places our achievements in the Pacific on the same plane as those of the sailors and soldiers of his king in Africa, Asia, and Europe.

According to the news release about the Nobel Prize, it was conferred on Churchill not only for his books, but for his oratory. And his oratory is indeed superb. We all know his aphorisms, such as "blood, sweat, and tears." One of the finest set speeches I have ever listened to was his when he received an honorary degree at Harvard in September 1943. Note the boldness and truth of this one paragraph:

Twice in my lifetime the long arm of destiny has reached across the ocean and involved the entire life and manhood of the United States in a deadly struggle. There was no use saying: "We don't want it, we won't have it; our forebears left Europe to avoid those quarrels; we have founded a new world which has no contact with the old" — there was no use in that. The long arm reaches out remorselessly and everyone's existence, environment, and outlook undergo a swift and irresistible change.

After the official ceremonies were over Churchill was asked informally to address the young soldiers and sailors then training at the university. He was unprepared; he had not even been told that this was expected of him; but this is what he said, in part (and, remember, this was before Salerno, before Tarawa, before Normandy):

I have no reason to suppose that the climax of the war has been reached. I have no reason to suppose that the heaviest sacrifices in blood and life do not lie before the armed forces of Britain and America. I know of no reason for supposing that the climax of the war has been reached even in Europe, and certainly not in Asia . . . I bid you all good fortune and success, and I earnestly trust that when you find yourselves alongside our soldiers and sailors you will feel that we are your worthy brothers in arms. And you shall know that we will never tire nor weaken. We shall march with you into every quarter of the globe to establish a reign of justice and law among men.

In that time and setting this was the most eloquent extempore address I have ever heard.

Nobody, and certainly not Churchill, will claim that his *Second World War,* of which the sixth and final volume will shortly appear, is "objective." He was too close to events, too much a part of them. He had neither the time nor the staff to sift everything to the bottom; consequently some assumptions of the time are accepted as facts, when the facts turn out to be different. But the general impression is correct. It is splendid history; magnanimous to our enemies; understanding and generous to England's allies, even to those who have sadly defected since 1945; vibrant with the passion and fervor of the time; written in muscular, virile prose.

So, here's a "Hurrah!" for the Nobel Prize Committee, and a three-times-three for "Winnie." And if any historian, British or American, won't join in the cheer, let him be condemned to sit forever in a college library, reading Ph.D. dissertations!

4

History As a Literary Art

From BY LAND AND BY SEA (New York: Alfred A. Knopf, 1953), *Chapter XIII*.

In the period between the two world wars, I became exercised over the bad English used by students of history, especially graduate students, and over the dull, pedantic manner in which many historical monographs were being presented. The hortatory essay that follows was first composed for my seminar in American history. In 1946 my friend Walter Whitehill asked me to contribute something toward starting a new series of Old South Leaflets. I offered him this, he accepted it, and to our astonishment it had an unexpected success as a twenty-five-cent pamphlet. You can still buy it at that price from the Old South Meeting House, Boston. It was even reviewed in THE SATURDAY REVIEW OF LITERATURE *and mentioned in* THE AMERICAN HISTORICAL REVIEW!

Since the essay incorporates a major part of my message to readers, students, and writers of history, I have included it here.

EXPLORING AMERICAN HISTORY has been a very absorbing and exciting business now for three quarters of a century. Thousands of graduate students have produced thousands of monographs on every aspect of the history of the Americas. But the American reading public for the most part is blissfully ignorant of this vast output. When John Citizen feels the urge to read history, he goes to the novels of Kenneth Roberts or Margaret Mitchell, not to the histories of Professor this or Doctor that. Why?

Because American historians, in their eagerness to present facts and their laudable concern to tell the truth, have neglected the literary aspects of their craft. They have forgotten that there is an art of writing history.

Even the earliest colonial historians, like William Bradford and Robert Beverley, knew that; they put conscious art into their narratives. And the historians of our classical period, Prescott and Motley, Irving and Bancroft, Parkman and Fiske, were great literary crafts-men. Their many-volumed works sold in sufficient quantities to give them handsome returns; even today they are widely read. But the first generation of seminar-trained historians, educated in Germany or by teachers trained there, imagined that history would tell itself, provided one was honest, thorough, and painstaking. Some of them went so far as to regard history as pure science and to assert that writers thereof had no more business trying to be "literary" than did writers of statistical reports or performers of scientific experiments. Professors warned their pupils (quite unnecessarily) against "fine writ-ing," and endeavored to protect their innocence from the seductive charm of Washington Irving or the masculine glamour of Macaulay. And in this flight of history from literature the public was left behind. American history became a bore to the reader and a drug on the market; even historians with something to say and the talent for say-ing it (Henry Adams, for instance) could not sell their books. The most popular American histories of the period 1890–1905 were those of John Fiske, a philosopher who had no historical training, but wrote with life and movement.

Theodore Roosevelt in his presidential address before the Ameri-can Historical Association in 1912 made a ringing plea to the young historian to do better: "He must ever remember that while the worst offense of which he can be guilty is to write vividly and inaccurately, yet that unless he writes vividly he cannot write truthfully; for no amount of dull, painstaking detail will sum up the whole truth unless the genius is there to paint the truth."

And although American historians cannot hope, as Theodore Roo-sevelt did, to "watch the nearing chariots of the champions," or to look forward to the day when "for us the war-horns of King Olaf shall wail across the flood, and the harps sound high at festivals in forgotten halls," we may indeed "show how the land which the pioneers won slowly and with incredible hardship was filled in two generations by the overflow from the countries of western and central Europe." We may describe the race, class, and religious conflicts that immigration has engendered, and trace the rise of the labor movement with a lit-erary art that compels people to read about it. You do not need chariots and horsemen, harps and war-horns, to make history inter-esting.

Theodore Roosevelt's trumpet call fell largely on deaf ears, at least in the academic historical profession. A whole generation has passed without producing any really great works on American history. Plenty of good books, valuable books, and new interpretations and explorations of the past; but none with fire in the eye, none to make a young man want to fight for his country in war or live to make it a better country in peace. There has been a sort of chain reaction of dullness. Professors who have risen to positions of eminence by writing dull, solid, valuable monographs that nobody reads outside the profession, teach graduate students to write dull, solid, valuable monographs like theirs; the road to academic security is that of writing dull, solid, valuable monographs. And so the young men who have a gift for good writing either leave the historical field for something more exciting, or write more dull, solid, valuable monographs. The few professional historians who have had a popular following or appeal during the last thirty years are either men like Allan Nevins who were trained in some juicier profession like journalism, or men and women like the Beards who had the sense to break loose young from academic trammels.

In the meantime, the American public has become so sated by dull history textbooks in school and college that it won't read history unless it is disguised as something else under a title such as *The Flowering of Florida, The Epic of the East,* or *The Growth of the American Republic.* Or, more often, they get what history they want from historical novels.

Now, I submit, this is a very bad situation. The tremendous plowing up of the past by well-trained scholars is all to the good, so far as it goes. Scholars know more about America's past than ever; they are opening new furrows and finding new artifacts, from aboriginal arrowheads to early twentieth-century corset stays. But they are heaping up the pay dirt for others. Journalists, novelists, and free-lance writers are the ones who extract the gold; and they deserve every ounce they get because they are the ones who know how to write histories that people care to read. What I want to see is a few more Ph.D.'s in history winning book-of-the-month adoptions and reaping the harvest of dividends. They can do it, too, if they will only use the same industry in presenting history as they do in compiling it.

Mind you, I intend no disparagement of historians who choose to devote their entire energies to teaching. Great teachers do far more good to the cause of history than mediocre writers. Such men, for instance, as the late H. Morse Stephens, who stopped writing (which he never liked) as soon as he obtained a chair in this country, and the late Edwin F. Gay, who never began writing, inspired thousands of young men and initiated scores of valuable books. Thank God for these gifted teachers, I say; universities should seek out, encourage, and promote them far more than they do. My remarks are addressed to young people who have the urge to write history, and wish to write it effectively.

There are no special rules for writing history; any good manual of rhetoric or teacher of composition will supply the rules for writing English. But what terrible stuff passes for English in Ph.D. dissertations, monographs, and articles in historical reviews! Long, involved sentences that one has to read two or three times in order to grasp their meaning; poverty in vocabulary, ineptness of expression, weakness in paragraph structure, frequent misuse of words, and, of late, the introduction of pseudoscientific and psychological jargon. There is no fundamental cure for this except better teaching of English in our schools and colleges, and by every teacher, whatever his other subject may be. If historical writing is infinitely better in France than in America, and far better in the British Isles and Canada than in the United States, it is because every French and British teacher of history drills his pupils in their mother tongue, requiring a constant stream of essays and reports, and criticizing written work, not only as history, but as literature. The American university teacher who gives honor grades to students who have not yet learned to write English, for industrious compilations of facts or feats of memory, is wanting in professional pride or competence.

Of course, what we should all like to attain in writing history is style. "The sense for style," says Whitehead in his *Aims of Education*, "is an aesthetic sense, based on admiration for the direct attainment of a foreseen end, simply and without waste. Style in art, style in literature, style in science, style in logic, style in practical execution, have fundamentally the same aesthetic qualities, namely, attainment and restraint. Style, in its finest sense, is the last acquirement of the educated mind; it is also the most useful. It pervades the whole being . . . Style is the ultimate morality of mind."

Unfortunately, there is no royal road to style. It cannot be attained by mere industry; it can never be achieved through imitation, although it may be promoted by example. Reading the greatest literary artists among historians will help; but do not forget that what was acceptable style in 1850 might seem turgid today. We can still read Macaulay with admiration and pleasure; we can still learn paragraph structure and other things from Macaulay; but anyone who tried to imitate Macaulay today would be a pompous ass.

Just as Voltaire's ideal curé advises his flock not to worry about going to heaven, but to do right and probably by God's grace they will get there, so the young writer of history had better concentrate on day-by-day improvement in craftsmanship. Then, perhaps, he may find someday that his prose appeals to a large popular audience; that, in other words, he has achieved style through simple, honest, straightforward writing.

A few hints as to the craft may be useful to budding historians. First and foremost, *get writing!* Young scholars generally wish to secure the last fact before writing anything, like General McClellan refusing to advance (as people said) until the last mule was shod. It is a terrible strain, isn't it, to sit down at a desk, with your notes all neatly docketed, and begin to write? You pretend to your wife that you mustn't be interrupted; but, actually, you welcome a ring of the telephone, a knock at the door, or a bellow from the baby as an excuse to break off. Finally, after smoking sundry cigarettes and pacing about the house two or three times, you commit a lame paragraph or two to paper. By the time you get to the third, one bit of information you want is lacking. What a relief! Now you must go back to the library or the archives to do some more digging. That's where you are happy! And what you turn up there leads to more questions and prolongs the delicious process of research. Half the pleas I have heard from graduate students for more time or another grant-in-aid are mere excuses to postpone the painful drudgery of writing.

There is the "indispensablest beauty in knowing how to get done," said Carlyle. In every research there comes a point, which you should recognize like a call of conscience, when you must get down to writing. And when you once are writing, go on writing as long as you can; there will be plenty of time later to shove in the footnotes or return to the library for extra information. Above all, *start* writing. Nothing is more pathetic than the "gonna" historian, who from graduate school on is always "gonna" write a magnum opus but never completes his research on the subject, and dies without anything to show for a lifetime's work.

Dictation is usually fatal to good historical writing. Write out your first draft in longhand or, if you compose easily on the typewriter, type it out yourself, revise with pencil or pen, and have it retyped clean. Don't stop to consult your notes for every clause or sentence; it is better to get what you have to say clearly in your mind and dash it off; then, after you have it down, return to your notes and compose your next few pages or paragraphs. After a little experience you may well find that you think best with your fingers on the typewriter keys or your fountain pen poised over the paper. For me, the mere writing of a few words seems to point up vague thoughts and make jumbled facts array themselves in neat order. Whichever method you choose, composing before you write or as you write, do not return to your raw material or verify facts and quotations or insert footnotes until you have written a substantial amount, an amount that will increase with practice. It is significant that two of our greatest American historians, Prescott and Parkman, were nearly blind during a good part of their active careers. They had to have the sources read to them and turn the matter over and over in their minds before they could give anything out; and when they gave, *they gave!*

Now, the purpose of this quick, warm synthesis between research, thinking, and writing is to attain the three prime qualities of historical composition — clarity, vigor, and objectivity. You must think about your facts, analyze your material, and decide exactly what you mean before you can write it so that the average reader will understand. Do not fall into the fallacy of supposing that "facts speak for themselves." Most of the facts that you excavate, like other relics of past human activity, are dumb things; it is for you to make them speak by proper selection, arrangement, and emphasis. Dump your entire collection of facts on paper, and the result will be unreadable if not incomprehensible.

So, too, with vigor. If your whole paragraph or chapter is but a hypothesis, say so at the beginning, but do not bore and confuse the reader with numerous "but"s, "except"s, "perhaps"s, and "possibly"s. Use direct rather than indirect statements, the active rather than the passive voice, and make every sentence and paragraph an organic whole. Above all, if you are writing historical narrative make it move. Do not take time out in the middle of a political or military campaign to introduce special developments or literary trends, as Mc-Master did to the confusion of his readers. Place those admittedly important matters in a chapter or chapters by themselves so that you do not lose your reader's attention by constant interruption.

That brings us to the third essential quality — objectivity. Keep the reader constantly in mind. You are not writing history for yourself or for the professors who are supposed to know more about it than you do. Assume that you are writing for intelligent people who know nothing about your particular subject but whom you wish to interest and attract. I once asked the late Senator Beveridge why his *Life of John Marshall,* despite its great length and scholarly apparatus, was so popular. He replied: "The trouble with you professors of history is that you write for each other. I write for people almost completely ignorant of American history, as I was when I began my research."

A few more details. Even if the work you are writing does not call for footnotes, keep them in your copy until the last draft, for they will enable you to check up on your facts, statements, and quotations. And since accuracy is the prime virtue of the historian, this checking must be done, either by the author or by someone else. You will be surprised by the mistakes that creep in between a first rough draft and a final typed copy. And the better you write, the more your critics will enjoy finding misquotations and inaccuracies.

The matter of handling quotations seems to be a difficult one for young historians. There is nothing that adds so much to the charm and effectiveness of a history as good quotations from the sources, especially if the period is somewhat remote. But there is nothing so disgusting to the reader as long, tedious, broken quotations in small print, especially those in which, to make sense, the author has to interpolate words in brackets. Young writers are prone to use quotations in places where their own words would be better, and to incorporate in the text source excerpts that belong in footnotes or appendices. Avoid ending chapters with quotations, and never close your book with one.

Above all, do not be afraid to revise and rewrite. Reading aloud is a good test — historians' wives have to stand a lot of that! A candid friend who is not an historian, and so represents the audience you are trying to reach, is perhaps the best "dog" to try it on. Even if he has little critical sense, it is encouraging to have him stay awake. My good friend Lucien Price years ago listened with a pained expression to a bit of my early work. "Now, just what do you mean by that?" he asked after a long, involved, pedantic, and quote-larded paragraph. I told him in words of one syllable, or perhaps two. "Fine!" said he. "I understand that. Now write down what you said; throw the other away!"

Undoubtedly the writer of history can enrich his mind and broaden his literary experience as well as better his craftsmanship by his choice of leisure reading. If he is so fortunate as to have had a classical education, no time will be better spent in making him an effective historian than in reading Latin and Greek authors. Both these ancient languages are such superb instruments of thought that a knowledge of them cures slipshod English and helps one to attain a clear, muscular style. All our greatest historical stylists — notably Prescott, Parkman, Fiske, and Frederick J. Turner — had a classical education and read the ancient historians in the original before they approached American history.

If you have little Latin and less Greek and feel unable to spare the time and effort to add them to your stock of tools, read the ancient classics in the best literary translations, such as North's Plutarch, Rawlinson's Herodotus, Gilbert Murray's Euripides, and, above all, Jowett's or Livingstone's Thucydides. Through them you will gain the content and spirit of the ancient classics, which will break down your provincialism, refresh your spirit, and give you a better philosophical insight into the ways of mankind than most of such works as the new science of psychology has brought forth. Moreover, you will be acquiring the same background as many of the great Americans of past generations, thus aiding your understanding of them.

The reading of English classics will tend in the same direction, and will also be a painless and unconscious means of improving your literary style. Almost every English or American writer of distinction is indebted to Shakespeare and the English Bible. The Authorized Version is not only the great source book of spiritual experience of English-speaking peoples; it is a treasury of plain, pungent words and muscular phrases, beautiful in themselves and with long associations, which we are apt to replace by smooth words lacking in punch, or by hackneyed or involved phrases. Here are a few examples chosen in five minutes from my desk Bible: I Samuel 1: 28: "I have lent him to the Lord." What an apt phrase for anyone bringing up his son for the Church! Why say "loaned" instead of "lent"? Isaiah 22:5: "For it is a day of trouble, and of treading down, and of perplexity." In brief, just what we are going through today. But most modern historians would not feel that they were giving the reader his money's worth unless they wrote: "It is an era of agitation, of a progressive decline in the standard of living, and of uncertainty as to the correct policy." Romans 11:25: "Wise in your own conceits." This epigram has often been used, but a modern writer would be tempted to express the thought in some such cumbrous manner as "Expert within the limits of your own fallacious theories."

Of course much of the Biblical phraseology is obsolete, and there are other literary quarries for historians. You can find many appropriate words, phrases, similes, and epigrams in American authors such as Mark Twain, Emerson, and Thoreau. I have heard an English economist push home a point to a learned audience with a quotation from *Alice in Wonderland;* American historians might make more use of *Huckleberry Finn.*

The historian can learn much from the novelist. Most writers of fiction are superior to all but the best historians in characterization and description. If you have difficulty in making people and events seem real, see if you cannot learn the technique from American novelists such as Sherwood Anderson, Joseph Hergesheimer, and Margaret Mitchell. For me, the greatest master of all is Henry James. He used a relatively simple and limited vocabulary; but what miracles he wrought with it! What precise and perfect use he makes of words to convey the essence of a human situation to the reader! If you are not yet acquainted with Henry James, try the selection of his shorter novels and stories edited by Clifton Fadiman, and then read some of the longer novels, like *Roderick Hudson* and *The American.* And, incidentally, you will learn more about the top layers of American and European society in the second half of the nineteenth century than you can ever glean from the works of social historians.

What is the place of imagination in history? An historian or biographer is under restrictions unknown to a novelist. He has no right to override facts by his own imagination. If he is writing on a remote or obscure subject about which few facts are available, his imagination may legitimately weave them into a pattern. But to be honest he must make clear what is fact and what is hypothesis. The quality of imagination, if properly restrained by the conditions of historical discipline, is of great assistance in enabling one to discover problems to be solved, to grasp the significance of facts, to form hypotheses, to discern causes in their first beginnings, and, above all, to relate the past creatively to the present. There are many opportunities in historical narrative for bold, imaginative expressions. "A complete statement in the imaginative form of an important truth arrests attention," wrote Emerson, "and is repeated and remembered." Imagination used in this way invests an otherwise pedestrian narrative with vivid and exciting qualities.

Finally, the historian should have frequent recourse to the book of life. The richer his personal experience, the wider his human contacts, the more likely he is to effect a living contact with his audience. In writing, similes drawn from the current experience of this mechanical age, rather than those rifled from the literary baggage of past eras, are the ones that will go home to his reader. Service on a jury or a local committee may be a revelation as to the political thoughts and habits of mankind. A month's labor in a modern factory would help any young academician to clarify his ideas of labor and capital. A camping trip in the woods will tell him things about Western pioneering that he can never learn in books. The great historians, with few exceptions, are those who have not merely studied, but lived; and whose studies have ranged over a much wider field than the period or subject of which they write.

The veterans of World War II who, for the most part, have completed their studies in college or graduate school should not regard the years of their war service as wasted. Rather should they realize that the war gave them a rich experience of life, which is the best equipment for an historian. They have "been around"; they have seen mankind at his best and his worst; they have shared the joy and passion of a mighty effort; and they can read man's doings in the past with far greater understanding than if they had spent these years in sheltered academic groves.

To these young men especially, and too all young men I say (as the poet Chapman said to the young Elizabethan): "Be free, all worthy spirits, and stretch yourselves!" Bring all your knowledge of life to bear on everything that you write. Never let yourself bog down in pedantry and detail. Bring history, the most humane and noble form of letters, back to the proud position she once held; knowing that your words, if they are read and remembered, will enter into the stream of life, and perhaps move men to thought and action centuries hence, as do those of Thucydides after more than two thousand years.

VI

Reminiscences and Adventures

1

One Boy's Boston, 1887–1901

Extracts from my book of that name, published by Houghton Mifflin in 1962.

The public owes this book to my late wife, Priscilla. During the winter of 1961 I caught one of the kinds of flu that are always blowing around New England, and was ordered by the doctor to stay in bed. This I found very boring, and kept sneaking out of bed to my library on the same floor to get books. Said Priscilla: "This has got to stop! Let me get you one of your favorite yellow blocks and a soft pencil, and write down some of those yarns you have been telling me about your family and your childhood in this house. Might even make a paper for the Massachusetts Historical Society!" That's what she did, and I did. To my surprise, if not hers, it was snapped up by Houghton Mifflin for a small book, published in 1962. Here are some of the funniest parts.

The Eliots and the Otises

ONE AUTUMN DAY in 1887, Dr. Charles Montraville Green, "with his little round hat and his walking stick and his beard of pubic hair" (as the famous "Ballad of Chambers Street" describes him), was walking along Brimmer Street, at the foot of Beacon Hill, in Boston. As he approached Number 44, his astonished gaze beheld a baby carriage, unattended, bouncing down the stone steps. Upon hitting the sidewalk it pitch-poled, hurling the contents — one mattress, one pillow, and one baby — into Brimmer Street. By a strange quirk of fate, the mattress landed first, with baby on top and the pillow on top of him. Dr. Green rushed forward, expecting to administer first aid to the howling infant, but found him unhurt, and identified him as Samuel Eliot Morison, whom he had brought into the world at the same house on the previous 9th of July.

What had happened was simply this: nurse Lizzie Doyle, pausing at the top of the steps to gossip with the parlormaid, momentarily released the perambulator's handle. Since no harm ensued, Lizzie was forgiven, and she continued as my nurse long enough to be remembered with deep affection.

Number 44 Brimmer Street, where I was born and still live, had been built by my maternal grandparents, the Samuel Eliots, during the winter of 1869–70, which they spent in Paris. They started home just before the Franco-Prussian War broke, taking passage in the Cunard side-wheeler *Scotia*. She was commanded by a bearded captain who always made a point of kissing the first-class lady passengers goodbye at the end of the voyage. Before reaching this osculatory terminus at Boston, *Scotia* called at Halifax and anchored in the stream. The gentleman passengers, who included James Bryce and A. V. Dicey, were mad to get at the Halifax newspapers and read news of the war; but the captain insisted on all the newspapers' being deposited in his cabin, and reading them himself, before he would allow any to go out.

Samuel Eliot, born in Boston in 1822, was a grandson of the Samuel Eliot who founded a professorship of Greek at Harvard, after accumulating a fortune in the mercantile business, most of which was dissipated in the next generation. My great-grandfather, William Havard Eliot, who lived at Number 56 Beacon Street, invested most of his patrimony in shares of the Tremont House, on the corner of Beacon and Tremont streets, which for many years was accounted the best hotel in the United States. Upon his untimely death, in 1830, his widow followed the bad advice of an executor by throwing these shares on the market at a fraction of their cost, and became a comparatively poor woman. This meant that my grandfather Samuel Eliot, after graduating from Harvard first in the Class of 1839 (Edward Everett Hale being second, and my other grandfather, Nathaniel Holmes Morison, third), had to go to work, and that his younger brother never did enter college.

Samuel Eliot prepared (the old word was "fitted") boys for college for several years. He then attained a chair of history at Trinity College, Hartford, and became president of the college in 1860. During a winter's trip to Europe, for his wife's health, he was eased out of that position owing to a faculty intrigue, and the Eliots returned to Boston to live. There, my grandfather, who was wholly devoid of

false pride, accepted the position of first headmaster of the Girls'
High School, which he raised to such a standard of excellence that it
was attended by many young girls of my mother's social set. He was
then appointed superintendent of schools of Boston for one term, but
failed to be reappointed because he published a very bowdlerized
edition of *The Arabian Nights* for school use. A rival who wanted the
job twisted this into "Corrupting our Youth with the Licentious Tales
of an Oriental Despotism," and Dr. Eliot returned to private life. He
accepted this humorously and philosophically — as he did all losses
and crosses in life; an attitude doubtless made easier because his wife
had brought enough money into the family for them to live comfortably without the aid of a salary.

She was Emily Marshall Otis, daughter of the one-time celebrated
beauty Emily Marshall, and of William Foster Otis, son of Harrison
Gray Otis, the Boston grandee. The Otises were genial, worldly, and
luxurious in their tastes; the Eliots were frugal and ascetic, dedicated
to literature and other good works. Although Harrison Gray Otis had
been a leader in Federalist politics and senator from Massachusetts,
he was better known for his wit, charm, and hospitality.

My great-grandmother, Emily Marshall Otis, died in childbirth in
1836. Her two little girls — Emily, my grandmother, and Mary,
who became Mrs. Alexander H. Stevens — and George (a childhood
friend of Henry Adams's), then lived in their Grandfather Otis's mansion at 45 Beacon Street, where they were brought up under the care
of a widowed aunt. My grandmother assured me that there was no
plumbing of any description in that great house; all the water had to
be brought in from a well in the yard. She, Mary, and George were
marched to the Tremont House once a week for a tub bath.

Samuel Eliot, a poor but handsome and popular young man,
courted and won Emily Otis. Emily Marshall Eliot, as she now became, inherited the Otis charm and sociability. I have never seen a
more gracious smile on any woman. She had a genius for making
people of any age feel at home; although, as far as small children were
concerned, this gift was assisted by her unique institution, the
"present drawer." In her downtown shopping expeditions she kept
an eye open for things that little boys and girls might like. These
were wrapped up, marked with their contents, and placed in two
bureau drawers in her bedroom, one for boys and one for girls.
Every child who came to the house was led to this bureau and al-

lowed to make his or her choice. That was what did the trick — you could pick out what you wanted.

Grandfather did not much care for evening parties, but Grandmother loved them, and even, on occasion, went without him. Once, when hoop skirts were still in fashion, she returned to 44 Brimmer Street alone after a dinner, dismissed the carriage, found she had no latch key, and could awaken nobody with the doorbell. So, she hung the hoop skirt on the back fence, climbed over, and got in by the dining room window, fortunately unlatched. At that juncture a constable came along, saw the hoop skirt hanging in a horrible attitude on the fence, assumed that there had been foul play, blew his whistle, and summoned reinforcements; so that before long, everyone in the house, and the neighborhood, too, was awake. Explanations were given, beer was produced for the cops, and all ended in laughter, as things generally did in that household.

The Eliots went in for education, literature, and scholarship. President Eliot and Charles Eliot Norton were my grandfather's first cousins, and he served on the board of almost every major charitable institution in and around Boston. But the Otises, like W. S. Gilbert's

>. . . House of Peers, throughout the war,
>   Did nothing in particular.
>   And did it very well.

Mother was very fond of her cousins Harry, Bertie, and Willy Otis, gay dogs and benevolently delightful to small boys like myself.

A typical Otis story about the "Otis boys" I heard much later. Johnny, as we shall call him, was married to a Miss Root. They had no children, but Johnny kept a mistress in a house on Shawmut Avenue, and had two or three children by her. There he was known as Mr. Jones, a clerk in the Customs House, whose duties required long, unexplained absences. During the summer the Otises kept a cottage at Nahant. Johnny used to take the morning boat to Boston, visit the downtown office, where he had nothing to do but clip coupons, lunch at his club, spend the afternoon at the Shawmut Avenue love nest, and catch the 5:00 P.M. boat back to Nahant. Johnny's wife adored him; but her mother hated him, put detectives on his trail, found out about his double life, and confronted her daughter with the evidence. She refused to believe a word of it. So Mamma decided to get the evidence for herself. She hired a cab, waited outside the

Shawmut Avenue house, and when Johnny came down the front steps, kissing his children goodbye, she flounced out, crying "Now John, you rascal, I've caught you! And I am going straight home to tell your poor deceived wife."

Johnny, apparently unperturbed, bowed deeply. "Madam, you are mistaken; I am Mr. Henry Jones of the United States Customs Service" — handing her the visiting card especially engraved for such emergencies. "Nonsense!" said the old lady, tearing the card in two, "You are wicked Johnny Otis, my son-in-law, and I am going right down to Nahant to tell your poor trusting wife about your despicable conduct." Snorting loudly, she got into the cab, and drove slowly off.

Johnny did some quick thinking. He sent one little boy to the nearest Western Union office with a telegram to a livery stable at Lynn, near the depot, ordering his favorite fast trotter to be harnessed to a buggy, and with driver to meet him on the arrival of the 4:30 train. Figuring that his mother-in-law, with her tired old cab horse, would miss that train, and guessing that upon arrival at Lynn she would await the hourly horse bus to Nahant, he sent a second boy to fetch a cab that stood on a nearby corner to serve sporting gents, and offered the cabby ten dollars to catch the 4:30. The cab galloped down Charles and Cambridge streets, passing Mamma's slow-moving vehicle with ease, and Johnny was just in time to swing onto the rear car of the 4:30 as it started. At Lynn, the horse and buggy were ready. The driver drove it over Lynn Beach as though competing in a trotting race. At the foot of the hill that leads to Nahant village, Johnny left his buggy, tipped the driver heavily, instructing him to walk the horse all the way back to Lynn, and himself walked up the hill. There, he was greeted by his trusting wife on the front porch of the Otis cottage.

"Why Johnny dear, why are you home so early?"

"Darling, I had such a hot, tired day at the office that I took an early train home, and I'm quite exhausted!"

"You poor dear, go right upstairs and get into bed, and I'll bring you some cool lemonade."

"Thank you, darling, I believe I will" — and did.

Johnny's calculations were correct. Mamma missed the 4:30 train, and, when the 5:00 arrived at Lynn, waited for the next slow bus. A good hour after Johnny's arrival she bustled up the steps, announcing, "Now my dear, will you believe me? This very afternoon I caught your wicked husband on Shawmut Avenue, surrounded by his little bastards!"

"Why, Mamma, why will you say such things about dear Johnny? The poor boy came home early from the office and is now upstairs asleep in bed!"

Mamma flung up her hands, exclaiming, "Well, I give up!"

She made no further efforts to disillusion her daughter, and the marriage lasted happily ever after.

A Horsey Neighborhood

The horse that entered this story as the savior of Cousin Johnny Otis's marriage was my companion from earliest childhood; I began riding at the age of five, and ours was the horsey end of town. Almost the entire square between the backs of Beacon, River, and Mt. Vernon streets and the river was occupied by stables big and little — livery stables, which let out "seagoing" hacks and coupés; boarding and baiting stables, where gentlemen who drove in from the suburbs behind fast trotters left their rigs during the day; club stables, where individuals could board one or two horses; and dozens of private stables. Chestnut Street between Charles and the river was called "Horse-Chestnut Street" in derision. Near the corner of River Street was Joe Pink's harness shop, redolent of saddlery, where horse tack was made and repaired, and the fraternity made horse deals around the potbellied stove. On Lime Street, there were at least two blacksmith shops, where the cheerful ringing of hammer on anvil could be heard from 7:00 A.M. to late afternoon. There was Chauncy Thomas's carriage factory on lower Chestnut Street, where beautiful sleighs, victorias, broughams, and other horse-drawn vehicles were built; Frederic J. Fisher, the famous designer of automobile bodies, there had his training. All this afforded abundant opportunity for an inquiring small boy to advance his education by picking up learned opinions from stablemen, coachmen, and blacksmiths on how to select and breed a horse, on treating equine maladies, on proper horseshoeing, and the like; information that the jolly Irishmen who practiced these arts were only too ready to impart. Horse lore was often expressed in rhymes, such as:

> One white stocking, try him;
> Two white stockings, buy him;

Three white stockings and a white nose,
Strip off his skin and feed him to the crows.

My descendants will find it hard to believe that I once kept a horse at the Beacon Club Stable for daily rides to Jamaica Pond or beyond, or for driving a girl to the Country Club on Sundays; and that even after becoming Professor Hart's assistant at Harvard, I would combine business with pleasure by riding my gray gelding, Blanco, to Cambridge, tying him to a tree in the Yard, and loading the saddlebags with students' papers that had to be corrected.

One center of interest for horse enthusiasts was Fire Engine Company Number 10, in its present location at the corner of Mt. Vernon and River streets. Number 10 kept four magnificent dapple-gray horses, which the firemen exercised between fires, riding them bareback up and down the street. A wonderful spectacle was touched off by the fire alarm. Doors to the horse stalls opened automatically; each horse went to its place at engine or hose wagon; the harness, even the collars, dropped into place on their backs and necks; firemen slid down poles, buckled the tackle, lit the fire under the brightly polished brass boiler; and within sixty seconds of the first bell, engine and hose went roaring out into the street, the horses at full gallop. Lucky was the boy who happened to be on hand, to catch a ride to the fire on the tail of the hose wagon.

It was a great mortification to the neighborhood that Number 10's apparatus happened to be helping at a distant fire when the greatest fire in Brimmer Street history broke out, in Brown's stable between Chestnut and Byron streets. This occurred after Brown had compromised with the automobile to the extent of letting his stable be used as a garage and filling station. The fire quickly spread to the gasoline tank. I heard the explosion, looked out, and saw a great flame shooting across Brimmer Street, menacing the wooden stable on the site of Emerson College. That was saved, but Brown's burned to the ground. It was replaced by the brick Brimmer Garage.

This horsey atmosphere, delicious to the rising generation, was less favorably savored by our elders. It gave the air a rich equine flavor, especially on days when the stablemen were pitching manure into the market gardeners' trucks that came to take it away. Swarms of flies penetrated 44 Brimmer Street in spite of the screens, pirouetting gaily around the chandeliers when not attempting to share our meals.

My grandmother, in desperation, offered me a cent for every fly I could kill indoors, and for several days I was in the money; but after I had incautiously run up the score to $1.12 in one day, the tariff came down sharply. Sticky flypaper was then substituted for Sammy and his swatter, to the discomfiture of family cats. Reader, if you have never seen a lively kitten mixing it up with a sheet of "Tanglefoot" flypaper, you have really missed something in life.

All this depressed real estate and made Brimmer Street unfashionable. That made no difference to our family, but the maids used to say to me, "Master Sammy, do persuade your grandpa to move to a swell neighborhood, like Commonwealt' Avenoo!" The revenge of time has reversed these values. With the passing of the horse, stables and blacksmith shops were pulled down or converted to dwellings, and a syndicate of enterprising young men, led by Matthew Hale, put up the neat, neo-Georgian brick houses that now line lower Brimmer Street, Lime Street, and Charles River Square. The smells departed with the horse; but so, alas, did the rather sporty and raffish atmosphere of the neighborhood. It has become eminently respectable, and property there or on Beacon Hill is at a premium, over that of the once-proud Back Bay.

Horse-drawn, too, was our public transportation until I was six or seven years old. A much-quoted ditty was the satirical poem of a Bostonian expatriate:

Oh! to be born in Boston, in the chill of a winter day,
To the family tree of a social grandee, and the tap of a pap-frappé;
With a cousin at every corner, and on every street an aunt;
To be known "who you are" on the Little Green Car,
And your family seat at Nahant.

With your "old man" strong in the market, and in mourning "Mamma so missed";
A hunter or two, and a Trinity pew, and a vanishing visiting list.
Ah yes, to be born in Boston, introduced by a spectacled stork;
In our great social spawn 'tis the place to be born —
But, ye gods, let me live in New York!

This Little Green Car was the horse-drawn car that started somewhere on Massachusetts Avenue, trotted down Marlborough Street, skirted the Public Garden to Charles, passed along Cambridge to Staniford, and descended the West End hill to the North Station.

Lying in bed at night, I could hear it tinkling past Brimmer and Beacon, then again past Charles and Mt. Vernon; hear the one bell that signaled the horses to stop, and two bells to start. The Little Green Car stopped anywhere on signal, not only at corners. The conductors knew everyone along the route, and the residents knew their names, and even those of the horses. A lady would put a small tot on board and say to the conductor, "Mr. Kelly, would you please see that little Mary gets off at her Aunt Anna's — Number 152 you know?" and Mr. Kelly would, and did.

I do not wish to sentimentalize the horse age. Motor transport is responsible for many ills, but it certainly has saved the world an enormous amount of equine and even human misery. Not every man and boy who handled a horse knew how to do it properly. Privately owned saddle horses, horsecar horses, and the sleek, well-fed animals in private stables were well treated, but the workhorses were commonly overworked, underfed, and subjected to senseless beatings by ignorant or brutal drivers. A frequent sight in winter was that of a horse falling down in harness, through slipping or sheer exhaustion; and I recall one occasion when a driver was whipping an animal that was prostrate in the snow to make him get up. My father intervened, stopped the cruelty, and showed the man how to unbuckle the harness and free the horse so that he could get up. My mother tried to intercede with an express company to stop one of its drivers from galloping his horse past our house every evening, bringing him to the nearby stable all hot and sweaty, so that the man could go off duty a few minutes earlier.

So, too, with the cab and hack drivers. I used to wonder why they were so gruff; it was partly, no doubt, that they got no tips, since that was not a tipping age — tipping was supposed to be decadent, servile, a European relic. Mostly, however, the cabbies' gruffness was caused by their patrons' lack of consideration, keeping them waiting for hours on a cold night while they dallied at a party. It was a frequent sight to see hack drivers walking up and down, slapping their sides with their arms to restore circulation, while the horses stood shivering under a blanket. Once, walking home on a night when the temperature was around zero, I passed a house where several hacks were waiting for dinner guests to get ready to leave; one of the drivers, looking toward the front door, exclaimed, "If those goddam rich bastards don't come out quick, I'm going in there to tell them to hell with them and they can walk home; I'm not going to stay here and freeze to death." So, I'm not shedding any tears over the passing of the horse from our cities, where, with few exceptions, he lived a short and miserable life, tended and driven by overworked and underpaid men.

Beverly Farms and Northeast Harbor

Beverly Farms was my grandparents' summer home in the 1890's. They hired the Knowlton house near the railway station, so close to the road that they named it "Roadside." A later owner has moved it well back into the field, which was then an apple orchard. There was an old barn that my cousin Mac and I invested with imaginary ghosts, celebrating an annual "revel day" every June. We were mad about bicycling, and must have covered almost every dirt road of Essex County, then far more open than today: a series of farms. I remember particularly the vast sweep of apple blossom in the late spring, the great heaps of golden squash and pumpkin in the autumn, and Sunday walks with my father, Mac, and his sisters on Beverly Commons, then an open hilly pasture. In Beverly Farms my nurse introduced me to one of the new inventions, the gramophone. One was owned in the village, and the proud owner invited friends and neighbors occasionally to listen to the marvelous thing; one left a nickel or dime in a plate at the door as a token admission fee. The selections were mostly popular or sentimental songs, or skits such as the town meetin' voting to construct the new skule house outen the materials of the old skule house, but not to pull down the old skule house till the new one was built. These were recorded on soft, wax-covered cylinders, which had to be handled very gingerly and brushed off with a camel's-hair brush.

A noted figure at "The Farms," as the natives called it, was Mrs. Henry Whitman, who let us use the section of West Beach in front of her house. Mr. Whitman, a shadowy figure in comparison with his wife, owned a small side-wheeler steam yacht, which he used for commuting to Boston. His wife was a disciple of Ruskin's. She not only cherished pre-Raphaelite art and artists, but set up a little factory of stained glass near Park Square, Boston, where she designed and executed some notable works in that medium. My parents first brought me to see her when I was seven or eight years old. She had no children of her own, but her heart seemed to go out to me, and mine to her; she encouraged me to call, received me as graciously as if I had been her friends Henry James or John Jay Chapman (whom I first met there), and carried on an intellectual conversation at my level, although I neither noted nor suspected any condescension. Every Christmas she gave me something beautiful to help form my taste: a framed photograph of an old master, or a small piece of stained glass to hang against a window. I count her as my dearest friend of that generation — about halfway between those of parents and grandparents — and as one of those who encouraged me very early in the way that eventually I chose.

Moving day to Beverly Farms, in mid-May, was a great day in the 44 Brimmer Street household. For a week previous, trunks had been packed, toys selected, bicycles stacked, even favorite chairs and other pieces of furniture collected. Early on the appointed day, two-horse wagons of Curtis and Croston, movers, pulled up at the front door. They drove the baggage all the way, over the Lynn marshes, through Salem and Beverly, arriving at Roadside in the early afternoon, while family and servants took the train; and about mid-October the process was repeated in reverse.

There is nothing to a boy like a real pal; Mac was mine at Beverly Farms. We shared the same secrets; went into spasms of laughter over our own jokes. As a sample of this adolescent wit, we were always playing the changes on a local character, Hanable by name, who let out dories and sold bait on West Beach. He became successively Hannibal, Hasdrubal, Hamilcar, Hanno, and the Noble Carthaginian, each new pseudonym dissolving us in idiotic laughter. Absurd conversations were evolved from the billboards we observed from the Boston & Maine Railroad — such as "Magee Furnaces and Ranges are the Best." "Yes, but you must shop when in Salem at Almy, Bigelow & Washburn's." "Of course, but don't forget Fletcher's Castoria — Children Cry For It," and so on, to the utter disgust of our elders.

My parents spent every July and August at the old Rockend Hotel in Northeast Harbor, Maine. It was there that I acquired my almost passionate love for the sea and for Mount Desert Island. There, too, one met children from New York, Philadelphia, Albany, and Baltimore; notably, the Gardiner grandchildren of Bishop William Croswell Doane, an old family friend, who had first shown my parents the beauty of that place. At Northeast Harbor, Sam Vaughan was the pal. We rowed skiffs and fished for flounders together; we spent hours in a discarded upright-piano box, which we named the "*Cimbria*," after a local steamboat, striking the bells on a section of drainpipe that passed for a smokestack, and calling all the landings from Bangor to Bar Harbor. The great moment came when the actual *Cimbria* passed, and returned our frantic wavings and shoutings with a real steam-whistle salute. From these childish games we graduated to sailing North Haven dinghies *Rena* and *Leda*. In sailing these little cat-rigged craft I first felt the exhilaration, the peculiar, indescribable delight of sea transport under sail. Luckily for us, the gasoline motor had not yet come in; we learned our sea lore from men who had made their living from the ocean, and who taught us how to "hand, reef, and steer" in the traditional manner.

2

Reminiscences of Charles Eliot Norton

From THE NEW ENGLAND QUARTERLY, September 1960.

This memoir was sparked by my last talk with Bernard Berenson, when we discussed Norton. I felt that "B.B." was rather disparaging of the old gentleman, and so jotted down what I knew and remembered of him.

CHARLES ELIOT NORTON was first cousin to Charles William Eliot, president of Harvard University, and to my grandfather Samuel Eliot. The Nortons, of the New England "Brahmin caste" of scholars and divines, married into the "North End Eliots," so called to distinguish them from the "South End Eliots," descendants of the Prophet to the Indians, who for the most part had been earthy and mercantile. Samuel Eliot, a Boston merchant who lived most of his life in the eighteenth century, made a fortune as a merchant-importer, but also became a patron of learning. He endowed a chair of Greek literature at Harvard College, probably at the suggestion of his cousin the Reverend Andrew Eliot, from whom T. S. Eliot is descended.

Even before Samuel Eliot died, in 1820, the North End Eliots decided that they had made enough money, and, like other old Boston families, devoted themselves largely to learning, education, and various good causes. Samuel Eliot's two sons lost their share of his fortune, one by bad investments and the other (President Eliot's father) in the panic of 1857; but his daughters, Catharine and Anna, kept their share, which enabled their scholarly husbands, the Reverend Andrews Norton and George Ticknor, to live like gentlemen. The Eliots, however, were never a close family corporation like the Cabots, Adamses, or Lowells. They did not marry within the family group or attempt to bring up their children together or live in the same city block. Thus, Charles Eliot Norton did not loom large in my young life, although he and my grandparents were warm friends.

I find in a notebook of parties given at 44 Brimmer Street in 1883 a "Party for Sally Norton," a daughter of Charles's who was coming out. No fewer than forty-three girls and fifty-five men assembled in this small town house to honor Sally; they danced on cloth-covered carpets to a three-piece orchestra, and at supper consumed, according to the hostess's record, five quarts of creamed oysters, a salad of which the basis was twenty-five pounds of lobster, a twelve-pound fillet of beef, two twelve-pound turkeys, eleven chickens, eight dozen rolls, six dozen individual ices, and four quarts of plain ices. Yet the alcoholic consumption was limited to a case of champagne, and a few bottles of sauterne and claret. Cocktails and whiskey, in those days, were not drawing-room beverages.

This feast took place before I was born. Norton first came into my life through his series of readers called *The Heart of Oak Books*, which appeared in the 1890's. Renewing acquaintance with them after sixty years, I note in the Preface of Volume II that Norton made his selections to help "the cultivation of the taste, and to the healthy development of the imagination." That, they certainly did; and there has been no other set of readers like them since. One rainy day, leafing through one of the volumes in my grandfather's library, I came across Thackeray's *Chronicle of the Drum*. And that sparked off a lifelong interest in the French Revolution.

My earliest recollection of Norton himself comes from an ocean voyage to England in the Dominion liner *New England*, in 1900. He was the life of the first cabin, presided genially at the inevitable concert, and made friends with everyone. My father was talking to a shoe salesman in the smoking room when Norton joined them. On being introduced, Norton put the salesman at his ease, with the question, "Do they still make those boots with elastic gussets let into the sides?"

"You mean 'Congress boots' don't you?"

"Yes."

"Oh, no, they went out long ago."

"I never thought they were very good style, did you?"

"No, completely second-rate"; and so on.

After Norton excused himself and left the group, the shoe salesman turned to my father and exclaimed, "What a delightful old gentleman! Interested in everything and everybody."

He certainly was; and that part of his life which was not devoted to teaching and scholarship was spent in trying to do something to help the poor and unfortunate. He opened in 1846 what was probably the earliest university extension night school, run by college students and professors for the benefit of boys and men who had had to cut their education short and go to work. When Cambridge and Somerville spread out and engulfed the Norton ancestral estate, Shady Hill, the Catholic Church put up, not half a mile from the Nortons, a hideous yellow brick institution with the name (now mercifully changed) of Hospital for Incurables. It was staffed by the Gray Nuns. Some of the neighbors resented its presence, but Charles came to terms with it in characteristic fashion.

The late Pierre La Rose told me in 1936 that an archbishop of Boston, inspecting this hospital, ascertained that some of the permanent patients were Protestants. He ordered the sister superior to get rid of them. She protested. "Why, what have the Protestants done for us?" asked the archbishop. "Well, a Protestant gentleman eighty years old comes here twice a week to read aloud to my patients, in a beautiful, cultivated voice, and he always asks me to send him to the poorest and most unfortunate of our inmates. His visits are the one thing they have to look forward to."

"Who is this man?"

"Charles Eliot Norton."

The archbishop said no more.

Norton established a friendly but critical relationship with the leading literary people of America and England — Parkman, Lowell, Henry James, Mrs. Wharton, Ruskin, Carlyle, Clough, Matthew Arnold, and a host of others. The relationship was not that of an adoring disciple to master, or, in the case of those younger than himself, the reverse. Norton stimulated and lectured, even scolded them; but in such friendly fashion that they loved him the more. Ruskin himself said that Norton was his "first real tutor," who exercised "a kind of paternal authority over" him, "and a right of guidance." As editor of *The North American Review,* Norton accepted Henry James's first critical review, gently impelled him into the life of letters, and gave him his first letters of introduction to Englishmen. Norton was the first critic of any importance to hail Edith Wharton's *Valley of Decision* as a great work, and he was one of the men whose advice she sought because, as she wrote, he "was supremely gifted" as an "awakener."

When *The Letters of John Ruskin to Charles Eliot Norton* was published in 1904, Norton's cousin Harriet Guild remarked, "I cannot understand how Charles Norton, who did not write much himself, became so intimate with these great men of letters." To which I replied, "It is because Mr. Norton has an infinite capacity for friendship, and great men are lonely; they need friends." But it was something more than that — it was "Norton's unique gift of discriminating sympathy."

Two or three years ago Bernard Berenson, who received from Norton the first shove on his road to fame, was quoted in *The Saturday Review* as having disparaged the old master. I brought this up in conversation with B.B. at Villa I Tatti in May of 1958. Berenson said that he had been misquoted; so I asked him what he really thought of Norton after all these years. "Norton knew nothing about art," said B.B.; "only theories of art — especially Ruskinesque. But he was a cultured New England gentleman of the best sort. He lectured his students on manners, and the values that an educated American should live by. I read through Dante with him in his study class; it was a revelation." Berenson added, however, that Norton had one blind spot: he refused to admit that anything that did not stem from Greece could belong to the fine arts. Although president of the American Archaeological Society, he wished the members to confine their researches to the Old World, doubting whether anything of artistic value would be discovered in the New. When B.B., in his *Venetian Painters of the Renaissance*, compared the work of a Renaissance painter (Catena, I think) to the Japanese, Norton scolded him for his presumption. Nothing Oriental or pre-Columbian American was to be mentioned in the same breath with the Italians!

There is no doubt that Italy was Norton's spiritual home, but he was of too tough a fiber, too deeply rooted in New England, too conscious of his duty toward his country, ever to become an expatriate. In the spring of 1908 I attended one of his evening *conversazioni* at Shady Hill. These were evening parties where one talked and talked, with no other refreshment than a glass of sherry. Norton expressed a kindly interest in my going to Europe to continue my studies; he hoped I would change my field from American to European history, because American history had so little "depth," and American achievements had not come up to our youthful promise. I bridled at this, and referred to our digging the Panama Canal after the French company had failed. He remarked, "How will it advance civilization to save two weeks in sending ships from the Atlantic to the Pacific?" I then quoted, as an example of depth in American history, Parkman's *Pioneers of France in the New World.* "Yes," he said quietly, "that is all very well — but think of Italy!" As he said it, his aged eyes glowed as with a hidden fire. His words seemed a far-off echo of those superb lines in which Virgil describes the feelings of Aeneas and his companions when first they sighted the peninsula:

> . . . *Italiam primus conclamat Achates;*
> *Italiam laeto socii clamore salutant.*

That was the last time I saw Charles Eliot Norton. He died on October 21, 1908, when I was about to begin my year's study in Paris, wondering whether he was not right after all.

3

A Summer Cruise in the Aegean

From SPRING TIDES *(Boston: Houghton Mifflin, 1965), pages 62–80.*

As the reader will see, this needs no introduction.

A DREAM of my boyhood was realized in 1934. Some thirty years earlier, studying Greek history at school, I traced in my *Atlas Antiquus* imaginary routes among the islands of the Aegean, and sailed in fancy the circle of the Cyclades. And I waited to visit Greece until I could do so by sea, as the ancients did; in a sailing vessel that can go anywhere, whose smooth motion is in harmony with the sounds of wind and waves, whose white wings make symmetry with mountains, native lateeners, and the wine-dark sea of Homer.

My old friend and shipmate Dr. Alexander Forbes made the dream come true, and his medium was the schooner *Ramah* of Boston. She was a sturdy, able vessel, 100 feet over all, Nova Scotia–built and Gloucester-fisherman in design; long black hull, and graceful sheer and lofty masts. Her sail plan consisted of a whacking great gaff-headed mainsail that needed two stout fellows on either halyard, a gaff-headed foresail, jumbo, jib, jib-topsail, and fisherman-staysail. No troublesome genoas with their clacking winches, no bellying spinnaker, no brasswork, brightwork, or other yachting refinements; all inside ballast and an old-fashioned backbreaker windlass that never jammed or slipped. *Ramah* was built by Columbus Iselin for his oceanographic work; Dr. Forbes installed an auxiliary engine and refitted her for a surveying expedition to northern Labrador, and after that was accomplished, sailed her in the summer of 1933 from Gloucester to Naples with an amateur crew.

Our auxiliary engine was not strictly necessary, but highly desirable for making schedule in the limited time at our disposal. We had about the same proportion of light, baffling airs and calms that dog yachtsmen in Long Island Sound in August. But more often there blew a brisk nor'wester that whipped up whitecaps and sent *Ramah* along at 8 or 9 knots. The wind almost always died away to a gentle zephyr at night, when *Ramah* would ghost along, making no sound except the slap of vang and topping lift against the mainsail.

A pair of shorts and sandals and a sun hat formed the usual male costume on board; ditto for the girls, plus one of those handkerchief arrangements that tie around the neck. Wendy Morison, Kitty Forbes, and Janet Forbes made as lovely modern replicas of Hera, Aphrodite, and Athena as one could find anywhere; and little Florrie Forbes, piping on a clarinet, became our god Pan and all the rest of us joined the girls in song.

The crew were all amateurs, chosen with an eye to work as well as friendship. At Cos, the Italian authorities objected to the girls' being entered on our yacht's papers as "stewardesses," the point being that as "passengers" they could have been taxed. They threatened to keep our documents until we paid up. So we put on a show for them. One morning all men and boys went below; the four girls made sail and weighed anchor with an occasional assist from their mothers, but none from the men and boys. Upon our returning to port that evening, our impounded ship's papers were courteously returned and no more was said about taxes. The Italians were so impressed that the story of this exploit preceded us to Rhodes, where a friend seeking news of us was asked, "You mean the yacht sailed by a crew of pretty girls?"

My rating on board *Ramah* is best described as that of the ancient *mystagogus*, guide and initiator to the mysteries. I was supposed to sell Hellenic culture to the youngsters, who, belonging to a generation deprived of its intellectual heritage, a sound classical education, knew next to nothing of Greek history or literature. Almost every day on board I read aloud for an hour or two from translations of Greek authors relevant to places in our itinerary, or the works of Zimmern and Livingstone. Theocritus and Herodotus were the favorites; the one portrays the rural life like that we saw in the islands, still going on very much as in the third century B.C.; and in the historian's pages we followed the progress of Xerxes' army and fleet to its disasters at Plataea and Mycale. What a grand old fellow Herodotus was! Far from being the uncritical raconteur that many have asserted, he writes with the most subtle art, bringing out the characters of individuals and places. And he never forgets what so many modern historians never learn, that history is primarily a story of mankind; not economics, sociology, or wisecrackery.

Alexander Forbes, owner and skipper of *Ramah*, and, at the age of fifty-two, the oldest person on board, is a truly remarkable character and one of the most versatile men of our era. An expert navigator, he became a physiologist by profession. An inventor too, he helped install radio direction finders in our destroyers in the First World War, and as a commander in the U.S. Naval Reserve in the Second World War, he provided some new devices for the military photographers. As dead-reckoning and celestial navigator, he is quicker and more accurate than most younger men in working out a position. An explorer, he had already surveyed and charted northern Labrador in *Ramah*.

The one paid hand in our ship's company of seventeen was the cook, Antonio Francesco, of Naples. Although he was supposed to be trilingual, his Greek was entirely expressed by signs, and his English was limited to "dirty Greeks," "fry-'em-up-eggs," "galley damn hot," and "finish." This last word came out when we tacked unexpectedly in a stiff breeze. The icebox door flew open and the contents fetched up on Francesco, on the lee side of the galley. When discovered fighting off a quarter of lamb, a bowl of cold macaroni, two quarts of milk, several dozen eggs, and a mass of broken crockery, he remarked, with great emphasis, "Feenish!" But he didn't finish, and was soon combing the egg out of his hair and cheerfully preparing the next meal. His culinary repertoire was limited to what he had learned in the Italian merchant marine. This became apparent at our first breakfast on board. Hoping to order something easy, Bessie Morison, the only person on board who could speak Italian, ordered boiled eggs. Francesco threw four dozen eggs into a cauldron of cold water, brought them to a boil, and boiled them for an hour. Bessie suggested that next time he bring the water to a boil, drop in the eggs — here Francesco interrupted, "If you do that they go *pouf!*" throwing up his hands to imitate an explosion. Possibly the grade of eggs issued to the Italian merchant marine did just that, but ours were of somewhat superior quality. Nevertheless, Francesco could not soft-boil eggs properly, so "fry-'em-up-eggs" became the daily breakfast dish. His spaghetti, however, was the real stuff; his soups and stews were excellent.

We were not altogether dependent on Francesco's culinary art. All

Greek seaports are oriented to the waterfront, and the best restaurant is apt to be a few yards from the anchorage. While our chain was rattling out of the hawsepipe, the waiters would rush a bevy of tables to the edge of the quay and make signs to us that food and drink were awaiting us ashore. We often fell for them, and found Greek cooking excellent. Aristophanes reminds us that Euripides' mother sold pot herbs for a living; and a skillful use of herbs still gives Greek food a peculiar flavor and zest.

The wine is even better than the food. Greece produces several hundred varieties, from the humble *retsinata,* which tastes like spruce gum (and explains why Dionysus sports a pine cone on his thyrsus), to the red, fruity *malvoisie,* the malmsey of mediaeval England, in a butt of which a certain Duke of Clarence met a pleasant if dishonorable death. Every island has its own vintages, none without some virtue, and most of them good and incredibly cheap.

To our great regret, we were unable to land in Asia Minor, for the Turks in 1934 were in a highly suspicious humor toward foreigners. Even with a Turkish visa we would have had to visit Smyrna to obtain a permit to touch at any part of King Croesus' ancient kingdom. So we had to be content with a telescopic view of the white marble castle at Budrum, the ancient Halicarnassus. One day, while we were rounding the lighthouse at the tip of the Bybassian Chersonese and passing within a quarter mile of the site of ancient Cnidus, deserted and as yet unexcavated by Turk or Giaour, some of our young men were for going ashore to see what they could pick up; but elderly prudence forbade. A few days earlier, as we subsequently learned, two British naval officers, swimming from a cutter near the Turkish shore, were shot at by a sentry, and one was killed. It was all a tragic mistake. The Turks beckoned to the British to approach for examination, but they turned the other way; for the Turks beckon with the palm of the hand toward you; so, naturally, the British thought they were being ordered to sheer off, and the sentry fired to stop them.

Bathing is delicious in the Aegean, and we were in and out of the water several times a day. One was sensible of the greater saltiness compared with the Atlantic. The color is a sapphire-blue under the summer sun, turning smaragdine in the shoals, and, in a calm, reflecting all the colors of the mountains. Toward nightfall it turns deep purple, the wine-dark of Homer. Bottom is often visible at ten fathoms. We missed the tides of our New England coast, and the variety that they give the shoreline. With a rise and fall of but a foot or two, there is no scope for seaweed, clams, or mussels to flourish; and the hard line where earth meets sea has the monotonous regularity of a lake shore. But raise the eyes above that, and you find a mountain landscape hard to match anywhere. Some of the mountain slopes hung heavy with vineyards, terraced cornfields where the red-ocher earth was breathing after the summer harvest and before the fall planting. Other slopes were planted with olive, each tree having its own retaining wall and morsel of earth. Still others were all gray rock and scrub, affording pasturage only to goats; and in some places there were cliffs gay with color as those of Martha's Vineyard. Almost all the flowers had gone to seed, and pine-clad slopes were rare; but one soon learns to ignore detail, or even color, and to look for form and mass. For pure form, the Greek mountains are completely satisfactory to the eye, as Monadnock is to a Yankee; one feels that they are what mountains should be. No long, even ridges or bizarre pinnacles, but hills molded by an unseen artist into noble shapes. Greek mountains are always varied, never monotonous; every few miles they part to admit a valley with bright green vineyards, gray-green olive groves, and often a bright little town of white, blue-trimmed houses, ending in a tiny quay with a fleet of lateener fishing boats. Under our skipper's expert navigation, it became one of our greatest pleasures to feel the way with leadline after dark into some nameless valley cove, anchoring as soon as the leadsman cried, "By the mark, five!" and awakening to the tune of goat bells in a new scene of Arcadian beauty. We did this at Voudia Bay in Melos, and at several other harbors that are not even named on the Admiralty chart.

We had been to Athens and wished to visit the site of her stern rival, although little there is to recall Sparta but her site, as Thucydides predicted. The deserted Byzantine town of Mistra, on the slope of Taygetus, offered more of interest than the ruins of Sparta, once the terror of Greece. But her defeated rival, Athens, still lives, through the deathless glory of her intellectual and artistic achievements. Indeed, it was for these that she was chosen the capital of modern Greece, and has become once more a great and populous city. It may be well for Americans to reflect that arts and letters go on paying material dividends to a country long after business has cracked and liberty vanished.

Not that Athens neglected the manly virtues: we had a spectacular illustration of that on our approach. With mainsail and jib-topsail set, we beat against a refreshing easterly from Eleusis through the Strait of Salamis, site of the naval battle in which Greece, under Athenian leadership, saved Europe. There was the site of Xerxes' ringside seat, and all the familiar land- and seamarks that we had read of in Herodotus' prose, and in the poetry of Aeschylus, himself a combatant. After clipping the waves where the fight had been thickest on that September day 2400 years ago, we emerged into the Gulf of Aegina and there, sweeping the Attic coast with marine glasses, caught Athena's rock and the glorious Parthenon. Before that immortal and perfect monument, the modern city faded into nothing. And as we swung into the wind and dropped anchor in Phaleron Bay at sunset, Athens for us put on her violet crown.

As I look back on the cruise, it seems studded with rare moments when present beauty, past association, and congenial shipmates struck the contrapuntal harmony that one finds in a composer such as Brahms. There was the morning in the Gulf of Corinth when dawn over Parnassus conjured out of the night a mountain amphitheater around an ocean orchestra, on which the quickening land breeze played, shoving our lee rail awash. There was another cool morning off Cape Sunium, when the sun rose from the Aegean and kindled the frosty white columns of Poseidon's temple to pure gold, and we landed from the schooner's dory on the ancient stone slipway built for biremes and viewed the temple with nobody else about but Greek goatherds. They, eager to please their unexpected visitors, plucked big leaves and rolled them into cornucopias, into which they milked a complaisant nanny, and proferred us the doubtful refreshment of warm, fresh goat's milk. There was an evening when we watched the sun god sink into the sea from his own Mount Cynthus, overlooking his island birthplace of Delos, the slope from summit to water's edge paved with ancient marble. There was an afternoon when we lay becalmed under Ikaria, stretching along the glassy sea like a giant sea monster and breeding clouds from her lofty back. The engine was not working, the ice had melted, and there was no more bread or butter on board; but we spread an awning over the main boom and relaxed, and at nightfall a gentle breeze made up and wafted us to Patmos.

The Aegean was not a sea empty of all but pleasure craft, as along our New England coast today, but full of little native traders, *kaikēs*, or caïques, as they are called, lateen or fore-and-aft rigged, their top-sides painted vermilion and other gay colors like that "saucy girl" in *The Greek Anthology*. Cos, with the ruined temple of Aesculapius an appropriate place of pilgrimage for our skipper; the ancient monastery at Patmos, commemorating the cave where St. John the Divine received his Revelation. The approach by sea to Lindos on Rhodes, with its acropolis of the pre-Christian era, is magnificent, and the old Byzantine town clustering about it, of surpassing interest.

In Rhodes there were glimpses of rural life such as Theocritus described in his seventh Idyl: shepherds resting with their flocks by a spring, a smell of ripening figs in the air, cicadas creaking and chattering in the olive trees, and a day owl hooting musically. An evening walk along Mirabella Bay in Crete, while the mountains turned from gold to deepest purple, and the music of goat bells accompanied our march. Nights at sea, greeting friends like the Pleiades and Hyades, and Spica and Vega, in the country where Hesiod wrote about them 2700 years ago. Peaceful nights at anchor, when a light movement of the waters set the topmasts tracing arabesques among the stars at zenith.

When the cruise was over, I wrote in my journal, "I intend to return, and in any sort of sailing craft; for there are still several routes traced out by my schoolboy pencil in the *Atlas Antiquus* that *Ramah* had no time to follow." Thirty years have passed, and never have I been able to return, although yearly George Polychronides, my friend at Herakleion, begs me to come back. Pursuit of Columbus sent me to the Caribbean, and the Navy in World War II took me to the Pacific. In both seas one may find scenery comparable to the best in Greece; but Hellas enhances her present beauty by the writings of those imperishable writers and artists who once dwelt there, and the memory of St. Paul who threaded the islands in a sailing vessel and addressed the "men of Athens" from the Areopagus.

4

Spring Tides

From my book of that name, published by Houghton Mifflin, 1965.

One gorgeous spring high tide in Maine, when I could sail my boat right up to the trees, suggested the first chapter of this volume; but I could not have completed it but for certain stanzas in St.-John Perse's AMERS (SEAMARKS), *which he has kindly allowed me to translate and quote.*

The sea belongs to us all, and every aspect of it, from halcyon calm to howling hurricane, is fraught with beauty. In these pages I am trying to share with the reader what the sea has meant to me; to pass on to another generation the delight that salt water affords to those who will take the trouble to learn sea lore. To ply, unhurried, the blue deeps, or skirt the shining margents of the land, communing with the element whence life sprang, hearing no other sound but the plash of oar, the flap of sail, the whistling of wind in the rigging, and the swish and gurgle of cloven waves, revives one's strength and refreshes one's spirit. Here, the tiniest lad sailing a dinghy becomes partner to the great navigators and discoverers of history; here, too, borrowing St.-John Perse's bold metaphor, unity between earth and heaven is recovered, truth is brought to light like the flash of a steel sword blade drawn out of its sheath; and we, the guests, can share the same supper with our Host.

SPRING TIDES are not the tides of spring, as many landsmen suppose. They are the very high and very low tides that occur twice a month, with the new and the full moon, when solar and lunar magnetism pull together to make the circumterrestrial tide wave higher than at other times. The opposite to the spring tide is the neap tide, halfway between these phases of the moon; Down East, in Maine, there may be as much as five feet difference in range between springs and neaps.

Spring tides are beloved by all who live by or from the sea. At a spring low, rocky ledges and sandbars that you never see ordinarily are bared; the kinds of seaweed that require air but twice a month appear; sand dollars, like tarnished pieces of eight, are visible on the bottom. Clam specialists can pick up the big "hen" clams or the quahaugs, and with a stiff wire hook deftly flip out of his long burrow the elusive razor clam. Shore birds — sandpiper, plover, and curlew — skitter over the sea-vacated flats, piping softly and gorging themselves on the minor forms of life that cling to this seldom-bared shelf.

The rising flood, engendering swift currents, seems determined to overflow the land. St.-John Perse compares the full tides of the new moon to "the rising sea of desire," "when the female land opens to the salacious, supple sea, adorned with bubbles even in its lagoons, its salt marshes, where the sea high in the grass makes a sucking noise, and the night teems with little cracklings." These cracklings (*éclosions*) he calls "the song of bubbles on the sand" — a million little bubbles that the waves deposit, bursting with soft little pops like the soap bubbles that children blow.*

A spring high is the time to bathe off sun-drenched rocks, or the still dry, narrow strip of sand with no stretch of pebbles and shells to hurt your feet. And at a spring high, children row over the farthest stretches of the tide, peering down delightedly at the sea lavender and beach grasses that they usually see well out of water. Curious bits of light flotsam, driftwood in fantastic shapes, green glass net floats, derelict lobsterpot buoys, float up with the spring high and dry out on the shore until some beachcomber picks them up to sell to tourists, or another spring high carries them off. But not all springs are of equal range. The full moon spring of mid-August, for instance, has a range of 12.5 feet at Portland, Maine; but the mid-October and mid-November ones run to 13.2 feet. By contrast, a July neap in this same harbor ranges barely 6 feet. A northeast gale may build as many as 4 feet to a spring high, flooding wharves and drowning out cellars near the waterfront. The spring of mid-January 1963 overflowed the bridge to our summer float, lifted it clear of the piers, and carried it out to sea. It also played a joke on local lobstermen by rising so high that their pot buoys were pulled under water. Some

* St.-John Perse, *Amers* (*Seamarks*) (New York: Pantheon Books, 1958), page 102.

busybody ashore, observing waters once dotted with gaily colored pot buoys to be clean as a mirror, jumped to the conclusion that lobster thieves had been cutting warps, and notified the police, who called the Coast Guard. By the time the cutter arrived, the tide was ebbing and the pot buoys were popping to the surface.

Spring highs, for some scientific reason unknown to me, always come within an hour of noon or of midnight. The herring fishermen are waiting for them, as the little fish are borne by the flood into coves and shoal waters where they can be caught more easily. On a calm summer night, with the brimming tide, the tiny fish leap out of water in unison and fall back, making a sound like that of a sudden shower on a pond. Presently boats appear, with flares; and amid cheery shouts the eager fishermen run "twine," as they call nets, upheld by cork buoys, around that part of the cove where the herring have been heard and seen. This is the stop seine, to prevent the fish from escaping seaward when the tide turns and during the hours of ebb.

Hours pass. The Pleiades rise, followed in late summer by the Dog Star and Orion. The eastern sky grows pale, then red, heralding the sun, whose reflection on the quiet water, lightly furred by the dawn offshore breeze, turns it wine-dark, the Homeric color. Now is the moment for action. The fishermen suspend from a dory and attach to the stop seine the pocket or purse seine, like the pendant on a lady's necklace. Between it and the big net is an opening — the gates of the herring's hell. With a clacking of oars against their boats, and splashing and shouts, the fishermen encourage the herring that are foolishly swimming to and fro on the net's shore side to pass through the gate whence there is no return. Sea gull and tern, cognizant of what is going on, gather in flocks and, screaming with joy, snap up and swallow fingerlings as fast as they come to the surface.

By this time a big diesel sardine boat, summoned by telephone, with bags of salt piled on her deck and a weird contraption for scaling herring, is standing by. At the moment judged right by the fishermen, the gate to the purse is closed, and herring in silver streams are scooped up by a great dip net from the big boat. If the herring are the right size and the market is good, they are rushed to the factory, where they are canned as Maine sardines. Those too big for the can are run through the descaling machine, these scales having a new market with the makers of costume jewelry. The descaled herring in

Maine are generally sold for lobster bait; but at Grand Manan or other places in the Provinces they are cured by smoking, packed in wooden boxes, and shipped, mostly to the West Indies. You can sometimes buy them in city fish markets, and tasty morsels they are, the best hors d'oeuvres in the world.

Since high water of a spring tide comes at noon or midnight, low water occurs shortly before sunrise and sunset, depending on the season. The October spring low is something I would not miss. After a day of brisk northwest wind, the harbor is glassy calm, reflecting sunset clouds, the brilliant maples on the shore, and the white hulls of yachts waiting to be hauled out. Around the edge of the sand flats, well below the blue mussel beds, is a rod-wide belt of eelgrass catching its fortnightly chance to breathe plenty of oxygen. Big black-backed gulls walk through the grass with a dignified gait, stalking the tiny crabs and little fishes that normally obtain protection among the grass but are now laid bare to the piercing eye and hungry beak.

My favorite spring high on the rocky Maine coast comes in May. It is an aesthetic delight to sail in a gentle breeze close to shore when the shadbush is flinging out its white banners among the dark green spruce, the birches are putting forth leaves of the tenderest green, and the birds are "singing like crazy." Equally beautiful, however, are the spring highs on one of those halcyon days in October, when the blueberry bushes on top of the granite cliffs turn a brilliant crimson, and the maple near shore sends up torches of gold and scarlet among the evergreen, all reflected in the quiet waters. No birds sing, but the crickets are lively, and if you sail close to where a meadow touches the shore you can hear a violin concerto of their little *cri-cri*. Lovers of Vermont and other inland states assert that their regions display the world's most brilliant colors in the fall of the year. Perhaps so; for who could test them with a color card? But the maples of Maine and the Maritime Provinces at least seem more brilliant, because of their background of dark green spruce and bright blue sea.

The "salacious, supple sea" nibbles at the land in every spring high. One can observe the change in the shoreline over a series of years. Here a boulder is unbalanced and rolls onto the beach; there a spruce, which has hopefully stretched out over the water to gather sunlight, loses its balance when a spring high sucks at its roots, and falls overboard; a clump of birches, undermined by the sea viciously undercutting the sandbank where it has been growing, topples and lies forlorn, roots in air, unless someone cuts it up for firewood. This is why people who love their shoreline build stone sea walls to restrain the robber tide; but if the present trend continues, the sea will have its way in the end. Highland Light has had to be moved twice in our time, as the sea bites farther and farther into the skinny arm of Cape Cod.

Shakespeare has Brutus remark:

> There is a tide in the affairs of men,
> Which, taken at the flood, leads on to fortune.

True enough, as Shakespeare had ample opportunity to observe in London River. There, if a sailing barge "missed its tide" it had to wait twelve hours, half of them sitting miserably on the bottom alongside an odorous dock, to catch another ebb to take her down the Thames. You may still see what the tide can do every day in the Tagus off Lisbon. A fleet of *fragatas*, the sailing lighters, part drifts, part sails up that noble river with the flood. The wind drops, the tide turns, and of a sudden you hear the rattle of forty chain cables off Black Horse Square as every vessel bound upriver anchors to await the next unpredictable fair wind or predictable fair tide.

Their predictability explains why tides are the sailor's friend. With a tide and current table he can figure them out to a minute; and even without modern aids he knows the full-and-change factor for his neighborhood, and has been shown by his grandfather how the currents work. Years ago, struggling with engine against a flood tide current between East Quoddy Head and Cutler, I barely overtook a fisherman who, with no other means of propulsion than sweep and sail, worked the eddies so close to that ironbound coast that he made good progress against the strong tidal current. Shipbuilders loved the spring tide, which enabled them to build large vessels on convenient spots, at the very head of tidewater, in their very backyards; yet launch and float them at the top of a spring ebb. At low water, take a look from the head of tide in Kennebunkport, or over Duxbury Bay, now a green meadow of eelgrass, and you can hardly believe that hundreds of tall ships were there built, launched, and sailed or poled down to deep water. At the North River in Massachusetts, ships were built as high upstream as Hanover bridge, launched on a spring high, and towed downstream on the ebb; a gang of men with a hawser on each bank, and the pilot, at the knightheads, ordering, "A leetle more over toward Scituate!" or, "Marshfield side, and put more back into it!"

Since tides, like the movements of sun, moon, and stars, were phenomena that man could not influence, it was man's natural conclusion that they affected his life. Just as farmers regulated plowing and sowing by the phases of the moon, so sailors and fishermen believed that flood tide meant strength, and ebb tide, weakness. If an old salt lay at death's door, his family and friends watched the tide. If he survived an ebb he would improve with the flood, but he would always die on the ebb. It was a pretty conception that the sailor's spirit would wish to float out of harbor with the ebb and once more survey familiar scenes — kelp-marked ledges, foaming tide rips, circling sea birds, friendly lighthouses — before it left for another world. That this belief was not confined to the coast is attested by Walt Whitman on the Civil War:

"He went out with the tide and the sunset," was a phrase I heard from a surgeon describing an old sailor's death under peculiarly gentle conditions.

During the Secession War, 1863 and '64, visiting the army hospitals around Washington, I formed the habit and continued it to the end, whenever the ebb or flood tide began the latter part of day, of punctually visiting those at that time populous wards of suffering men. Somehow (or I thought so) the effect of the hour was palpable. The badly wounded would get some ease and would like to talk a little or be talked to. Intellectual and emotional natures would be at their best; deaths were always easier; medicines seemed to have better effect when given then; and a lulling atmosphere would pervade the wards.

Similar influences, similar circumstances and hours, day-close, after great battles, even with all their horrors. I had more than once the same experiences on the fields covered with the fallen or dead.*

Something of the same feeling comes over every lover of the sea at the turn of a spring tide, especially if the wind is offshore. His soul seems to be pulling his body seaward. He feels an almost irresistible impulse to knock off whatever he may be doing, launch the punt, row out to his sail or motor boat, make sail or start the engine, and speed out into blue water with the ebb, which on a spring tide will carry

---

* Quoted from *Walt Whitman's Civil War*, edited by Walter Lowenfels (Alfred A. Knopf, 1961), page 111.

him through the narrow channel with unusual speed. Around sunset, when the tide turns, he can point his prow home once more, and feel the ineffable delight of half-sailing, half-drifting to his mooring with the lightest of sea breezes, under a full moon; or in the new-moon spring, under stars that have guided mariners for thousands of years.

5

An August Day's Sail

From SPRING TIDES, *Chapter III.*

And here is another little piece that expresses everything I have felt about sailing from youth to old age in those Maine waters I have known since boyhood. Although the yawl has gone, I still retain the well-balanced little skiff, designed by Sam Crocker thirty years ago, that served as tender to Emily Marshall. *Frequently, I row the skiff up harbor to fetch the mail, and of a Sunday across the harbor to church, so I keep in close touch with the sea.*

A LIGHT, caressing southerly breeze is blowing; just enough to heel the yawl and give her momentum. The boy and I get under way from the mooring by the usual ritual. I take in the ensign, hoist the mizzen, cast off main sheet and slack the backstays; he helps me hoist the mainsail, sway the halyards, and neatly coil them. Now the wheel and the main sheet are in hand, the boy casts off the mooring rode and hoists the jib, and off she goes, like a lively dog let off the leash.

We make a long, leisurely beat to windward out of the Western Way, with tide almost dead low; the reefs, sprayed with brown rockweed, show up clearly. We pass the bell buoy and leave to starboard the naked reef known to proper chartmakers as South Bunkers Ledge, but to Mount Deserters as "Bunker's Whore."

Now we are in the open sea, nothing between us and Nova Scotia. The day is pleasantly cool and bright, with gathering cirrus clouds that sometimes obscure the sun. Old ocean today is green, heaving with a surge farflung from a blow somewhere between us and Europe. Visibility is so high that the horizon is a clean-cut line over which one can see the masts of fishing draggers whose hulls are concealed by the earth's bulge. Seaward, the Duck Islands seem to float on the emerald waters. Landward, the rocky shores of Great Cranberry Island are misty with the spray from a line of white breakers. One thinks of Heredia's line about Brittanny: *"Du Raz jusqu'à Penmarc'h la côte entière fume"* — the entire coast is smoky. Ocean swell makes the yawl roll and pitch, not unpleasantly but in harmonious cadence with the sea, the motion starting little snaps and whistles among the cordage, and the tapping of reef points on the mainsail.

This is the time for the lunch that Priscilla prepared for us — jellied eggs and baby carrots as hors d'oeuvres; mushroom soup in a thermos; succulent ham sandwiches freshly made with lettuce and mayonnaise; chilled beer from the icebox; homemade doughnuts, crisp outside and flaky-soft inside, as you find them only when made by a master hand in Maine.

Now we are off Bakers Island, where the long, flat granite ledges, washed clean by winter gales, hang over a reddish-brown apron of kelp and dulse, whirling in the breakers that roar in past the Thumper ledge. We round the groaner, the perpetually whistling buoy, haul our wind, and turn northward.

Here we face the superb panorama of Mount Desert Island and Frenchmans Bay. The westering sun kindles the granite summits of Sargent, Green, and Newport mountains to rose color; and the ocean between us and them is cobalt-blue. Spruce-dark Otter Cliff and bare, brown Great Head thrust out into Frenchmans Bay. Under this luminous northern sky, distant Schoodic stands out bold and clear; miles beyond, the summit of Pigeon Hill appears, and Petit Manan lighthouse tower, entrance post to the Bay of Fundy, pricks the eastern horizon.

We close-haul our sails, round the black can buoy, and glide out of the ocean swell into the smooth, sheltered anchorage of Bakers Island. Flood tide is only one-hour old; and my quest is for fresh mussels in that clear, unpolluted water. We shoot into the wind, avoiding the numerous lobsterpot buoys, hand the jib and mainsail, drop the anchor, and pay out scope on the cable. I pull the skiff alongside and row ashore. Spicy late summer fragrance wells out from the sun-drenched island — sweet grasses, goldenrod, aster; even some of the white and pink *Rosa rugosa*, for which this place is famous, are still in bloom. The colorful sea bottom appears; gray sand studded with big smooth pebbles tumbled and polished by millennia of winter gales, when the great combers at high water rip over the reef barrier that now makes this spot a sheltered harbor. Two more strokes of the oars, and the skiff grounds on a rock; bucket in one hand and boat painter in the other, I make a wobbly landing, unlike the fishermen who splash boldly ashore in their rubber boots. Mussels are there in great plenty, their dark blue shells with brown "beards" clinging in clusters to barnacled rocks and to the wooden ways laid years ago for the lighthouse-keeper's skiff. In ten minutes' time I have gathered a pailful, then shove the skiff off the rock where she grounded, and row back to the yawl, facing forward to admire her perfect proportions and the backdrop of mountains.

We make sail once more, weigh anchor, and the yawl pirouettes on her keel to head toward home. My young sailor, blond and lithe as one imagines ancient Greek sailors to have been in the Aegean, gazes, speechless, at sea and mountains. What is he, at nineteen, thinking of it all? Does the beauty of sun-washed shore and granite mountains mean the same to him as to me, four times his age? I respect the youth's right to his own thoughts and do not ask, fearing, perhaps, that he may break the spell by some offhand or discordant reply.

Now we close-haul the sails again to pass between Suttons Island and the two Cranberries. I turn my back on the Islesford shore, where the summer houses are pretentiously inappropriate, but linger lovingly on the south shore of Suttons, its little cottages built in the good, simple taste of a century ago, when Maine men knew how to create as beautiful a house as a ship. Suttons, with its memories of John Gilley and Mary Wheelwright, of picnics long ago, of clumps of blue harebell growing like weeds from the wild grass. In this bight of the bay we encounter the inevitable spell of calm. The yawl holds her headway for two or three hundred yards, her sail full although the surface of the sea has become a wavy mirror; the ripples from her bows making sweet music. Finally her headway ceases, the sails gently flap, the booms swing from side to side, and the reef points play a tattoo on the mainsail.

What makes this particular day so memorable is its freedom from the mutter of motors. All power yachts are following the annual race in Blue Hill Bay; no snarling outboards are about. The lobstermen have finished hauling their traps and are at home eating supper. There is no sound but the lapping of waves on the shore, the lazy clang of Spurlings Ledge bell buoy, and the distant bark of a dog.

After a breathless calm of a quarter-hour, the breeze returns, limp sheets stretch out taut with a clatter of blocks, sails fill, and the yawl heels to the last of the west wind.

Around the western point of Suttons, Bear Island makes out. Its white lighthouse tower and pyramidical bell house seem to look down like benign parents on three tiny sloops that flutter past, having a little race of their own as they did not rate the big cruise. How many thousands of sailing craft have passed that sea mark since 1839, when, at the suggestion of a naval captain, the government built the light station? How many seamen have blessed that winking white eye guiding them through Eastern or Western Way to the snug harbors within, or strained their ears to catch the deep-throated note of the fog bell?

Leaving the cliffs of Bear Island astern on the starboard quarter, we enter Northeast Harbor with the dying breeze, avoiding the ever-present "Kimball's Calms" on the port hand. My boy lowers and neatly furls the jib, then stands with boat hook, poised like a classic harpooner, to spear the mooring buoy. Main and mizzen sheets are hauled flat to give the yawl one last graceful curvet before her way is checked in the wind's eye. Then the mooring rode is secured to the forward bitts, and the yacht's white wings are folded for the night.

DATE DUE

SEP AUG 23 '83			
GAYLORD			PRINTED IN U.S.